W9-CTH-615

DATE DUE

			PRINTED IN U.S.A.

Authors & Artists for Young Adults

ISSN 1040-5682

Authors & Artists for Young Adults

VOLUME 17

Diane Telgen
E. A. Des Chenes
Editors

Thomas McMahon
Associate Editor

GALE

an International Thomson Publishing company I⒯P®

L. A. Des Chenes and Diane Telgen, *Editors*

Linda R. Andres, Shelly Andrews, Joanna Brod, Sharon R. Gunton, Alan Hedblad,
Motoko Huthwaite, Julie Karmazin, Thomas F. McMahon, Gerard J. Senick
Contributing Editors

Mindi Dickstein, David P. Johnson, Ronie-Richele Garcia-Johnson, Marian C. Gonsior,
Hollis E. Helmeci, Janet L. Hile, Laurie Collier Hillstrom, Nancy E. Rampson,
Megan Ratner, Kenneth R. Shepherd, Tracy J. Sukraw, Sara Verney
Sketch Contributors

Victoria B. Cariappa, *Research Manager*
Donna Melnychenko, *Project Coordinator*

Maria E. Bryson, Tamara C. Nott, and Norma Sawaya, *Research Associates*
Alicia Noel Biggers, Michelle Lee, and Cheryl L. Warnock, *Research Assistants*

Marlene S. Hurst, *Permissions Manager*
Margaret A. Chamberlain, Maria Franklin, *Picture Permissions Specialist*
Kimberly F. Smilay, *Permissions Associate*

Mary Beth Trimper, *Production Director*
Deborah Milliken, *Production Assistant*

Randy Bassett, *Image Database Supervisor*
Sherrell Hobbs, *Macintosh Artist*
Robert Duncan, *Imaging Specialist*
Pamela A. Hayes, *Photography Coordinator*

 The paper used in this publication meets the minimum requirements of American National Standard for Information Sciences—Permanence Paper for Printed Library Materials, ANSI Z39.48-1984.

I(T)P™   Gale Research, an ITP Information/Reference Group Company.
ITP logo is a trademark under license.

Library of Congress Catalog Card Number 89-641100
ISBN 0-8103-9369-7
ISSN 1040-5682

10 9 8 7 6 5 4 3 2 1

Printed in the United States of America

Authors and Artists for Young Adults

TEEN BOARD

———

The staff of *Authors and Artists for Young Adults* wishes to thank the following young adult readers for their teen board participation:

Contents

Introduction

Authors and Artists for Young Adults is a reference series designed to serve the needs of middle school, junior high, and high school students interested in creative artists. Originally inspired by the need to bridge the gap between Gale's *Something about the Author*, created for children, and *Contemporary Authors*, intended for older students and adults, *Authors and Artists for Young Adults* has been expanded to cover not only an international scope of authors, but also a wide variety of other artists.

Although the emphasis of the series remains on the writer for young adults, we recognize that these readers have diverse interests covering a wide range of reading levels. The series therefore contains not only those creative artists who are of high interest to young adults, including cartoonists, photographers, music composers, bestselling authors of adult novels, media directors, producers, and performers, but also literary and artistic figures studied in academic curricula, such as influential novelists, playwrights, poets, and painters. The goal of *Authors and Artists for Young Adults* is to present this great diversity of creative artists in a format that is entertaining, informative, and understandable to the young adult reader.

Entry Format

Each volume of *Authors and Artists for Young Adults* will furnish in-depth coverage of twenty to twenty-five authors and artists. The typical entry consists of:

—A detailed biographical section that includes date of birth, marriage, children, education, and addresses.

—A comprehensive bibliography or filmography including publishers, producers, and years.

—Adaptations into other media forms.

—Works in progress.

—A distinctive essay featuring comments on an artist's life, career, artistic intentions, world views, and controversies.

—References for further reading.

—Extensive illustrations, photographs, movie stills, cartoons, book covers, and other relevant visual material.

A cumulative index to featured authors and artists appears in each volume.

Compilation Methods

The editors of *Authors and Artists for Young Adults* make every effort to secure information directly from the authors and artists through personal correspondence and interviews. Sketches on living authors and artists are sent to the biographee for review prior to publication. Any sketches not personally reviewed by biographees or their representatives are marked with an asterisk (*).

Highlights of Forthcoming Volumes

Among the authors and artists planned for future volumes are:

Isabel Allende
William H. Armstrong
W. H. Auden
Clayton Bess
Jorges Luis Borges
Robbie Branscum
Terry Brooks
Lois McMaster Bujold
Octavia E. Butler
Betsy Byars
Patricia Calvert
Pam Conrad

Clive Cussler
Berlie Doherty
John Donovan
Michael Dorris
Clint Eastwood
Louise Fitzhugh
Ernest J. Gaines
Nancy Garden
Alan Garner
Michael Hague
Nathaniel Hawthorne
Ernest Hemingway

Lee Bennett Hopkins
James Houston
Monica Hughes
Irene Hunt
Patricia MacLachlan
Jay McInerney
K. M. Peyton
Pamela Sargent
Cindy Sherman
Mark Twain
Anne Tyler
H. G. Wells

The editors of *Authors and Artists for Young Adults* welcome any suggestions for additional biographees to be included in this series. Please write and give us your opinions and suggestions for making our series more helpful to you. Direct your comments to: Editors, *Authors and Artists for Young Adults,* Gale Research, 645 Griswold St., Suite 835, Penobscot Building, Detroit, MI 48226-4094.

Authors & Artists for Young Adults

Sandy Asher

■ Personal

Full name, Sandra Fenichel Asher; born October 16, 1942, in Philadelphia, PA; daughter of Benjamin (a physician) and Fanny (Weiner) Fenichel; married Harvey Asher (a professor), January 31, 1965; children: Benjamin, Emily. *Education:* Attended University of Pennsylvania, 1960-62; Indiana University, B.A. (English, with a minor in theater), 1964; graduate study in child development at University of Connecticut, 1973; Drury College, elementary education certificate, 1974. *Religion:* Jewish.

■ Addresses

Home—721 South Weller Ave., Springfield, MO 65802. *Office*—Department of Literature, Drury College, 900 North Benston, Springfield, MO 65802. *Agent*—Harold Ober Associates, Inc., 425 Madison Ave., New York, NY 10017.

■ Career

WFIU-Radio, Bloomington, IN, scriptwriter, 1963-64; Ball Associates (advertising agency), Philadel-phia, PA, copywriter, 1964; *Spectator*, Bloomington, drama critic, 1966-67; Drury College, Springfield, MO, instructor in creative writing, 1978-85, writer in residence, 1985—. Instructor in creative writing for children's summer programs, Summerscape, 1981-82, and Artworks, 1982; instructor, Institute of Children's Literature, 1986—. Guest Speaker at conferences, workshops, and schools. *Member:* The International Association of Theatre for Children and Young People (ASSITEJ; member of board of directors, 1989—), Dramatists Guild, Authors League of America, National Council of Teachers of English Assembly on Literature for Adolescents, Society of Children's Book Writers and Illustrators (Missouri advisor, 1986-89; member of board of directors, 1989—), Children's Reading Round Table of Chicago, Phi Beta Kappa.

■ Awards, Honors

Honorable mention from *Envoi* magazine, 1970, for poem, "Emancipation"; award of excellence from Festival of Missouri Women in the Arts, 1974, for *Come Join the Circus*; honorable mention, Unitarian Universalist Religious Arts Guild, 1975, for play *Afterthoughts in Eden*; poetry award from *Bitterroot* magazine, 1975; creative writing fellowship in playwriting from National Endowment for the Arts, 1978, for *God and a Woman*; first prize in one-act play contest from Little Theatre of Alexandria, 1983, and Street Players Theatre, 1989, for *The Grand Canyon*; first prize from Children's Musical Theater of Mobile contest and Dubuque

Fine Arts Players contest, both 1984, for *East of the Sun/West of the Moon;* Mark Twain Award nomination, 1984, for *Just Like Jenny;* University of Iowa Outstanding Books for Young Adults Award and Child Study Association Best Books Award, both 1985, for *Missing Pieces; Little Old Ladies in Tennis Shoes* was named best new play of the season by the Maxwell Anderson Playwriting Series, 1985-86, and was a finalist for the 1988 Ellis Memorial Award, Theatre Americana; *God and a Woman* won the Center Stage New Horizons contest, 1986, Mercyhurst College National Playwrights Showcase, 1986-87, and the Unpublished Play Project of the American Alliance for Theatre in Education, 1987-88; *Things Are Seldom What They Seem* was nominated for Iowa Teen Award and Young Hoosier Award, both 1986-87; Children's Theatre Indianapolis Children's Theatre Symposium playwriting awards, from Indiana University/Purdue University, 1987, for *Prince Alexis and the Silver Saucer,* and 1989, for *A Woman Called Truth;* Joseph Campbell Memorial Fund Award from the Open Eye, 1991-92, for *A Woman Called Truth; Dancing with Strangers* won playwriting contests sponsored by TADA!, 1991, and Choate Rosemary Hall, 1993; New Play Festival Award from the Actors' Guild of Lexington, Inc., 1992, for *Sunday, Sunday;* "Once, In the Time of Trolls" won a playwriting contest sponsored by East Central College in Union, MO, 1993; *A Woman Called Truth* was voted an Outstanding Play for Young Audiences by the U.S. Center of the International Association of Theatres for Children and Young People, 1993. *Just Like Jenny, Things Are Seldom What They Seem,* and *Everything Is Not Enough* were all *Junior Library Guild* selections.

■ Writings

FOR YOUNG ADULTS

Summer Begins, Elsevier-Nelson, 1980, published as *Summer Smith Begins,* Bantam, 1986.
Daughters of the Law, Beaufort Books, 1980, published in England as *Friends and Sisters,* Gollancz, 1982.
Just Like Jenny, Delacorte, 1982.
Things Are Seldom What They Seem, Delacorte, 1983.
Missing Pieces, Delacorte, 1984.
Everything Is Not Enough, Delacorte, 1987.
Out of Here: A Senior Class Yearbook (short story collection), Dutton/Lodestar, 1993.

FOR CHILDREN

Teddy Teabury's Fabulous Fact, Dell, 1985.
Teddy Teabury's Peanutty Problems, Dell, 1987.
Princess Bee and the Royal Good-night Story (picture book), illustrated by Cat Bowman Smith, A. Whitman, 1990.

"BALLET ONE" SERIES; FOR CHILDREN

Best Friends Get Better, Scholastic, 1989.
Mary-in-the-Middle, Scholastic, 1990.
Pat's Promise, Scholastic, 1990.
Can David Do It?, Scholastic, 1991.

PLAYS; UNDER NAME SANDRA FENICHEL ASHER

Come Join the Circus (one-act), first produced in Springfield, MO, at Springfield Little Theatre, December, 1973.
Afterthoughts in Eden (one-act), first produced in Los Angeles, CA, at Los Angeles Feminist Theatre, February, 1975.
A Song of Sixpence (one-act), Encore Performance Publishing, 1976.
The Ballad of Two Who Flew (one-act), published in *Plays,* March, 1976.
How I Nearly Changed the World, but Didn't (one-act), first produced in Springfield, at National Organization for Women Herstory Women's Fair, November, 1977.
Witling and the Stone Princess, published in *Plays,* 1979.
Food Is Love (one-act), first produced in Springfield at Drury College, January, 1979.
The Insulting Princess (one-act; first produced in Interlochen, MI, at Interlochen Arts Academy, May, 1979), Encore Performance Publishing (Orem, UT), 1988.
The Mermaid's Tale (one-act; first produced in Interlochen at Interlochen Arts Academy, May, 1979), Encore Performance Publishing (Vacaville, CA), 1988.
Dover's Domain, Pioneer Drama Service (Denver, CO), 1980.
The Golden Cow of Chelm (one-act; first produced in Springfield at United Hebrew Congregation, December, 1980), published in *Plays,* 1980.
Sunday, Sunday (two-act), first produced in Lafayette, IN, at Purdue University, March, 1981.
The Grand Canyon (one-act), first produced in the Little Theatre of Alexandria, Virginia, 1983.
Little Old Ladies in Tennis Shoes (two-act; first produced in Philadelphia, PA, at the Society Hill Playhouse, 1985), Dramatic Publishing Co. (Woodstock, IL), 1989.

East of the Sun/West of the Moon (one-act), first produced in the Children's Musical Theatre of Mobile, AL, 1985.

God and a Woman (two-act), first produced in Erie, PA, at the National Playwrights Showcase, 1987, produced in a one-act version entitled *A Woman Called Truth* (first produced in Houston, TX, at the Main Street Theatre, 1989), Dramatic Publishing Co., 1989.

Prince Alexis and the Silver Saucer (one-act), first produced in Springfield at Drury College, 1987.

The Wise Men of Chelm (one-act; first produced in Louisville, KY, at the Jewish Community Center, 1991), Dramatic Publishing Co., 1992.

All on a Saturday Morning (one-act), first produced in Columbia, MO, 1992.

Blind Dating (one-act), first produced in New York City at TADA!, 1992.

Perfect (one-act), first produced in New York City at The Open Eye: New Stagings for Youth, 1992.

Where Do You Get Your Ideas? (adapted for the stage from the author's book of the same title), first produced in New York City at The Open Eye: New Stagings for Youth, 1992.

Dancing with Strangers (three one-acts), first produced in Wallingford, CT, 1993.

Also author of play, "Once, in the Time of Trolls"; contributor of plays to anthologies, including *Center Stage*, Harper, 1990.

NONFICTION

(Under name Sandra Fenichel Asher) *The Great American Peanut Book*, illustrated by Jo Anne Metsch Bonnell, Tempo, 1977.

Where Do You Get Your Ideas?: Helping Young Writers Begin, illustrated by Susan Hellard, Walker & Co., 1989.

Wild Words!: How to Train Them to Tell Stories, illustrated by Dennis Kendrick, Walker & Co., 1989.

OTHER

Contributor of stories and articles to books, including *Visions*, edited by Don Gallo, Delacorte/Dell, 1987; *Speaking for Ourselves*, edited by Ruth Nathan, Christopher-Gordon, 1991; *Writers in the Classroom*, edited by Ruth Nathan, Christopher-Gordon, 1991; *Performing the Text: Reading, Writing, and Teaching the Young Adult Novel*, edited by Virginia Monseau and Gary Salvner, Heinemann-Boynton/Cook, 1992; *Authors' Perspectives: Turning Teenagers into Readers and Writers*, edited by Donald Gallo, Heinemann-Boynton/Cook, 1992. Contributor of stories and articles to periodicals, including *Highlights for Children, Humpty Dumpty's Magazine, Parents Magazine, ALAN Review, Journal of Reading, Spark!, Theater for Young Audiences Today,* and *Writer's Digest.*

■ **Sidelights**

When young adult novelist Sandy Asher was a young girl living in Philadelphia, a band of Gypsies would make occasional stops in her neighborhood. Asher and the other children in her class would know that these mysterious travellers were once again in their town when a young boy they called "John the Gypsy" would once more come to James G. Blaine Elementary school. "He informed us that John was his school name," Asher wrote in her *Something about the Author Autobiography Series (SAAS)* entry, "but that his Gypsy name was Four Roses and he knew what the wind that blew around the reservoir was saying. It said 'Go where you must go, and be what you must be,' he told us, in hushed tones that sent shivers along our spines. I've always wanted to put that scene into a book, but it's never quite fit. Maybe someday it will."

Although Asher has never managed to add John's sage advice into one of her books, she has been able to abide by it in her own life. From a young age, she had dreamed of becoming the author she eventually became. "On Sundays," Asher recalled, "my parents dropped me off at the Children's Reading Room entrance of the monumental Free Library of Philadelphia at Logan Square. They drove off to visit their friends; I raced down the long ramp and through the tall glass doors to visit mine: books. I adored their worn, dingy bindings all in neat rows and their musty, age-old smell. I believed wholeheartedly in the people I met within their covers: Jo March, Peter Pan and Wendy, Dorothy and the Scarecrow. I remember thinking how wonderful it would be to write a book someone would enjoy as much as I enjoyed those I read." Now the author of dozens of novels and plays for young audiences, Asher has listened to the wind and fulfilled her dream.

Asher is known for her realistic novels featuring teens overcoming the ordinary—though often traumatic—problems of growing up. Her characters, as she described them in *Twentieth-Century Young Adult Writers*, are typically "'nice kids'—the ones who rarely give a teacher a minute's trouble. . . . [These] young adults learn to deal with grief, loneliness, fear, jealousy, anger, frustration, confusion, love—and the lack of it—because nice kids must, and nice kids do." She gleans most of her material from events she experienced and people she knew in her own childhood.

Strawberry Mansion Days

Born after the beginning of World War II, Asher didn't see her father, Benjamin Fenichel, until she was almost three years old because he had been drafted before his daughter was born. When he returned, he resumed his medical practice from an office in the Fenichel home on Diamond Street in the Strawberry Mansion neighborhood of Philadelphia. Because the office was in the house, Asher and her older brother had to be quiet when they were inside. Outside, however, was a different story. Filled with "war babies" and "baby boomers," the streets of Strawberry Mansion were bustling with young children. They would all go to Fairmount Park to play or spend the day watching the double feature and film shorts at the Park Theater. Like many of her friends at the time, Asher dreamed of one day becoming a movie actress. "We acted out movies over and over again," she said in *SAAS*, "in backyards, in basements, in bedrooms, and the schoolyard. . . . The movies promised us lives of endless adventure, and we believed them."

The fantasy world of the movies was no more interesting than the fantasy world she fostered in her own imagination, however. "I learned early that inner space is worth exploring and that even when alone, you can find yourself in fascinating company. . . . I made up poems and songs, stories and plays, to fill my fantasy world and entertain myself. I read whole volumes of the *Book of Knowledge* encyclopedia and pages at a time out of the dictionary, eager to know everything about everything. Little did I know what excellent training for a writer those solitary hours up in my room would prove to be." Her parents, whose main goal for their daughter was that she get married and have children, didn't take their daughter's interest seriously. "That I wrote constantly, practically from infancy, was considered amusing by my family, but certainly not significant. That I had dreams of becoming a professional writer struck them as a safe enough way for me to pass the time until marriage and children came along. I can't blame them for the way they saw me. They were products of their time."

In addition to movies and books, Asher developed an early love for the stage. Inspired in the second grade by her teacher Mrs. Lomozoff, she was encouraged in school to write short plays, as well as poems. She also enjoyed music and taking ballet lessons, though she later gave up any notions of becoming a professional dancer, concluding that she didn't have the talent or physical strength necessary. These interests became even more important to the young Asher when she was ten years old and her family moved to Mount Airy, which is close to the Germantown area of Phila-

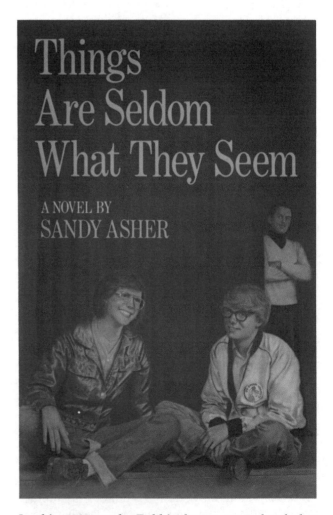

In this 1983 work, Debbie learns some harsh lessons about love, friendship and trust while trying to adjust to high school.

delphia. Asher found social life at her new school, Leeds Junior High, uncomfortable at best. No longer were her peers interested in movie stars; boys and clothes were the main concerns, as well as being part of the "in" crowd. "It's not that anyone teased me or that I was particularly unpopular," said Asher. "I simply felt uncomfortable all of the time." Fortunately, she found some fulfillment in the creativity of summer day camp at the Allens Lane Art Center. "It turned out to be my idea of paradise: five days a week devoted to art, dance, drama, and music, with some of the finest instructors in Philadelphia."

Dreams of the Stage, Dancing, and Writing

While her school friends gossiped about dating and the latest fashions, Asher said she "lived for my evening and weekend dance classes and performances with the Philadelphia Civic Ballet and the Philadelphia Civic Theater. . . . [The] real me came alive then." When she was sixteen, she won a dance apprenticeship at the Williamstown Summer Theater in Massachusetts, where she was lucky enough to meet playwright Thornton Wilder, who was helping the students with a production of his *Our Town*. Wilder left an indelible impression on the young Asher's psyche. Compared to her father, who had gone into medicine out of a sense of obligation to his mother and who always told his daughter to "do the unpleasant willingly," Wilder was possessed of a passion for his work that Asher found enlightening. "Never in my life had I seen someone his age so enthusiastic about his work, so passionate about the life he had chosen to lead . . . ," Asher wrote in *SAAS*. "His face seemed to radiate light and energy. Until his visit, I had no idea that kind of excitement could last a lifetime."

The excitement would indeed last a lifetime for Asher; unfortunately, actively pursuing her dreams became much more difficult for her in high school when her parents finally began to take notice of their daughter's genuine enthusiasm for the arts. Worried that she would abandon the security of home, marriage, and family for the much more risky career the stage offered, they imposed curfews and restricted the amount of time Asher could spend with her theater friends. "Arguments and tears only convinced my parents that I'd become too involved for my own good," wrote Asher. "My mother, the one who had taken me

Michael's well-planned life begins to unravel after he takes a busboy job at a small restaurant.

to ballets and plays even when I was too young to stay awake for the second act, feared she had created a monster." Asher attended the University of Pennsylvania for the first two years of college because her parents insisted she go to a college close enough for her to live at home. Before her junior year, however, she convinced her parents to let her go to Indiana University, assuring them that her cousin, Richie, who was also attending that university, would keep her out of trouble.

Asher felt much more at ease at Indiana, where "it was once again okay to be smart. . . . I felt right at home. I couldn't get enough of what was suddenly available to me. I took twenty-two hours a semester of writing courses, theatre courses, dance classes, psychology, French, anything I could squeeze in. I stayed up half the night talking with friends in the dorm about books and plays and The Meaning of Life." She continued to act in plays at Indiana, and in 1963 had the chance to spend the summer living and performing on the *Majestic*, "the last real traveling showboat in the United States."

After college, Asher worked briefly as a copywriter before marrying Harvey Asher, whom she had met at Indiana University and who—just like the husband of one of her favorite heroines, Louisa May Alcott's character in *Little Women*, Jo March—was a professor. Asher was also like Jo in that they both wanted to be writers. For Asher, though, this dream would be postponed for several years. Only after the birth of her two children—Benjamin was born in 1966 and Emily in 1968—and the family's move to Springfield, Missouri, where Asher's husband had found a job as a history professor at Drury College, did she begin to write in earnest. During the 1960s and 1970s, she concentrated on plays, short stories, and poems, for which she has won several prizes. Although she realized in the early seventies—after taking a class in children's literature—that the genre of young adult fiction had particular appeal, Asher didn't publish her first novel for teens until ten years later.

Stories Based on Experience

Asher bases many of her fictional characters on people she has known in real life. In her first published young adult novel, *Summer Begins*, Summer Smith's school principal, Dr. Kyle, is based on the stern man who held that job in Asher's own elementary school for a time, and the author combined three of her favorite junior and senior high school teachers into Summer's English teacher, Mrs. Morton. The central conflict of the book, as well as in several books that followed, is also grounded in Asher's own personal feelings in trying to become an individual, independent of her parents. In Summer's case, it is difficult for her to emerge from her parents' shadows. Her father is a famous literary critic, and her mother is a former Olympic swimmer. Believing that she is not very important, Summer finds security in anonymity, until one day when she writes an essay for the eighth-graders' school newspaper, suggesting that the school Christmas program also celebrate religions other than Christianity. The paper causes an uproar both at home and at school that compels Summer to assert herself as an individual. "In facing up to the controversy," wrote *Dictionary of Literary Biography*

contributor Judith S. Baughman, "she begins to assert herself and thus to initiate meaningful communication with her parents and friends."

The relationship between mothers and their daughters is a special part of the theme of children becoming individuals. It is an important feature in *Summer Begins*, as well as *Daughters of the Law* and *Missing Pieces*. As Asher stated in *SAAS*, however, these "mother/daughter relationships [are] not really like my mother's and mine, but [are] related to our struggle to understand one another, a struggle that ended too soon when she died." Asher actually began writing *Daughters of the Law* years before *Summer Begins*, though it was published a few months afterwards.

Daughters of the Law tackles another personal issue for Asher, who is Jewish: the Holocaust and its continuing effects on Jewish families even decades after the end of World War II. The story is set during the early 1970s when Ruthie Morgenthau is trying to come to terms with the horrors her mother Hannah endured in Europe at the hands of the Nazis. Unable to communicate with her mother, who is also mourning the recent death of Ruthie's father, Ruthie finds some escape by making drawings and in her friendship with Denise Riley, an idealistic girl who likes to crusade for just causes. Through Denise, Ruthie learns that the world is not all misery, and Denise discovers that the world is not as simple as she'd like it to be.

Asher's background in dancing served her well in *Just Like Jenny*, in which thirteen-year-old Stephanie Nordland envies Jenny Gianino's dancing ability. Still drawing on people she once knew, Asher turned her second-grade teacher Mrs. Lomozoff into Stephanie and Jenny's dynamic music teacher Mrs. Deveraux, and the author also transferred her desire to become a professional dancer into her young characters in this story. In her *SAAS* essay, Asher says she gave Jenny and Stephanie the dancing abilities she felt she did not possess herself, "so they could live out that dream for me." The story centers on Stephanie's difficulty in believing in herself. Her admiration for Jenny's dancing skill causes her to think less of her own abilities, which consequently leads her to turn down an opportunity to perform with a semiprofessional dance troupe. "The remainder of [the] novel," explained Baughman, "dramatizes the young protagonist's confused efforts to define

A SENIOR CLASS YEARBOOK

OUT OF HERE

SANDY ASHER

Nine graduating seniors face new and interesting challenges in Asher's 1993 novel.

more clearly both the nature of her friendship with Jenny and her own identity and goals."

Examining the Tough Questions

Things Are Seldom What They Seem touches upon an even more delicate issue: sexual abuse. When Asher was in the fourth grade, she had a music teacher who wasn't all that he appeared to be. Asher wrote, "I don't remember the music teacher's name. I know he was energetic and funny and we liked him. Except that he hugged and tickled us too much, and we didn't care for that. One day he just wasn't there anymore, and nobody would tell us why." Asher later figured out that the teacher had been discovered to be a child molester and lost his job. She felt it was important to write a story about this. *Things Are Seldom What They Seem* is a warning to young people, and it also points out that molesters are

not so easy to identify. "They aren't aliens," Asher observed. "They're human beings, just like the rest of us."

Even though Asher's novel concentrates on the reactions and emotions the young characters feel about their drama teacher Mr. Carraway's molestation of Karen Jackson and Margaret Palermo, rather than trying to sensationalize the problem, parents and teachers censored *Things Are Seldom What They Seem.* It was taken off library shelves around the country. In her *SAAS* essay, Asher doubted that such actions serve to protect children: "I suppose those adults think the world is a safer place for their children without my book and others like it. They're in for some cruel surprises. Unfortunately, so are their kids."

Some of the characters in *Things Are Seldom What They Seem* once more emerge from Asher's memories of herself and her friends and family. Debbie Palermo, the novel's narrator and younger sister of one of the molestation victims, faces some of the same crises Asher did in junior high and high school. A bright girl who was disgusted by the social cliques and posturing her peers did in junior high, she worries that high school will be just more of the same. Her fears are somewhat relieved when she meets Murray Gordon, a funny and smart oddball. He is based on a boy Asher first met in sixth grade who was a kind of nemesis for the author. "He sat right in front of me and turned every move we made into a competition," Asher remembered. "Murray really got on my nerves," she later added, "but he kept me busy. . . . Murray is goading me on still. He's my personal gadfly; I cannot get rid of him. He's Murray Gordon in *Things Are Seldom What They Seem*, Ralph Major in the 'Ballet One' series, Cory Sedgwick in the 'Teddy Teabury' books."

Although Asher has some personal experience with the topic addressed in *Things Are Seldom What They Seem,* a much closer subject to her heart is the loss of a family member, which is the theme of *Missing Pieces.* When she was in her twenties, she endured the loss of both of her parents, her grandmother, and her grandfather in the space of only a few years. "*Missing Pieces,*" she revealed in *SAAS,* " . . . deals with my feelings after my father's death." The novel is about a high school student named Heather Connelly and the enormous losses she suffers during one horrible year. After her father dies, her mother becomes withdrawn and uncommunicative; in addition to this, Heather's favorite uncle has become senile, her boyfriend runs away because of his own family problems, and Heather can't even talk to her brother, who has moved away. But Heather finds support from—and returns that support in kind to—her boyfriend Nicky and from Cara Dale; in this way they all find the strength to come to terms with their problems, as well as improve their relationships with their parents. Such friendships are an important theme in Asher's work, and many of her protagonists' best friends are based upon her own lifelong pal, Honey.

The setting for *Everything Is Not Enough* comes from Asher's yearly summer trips to Atlantic City, where she used to love going to the beach and strolling along the boardwalk. She turned this place into Braden's Port for her sixth young adult novel. When Michael Paeglis and his well-to-do family come to Braden's Port for the summer, Michael defies his father by getting a low-paying job as a busboy at the Jolly Mackerel restaurant to learn more about the real world. Michael has been protected by his parents all his life, and his father, an immigrant who has become a successful businessman, has given his son everything he needs and has big dreams for him. He disapproves of Michael's wish to work at such a menial job, but Michael prevails.

At the Jolly Mackerel, Michael meets Linda, who is trying to earn money to go to fashion school and has dreams of moving to New York City, Peter, a former sports hero turned cook and alcoholic, and Traci, Peter's wife. Life has been much less kind to the people Michael comes to know at the restaurant, especially Traci, who, Michael and Linda learn, is being physically abused by Peter. By entering the real world, Michael grows as a person, and by the end of the story he is considering a career in social work. His father, too, is impressed by the changes he sees in his son and decides that the busboy job was a good thing after all.

Moving Away from the Teen Novel

After *Everything Is Not Enough*, Asher moved away from young adult novels and concentrated more on stories for younger children, as well as continuing to write plays. Her most notable play of this period is probably *God and a Woman*, which she later retitled *A Woman Called Truth*,

her award-winning drama about Sojourner Truth. Asher also worked on the "Ballet One" series, which draws from her childhood experiences in dance class, and two humorous books for grade school children featuring her character Teddy Teabury.

It wasn't until 1993 that she returned to fiction for teenagers, publishing the short story collection, *Out of Here: A Senior Class Yearbook*. Though it isn't a novel, the nine stories in this book have a unifying theme. As Asher explained in *SAAS, Out of Here* reflects the problems she had trying to fit in at Leeds Junior High and Germantown High. Admitting that she never figured out most of the unwritten social rules the popular girls followed in school, she wrote, "I've tried to write about that confusion in . . . *Out of Here*." Set in a 1990s high school, each story in *Out of Here* centers on different senior class students who must face a particular coming-of-age problem. Calling the collection "an accurate portrayal of high school," a *School Library Journal* contributor said that "YAs will recognize themselves and their classmates in these teenagers."

Asher considers her role as a writer of fiction for young people an important responsibility not to be taken lightly. In a speech quoted by Baughman, Asher declared: "The biggest difference, it seems to me, between writing for adults and writing for young teenagers is that when you write for young teenagers, there's a very good chance some of your readers will take you seriously. . . . Knowing how vital a part I may play in some young person's life, I feel a heavy responsibility to be careful about what I say and how I say it." Having fulfilled her dream by listening to the wind's advice as told to her by a Gypsy boy long ago, Asher has become the writer she wanted to be; like a character in one of her books who has survived the story's denouement with dignity and independence in tact, she has come through the difficult years that followed Strawberry Mansion. "Slowly but surely," she concluded in *SAAS*, "I've repaired broken bridges to my past and laid old sorrows to rest. I hope I also show readers that this does happen."

■ Works Cited

Asher, Sandy, essay in *Something about the Author Autobiography Series*, Volume 13, Gale, 1992.

Asher, Sandy, essay in *Twentieth-Century Young Adult Writers,* first edition, edited by Laura Standley Berger, St. James, 1994.

Baughman, Judith S., "Sandy Asher," *Dictionary of Literary Biography Yearbook: 1983,* edited by Mary Bruccoli and Jean W. Ross, Gale, 1984, pp. 179-185.

Review of *Out of Here: A Senior Class Yearbook, School Library Journal,* July, 1993, p. 98.

■ For More Information See

PERIODICALS

ALAN Review, spring, 1995, p. 2.

Booklist, September 15, 1987, p. 140; November, 1989, p. 42; June 1, 1993, p. 1806.

Bulletin of the Center for Children's Books, December, 1987, p. 61.

Horn Book Guide, July, 1989, pp. 95, 144; spring, 1994, p. 85.

Junior Bookshelf, December, 1988, p. 312.

Kirkus Reviews, June 15, 1987, p. 921; December 15, 1989, p. 1832; July 1, 1993, p. 856.

Publishers Weekly, February 13, 1987, p. 94; June 14, 1993, p. 72.

School Library Journal, August, 1987, p. 88; September, 1987, p. 184; December, 1989, p. 98; January, 1990, p. 110; March, 1990, p. 184.

Voice of Youth Advocates, June, 1987, p. 74; February, 1990, p. 350; December, 1993, p. 286.*

—Sketch by Janet L. Hile

Charlotte Brontë

Emily Brontë

Charlotte and Emily Brontë

■ Personal

Daughters of Patrick (a priest in the Church of England) and Maria (maiden name, Branwell) Brontë.

Charlotte Brontë: Wrote under pseudonym Currer Bell; born April 21, 1816, in Thornton, Yorkshire, England; died March 31, 1855, in Haworth; married Arthur Bell Nicholls (a curate), June 29, 1854. *Education:* Attended Clergy Daughters' Schoo! at Cowan Bridge, 1824; Roe Head School, 1831-32; Pensionnat Heger, 1842-43.

Emily Brontë: Wrote under pseudonym Ellis Bell; born July 30, 1818, in Haworth, Yorkshire, England; died of tuberculosis, December 19, 1848, in Haworth. *Education:* Attended Clergy Daughters' School at Cowan Bridge, 1824; Roe Head School, 1835; Pensionnat Heger, 1842.

■ Career

Charlotte Brontë: Author. Also worked as a teacher and governess. Roe Head School, Desbury Moor, teacher, 1835-38; Stonegappe, near Lothersdale, governess, 1839; Rawdon, near Bradford, governess, 1841; Pensionnat Heger, Brussels, teacher, 1843-45.

Emily Brontë: Author. Also worked as a governess at Law Hill, Halifax, 1838.

■ Writings

COLLECTED POETRY AS CURRER AND ELLIS BELL

(With Anne Brontë as Acton Bell) *Poems by Currer, Ellis and Acton Bell*, Aylott & Jones, 1846, Lea & Blanchard, 1848.

NOVELS AND POETRY BY CHARLOTTE BRONTË

(As Currer Bell) *Jane Eyre: An Autobiography*, published in three volumes by Smith, Elder, 1847, published in one volume, Harper, 1950.

(As Currer Bell) *Shirley: A Tale*, published in three volumes, Smith, Elder, 1853, published in one volume, Harper, 1853.

(As Currer Bell) *Villette*, published in three volumes, Smith, Elder, 1853, published in one volume, Harper, 1953.

The Professor: A Tale, published in 2 volumes, Smith, Elder, 1857, published in one volume, Harper, 1857.

The Twelve Adventurers and Other Stories, edited by C.K. Shorter and C. W. Hatfield, Hodder & Stoughton, 1925.

Legends of Angria: Compiled from the Early Writings of Charlotte Brontë, edited by Fannie E. Ratchford and William Clyde De Vane, Yale University Press, 1933.

(With "Another Lady") *Emma* (the fragment of an unfinished novel, "Emma," finished anonymously), Everest House, 1981.

The Poems of Charlotte Brontë (a new annotated and enlarged edition of the Shakespeare Head Brontë), edited by Tom Winnifrith, Blackwell, 1985.

The Unfinished Novels, A. Sutton, 1993.

NOVEL, POETRY AND ESSAYS BY EMILY BRONTË

(As Ellis Bell) *Wuthering Heights*, published in 2 volumes, T. C. Newby, 1847, published in 1 volume, Coolidge & Wiley, 1848.

The Complete Poems of Emily Jane Brontë, edited by C. K. Shorter, Hodder & Stoughton, 1908, 1910.

Five Essays Written in French by Emily Jane Brontë, translated by Lorine White Nagel, edited by Fannie E. Ratchford, University of Texas Press, 1948.

■ Adaptations

Wuthering Heights was produced as a film with Merle Oberon and Laurence Olivier in 1939, and with Timothy Dalton and Anna Calder-Marshall in 1970; it was also adapted for the stage by Charles Vance, Samuel French, 1990; made into an opera by Bernard Herrmann; read by Michael Page and Laural Merlington for an audio version, Brilliance Corporation, 1992, as *Wuthering Heights Readalong*, Lake Publishing Co., 1994; and adapted for audio by various companies. *Jane Eyre* has been produced as a film several times, the most famous version being the one starring Orson Welles and Joan Fontaine (1944); it was also adapted on fifteen audio cassettes by BLKA, 1994; adapted as *Jane Eyre Readalong*, Lake Publishing Company, 1994; adapted on 2 cassettes by Durkin Hayes, 1993. *Villette* was adapted for an audio version.

■ Sidelights

Who would have guessed that Charlotte and Emily Brontë, the motherless daughters of a country curate, would someday be regarded as two of the best writers in the English language? They lived quiet lives far from sophisticated urban society, never received formal college degrees, and, to make matters worse—they were middle-class women living in nineteenth-century England. What made the sisters remarkable was their ability to turn every disadvantage to an advantage. They spent days at home reading the classics of English literature, making up their own stories, or roaming over the wild moors. They keenly observed the friends they met at various schools, and vividly remembered the horrors and traumas they experienced there. Finally, sometimes subtly, sometimes passionately—they expressed their repressed emotions in prose and poetry, through female and male voices. As a result, when their works were finally published, Charlotte and Emily Brontë sent English literature in new directions and set important examples for future female writers.

According to Herbert J. Rosengarten in *Dictionary of Literary Biography*, Charlotte's "explorations of emotional repression and the feminine psyche" in novels like *Jane Eyre: An Autobiography* "introduced a new depth and intensity to the study of character and motive in fiction." With four novels to her credit, she "made a significant contribution to the development of the novel." In addition, wrote Rosengarten, while Charlotte "was not in any formal sense a proponent of women's rights," she spoke "out strongly against the injustices suffered by women in a society that restricts their freedom of action and exploits their dependent status" in her books.

Emily's *Wuthering Heights,* which first shocked and puzzled readers with its seemingly unrestrained passion, is an enduring, overwhelmingly popular classic of romantic literature. Although, as Lionel Trilling wrote in an article in *The Morningside,* Emily's "merit as a poet is eclipsed by her own [fame] as a novelist," critics agree that her poetry deserves attention. *Saturday Review* included Emily Brontë with Elizabeth Barrett Browning and Christina Rossetti in a list of the three greatest female English poets of the nineteenth century.

As a reviewer for the *Times Literary Supplement* commented, the disparity between the Brontë sister's lives and their literary works is intriguing: "For most biographers and critics it is the sense of mystery about them, the enthralling problem of accounting for their peculiar genius in the context of their historical times and their private lives." Thanks to biographers and critics, and, especially, Elizabeth Cleghorn Gaskell, who wrote Charlotte's biography after her death, readers may attempt to gain an understanding of the writers' early lives.

Growing Up on the Moors of Yorkshire

The Brontë sisters' father, Patrick Brontë, was born in County Down, Ireland, and educated at St. John's College in Cambridge as an ordained priest of the Church of England. He met and married Maria Branwell, from Cornwall, in 1812, and the couple settled at Thornton, Bradford, Yorkshire. Charlotte, who was born April 21, 1816, was the Brontë's third daughter after Maria and Elizabeth; Patrick Branwell (June 26, 1817), Emily (July 30, 1818), and Anne (January 17, 1820) followed in quick succession.

In the spring of 1820 the family moved from Thornton to Haworth, a small mill town in Yorkshire. The Haworth parsonage, built of stone on a high hill, was placed in between the moors and the cemetery of St. Michael's Church. This unsanitary location undermined the Brontë children's fragile health. Their mother lived for just a few months at Haworth; she succumbed to her own exhaustion and the inhospitable environment in September, when Charlotte was just five years old and Emily was just three.

Maria Brontë's sister, Miss Elizabeth Branwell, came to the parsonage to live with the family. She was a stern woman who expected respect, rather than love, from the children. Yet with Aunt Branwell's care and their father's guidance, the Brontë children developed their intellects and indulged their imaginations. They wandered the moors, told each other stories, read books together, and even discussed the salient political issues of the day. Maria, the eldest Brontë child, led the younger children in the performance of short plays.

In August 1824, Charlotte was sent to the Clergy Daughters' School at Cowan Bridge, and Emily

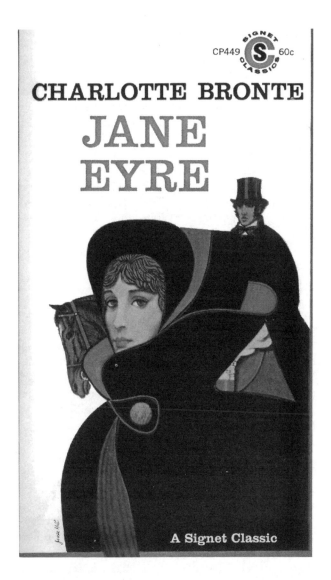

CP449 ⓢ 60c

CHARLOTTE BRONTE
JANE EYRE

A Signet Classic

This 1847 masterpiece by Charlotte Brontë follows a lonely orphan who becomes the governess at an estate and falls in love with the estate's owner.

followed in November. This school, located near Tunstall, Lancashire, was established to provide daughters of clergymen with an education and to train them to become governesses. As eager as she might have been to gain an education and join her older sisters, Maria and Elizabeth, Charlotte was disappointed with the Clergy Daughters' School.

William Carus Wilson, the school's founder, insisted that the girls observe his habits of self-restraint and denial. The girls were not allowed to play; they were always hungry and often sick. In 1825, Maria and Elizabeth contracted tuberculosis at school and were sent home, where first Maria, and then Elizabeth, died. Given the earlier death of their mother, the loss of their older sisters must have been traumatic for Charlotte and Emily. Some critics believe that the pain Charlotte felt at this time, her admiration for Maria, and her disdain for the school are reflected in *Jane Eyre*.

Charlotte and Emily returned home, where their father educated them himself. He encouraged them to read the books in his own collection and to visit the library at the Keighley Mechanics' Institute. It was not long before the girls were very familiar with the classics of English literature from Shakespeare to Byron. They read the *Arabian Nights Entertainments*, Whig and Tory newspapers, and a variety of magazines and annuals. Perhaps more importantly, however, the Brontë children began to write their own stories, essays, and poems.

The children's creativity soared after their father presented Branwell with a set of toy soldiers in June 1826. They named the soldiers and developed their characters, which they called the "Twelves." This led to the development of an imaginary world (complete with maps and watercolor renderings): the African kingdom of "Angria." The children kept themselves busy devising plots about the people of Angria, and its capital city, "Glass Town" (later called Verreopolis, and finally, Verdopolis). Charlotte and Branwell even wrote and crafted tiny magazines, describing current Angrian social and political issues which reflected those of England during their childhood. Emily and Anne abandoned Charlotte and Branwell's highly politicized and militaristic "Glass Town Confederacy" sagas to create their own alternative world in the Pacific: Gondal. These pursuits developed the girls' writing skills, allowed them to express repressed desires and emotions, and provided them with material for their

later, published works. In fact, both sets of Brontë children continued to write about their imaginary worlds as adults.

Studying and Teaching Away from Home

In 1831, Charlotte's godparents, the Atkinsons, agreed to help fund her education at a private school. Charlotte left her siblings and the toy soldiers to enroll at a school directed by Miss Margaret Wooler, in Roe Head, near Mirfield in East Yorkshire. At Roe Head, Charlotte made three important friends: Miss Wooler, with whom Charlotte would be friends for the rest of her life, and two students, Ellen Nussey and Mary Taylor. In addition to their companionship, these friends provided Charlotte with insight into a realm of English society heretofore unknown to her.

In 1832, Charlotte returned to Haworth, and began to tutor Emily and Anne. By July 1835, she was ready to return to Roe Head as an instructor, and, as part of her payment, Emily received free tuition. Emily did not enjoy Roe Head as much as Charlotte did, and she suffered from homesickness. When she finally returned to Haworth in October 1835, Anne was sent to Roe Head in her place. With Charlotte and Anne away, Emily and Branwell were left to talk and write together. While many critics have noted Branwell's influence on her work, and some even suggest that he, and not Emily, wrote *Wuthering Heights*, most scholars agree that Emily wrote her famous novel on her own. In any case, the period was one of growth for the fourth Brontë sister.

Emily left home again in 1838. This time, she served as an assistant teacher at Law Hill, near Halifax. Conditions at Law Hill were so difficult that Charlotte wrote a letter of complaint to its director, Miss Patchett. Nevertheless, Emily may have benefited somewhat from her time at Law Hill: the setting provided Emily with exposure to High Sunderland Hall, the house that scholars assert is the model for Wuthering Heights. Some scholars believe that Jack Sharp, a man who lived in Halifax, provided Emily with aspects of the famous *Wuthering Heights* character, Heathcliff. Emily could bear Law Hill for no longer than six months; she returned home in December 1838.

After Anne left the Wooler school in 1837, Charlotte's enthusiasm for her position there declined, and she returned home in May 1838. She worked for a time in 1839 as the governess for a family named Sidgwick, in Stonegappe, near Lothersdale; as the parents were condescending and the children rude, Charlotte soon relinquished this position and returned to Haworth.

Charlotte received two proposals of marriage in 1839, one from her friend Ellen Nussey's brother, Henry (a clergyman), and another from an Irish curate. Charlotte turned down both men. She was determined to marry a man she truly loved, and since she was almost certain that she never would truly love any man, she resigned herself to becoming an "old maid." Yet instead of becoming an old maid, Charlotte became a serious young writer. In late 1840, she sent one of her manuscripts to Hartley Coleridge, the son of Samuel Taylor Coleridge, to gain his opinion of her work. Despite her literary ambitions, Charlotte was unable to devote herself to writing full time. She went to work as a governess in March 1841 at the home of the White family in Rawdon, near Bradford, but this arrangement did not last long. Then Emily persuaded Charlotte to try to set up their own school, at their home in Haworth. Recognizing that they needed to supplement their qualifications as teachers, the two Brontë sisters set out for school in Brussels, where Mary Taylor was a student.

Schooling in Brussels

Accompanied by their father, Charlotte and Emily traveled to London, and then to Brussels, where they enrolled at the Pensionnat Heger in February 1842. Concentrating their efforts on French literature and some German, the young women studied diligently. Charlotte taught English, toured Brussels with Emily and the Taylors, and gradually began to look upon Constantin Heger, the husband of the school's owner, with unrequited affection. "Had she been younger," commented Herbert J. Rosengarten in the *Dictionary of Library Biography*, "her feelings might have taken the form of a schoolgirl infatuation, quickly roused and quickly quenched; but at twenty-six she had deeper yearnings, desires which possibly she did not understand herself."

A series of traumatic events led to the young women's return to England. First, in September 1842, William Weightman, their father's curate,

died, and then, in October, Martha Taylor died of cholera. When Aunt Branwell died at the end of that same month, Charlotte and Emily hastily returned to Haworth.

In late January 1943, Charlotte traveled to Brussels alone and, as Rosengarten noted, experienced "difficulties much like those she later bestowed on Lucy Snowe, who makes a similar journey in *Villette.*" Charlotte spent another year at the Heger school, where she held new duties as an English teacher. She also studied German and spent her free time visiting friends. As the year progressed, however, Charlotte grew increasingly lonely; Madame Heger's seeming knowledge of her affection for Monsieur Heger and his evasive attitude made matters worse. Charlotte left the school for good in January 1844.

As Branwell and Anne were living and working at Thorp Green, Emily was the only Brontë child at home in 1843. She spent much of her time writing poetry, and in February, not long after Charlotte's return, she collected the poems she'd been working on into two notebooks, one of which was labeled "Gondal Poems." During her time home alone, Emily also thought about ways to utilize the money Aunt Branwell had left the three Brontë sisters. As Charlotte had received a diploma from the Heger school, Emily and Charlotte began making serious plans for their own school. Yet "The Misses Brontë's Establishment for the Board and Education of a limited number of Young Ladies" failed to attract any applicants, and the young women were forced to abandon their plans.

The years 1844 and 1845 proved to be difficult ones for the Brontë family. Mr. Brontë's health was poor. Branwell was dismissed from his work as a tutor for the Robinson family in Thorp Green in July of that first year for inappropriate behavior. Instead of becoming a brilliant painter, he became an uncooperative alcoholic. The three Brontë sisters were disappointed with the outcome of their school initiative. Charlotte was still pained by her separation from Heger; his refusal to answer her anxious letters tormented her.

The Brontë Sisters Publish Their Poetry

Despite such troubles, or perhaps because of them, Emily continued to add poems to her notebooks. When Charlotte found and read one of them, in autumn 1845, she was impressed and told Emily that the poems should be published. Initially, Emily was very upset that Charlotte had read her work without her permission; she certainly was not willing to let strangers read her private poems. Nevertheless, Charlotte's persistence persuaded Emily to select twenty-one of her poems to add to some of Charlotte's and Anne's for publication. Emily retitled and revised many of the poems she chose; she also deleted references to Gondal.

With Aunt Branwell's money, the Brontë sisters paid thirty-six pounds, ten shillings, to have the collection published by Aylott and Jones. Afraid that their work would be judged differently if they revealed their identity as women, they chose masculine pseudonyms: Currer, Ellis and Acton Bell. *Poems by Currer, Ellis and Acton Bell* was available for sale in May 1846, for four shillings. It sold just two copies in one month.

After the publication of their poems, the sisters embarked upon a project they'd been thinking of for some time—publishing their own novels. Charlotte finished the manuscript for *The Professor: A Tale,* Emily contributed *Wuthering Heights,* and Anne presented *Agnes Grey* by late June 1846. They hoped to published the three novels together, and sent the manuscripts to publishers as a collection. After several complete rejections, Thomas Cautley Newby of London agreed to publish *Wuthering Heights* and *Agnes Grey,* but not *The Professor.* Ellis and Acton were obliged to pay fifty pounds to help meet the publishing costs, and the novels were finally published in December 1847. Critics did not know what to think about Emily's *Wuthering Heights,* and it was poorly received at first.

Charlotte continued her efforts to publish *The Professor.* When the manuscript found its way into the hands of William Smith Williams, a reader for the publishing firm of Smith, Elder, he rejected it, but suggested that Currer Bell send him something else. Charlotte had been working on *Jane Eyre* since August, 1846, when she was caring for her father after a cataract operation, and the novel was now complete. Smith, Elder accepted this manuscript for publication and paid Charlotte 500 pounds; the novel appeared for sale for thirty-one shillings, sixpence, in three volumes in October 1847, as *Jane Eyre: An Autobiography.*

Emily Brontë's pencil drawing of a fir tree adorns the cover of this collection of her poems.

Jane Eyre, "edited" by Currer Bell, was an instant success. The novel was published in a second edition, and then a third, by April 1848; the great novelist Thackeray sent Charlotte appreciative comments. Charlotte continued work on her next novel, *Shirley: A Tale,* and Newby agreed to publish Anne's *The Tenant of Wildfell Hall* in 1848. Yet Emily seems to have stopped writing. She hadn't written any original poems since September 1846, and the notion that she was working on a second novel remains unfounded. Critics will probably never know whether Emily stopped writing poems because of the publication of her first works, or because she was busy with a second version of *Wuthering Heights,* or just because she was busy caring for Branwell.

Given his alcoholism and opium addiction, Branwell's health had been deteriorating since

1845. Despite the loving care of his sisters, he finally died on September 24, 1848. Charlotte grieved intensely for Branwell for weeks, only to find that Emily (who, according to popular legend, refused to accept treatment for her own consumptive cough) was growing sicker. In the words of Lionel Trilling in *The Morningside*, Emily "died at twenty-nine longing very intensely for something she will not define and never got," on December 19. Although Charlotte and her friend Ellen Nussey tried to save Anne by taking her to the Scarborough shore, she died on May 28.

Alone at Haworth with her father, Charlotte grieved the death of her siblings. In search of solace, she quickly completed her third novel; *Shirley: A Tale* was published in 1849 in three volumes. Charlotte spent the next few years caring for her father, writing, and editing. For Smith, Elder, she wrote a Biographical Notice, selected some of Emily and Anne's poems, and added them to her corrected and revised edition of *Wuthering Heights* and *Agnes Grey* for publication. Charlotte also met and visited other writers, including Thackeray, G. H. Lewes, Samuel Rogers, and Elizabeth Cleghorn Gaskell, who would later write Brontë's biography, *The Life of Charlotte Brontë*. Charlotte also developed a friendship with George Smith, of Smith, Elder publishers.

Before *Villette*, Charlotte's third published novel, was published in late January 1853, she had received a proposal from Arthur Bell, another of her father's curates. Although Charlotte at first refused him, he persuaded her to marry him. The couple was engaged in April 1854, and they married on June 29, 1854. Charlotte's writing career was finished; she never completed "The Story of Willie Ellin," and "Emma," both fragments of novels. Soon after Charlotte realized she was pregnant, in January 1855, she was seriously weakened by nausea and vomiting, and died on March 31, 1855.

The Brontë Sisters' Legacy: Their Novels

After Charlotte's death, Gaskell found the manuscript for the *Professor* among her things at Haworth, and Sir James Kay-Shuttleworth encouraged her to publish it after some revision by Arthur Bell Nicholls. *The Professor*, Brontë's first novel, differs from her other novels because its protagonist and narrator, William Crimsworth, is male. Like Charlotte, however, this character becomes a teacher in a Brussels school. Here, his superior, Madame Reuter, attempts to gain his affections; William expertly evades her and increases her passion for him at the same time.

While, according to Rosengarten, the novel "suffers . . . from awkwardness in construction and in the handling of the plot," it has "real power in its delineation of character and in its exploration of the individual's struggle to find emotional fulfillment despite socially repressive circumstances." Rosengarten remarked that if *The Professor* "is sometimes slow, even dull," it focuses "on the pains and pleasures of a recognizably ordinary life." This focus "places Charlotte Brontë at the forefront of developments in modern literary realism."

It was *Jane Eyre* which made Charlotte famous during her lifetime and which has proved to be an enduring classic. In fact, according to Nancy R. Ives, writing in *Library Journal*, *Jane Eyre* is "often the book that introduces students to serious literature." Jane, who narrates her own story, is an unattractive, lonely orphan surrounded by the members of a surrogate family, the Reeds, who neglect, humiliate, and abuse her. She takes comfort in books and her own stories, but the doll she clutches cannot fulfill her need for love. Jane must call upon her strength and integrity to find a happier life.

She leaves the Reed home for the Lowood Institution, which Rosengarten describes as "a thinly veiled reminiscence of [Charlotte's] life at the Clergy Daughters' School at Cowan Bridge." Jane Eyre's friend, the tolerant, meek Helen Burns, according to Rosengarten, was modeled after Charlotte's elder sister Maria. Jane takes a position as a governess at Thornfield Hall when she is just eighteen. Thinking that the mistress of Thornfield is dead, she develops a romance with Edward Fairfax Rochester and even agrees to marry him. Before the ceremony can take place, however, Jane discovers that Rochester's wife is alive, though insane, at Thornfield Hall. Jane refuses to live with Rochester and runs away to live with her cousins. When she finally returns to Thornfield, Rochester's wife dies. The lovers marry, and Jane finds happiness as the new mistress of Thornfield Hall.

As Rosengarten noted, "Victorian readers were disturbed by the novel's suggestion that women need not always be passive or submissive, and by its treatment of love, which, by contemporary standards, seemed coarse and offensive." These initial readers also questioned Brontë's treatment of Christianity. Nevertheless, wrote Rosengarten, while "modern critics, often eager to see in Jane a prototype of the modern liberated woman, rightly emphasize her spirit of independence and self-reliance, it should also be recognized that in her quest for earthly happiness Jane is guided by a simple faith that gives her the inner strength to continue her search."

Unlike *Jane Eyre, Shirley* follows the lives of several characters, is set in the context of a historical event, and broaches a political issue. As Rosengarten noted, the "novel is set in the West Riding of Yorkshire during the troubled years of 1811-1812, when the economic hardships ensuing from the war with France . . . led to massive unemployment and widespread rioting in the wool-producing districts." The first part of the book, written before Emily's death, portrays the relationship between Caroline Helstone and her cousin Roger Moore, a mill owner. Shirley Keeldar, a beautiful, witty landowner, is introduced later in the book. When Caroline thinks that Shirley has won the love of Robert, she becomes ill. Yet Shirley directs her affection toward Robert's brother Louis, and they marry despite the fact that he is a tutor and she is an heiress. Caroline is nursed back to health by a woman who turns out to be her long-lost mother, and Robert, who has been shot during an 1812 Luddite uprisings caused by the turmoil abroad, heals and professes his love for her.

Brontë researched the historical context of *Shirley* thoroughly. The "result" of this research, in the words of Rosengarten, "is an authentic recreation of the period in which local events are merged with issues of national policy, and fiction is expertly blended with historical fact." Her novel also "offers an oblique comment on the need for more tolerant attitudes on the part of the governing class in the England of 1848." After noting that

The windswept moors of Top Withens are believed to have inspired the setting of Emily Brontë's 1847 work, *Wuthering Heights*.

many critics were disappointed because *Shirley* was so unlike *Jane Eyre*, Rosengarten asserted that *Shirley* "may lack the concentration, the driving force of a single vision that gives *Jane Eyre* its power; but in its treatment of complex social issues and its panoramic study of a turbulent period of English History, *Shirley* ranks with novels like Disraeli's *Sybil* (1845), Mrs. Gaskell's *Mary Barton* (1848), or Dicken's *Hard Times* (1954) as a significant contribution to the Victorian debate about the goals and values of industrial capitalism."

Villette is the story of Lucy Snowe, told in an autobiographical manner. Lucy introduces herself when she is just fourteen and living with Louisa Bretton, her grandmother, and Bretton's son, John; a motherless girl, Paulina, joins the household later. Lucy leaves the Bretton household to provide for herself, and gains employment caring for Miss Marchmont, an elderly woman. When Marchmont dies, Lucy travels to Villette to teach at a school, and it is not long before she meets the Brettons again. Lucy gradually falls in love with John, who is now a doctor, but the school's owner Madame Beck, and one of the school's students, competes for his love as well. When Paulina re-enters the story, John falls in love with her, and Madame Beck's cousin Paul, another teacher, falls in love with Lucy. He helps her set up her own school in Villette, and sets off for the West Indies promising to return. Although Lucy waits for Paul for three years, he drowns at sea during a shipwreck on his way home.

According to Rosengarten, "Lucy Snowe embodies much of Brontë's own experience and outlook, and in many respects is a projection of her creator's inner self." This book is "colored even more highly than *The Professor* by Brontë's recollections of her two years at Pensionnat Heger": characters, settings, and events are modeled after those people she met and places she visited in Brussels and London.

At the time it was published, many readers found fault with *Villette's* ambiguous ending. Other critiques complained that the book focused on pain and hunger to its detriment. Rosengarten asserts that these latter judgements "reflect an ineluctable truth: the source of the novel's great strength, its power to arouse and disturb, does lie in the author's painful attempt to reconcile the conflict between her desires and her sense of inadequacy."

While *Jane Eyre* is one of the most popular and widely cited novels in the canon of English literature, as a critic for the *Washington Post Book World* noted, some readers consider *Villette* to be Charlotte Brontë's "masterpiece."

Charlotte left two unfinished novels, "The Story of Willie Ellin" (1853), and "Emma" (1853), when she died. "The Story of Willie Ellin" describes the sad relationship between two brothers, Edward and William; Edward, the eldest, treats ten-year-old Willie with cruelty and whips him when he tries to run away. "Emma," a ten-page manuscript, begins the story of Matilda Fitzgibbon. Her father leaves her at a girls' school after leaving the staff with the idea that she is an heiress. When Miss

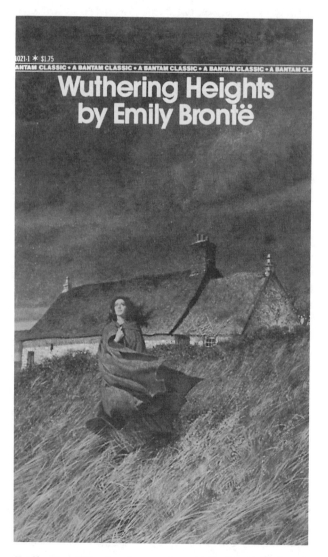

Emily Brontë's classic novel, written in 1847, just a year before her death, tells a powerful tale of passion and evil.

Wilcox, who runs the school, discovers that Matilda's father has given her a false address and has disappeared, she confronts the girl. The fragment ends as Matilda collapses and is cared for by a man named Mr. Ellin. In 1981, "Another Lady" attempted to finish the "Emma," but, according to Patricia Meyer Spacks in the *New York Times Book Review, Emma* "lacks the symbolic depth of Charlotte Brontë's fiction and its characteristic energizing undercurrent of rage."

Wuthering Heights

Emily Brontë tells a story of passion, evil, and violence in *Wuthering Heights.* After Lockwood's arrival at Thrushcross Grange in the Yorkshire moors, he visits his landlord, Heathcliff, at an odd, imposing home called Wuthering Heights. Lockwood learns the strange history of the house's inhabitants from Nelly Dean, a maidservant, when he returns to Thrushcross Grange. According to Dean, Mr. Earnshaw, Wuthering Heights's owner, brought Heathcliff as a young child to live with the Earnshaw family. Although Heathcliff and the Earnshaw daughter, Catherine, develop a close relationship, the Earnshaw son, Hindley, detests and mistreats him. To stay away from Hindley and enjoy each other's company, Catherine and Heathcliff roam the moors. They meet the young people living in a nearby home called Thrushcross Grange, Edgar and Isabella Linton.

When Edgar Linton proposes marriage to Catherine, she discusses the matter with Nelly Dean, and remarks that Hindley has debased Heathcliff to the extent that she shouldn't marry him. Heathcliff, who has been eavesdropping, hears this comment and, enraged and humiliated, rushes away before he can hear Catherine testify to her love for Heathcliff. Heathcliff is away from Wuthering Heights for three years; just before his return, Catherine finally marries Edgar. Heathcliff is now a rich man, and he persuades Isabella to marry him.

Catherine, who has been ill since the disappearance of Heathcliff, dies after a clandestine and heartfelt conversation with Heathcliff and after giving birth to a baby girl, Cathy. Heathcliff and Isabel also have a son, Linton, who lives in Wuthering Heights after his mother's death. Hindley gambles away his ownership of Wuthering Heights, and upon his death it is transferred to Heathcliff along with the guardianship of

Hindley's son, Hareton. With evil and greedy intentions, Heathcliff forces Cathy and Linton to marry, so that he will own Thrushcross Grange when Linton dies (as a woman, Cathy had no rights to her father's home).

On a later visit to Thrushcross Grange and Wuthering Heights, Lockwood finds that Heathcliff is dead. Cathy and Hareton are to marry and abandon Wuthering Heights to a servant. Lockwood hears tales of the ghost of Heathcliff roaming the moors with a woman, perhaps Catherine. With that, the novel ends, and readers cannot be certain of the story's message; despite the labors of numerous literary critics, no single interpretation can satisfactorily explain the book. As Tom Winnifrith wrote in the *Concise Dictionary of British Literary Biography*, "Perhaps the only certain message of *Wuthering Heights* is that nothing is certain. Brontë's defiance of rigid categories and her refusal to divide people into saints and sinners, gentry and servants, good and bad is very unVictorian, but does not seem out of keeping with what is known of her temperament."

As Winnifrith explained, *Wuthering Heights* gradually won respect from critics. In fact, "it was only in 1899, with the publication of the Haworth Edition of the Brontë novels, that Emily was finally established as a novelist superior to Charlotte in the introductions of Mrs. Humphrey Ward." The fact that Charlotte Brontë is "an author so much easier to tie down to a definite meaning than Emily, has meant that Emily has slightly lost ground at her sister's expense, although *Wuthering Heights* remains the most popular and the most typical Brontë novel in both academic and popular circles."

Without denying the popularity of *Wuthering Heights*, Rosengarten remarked that while the "stark and mythopoeic qualities of *Wuthering Heights* undeniably reflect a genius and a vision beyond Charlotte's capacities . . . Emily's enigmatic romance, unique of its kind, was a dead end in English fiction." He asserted that "the painful realism of Charlotte's studies of the human heart gave a fresh impetus and a new direction to the genre of the novel."

Poetry

Since the publication of the sisters' poems in 1846, Emily's poetry has been generally favored by critics. Some readers have even declared that Charlotte Brontë was the worst poet among the Brontë children. According to Grevel Lindop in the *Times Literary Supplement*, Charlotte's poetry "is simply mediocre—the tepid, Romanticizing verse exercises, one would think, of an early-Victorian young lady unremarkable in everything but her addiction to pen and paper." Nevertheless, many critics, like Lindop, consider Charlotte Brontë's poetry worth reading because it holds "much that is of biographical and contextual interest for a reading [of her] mature work."

Although *Poems by Currer, Ellis and Acton Bell* did not sell well at first, the popularity of Charlotte's *Jane Eyre* and the re-evaluation of Emily's *Wuthering Heights* in later years sparked new interest in Emily's poetry; stirring poems like "No Coward Soul" and "Cold in the Earth" have especially fascinated critics. Interpreting Emily's poetry, however, is a difficult task. As Angela Leighton explained in the *Times Literary Supplement*, the meanings of Emily's poems were transformed when she revised them for publication in *Poems by Currer, Ellis and Acton Bell*. Depending on which version of the original poem "R Alcona to J Brenzaida" (first published as "Remembrance") one reads, for example, the poem may be interpreted as "an externalized Romantic melodrama or an internalized Victorian elegy . . ." Scholars have yet to decide whether Emily's Gondal poems should be understood in the context in which they were written, or as they were revised by an older, more mature young woman. C. Day Lewis, a Poet Laureate of England, decided that "the Gondal saga was a mere scaffolding, which, having enabled the construction of a number of poems, could then be dismantled and dismissed."

Generally, scholars agree on two points about Emily's poetry: Emily did not have the poetic tools of her contemporaries and produced direct, unembellished, often masculine poetry (influenced by the poet Cowper and her Protestant background), but she did possess deep, if often suppressed, passion. As a critic for the *Saturday Review* asserted, "Her creative power, it must be admitted, is not great. . . . But she has passion, energy of thought, and daring—the daring to lay hold of those problems which arise, not from a large experience, but from the very constitution of our being."

Similarly, Robert Bridges, the Poet Laureate of England from 1913 to 1930, remarked in an essay in the *Times Literary Supplement* that Emily's poems suffered from an "indifference to artistic beauty" and that Emily was "certainly not delicately conscious of the music either of her rhythm or of her rhyme," yet he asserted that "a genius" was speaking in her poems: "when one has got accustomed to her voice it is wonderful what a range it covers, and how various are her successes." "Art for art's sake is the very last phrase one could apply to her work," wrote C. Day Lewis in *Brontë Society Transactions.*

Some one hundred years after the first publication of Emily's poetry, critics were still trying to determine the source of Emily's passion. Supported by Charlotte Brontë's own opinion of her sister, C. Day Lewis insisted in 1954 that Emily's "ruling passion" was freedom, and that "the source of Emily Brontë's proud recalcitrance, her preoccupation with themes of captivity, exile and freedom, was her sex; the limitation of not being a man." According to Lewis, this doesn't mean that Emily "consciously rebelled against being a woman."

In 1980, in *Women's Studies: An Interdisciplinary Journal*, Christine Gallant stated that Brontë's "poetry was significantly shaped by her experience of what it was to be a woman in nineteenth-century England." Teddi Lynn Chichester suggested in 1991 in *Victorian Poetry* that, because of the deaths of her "beloved female family members," femininity was particularly vulnerable to Emily, and thus she possessed a "desire for alternative selfhoods, as expressed in her poetry."

Critics have enjoyed exploring the relationship between Emily's poetry and *Wuthering Heights,* which C. Day Lewis called a "great, mad poem in prose." Leighton, for one, remarked in the *Times Literary Supplement* that Brontë is "a poet of first lines," her "taut hymns and songs are the voice of a poet, perhaps all the more impressive for being one who, essentially, was practising for greater prose."

Clearly, despite their short lives, Charlotte and Emily Brontë provided critics with much to contemplate. Scholars are continually seeking fresh interpretations of the Brontës' novels and poetry. Others search for hidden links between their personal histories and their works. The debate about which Brontë sister was the better writer continues. Yet more casual readers may be more interested in Patricia Meyer Spacks's claim in the *New York Times Book Review* that "[t]here's nothing like a 19th-century novel." Given Charlotte and Emily's contributions to the genre, we may conclude that one of the most satisfying aspects of the Brontë's gift to later generations lies in the pleasure of reading *Jane Eyre* and *Wuthering Heights*.

■ Works Cited

Bridges, Robert, "The Poems of Emily Brontë," *Times Literary Supplement*, January 12, 1911, pp. 9-10.

Chichester, Teddi Lynn, "Evading 'Earth's Dungeon Tomb': Emily Brontë, A. G. A., and The Fatally Feminine," in *Victorian Poetry*, Volume 29, Number 1, Spring, 1991, pp. 1-15.

"The Fascinations of the Brontës," *Times Literary Supplement*, December 25, 1969, p. 1464.

Gallant, Christine, "The Archetypal Feminine in Emily Brontë's Poetry," in *Women's Studies: An Interdisciplinary Journal*, Volume 7, Number 1, 1980, pp. 79-94.

Leighton, Angela, "Famous First Lines," *Times Literary Supplement*, January 15, 1993, p. 24.

Lewis, C. Day, "The Poetry of Emily Brontë," in *Brontë Society Transactions*," Volume 13, No. 3, 1957, pp. 83-99.

Lindop, Grevel, "Precociously Poetical," *Times Literary Supplement*, August 9, 1985, p. 872.

"Poetesses," in *Saturday Review*, May 23, 1868, pp. 678-9.

Rosengarten, Herbert J., "Charlotte Brontë," *Dictionary of Literary Biography: Victorian Novelists Before 1885*, Volume 21, Gale, 1983, pp. 25-54.

Spacks, Patricia Meyer, "Family History," *New York Times Book Review*, July 12, 1981, p. 13.

Review of *Villette*, *Washington Post Book World*, November 16, 1986, p. 12.

Trilling, Lionel, "The Poems of Emily Brontë," in his *Speaking of Literature and Society*, edited by Diana Trilling, Harcourt Brace Jovanovich, 1980, pp. 3-6.

Winnifrith, Tom, "Emily Brontë," *Concise Dictionary of British Literary Biography: Victorian Writers, 1834-1890*, Volume 4, Gale, 1991, pp. 60-73.

■ For More Information See

BOOKS

Bloom, Harold (editor), *Heathcliff*, Chelsea House, 1993.

Boumelha, Penny, *Charlotte Brontë*, Indiana University Press, 1990.

Frank, Katherine, *A Chainless Soul: A Life of Emily Brontë*, Houghton Mifflin, 1990.

Gardiner, Juliet, *The Brontës at Haworth*, Clarkson Potter, 1992.

Gaskell, Elizabeth Cleghorn, *The Life of Charlotte Brontë*, J. M. Dent, 1992.

Gates, Barbara Timm (editor), *Critical Essays on Charlotte Brontë*, Boston, MA, G.K. Hall, 1990.

Gerin, Winifred, *Emily Brontë: A Biography*, Oxford University Press, 1971.

Gerin, Winifred, *Charlotte Brontë: The Evolution of Genius*, Oxford University Press, 1991.

Ghnassia, Jill Dix, *Metaphysical Rebellion in the Works of Emily Brontë: A Reinterpretation*, St. Martin's Press, 1994.

Grove, Robin, *Emily Brontë's "Wuthering Heights,"* Sydney University Press in association with Oxford University Press, 1994.

Nestor, Pauline, *Charlotte Brontë's "Jane Eyre"*, St. Martin's Press, 1992.

Tayler, Irene, *Holy Ghosts: The Male Muses of Emily and Charlotte Brontë*, Columbia University Press, 1990.

Wheat, Patricia H., *The Adytum of the Heart: The Literary Criticism of Charlotte Brontë*, Fairleigh Dickinson University Press, 1992.

PERIODICALS

Booklist, January 15, 1992, p. 932.
Brontë Society Gazette, May, 1990.
Publishers Weekly, April 24, 1978, p. 76.
School Library Journal, February, 1993, p. 33.
Times Literary Supplement, January 10, 1992, p. 8.

—*Sketch by R. Garcia-Johnson*

James L. Brooks

■ Personal

Born May 9, 1940, in Brooklyn, NY; son of Edward M. and Dorothy Helen (Sheinheit) Brooks; married Marianne Catherine Morrissey, July 7, 1964 (divorced, 1971); married Holly Beth Holmberg, July 23, 1978; children: (first marriage) Amy Lorraine; (second marriage) Chloe, Cooper, Joseph.

■ Addresses

Office—Gracie Films, Columbia Pictures, Poitier Building, 10202 W. Washington Blvd., Culver City, CA, 90232. *Agent*—International Creative Management, 8899 Beverly Blvd., Los Angeles, CA, 90048.

■ Career

Writer, producer, and director. Columbia Broadcasting System (CBS) News, New York City, reporter and writer, 1964-66; Wolper Productions, Los Angeles, CA, writer and producer of documentaries, 1966-67; American Broadcasting Company (ABC),

Los Angeles, executive story editor and creator of television series *Room 222*, 1968-69; CBS, Studio City, CA, executive producer and creator of television series *The Mary Tyler Moore Show*, 1970-77; founder of Gracie Films, 1984. Producer, co-creator, and writer for numerous television series and films, 1968-94, including *Thursday's Game*, *Cindy* (musical), *Rhoda*, *The New Lorenzo Music Show*, *Friends and Lovers*, *Lou Grant*, *Taxi*, *The Associates*, *Terms of Endearment*, *Starting Over*, *Broadcast News*, *I'll Do Anything*, *Sibs*, *The Tracey Ullman Show*, *The Simpsons*, and *The Critic*; also producer of the films *Big*, 1988, *War of the Roses*, 1989, and executive producer of *Say Anything*, 1989; producer and director of the play *Brooklyn Laundry*, 1991. Appeared as an actor in the film *Modern Romance*, 1981. Guest lecturer, Stanford Graduate School of Communications. *Member:* Writers Guild of America, Directors Guild of America, Television Academy of Arts and Sciences, Screen Actors Guild, Academy of Motion Picture Arts and Sciences.

■ Awards, Honors

Emmy Award, best new series, National Academy of Television Arts and Sciences, 1969, for *Room 222*; Emmy Awards, outstanding comedy writing, 1971, 1974-77, outstanding comedy series, 1975-77, Emmy Award nominations, outstanding comedy series 1971-74, outstanding writing in a comedy series, 1973, Writers Guild of America Award nomination, best comic episode, 1972, Peabody Award, Writers Guild of America Award nomination, best teleplay, TV Critics Achievement in Comedy Award, TV Critics Achievement in Series Award, and Humanitas Prize, 1977, all for *The Mary Tyler Moore Show*; Golden Globe Award, 1974, Emmy Award nominations, outstanding writing in a comedy series and outstanding comedy series, 1975, and Humanitas Prizes, 1977 and 1982, all for *Rhoda*; Peabody Awards, 1977 and 1978, Emmy Awards, outstanding writing in a drama, 1978-82, and Emmy Award nomination, outstanding drama series, 1978, all for *Lou Grant*; TV Film Critics Circle Awards, achievement in comedy and in a series, 1977, Golden Globe Awards, best comedy, 1978-80, Humanitas Prize, 1979, Emmy Awards, outstanding comedy series, 1979-81, and Emmy Award nominations, outstanding comedy series, 1982-83, all for *Taxi*; Writers Guild of America Award nomination, outstanding script, 1978, for *Cindy*; Academy Awards, best film, best direction, and best adapted screenplay, American Academy of Motion Picture Arts and Sciences, 1984, Golden Globe Award, and New York Film Critics Circle Award, all for *Terms of Endearment*; numerous Emmy Awards and nominations, 1986-90, for *The Tracey Ullman Show*; Academy Award nominations, best picture and best original screenplay, 1987, and New York Film Critics Circle Awards, best picture, best direction and best original screenplay, 1987, all for *Broadcast News*; Emmy Awards, outstanding animated special and outstanding animated program, 1990, for *The Simpsons*.

■ Writings

SCREENPLAYS

(And co-producer) *Starting Over*, Paramount, 1979.
(And co-producer and director) *Terms of Endearment*, Paramount, 1983.
(And producer and director) *Broadcast News*, Twentieth Century-Fox, 1987.
(And co-producer and director) *I'll Do Anything*, Columbia Pictures, 1994.

TELEVISION SERIES

(And creator) *Room 222*, ABC, 1968-69.
(And co-creator and executive producer) *The Mary Tyler Moore Show*, CBS, 1970-77.

Also writer for other television series, including (producer) *Paul Sand in Friends and Lovers*, 1974;

(co-creator and co-executive producer) *Rhoda*, 1974-82; *The New Lorenzo Music Show*, 1976; (co-creator and executive producer) *Taxi*, 1976-83; (co-creator and producer) *Lou Grant*, 1978-82; (co-writer and co-executive producer) *Cindy*, 1978; (co-creator and executive producer) *The Associates*, 1979; (co-creator, co-executive producer, and executive producer) *The Tracey Ullman Show*, 1986-90; (executive producer) *The Simpsons*, 1990-94; (co-creator and executive producer) *Sibs*, 1991-92; and (co-executive producer) *The Critic*, 1993.

TELEVISION FILMS

(Co-writer and co-producer) *Thursday Game*, 1971.

■ Sidelights

James L. Brooks is variously described as a mercurial man who can bubble effusively one minute and turn apprehensive the next, and an engaging eccentric who has made a career of turning his own inner turmoil into comedy. The tall, bearded Brooks was born in Brooklyn, New York, in 1940 and raised in a lower-middle-class section of North Bergen, New Jersey across the Hudson River. "I was early latchkey," he told *Interview* reporter Wayne Stambler in 1988. "My father wasn't a regular financial contributor in the home and my mother worked very hard: So I was alone a lot. My mother was an enormous influence on me."

In the late 1950s Brooks attended New York University in Greenwich Village, but after a few courses of study dropped out of college to take a job as a copy boy for CBS News in New York. After four years of toil in the newsroom (later the source for his television news-based *The Mary Tyler Moore Show* and *Broadcast News*), he managed to work his way up to newswriter and reporter, and by 1966 he was ready to leave New York City for Los Angeles.

In Hollywood Brooks wrote and produced documentaries for David L. Wolper (who, in 1984, would be the producer of the television coverage of the Olympics in Los Angeles), and began writing for television—primarily as a freelancer, at first writing and selling scripts for various situation comedies. Before landing a job at ABC in 1968 as executive story editor, where he went on to create the award-winning television series *Room 222*,

One of Brooks early successes, for which he served as the executive story editor and creator, was the 1960s television series *Room 222*, which focused on life at an integrated Los Angeles high school.

Brooks contributed to such programs as *The Andy Griffith Show, Hey Landlord, That Girl* and *My Mother the Car.*

The 1970s: Defining Television Comedy

These early beginnings in television writing led to the show Brooks is perhaps best known for, *The Mary Tyler Moore Show.* Acting as creator, writer, and producer, Brooks found success in this long-running television comedy that, after seven years on television, garnered numerous awards and honors. The show features a single woman, Mary Richards, in pursuit of a career and mirrors the times in its reflection of American women's efforts at social and economic liberation. During her seven years in WJM's newsroom, Mary moves up the ladder, eventually earning the title and

responsibilities of Associate Producer. The program typifies what have become hallmarks of the Brooks style: wit, sentiment, and originality.

During the 1970s Brooks created a string of television hits that each, in their way, reflected their times and exemplified a high standard of television writing. In 1976 he created *Rhoda,* a spin-off from *The Mary Tyler Moore Show* that features Mary's best friend, Rhoda, as she pursues her dreams and goals in Manhattan. During the series' six year run Rhoda experiences her share of economic and social woes along with the nation, including marital problems that eventually lead to divorce. Another spin-off from *The Mary Tyler Moore Show* was the dramatic series *Lou Grant,* which emerged in the late 1970s and was typified by a sense of social responsibility. Story lines feature reporters uncovering the truth behind the lies, much as Woodward and Bernstein uncovered the truth, a few years prior to the show's debut, about Watergate.

Brooks also created *Taxi* in the late 1970s, a show that more reflected his trademark rapier wit. *Taxi*, as distinctive a series as any of its predecessors, captures with comic gusto the flip side of disenchantment—not the despair, but the devil-may-care attitude that emerges when one realizes, after all, that there is really nothing to lose but one's sense of humor. In typical Brooksian style, the series always manages to zero in on the people, to focus on the sentimental notion (for some this is a criticism, for others praise) that what matters most in life is what transpires between individual friends and lovers.

The Transition from Television to Movies

By the end of the 1970s Brooks, with three hit television series running concurrently (*Taxi, Rhoda,* and *Lou Grant*), made the leap into films. Testing the waters gingerly (for him) he confined his efforts to writing and producing. This first film, *Starting Over* (released by Paramount in 1979, starring Burt Reynolds and Jill Clayburgh), mines the rich territory of Brooks's own 1971 divorce from his first wife and 1978 marriage to his second. Armed with a moderate success as a writer and an even better one as a producer, Brooks optioned the rights to a novel by Larry McMurtry, wrote an adaptation, and began plans for his directing debut. The only trouble was that he received no encouragement whatsoever from the major studios.

Brooks scored another hit with the Emmy Award-winning *The Mary Tyler Moore Show,* featuring Moore as a single working woman on the news staff of a Minneapolis television station and also starring Ed Asner, Ted Knight, Gavin MacLeod, and Betty White.

According to the studio brass, this film, *Terms of Endearment,* which focuses on a problematic mother-daughter relationship, was too uncommercial, too downbeat. But somehow Brooks got Paramount to back the project, and in 1983 the film opened to rave reviews. Starring Debra Winger, Shirley MacLaine and Jack Nicholson, *Terms of Endearment* was lauded for its comic richness despite a story mired in the touchy subject of death and cancer. Indeed, the success was stupendous. As Brooks told Stambler: "With 'Terms,' a lot of smart people told me that in ways I couldn't imagine it would be rocky going. And it was."

"In adapting [McMurtry's] entertaining and affecting but dramatically diffuse novel, Brooks has contrived to finesse most of the structural defects built into its rambling, episodic nature," wrote film critic Gary Arnold in the *Washington Post.* "*Terms of Endearment,*" stated Vincent Canby in the *New York Times,* "is not a perfect movie . . . [it] meanders around a plot that covers approximately 30 years. It contains one more fatal illness than you may want to witness . . . [but this work] must be one of the most engaging films of the year, to be cherished as much for the low-pressure way in which it operates . . . as for the fact that it contains what are possibly the best performances ever given by Shirley Maclaine and Jack Nicholson." The film won three major Academy Awards, including best picture and best screenplay adaptation for Brooks, and made a writing/producing/directing movie star (a "triple threat") out of him in the process.

Broadcast News

In 1987, Brooks returned to the fertile ground of his newsroom experience and knowledge to produce, write, and direct *Broadcast News.* The story concerns a love triangle—among Jane, a savvy, spitfire of a news producer played by Holly Hunter, Aaron, a brilliant but uncharismatic reporter played by Albert Brooks, and Tom, an attractive but less-gifted anchorman played by William Hurt. Complicated, witty, urbane, intelligent, and ultimately an exploration of individuals in the news rather than an expose of the business itself, *Broadcast News* was nonetheless a popular and critical success.

The film, Brooks told Stambler, was "very much about how we use work to fill these voids we have in our lives. Work is family. People are always saying that when you make work such a large part of your life, it is an abandonment . . . of all your other values . . . an attempt to distort work into something that it wasn't meant to be."

Writing about *Broadcast News* in *Nation,* James Lardner observed that Brooks "said that he intended to make a romantic comedy rather than a social commentary, and through most of the movie his observations of the milieu have a nicely incidental flavor: This is how things are, he is saying, make of them what you will." Lardner lauded the film for rising above its potential for sit-com in its essential premise, observing a sense of reality in the interweaving of plot and character. "Work is more than a background for these characters," Lardner wrote. "Take away their jobs and they would have nothing to say to each other, and nowhere to go. This is not only a plausible description of such a relationship in the movie's chosen context but a great relief in the context of recent movies. For once, we get to watch two people fall in love (more or less) without going through one of those gauzy, touristic montage sequences . . . with which Hollywood is wont to camouflage its ignorance of the human heart." Lardner continued: "Insofar as Brooks has succumbed to the temptation to comment on what's wrong with TV news, he tends to ally himself with the view that there's nothing wrong that a little vigilance couldn't cure."

People writer Peter Travers called the film "the best and most perceptively hilarious movie of the year." Tom O'Brien, reviewing the film for *Commonweal,* found it "genuinely witty" and applauded the way it "neatly" fused "romance, studio soap opera, and social satire." He, like Lardner, though, found some fault with the film, noting that "director Brooks allows the love triangle to go on too long; he also stacks the deck too patly in the ugly duckling's favor." Nonetheless, O'Brien credited Brooks with shaping "the best comic performance in some time by Jack Nicholson" and adds that "the screenplay is both fun and biting. There are lines with such a precise quality that you know James Brooks heard or thought of them long ago, then saved them for occasions like these."

Writing in the *New Republic,* critic Stanley Kauffmann found the film "much more bourgeois

Holly Hunter, William Hurt, and Albert Brooks starred in the 1987 romantic comedy *Broadcast News*, which Brooks wrote, produced, and directed.

than 'Terms,'" which had been blasted by some critics in 1983 for being too common and sentimental. "The people in 'Terms' lived in a more or less enclosed society," Kauffmann wrote, "and coped with what came along in terms of society. But the leading characters in the new film, although shown to be of bourgeois origins, are now part of a smart set distanced from these origins, are privy to the trimmings and betrayals of bourgeois culture."

But Kauffmann, like many other critics, found that despite the film's shortcomings, its "dialogue is shrewd, so bright that it almost visibly glistens as it races past" and "the story is well-built." Indeed, wrote Kauffmann, though his directing lacks "cameo moments like the brief summerhouse scene between Nicholson and Shirley MacLaine in 'Terms' . . . the slapstick sequence aside, his work is authoritative, fluent." Kauffmann's main problem with the film is its lack of bite: "Does it show prejudice to expect a film about TV news to be critical of it? To me, criticism seems inseparable from this choice of setting. To accept the setting as simply one out of a thousand possibilities, without the imperative of criticism, is to accept the limitations of TV news itself." He went on to conclude that the film is "highly amusing. But its cleverness has no bite—worse, is not meant to have any. Like the caustic comedies of George S. Kauffmann and Neil Simon, it is finally part of its own subject."

Broadcast News was the first picture released by Brooks's own film company, Gracie Films, named for the famous female half of the comedy team known as Burns and Allen in the 1940s and 1950s, Gracie Allen, the late wife of the ageless George Burns. Brooks created Gracie Films as a refuge for the writer, and while in some more recent cases that have placed Brooks the director at odds with Brooks the screenwriter, by and large Brooks has remained true to his vision: "The justification for Gracie was to try this idea out," he told *American Film* writer Sean Mitchell, "that we'd consider it a personal failure if more than the original writer's name appeared on the credits. . . . We wanted authorship of movies," he added, "not the latest draft from the latest person hired." Indeed, the quality of Brooks's work on big screen and small has come from his commitment to the fidelity of the written word.

The Simpsons

David Ansen, in a *Newsweek* blurb on the 1989 opening of a new film produced by Brooks (*Say Anything*), noted that whether he is the writer-director or the producer, "Brooks always embroiders his movies with quirky, specific touches that make familiar genres fresh." The same can also be said of his television programs, which from the early 1970s (*The Mary Tyler Moore Show*) to the 1990s (*The Simpsons*) have managed to capture the spirit of the times with language, characters, and situations that are at once unique and universal. There may be critics who dislike this or that aspect of a film or television program produced, written, and/or directed by Brooks, but few fail to praise his cleverness and originality, or his eye for the current moment.

In 1986 Brooks returned to his home ground, television, producing *The Tracey Ullman Show*, which ran on the Fox television network for four years. Though it never garnered the kind of ratings Brooks's 1970s network series raked in, *The Tracey Ullman Show* was widely respected (and awarded) for its comedy writing and format, and bears the distinction of being the show where *The Simpsons*, the 1990s animated television series phenomenon, got its start, thanks to executive producer Brooks.

Bill Zehme, writing in *Rolling Stone*, stated that "without Brooks, of course, it is doubtful Simpsonia would have gripped the land. He sponsored the Simpsons' rise by hiring [Matt] Groening . . . to contribute his incisive cartoonery to 'The Tracey Ullman Show.' . . . Each week, the Simpsons, in skitlet form, bracketed Ullman's commercial breaks." When the show was "spun off" in 1989, the Simpsons became "the soul of Fox Broadcasting, dependably notching Top Twenty Nielsen ratings."

I'll Do Anything

The renewed television success brought to Brooks by *The Simpsons*, however, has not interfered with his movie projects. One of Brooks's more recent films, *I'll Do Anything*, is a satire of Hollywood that was originally conceived as a musical film but ended up being reshaped into a comedy-romance with one song. The venture is typical of Brooks's passion for ideas—for years, he said in

Brooks's popular animated series *The Simpsons* introduced one of televison's favorite wisecrackers, the irrepressible Bart Simpson.

an interview with Nancy Griffin for *Premiere*, "I knew I wanted to somehow sort out my feelings about Hollywood." Because he felt there was a lot of prejudice in people's minds about what Hollywood was and wasn't, he continued in his *Premiere* interview, "I thought that required music to get around, to bring people in to some of the emotional truths. . . . You couldn't attempt to put a psychological thought into a child's mouth without a song . . . or to make a sad ballet out of tablehopping in a Hollywood Restaurant."

Featuring a score largely written by Prince and choreography by the eminent modern dancer Twyla Tharp, *I'll Do Anything* exhibited "the kind of crackling comedic dialogue that is a hallmark of all of Jim Brooks's work," described Griffin, adding that the songs themselves in the context of the emotionally strong father-daughter story just didn't work. When the original cut of the musical film was a disastrous failure in audience screenings, Brooks realized he had to delete the

songs to make the story work. As Griffin observed, though, "What remains is, incredibly enough, a dazzling, urbane comedy of which Brooks can be justly proud, rich in its navigation through the ethical flytraps and seductions of the entertainment industry." Perhaps, as Brooks stated, the failure was a lack of simplicity—which is necessary to a successful musical. "There is something about me that's at war with simplicity," he told Griffin. "And if it is true that the form requires some simplicity, maybe that is it."

Throughout his career Brooks has remained, above all, a writer with an ear for snappy dialogue that lashes out at the listener, that has the ring of comedy, that tells the viewer: here is something you have never heard before. And he has remained, too, an iconoclastic, almost capricious teller of darker truths. "I'm telling you," Brooks told Griffin emphatically, "I'm a guy trying to get the people right." And as if that wasn't hard enough, he is also, as he told Mitchell, "always alarmed. I live in a state of being alarmed." Perhaps he would do best to heed his own advice: "The truth about making movies," he told Stambler, "the overwhelming thing about making movies—is God help us if it's all that important."

■ **Works Cited**

Ansen, David, "A Crowe's-Eye View of Teen Love," *Newsweek*, April 17, 1989, p. 72.

Arnold, Gary, review of *Terms of Endearment*, *Washington Post*, November 23, 1983.

Canby, Vincent, review of *Terms of Endearment*, *New York Times*, November 20, 1983.

Griffin, Nancy, "The Way the Music Died," *Premiere*, March, 1994, p. 49.

Kauffmann, Stanley, review of *Broadcast News*, *New Republic*, February 1, 1988, p. 26.

Lardner, James, review of *Broadcast News*, *Nation*, January 23, 1988, p. 94.

Mitchell, Sean, "Don't Worry, Be Unhappy," *American Film*, May, 1989, p. 44.

O'Brien, Tom, review of *Broadcast News*, *Commonweal*, January 29, 1988, p. 49.

Stambler, Wayne, "Our Mr. Brooks," *Interview*, April, 1988, p. 92.

Travers, Peter, review of *Broadcast News*, *People*, December 21, 1987, p. 10.

Zehme, Bill, "The Only Real People on TV," *Rolling Stone*, June 28, 1990, p. 41.

■ For More Information See

PERIODICALS

Cosmopolitan, February, 1988, p. 40.
Forbes, November 12, 1990, p. 188.
Movieline, April, 1994, p. 36.
Ms., March, 1988, p. 26.
National Review, February 5, 1988, p. 56.
New York, February 1, 1988, p. 54.
New Yorker, January 11, 1988, p. 76.
Premiere, September, 1989, p. 105.
Vogue, February, 1988, p. 86; April, 1988, p. 198.

—Sketch by Mindi Dickstein

Jim Carroll

■ Personal

Born August 1, 1951; son of Thomas J. (a bartender) and Agnes (Coyle) Carroll; married, wife's name: Rosemary; children: Aaron, Cassandra. *Education:* Attended Wagner College and Columbia University. *Politics:* "Peace." *Religion:* "God."

■ Addresses

Agent—c/o Viking Publicity, 375 Hudson, New York, NY 10014-3657.

■ Career

Poet, writer, and musician. Teacher at poetry workshops and poetry projects in New York City, 1968-71; *Art News*, New York City, critic, 1969; has given poetry readings at New York area colleges and churches.

■ Awards, Honors

Random House Young Writers Award, 1970, for excerpt from *The Basketball Diaries* published in *Paris Review.*

■ Writings

NONFICTION

The Basketball Diaries: Age Twelve to Fifteen, limited edition, Tombouctou, 1978, Bantam, 1980, Penguin, 1987.
Forced Entries: The Downtown Diaries, 1971-73, Penguin, 1987.

POETRY

Organic Trains, Penny Press, 1967.
Four Ups and One Down, Angel Hail Press, 1970.
Living at the Movies, Van Grossman, 1973, Penguin, 1980.
The Book of Nods, Penguin, 1986.
Fear of Dreaming: Selected Poems, Penguin, 1993.

Contributor to anthologies, including *The World Anthology,* edited by Anne Waldman, Bobbs-Merrill, 1969; *Another World,* edited by Waldman, Bobbs-Merril, 1972; *The Young American Poets,* Volume II, edited by Paul Carroll, Random House, 1973; and *Angel Vision,* edited by Jay Gaines, Huntington House, 1992. Also contributor to "The Authors and the Artists" series, 1977.

MUSICAL RECORDINGS

(With the Jim Carroll Band) *Catholic Boy,* ATCO, 1980.

Dry Dreams, ATCO, 1982.
I Write Your Name, Atlantic, 1983.
Praying Mantis (spoken word), Giant/Reprise, 1992.
The Best of the Jim Carroll Band, Rhino Records, 1993.

■ **Adaptations**

The Basketball Diaries was adapted as a screenplay by Bryan Goluboff, New Line Cinema, 1995.

■ **Sidelights**

Jim Carroll was an emerging basketball star when, at age thirteen, he began shooting heroin. Remarkably, Carroll was witness to his own decline in a series of diaries he kept. Populated by the lovers, addicts, and perverts Carroll knew from the ages of thirteen to fifteen, the diaries document the sordid nature of street life in New York City. As autobiography, the diaries chronicle Carroll's descent into increasing drug use, sexual promiscuity, and crime. As Carroll approached adulthood, selections from the diaries were published, prompting beat-generation novelist Jack Kerouac (in an oft-reprinted quotation) to proclaim, "At thirteen years of age, Jim Carroll writes better prose than eighty-nine percent of the novelists working today."

By the time he was eighteen, Carroll was established among the leading poets and writers of New York City's beat community. Initially recognized as an adolescent diarist, Carroll has proven himself a versatile contemporary artist. He has published five collections of poetry, a sequel to his early diaries, recorded a spoken word performance, and has forayed into rock music as the lyricist and vocalist of the Jim Carroll Band.

Carroll was raised in the poorer Irish neighborhoods of Manhattan and the Bronx, where his father and grandfather were bartenders. His early passion was basketball, and by all accounts he was an outstanding player. In his early teenage years, Carroll's dreams of basketball greatness began to give way to the allure of the street. Carroll was a heroin addict by the age of fifteen; his athletic gifts squandered. In an act that seems fortuitous in retrospect, Carroll recorded his experience. The work which resulted has been con-

sistently praised for its unequivocal portrait of drug use among teens.

Excerpts of the diaries began to appear in literary magazines in New York City in the late 1960s, adding to Carroll's growing reputation as a young poet. A diary excerpt published in the *Paris Review* earned Carroll the Random House Young Writers Award in 1970. The diaries weren't published in their entirety, however, until 1978, when they were compiled and released under the title *The Basketball Diaries*.

The Basketball Diaries opens with Carroll's introduction to organized basketball. In a so-called "biddy" league with an age-limit of twelve, Carroll is a thirteen-year-old with a fake birth certificate provided by his coach. Carroll and his teammates,

> *"The more I read the more I know it now, heavier each day, that I need to write."*

many of whom also exceed the age-limit, shine on court, defeating better-funded and better-coached teams. Off court they pilfer from opponent's lockers, shoplift, sniff glue, and get drunk. While running down the sources of income that fund their drug use, the thirteen-year-old Carroll noted, "All of us little crooks down here on the Lower East Side got one specialty in common: snatching bags off ladies." During this period Carroll also began using heroin, while resisting marijuana, because he mistakenly thought it was the less addictive drug. Despite the risks and damages he incurred off court, Carroll continued to excel as an athlete. Following his eighth-grade season, he earned a basketball scholarship to prestigious Trinity High School in Manhattan.

At Trinity, Carroll was immersed in an unfamiliar and demanding environment. On the first day of class he shocked his Latin instructor by responding in the affirmative with "Yah," rather than "Yes sir." The teacher kept him after class, Carroll recalled, "and explains how he understands, with mounds of sympathy, how my family are lowly slobs and all but to discipline myself to proper replies and classroom etiquette. Sure thing." The petty elitism of the school was a strain on Carroll, but he left Trinity that first day "secretly loving everything about this crazy place."

Carroll distinguished himself almost immediately as an athlete (eventually becoming an All-City and National High School All Star selection), and dealt with the stresses of student life by cutting class to smoke marijuana or shoot heroin. He and a few friends became so intensely involved in drugs that their lives included little other than getting high and playing ball. Carroll finally jeopardized his athletic career when he began taking drugs before games. On one occasion he and his drug-using teammates were unable to distinguish between the amphetamines and depressants they had on hand. Shortly before the game they resolve to choose pills out of a hat, and inadvertently take overpowering depressants. "My legs began to get the feeling someone slit a nice little hole at the top of my thighs and poured in a few gallons of liquid lead, I had a head on that felt like the Rock of Gibraltar," Carroll observed.

Throughout the diaries Carroll's mordant sense of humor surfaces, turning the merely shameful into the hilarious; he and his cronies never fail to laugh at the sight of blood. In the midst of his depravity, however, Carroll turns his attention to poetry. "The more I read the more I know it now," he acknowledged, "heavier each day, that I need to write. I think of poetry and how I see it as just a raw block of stone ready to be shaped, the way words are never a horrible limit to me, just tools to shape."

Sentenced to Reformatory

In the winter of 1966, Carroll was sentenced to three months in Riker's Island Juvenile Reformatory for the possession of heroin and a syringe. His mother refused to visit him. Confined for the first time in his life, Carroll expressed the depth of his depression. "I'm not interested in keeping this diary going while I'm here. Maybe later," he wrote. "Right now I'm not interested in anything." While he was in the reformatory Carroll toyed with the idea of kicking his drug habit. Due to pleas on his behalf from his school's headmaster, Carroll was released after serving only a month of his sentence. "I almost refused," Carroll wrote

of the first heroin offered to him after his stint at the reformatory. "It was a moment I had dreamt of passionately and cursed even more . . . but with the dream in front of me I found that it was quite easy to curse . . . but so much harder to refuse."

To raise the money necessary to support his addiction, Carroll worked as a homosexual prostitute, robbed pedestrians at knife point, and stole a car, only to have it towed by the city before he could deliver it to a buyer. At the conclusion of *The Basketball Diaries*, it is clear that Carroll is spiraling out of control, but not without hope, as he writes, "I gotta go in and puke. I just want to be pure. . . ."

American Book Review critic Jamie James found the assembled diaries evidence of Carroll's extraordinary maturity as a writer. The occasional publishing of excerpts made the diaries seem "the charming but trivial work of a precociously gifted young writer," James asserted. Reading the complete work, however, created an altogether different impression. "Despite the adolescent egoism and occasional tendency towards smart-aleckiness, the theme that reverberates through the whole, like the recurring melody of a jazz improv, is the struggle of a boy to hold on to his sense of himself," wrote James. He also points out that *The Basketball Diaries* isn't literature in the conventional sense, but commanding storytelling. "It suffers from all the faults of the genre, too," James concluded, "some of the stories sound made up, others are stock footage from anyone's adolescence." *The Basketball Diaries* was adapted as a screenplay by Bryan Goluboff, and a film of the same title directed by Scott Kalvert was released in 1995. Young actor Leonardo Di Caprio starred in the role of Jim Carroll.

Eleven years after the publication of *The Basketball Diaries* Carroll released the sequel, *Forced Entries: The Downtown Diaries, 1971-73*. As the diary opens it is clear that Carroll's basketball career has ended. His poetry, however, came to the attention of several important figures in New York's literary community, most notably the poet Ted Berrigan. Carroll honed his craft in a series of writing workshops led by Berrigan, and published his first collection of poetry, *Organic Trains*, in 1967. With his penchant for excessive drug use Carroll slipped easily into the New York art scene. He occasionally worked for renowned pop artist

Andy Warhol at his Factory, a collaborative for the production of avant-garde work. As a rising young poet Carroll also met folk singer Bob Dylan, and beat writers Allen Ginsberg and William S. Burroughs. "When Carroll is not busy scoring dope or sex, he is scoring celebrities," quipped a *Publishers Weekly* reviewer, "but his peculiar aura of choirboy innocence transforms even the most decadent happenings into a good-natured romp." The writer's "voice is grown up now," *New York Times* reviewer Christopher Lehmann-Haupt observed of *Forced Entries*, "the whine and the adolescent strutting are gone." Although both diaries "remain similar in their quest for extreme sensations and their eagerness to shock the reader," the author's concerns are no longer those of the adolescent who wrote *The Basketball Diaries*, concluded Lehmann-Haupt. Carroll no longer relished the dissolute thrills or vacant company of the addict's life. After nearly a decade, Carroll attempted to kick his heroin habit. In *Forced Entries* Carroll describes his subsequent addiction to methadone (a heroin substitute used to alleviate the symptoms of withdrawal), and his eventual recovery in a California drug treatment center. "But whether or not one believes Jim Carroll's redemption," Lehmann-Haupt wrote, "his two diaries constitute a remarkable account of New York City's lower depths. At the very least, they should serve further to demystify the usefulness of drugs to writers. Finally, the main reason Carroll decides to kick his habit is for the sake of his art."

Carroll as Poet

Apart from his diaries, the majority of Carroll's literary output has been poetry. His first two collections, *Organic Trains* and *Four Ups and One Down*, garnered little attention outside his circle of friends and well-wishers. Carroll's notoriety increased with the publication of *Living at the Movies* in 1973. *Booklist* reviewer Benjamin Segedin characterized the poetry of *Living at the Movies* as a "brand of free-verse at once hallucinatory and sharply focused." "On the whole Jim Carroll has the confidence of a true artist," Gerald Malanga of *Poetry* wrote, "meaning he is confident about the right things. He is steeped in his craft. He has worked only as a man of inspiration is capable of working, and his presence has added great dignity to the generation of poets of the 'seventies to which he belongs."

Carroll's follow-up to *Living at the Movies* was a collection of prose poems, *The Book of Nods*. Daniel L. Guillory of *Library Journal* asserted that Carroll's juxtaposition of imagery in these works rapidly loses its effectiveness. "*The Book of Nods* is always interesting if sometimes uneven," Guillory concludes. Frank Allen, also of *Library Journal*, characterized the prose poems, or "nods," as "kinetic and ebullient."

Begins Career as Rock Musician

Carroll began his career as a rock musician in the early 1980s. Following the success of *The Basketball Diaries*, Patti Smith, a former girlfriend who made the leap from poetry to punk, encouraged Carroll to try his hand at song writing. Smith also invited Carroll and his band to perform with her in San Francisco and New York. Having chosen rock and roll as a forum for his lyrical poetry because of its wide audience appeal, "the gangly Carroll delivers his cathartic songs with a refreshingly unpolished stage manner whose very vulnerability suggests courage and commitment," commented *Variety* critic Richard Gold. After just two shows the Jim Carroll Band was signed to a recording contract, and their first album, *Catholic Boy*, was released in 1980.

Carroll's song lyrics explore themes familiar to his diaries and poetry. "Not since Lou Reed wrote 'Walk on the Wild Side' has a rock singer so vividly evoked the casual brutality of New York as has Jim Carroll," declared *Newsweek* reviewer Barbara Graustark. "To some his songs will sound like the glorification of the decadent, and indeed Carroll is carrying on the beat tradition of celebrating life on the edge." On the album's single, "People Who Died," Carroll grinds through a long inventory of the grisly deaths that have taken so many of his friends and loved ones. *Stereo Review* critic Steven Simels found the song "arresting," and noted its peculiar mixture of sadness and celebration. While Carroll sincerely expresses his loss and regret over the needless deaths of his associates, Simels pointed out, the song's "gospel-derived choruses in the traditional 'rock-anthem' manner are so exhilarating that it soon becomes apparent that he *admires* their 'romantic' exits, viewing his own survival as a kind of artistic failure."

Carroll moved slightly away from his earlier influences on his band's second album, *Dry Dreams*, remarked *Rolling Stone* reviewer Michael Goldberg, "creating a distinctly urban brand of rock & roll that's equal parts New York intellectual and savvy street hipster." Despite Carroll's growth as a vocalist, *Dry Dreams* failed to live up to the expectations generated by *Catholic Boy. Audio* reviewer Michael Tearson admitted that the band had maintained the hard-driving, straight-ahead sound of their first album, but added, "Carroll's songs are not as strong as the previous crop with the obvious exception of 'Jealous Twin,' the clear standout."

"I want kids to know it's not hip to indulge yourself at the bottom unless you're planning one helluva resurrection."

The Jim Carroll Band's third and final album, *I Write Your Name*, also received mixed reviews. The album demonstrates that Carroll has "yet to fulfill his promise" as a rock artist, wrote Christopher Connelly of *Rolling Stone*. While the album has its shortcomings, its high-minded literary sensibility made it a welcome alternative to Michael Jackson, Duran Duran, and Boy George, asserted *Wilson Library Bulletin* reviewer Bruce Pollock. While Pollock found the majority of the album frustrating because of lack of coordination between Carroll's vocals and the band's "typical rock scores," he considered the title song Carroll's best since "People Who Died." The song "deserves to be considered as a kind of rock and roll *Howl* of the eighties," Pollock concluded.

In 1992 Carroll released his first spoken word recording, *Praying Mantis*, a collection of comedic readings, monologues, and poetry recorded at St. Mark's Church in New York City. "Reciting wryly, and with a hefty dose of self-deprecation, Carroll recounts some of the odder moments of his altogether unusual life," wrote *Wilson Library Bulletin* reviewer Toby Goldstein.

From the diaries to the rock and roll recordings, Carroll's work has consistently documented the underside of the urban experience in New York City. His evocation of the playgrounds, drug houses, and streets, as well as his depictions of the athletes, addicts, artists, and hustlers he has known, comprise a portrayal of life that gnaws at the values and presumptions of the mainstream. More importantly, perhaps, Carroll's writing is a story of redemption, his own redemption from the addictions that destroyed the lives of so many around him. Readers are fortunate that Carroll escaped that destruction to produce what must ultimately stand as testament against life on the streets. As Carroll told Barbara Graustark, "I don't want to glorify junk. Susan Sontag once told me that a junkie has the unique chance to rise up and start life over. But I want kids to know it's not hip to indulge yourself at the bottom unless you're planning one helluva resurrection."

■ Works Cited

Allen, Frank, review of *Fear of Dreaming, Library Journal*, October 15, 1993, p. 68.

Carroll, Jim, *The Basketball Diaries*, Penguin Books, 1995.

Connelly, Christopher, review of *I Write Your Name, Rolling Stone*, March 29, 1984, pp. 74, 76.

Review of *Forced Entries: The Downtown Diaries, 1971-73, Publishers Weekly*, June 5, 1987, p. 73.

Gold, Richard, "Jim Carroll," *Variety*, June 9, 1982, p. 56.

Goldberg, Michael, review of *Dry Dreams, Rolling Stone*, July 8, 1982, p. 50.

Goldstein, Toby, review of *Praying Mantis, Wilson Library Bulletin*, February, 1992, pp. 64-65.

Graustark, Barbara, "Mean Streets," *Newsweek*, September 8, 1980, pp. 80-81.

Guillory, Daniel L., review of *The Book of Nods, Library Journal*, April 15, 1986, p. 84.

James, Jamie, review of *The Basketball Diaries, American Book Review*, February, 1980, p. 9.

Lehmann-Haupt, Christopher, review of *Forced Entries, New York Times*, July 9, 1987, p. C-23.

Malanga, Gerald, "Traveling & Living," *Poetry*, December, 1974, pp. 162-65.

Pollock, Bruce, review of *I Write Your Name, Wilson Library Bulletin*, June, 1984, pp. 746-47.

Segedin, Benjamin, review of *Living at the Movies, Booklist*, October 15, 1993, p. 412.

Simels, Steven, "Jim Carroll," *Stereo Review*, February, 1981, p. 40.

Tearson, Michael, review of *Dry Dreams, Audio*, August, 1982, p. 23.

■ For More Information See

PERIODICALS

Booklist, October 15, 1993, p. 412.
Los Angeles Times Book Review, October 18, 1987, p. 10.
New York Times Book Review, August 2, 1987, p. 8.
School Library Journal, September, 1992, p. 150.

—Sketch by David P. Johnson

Alden R. Carter

■ Personal

Full name, Alden Richardson Carter; born April 7, 1947, in Eau Claire, WI; son of John Kelley (a lawyer) and Hilda Small (Richardson) Carter; married Carol Ann Shadis (a social worker), September 14, 1974; children: Brian Patrick, Siri Morgan. *Education:* University of Kansas, B.A., 1969; Montana State University, teaching certificate, 1976. *Politics:* Democrat. *Hobbies and other interests:* Canoeing, camping, hiking, reading.

■ Addresses

Home and office—1113 West Onstad Dr., Marshfield, WI 54449. *Agent*—Lazear Agency, 430 First Ave. N., Suite 416, Minneapolis, MN 55401.

■ Career

Writer. Taught high school English and journalism for four years in Marshfield, WI. Speaker at workshops, including ALAN Workshop on Young Adult Literature and National Council of Teachers of English. *Military service:* U.S. Navy, 1969-74; became lieutenant senior grade. *Member:* Society of Children's Book Writers and Illustrators, Society of Midland Authors, Council on Wisconsin Writers, Sierra Club.

■ Awards, Honors

Best Book for Young Adults citation, American Library Association (ALA), 1984, for *Growing Season;* Best Book for Young Adults citations, ALA, New York Public Library, Los Angeles Public Library, and Child Study Association, Best Book for Reluctant Readers citation, ALA Young Adult Services Committee, all 1985, all for *Wart, Son of Toad;* Best Book for Young Adults citations, ALA and Los Angeles Public Library, and Best Book for the Teenage citation, New York Public Library, all 1987, all for *Sheila's Dying;* Children's Book Council/National Science Teacher's Association Outstanding Science Trade Book for Children citation, 1988, for *Radio: From Marconi to the Space Age;* Best Book citation, ALA, and Best Book for the Teenage citation, New York Public Library, both 1989, both for *Up Country;* Best Book for the Teenage citation, 1990, and Best Children's Fiction Book of the Year citation, Society of Midland Authors, both 1990, both for *RoboDad.*

■ Writings

YOUNG ADULT NOVELS

Growing Season, Coward-McCann, 1984.
Wart, Son of Toad, Putnam, 1985.

Sheila's Dying, Putnam, 1987.

Up Country, Putnam, 1989.

RoboDad, Putnam, 1990, published as *Dancing on Dark Water,* Scholastic, 1993.

Dogwolf, Scholastic, 1994.

Between a Rock and a Hard Place, Scholastic, 1995.

YOUNG ADULT NONFICTION

(With Wayne Jerome LeBlanc) *Supercomputers,* F. Watts, 1985.

(And photographer with wife, Carol S. Carter) *Modern China,* F. Watts, 1986.

(With Wayne Jerome LeBlanc) *Modern Electronics,* F. Watts, 1986.

Radio: From Marconi to the Space Age, F. Watts, 1987.

Illinois, F. Watts, 1987.

The Shoshoni, F. Watts, 1989.

Last Stand at the Alamo, F. Watts, 1990.

The Battle of Gettysburg, F. Watts, 1990.

The American Revolution: War for Independence, F. Watts, 1992.

The Civil War: American Tragedy, F. Watts, 1992.

The Spanish-American War: Imperial Ambitions, F. Watts, 1992.

The Colonial Wars: Clashes in the Wilderness, F. Watts, 1992.

The War of 1812: Second Fight for Independence, F. Watts, 1992.

The Mexican War: Manifest Destiny, F. Watts, 1992.

Battle of the Ironclads: The Monitor and the Merrimack, F. Watts, 1993.

China Past—China Future, F. Watts, 1994.

"THE AMERICAN REVOLUTION" SERIES

Colonies in Revolt, F. Watts, 1988.

The Darkest Hours, F. Watts, 1988.

At the Forge of Liberty, F. Watts, 1988.

Birth of the Republic, F. Watts, 1988.

■ Sidelights

"I like to write for young adults," Alden R. Carter wrote in his entry in the *Something about the Author Autobiographical Series (SAAS),* "because they have yet to develop the protective layers of emotional experience that desensitize our adult recollection of what it felt like to be teenagers." Carter, who has also written a great deal of nonfiction for teens, has won numerous accolades for his young adult novels, which often deal with very grim issues, such as death, alcoholism, and mental illness. Aware that these serious problems could weigh his stories down if not balanced by some lightheartedness, Carter said in *SAAS,* "I'm always concerned that my novels sound bleak, when actually there's a fair amount of humor in all of them." The mixture of happiness and pain that his characters experience in his books is somewhat reflective of the author's own life, especially his feelings about growing up with an alcoholic father.

The second of three children, Carter was born on April 7, 1947, in Eau Claire, Wisconsin. He was given the name Alden after John and Priscilla Alden, two pilgrims who arrived in America on the *Mayflower,* and whom Carter's mother counted among her family's ancestors. Carter, however, never liked the name and quickly shortened it to Al. His father, a lawyer by profession, had moved to Eau Claire in 1941 when his uncle passed away, leaving him with a good deal of property in the downtown area to manage. Although he made a good living, Carter's father "was frustrated by the interruption of his legal career and deeply disappointed when poor eyesight kept him out of World War II," said the author. "A heavy drinker since his youth, he began drinking even more, and his long battle with alcohol would become a central theme of my growing up."

Still, Carter remembered his childhood as being a happy one for the most part. His family lived in a prosperous area of Eau Claire called the Third Ward, where the streets were lined with elm trees, and peaceful rivers flowed nearby. Carter and his siblings attended Campus School, where he considered himself to be only a fair student. However, he had a great fondness for reading. By the time he reached the end of elementary school, books had become even more important to him, serving as a place to escape to when his father's alcoholism worsened.

Later, his experiences as the child of an alcoholic parent would be the inspiration for his novel, *Up Country,* and it wasn't until Carter conducted research on the subject in preparation for writing the book that he learned what a typical example he was of a child with a parent suffering from this illness. "I wish I had known more as a child," the author reflected, "because maybe then I

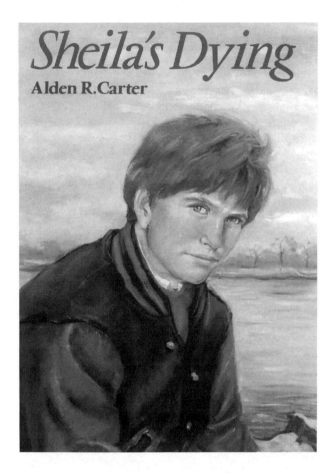

Sheila's Dying

Alden R. Carter

This much-praised 1987 work concerns a terminally ill teenage girl and the friends who share in the experience.

wouldn't have felt that we were somehow uniquely flawed. In reality, we were frighteningly typical: my father, the alcoholic denying his addiction; my mother, the 'enabler,' taking on so many of the family responsibilities that she ironically made it easier for him to booze; my brother, the super-achieving eldest child; me, the rambunctious and often rebellious middle child; and my sister, the silent youngest child."

Still a Happy Childhood

Despite his father's problem, however, Carter was never abused as a child—a common occurrence in such families—and his parents were both kind and loving to him. They encouraged their son's fondness for books, and his father often read to him in bed. Furthermore, they were strongly opposed to television, which was just coming into wide use in the 1950s when Carter was growing

up, and they didn't own a television set until the author was a teenager. They didn't discourage their children from going to the picture show, however, and Carter has fond memories of going to the movies to see such films as *Gunfight at the OK Corral* and *The Guns of Navarone*.

Carter's favorite stories as a child included "dog stories, pirate sagas, and Westerns," but he was inspired to write his first story—at the early age of eight—by a song he remembers his mother singing called "Beloved Old Percy." Loosely based on the lyrics, the young Carter wrote a rather gruesome tale about a retired racehorse who is allowed to run one last race only to die in an unsuccessful attempt to jump a picket fence. Although not exactly a great story, Carter recalled reading it to his younger sister, who cried when Percy the horse died. "From that day my sister cried," Carter wrote in *SAAS*, "I dreamed about becoming a writer."

Although junior high was difficult for Carter, just before he moved on to high school an important change occurred in his family: his father finally realized he had gone too far with his drinking and managed to quit. There "was always the fear that he would backslide, [but] the next couple of years were among the happiest of my youth." Carter started attending Eau Claire Memorial High School, where he became heavily involved with the school newspaper. While still in high school, Carter's father became ill from throat cancer, and he died not too many months after the diagnosis. Because the family's finances suffered due to the resulting medical bills and other expenses they incurred, Carter accepted a navy ROTC scholarship to the University of Kansas rather than going to another university without tuition assistance. Before moving to Kansas, however, he spent the summer at his family's cabin in northern Wisconsin, where he met his future wife, Carol Ann Shadis, whom he got to know through their mutual love of canoeing.

Carter devoted the next nine years of his life to the navy, taking the courses required of him at the University of Kansas and spending most of his summers during the first four years gaining experience on naval vessels. With his degree in English, Carter went on to become a communications officer for the navy for almost five more years as an ensign and, later, a lieutenant. Whenever he could, he would go back to Wisconsin to see Carol and his family. Resigning his commission in 1974, Carter married Carol and the next year enrolled at Montana State University to earn his teaching certificate. Certificate in hand, he went on to teach English and journalism back in Wisconsin.

Struggling Toward That First Novel

"All the time I was in college and the navy," Carter said in *SAAS*, "I never gave up my ambition to become a writer. I became a teacher because I loved literature, liked young people, and suffered under the delusion that the long vacations would give me a chance to write. (Teachers who read this will find the last reason a real howler.) But teaching is an all-consuming profession, and most teachers spend their vacations studying or just trying to recover from the months in the classroom." In addition to his regular teaching duties, Carter was responsible for serving as the advisor to the school's newspaper and yearbook and preparing the superintendent's newsletter and the Future Farmers of America newspaper, all of which left little time for writing. He did try to write two novels during his teaching years, but neither one was published, and Carter felt he would never get good enough if he was spending up to sixteen hours a day at school.

Finally, in 1980, he quit his job to pursue his writing ambitions. "If I'd known how difficult it was going to be," Carter revealed in his *SAAS* essay, "I probably would have begged for my teaching job back or called the local navy recruiter to see if I could get aboard a warship going somewhere." After many rejection letters from publishers, however, Carter finally received an interested nibble from an editor for his manuscript for *Growing Season.* Before she would accept the book, though, the editor demanded major rewrites of the story. Working for months and revising almost every word, Carter resubmitted the novel only to have it rejected again. Always tenacious, he refused to give up on the book and sent the rewritten version back to another publisher, Coward-McCann, which had rejected the original. This time it was accepted, though the publisher did ask for some more revisions. "I now look back on that day as one of the grandest in my life," Carter declared.

Growing Season, which was cited as a Best Book for Young Adults by the American Library Asso-

ciation, is a coming-of-age novel about a teenager named Rick Simon who learns more about himself and family responsibilities when his parents decide to move from the city to a dairy farm in Wisconsin. Critics praised the novel for its realistic, unromanticized depiction of farm life and family relationships. Calling the novel "a welcome, truthful rendering of farm life," Hope Bridgewater also commented in *School Library Journal* that Carter's description of "a boy becoming a man is especially well done." *Voice of Youth Advocates* contributor Mary K. Chelton similarly remarked that "it is the superior characterizations which readily distinguish the high level of quality in this fine first . . . novel." And Ethel R. Twichell, writing in *Horn Book,* called the story a "fine, honest novel in the tradition of Robert Newton Peck's *A Day No Pigs Would Die.*"

Carl, the sixteen-year-old son of an alcoholic, is sent "up country" to live with relatives after his mother is arrested for causing an accident while driving under the influence in this 1989 novel.

"Revising *Growing Season* with the help of a skilled editor taught me a great deal about developing characters, writing dialogue, and pacing the flow of a novel," the author revealed in a promotional piece released by the Putnam Publishing Group. Through the urgings of his new literary agent, Carter also learned about writing nonfiction for teenagers. Forming a partnership with his sister's husband, Wayne LeBlanc, Carter wrote *Supercomputers* and *Modern Electronics*. Later, with the help of LeBlanc as his advisor, Carter won an Outstanding Science Trade Book for Children citation for *Radio: From Marconi to the Space Age*. Since then, most of the author's nonfiction works have been about American history.

"The reasons why I've written so much nonfiction are varied," Carter commented in his *SAAS* entry. "There are the practical reasons of earning a living and expanding my credit list, but there's more to it. I'm fascinated with history and believe strongly that young people need to learn about the past. . . . I also enjoy research and the process of expanding and reexamining my own knowledge." But, Carter later added, "As much as I enjoy writing nonfiction, fiction is my first love, and I think of myself primarily as a novelist."

Wart, Son of Toad

Carter's second novel, *Wart, Son of Toad*, was even more lauded than his first, winning awards from the American Library Association, the Child Study Association, and the New York and Los Angeles Public Libraries. A study in the tragic loss of loved ones and father-son relationships, *Wart, Son of Toad* is about a teenager named Steve Michaels whose mother and sister have been killed in an automobile accident. His father, an unpopular high school science teacher whom students call "Toad," is having trouble dealing with his loss and doesn't know how to raise his son, whose modest ambitions to become a car mechanic he can't understand. Steve's father feels he should do better at school, but Steve has a hard time relating to his father's arguments to study harder, and this only creates more tension between them.

Steve, who attends the same high school at which his father teaches, is nicknamed "Wart" by his peers because of this relationship. Steve is considered to be a "dirt," a clique defined by its members' tendency to skip classes, get poor grades, and drink and smoke a lot. The dirts are at odds with the school's athletic clique, or "jocks." Because they do not like his father, the jocks pick on Steve, which leads to a fight between Steve and the school's star football player. The two teens are punished for fighting and sent to the assistant principal. A twist of fate occurs when the assistant principal has a heart attack and the two boys save his life, resulting in a new, though tentative, friendship. Just as an understanding between Steve and the jocks develops, Steve and his father also slowly come to understand one another as they come to terms with their personal losses.

Although one *Kirkus Reviews* critic felt the book was "static, sappy, and relies much too heavily on contrivance," many other reviewers had positive remarks for *Wart, Son of Toad*, especially with regard to Carter's sense of characterization. "Carter does a convincing job of portraying a father/son relationship that, while gone terribly askew, is rooted in real caring," observed Stephanie Zvirin in *Booklist*. Robert Unsworth further expounded in *School Library Journal* that "Steve is a refreshing protagonist," noting that the teenager's "father, with his faults uncovered, is nonetheless presented with empathy." As Carter himself stated in his *SAAS* entry, characters are very important to him: "I devote a lot of time to developing strong characters. I want my characters to breathe, talk, laugh, and cry like real people."

Carter's novels for young adults often address very tough issues without making any pretense that they have easy answers. In *Wart, Son of Toad*, the author does not conclude the novel with a happy ending in which father and son come to see each other completely eye to eye; their relationship, though improved, is still something that needs much work. Similarly, with books like *Sheila's Dying*, *Up Country*, and *RoboDad* (later published as *Dancing on Dark Water*), Carter refuses to reward his readers with simple solutions.

No Simple Solutions

In *Sheila's Dying*, the young teen of the title is suffering from uterine cancer and, indeed, dies from her illness. The story is as much about terminal disease as it is about how it can affect those around the afflicted person—in this case, Sheila's

In this 1993 tale, Shar's life is drastically altered when her father suffers a debilitating stroke.

boyfriend, Jerry, and her best pal, Bonnie. Although Jerry admits to himself that he is no t really in love with Sheila, he resolves to not leave her side; this brings him into close contact with Bonnie, who, compared to the empty-headed yet very funny Sheila, is much smarter and not nearly as sociable. Through their shared experience with Sheila's illness, however, Jerry and Bonnie become close and eventually evolve a caring relationship of their own. Winning several honors, *Sheila's Dying* was praised for its unsentimental and realistic treatment of terminal illness. "The author presents an unflinching view of death and conveys a real sense of Jerry's turmoil," wrote Zvirin in a *Booklist* review. Zena Sutherland also commented in the *Bulletin of the Center for Children's Books* that the novel offers "sturdy characteriza-

tion and dialogue, and makes a statement about responsibility without moralizing."

Carter's *RoboDad* is similar in some ways to *Sheila's Dying* in that both books deal with serious illness. The author's experience in researching nonfiction works—and his contacts with friends in the medical community—also served a purpose for both in the amount of technical detail he includes. As Janet Bryan remarked in her *School Library Journal* review of *Sheila's Dying*, this attention to detail pays off. "The outstanding feature of this novel is its realism concerning all aspects of illness," said Bryan. Carter tries to stay faithful not only to technical aspects, but also to the psychology of the patient—Sheila is neither a hero, nor a pathetic victim of circumstances, as Bryan pointed out.

The situation presented in *RoboDad* is, in some respects, even worse than terminal cancer in that there is no end in sight. Shar's father was once a caring, understanding parent whom she deeply loved. However, after he suffers from a massive stroke, his behavior changes dramatically. Although six months have gone by at the time the novel opens, all Shar's father does is sit in front of the television and eat. Even worse, he has become cruel and possibly incestuous toward Shar. Shar's mother hides from the situation by throwing herself into her job, and Shar, whose brothers are of no help, is left to run the house by herself, while trying to maintain her grades and still have time for her new boyfriend, Paul. That relationship ends, however, when Paul comes to visit one day for a cookout and her father acts frighteningly insane, scaring him out of the house and her life.

Though at the beginning of the story Shar hopes that her father will get better, by the novel's conclusion she comes to the realization that she will have to adjust to what has happened to her father. Finding that the story has "no happy ending," *Bulletin of the Center for Children's Books* contributor Ruth Ann Smith called the book "[p]owerful and disturbing," adding, "the story is told with compassion and honesty." "This conclusion is refreshingly realistic since there is no real ending to Shar or her family's predicament," Laura L. Lent also observed in *Voice of Youth Advocates*. And *Booklist* critic Leone McDermott concluded that "Carter is extraordinarily, almost painfully, perceptive about the dynamics of family life" in a crisis.

Children of Alcoholics

This understanding of how each member of a family interrelates when there is a serious problem stems from Carter's own experience with his alcoholic father. But, as the author explained in his *SAAS* entry, he still learned a lot when researching his very personal—though not autobiographical—novel, *Up Country:* "Arrogantly, I didn't think I needed to do any research when I was preparing to write about being the son of an alcoholic. . . . Hey, I'd been there, and no one could tell me anything about the experience. But one January night, I sat down to take just a glance at a book about adult children of alcoholics and had the most shocking intellectual and emotional experience of my life. I hadn't understood anything!" After reading more on the subject, Carter joined a support group and finally managed to come to terms with his past. Feeling much happier about life because of his newfound understanding, Carter tried to reach out to his readers with *Up Country* so that they might not, through the mere ignorance of the fact that their situation is shared by many other people, suffer the years of inner turmoil that he did.

The main character in *Up Country* is sixteen-year-old Carl, whose mother is an alcoholic. While she neglects him, Carl earns money by repairing stolen stereos, saving what he can for tuition money for engineering school. But Carl's life abruptly changes when his mother is arrested for a hit-and-run accident while driving under the influence of alcohol. Sent to live with his aunt and uncle in the countryside, the teenager at first resists the love his relatives try to give him; ironically, just when he does start to feel comfortable with his new family, the stolen equipment he stashed in the basement of his mother's home is discovered, and he is arrested and punished for his crime. Carl is eventually rehabilitated by the caring and understanding his aunt, uncle, and new girlfriend give him. Although some critics found the premise of *Up Country* not overly original, they were generally pleased by Carter's handling of his themes. Barbara Hutcheson, for example, called the story a "solid, unpreachy novel" in her *School Library Journal* review. Commenting that the author has created a memorable character in Carl, *Bulletin of the Center for Children's Books* reviewer Betsy Hearne concluded that *Up Country* "will make [YA readers] think about the ways they solve whatever problems loom in their own lives."

Although Carter writes in *SAAS*, "I do not set out to advise kids how to survive the teenage years," he maintains a certain faith that his writing can have some positive influence. "Young adult novels provide no miraculous cure for the age-old problems of growing up," he says in his essay. "Yet, a YA novel can offer a respite of sorts. For a few hours, the young adult reader can escape into the lives of fictional young people who are also fighting to make some sense of life: young people who are, in short, proving that the teenage years can be survived."

■ Works Cited

Bridgewater, Hope, review of *Growing Season, School Library Journal*, September, 1984, p. 126.

Bryan, Janet, review of *Sheila's Dying, School Library Journal*, May, 1987, p. 108.

Carter, Alden, *Alden Carter in His Own Words* (promotional piece), Putnam, October, 1987.

Carter, Alden, essay in *Something about the Author Autobiographical Series*, Volume 18, Gale, 1994, pp. 77-94.

Chelton, Mary K., review of *Growing Season, Voice of Youth Advocates*, October, 1984, p. 195.

Hearne, Betsy, review of *Up Country, Bulletin of the Center for Children's Books*, July-August, 1989, p. 270.

Hutcheson, Barbara, review of *Up Country, School Library Journal*, June, 1989, p. 121.

Lent, Laura L., review of *RoboDad, Voice of Youth Advocates*, December, 1990, pp. 277-78.

McDermott, Leone, review of *RoboDad, Booklist*, November 15, 1990, pp. 653-54.

Smith, Ruth Ann, review of *RoboDad, Bulletin of the Center for Children's Books*, February, 1991, pp. 138-39.

Sutherland, Zena, review of *Sheila's Dying, Bulletin of the Center for Children's Books*, July/August, 1987, p. 204.

Twichell, Ethel R., review of *Growing Season, Horn Book*, August, 1984, pp. 473-74.

Unsworth, Robert, review of *Wart, Son of Toad, School Library Journal*, February, 1986, pp. 93-94.

Review of *Wart, Son of Toad, Kirkus Reviews*, November 1, 1985, p. 1197.

Zvirin, Stephanie, review of *Wart, Son of Toad, Booklist*, November 15, 1985, p. 481.

Zvirin, Stephanie, review of *Sheila's Dying, Booklist*, June 1, 1987, pp. 1514-15.

■ For More Information See

BOOKS

Children's Literature Review, Volume 22, Gale, 1991,
    pp. 16-23.

PERIODICALS

Booklist, July, 1984, p. 1544; May 1, 1985, p. 1247;
    October 1, 1989, p. 344.
Kirkus Reviews, May 1, 1987, p. 716.
School Library Journal, May, 1988, pp. 48-49; No-
    vember, 1989, pp. 42-43.
Voice of Youth Advocates, August, 1989, p. 155;
    April, 1990, p. 68; October, 1994, p. 229.
Wilson Library Bulletin, November, 1985, p. 47.

—Sketch by Janet L. Hile

Gary Crew

■ Personal

Born September 23, 1947, in Brisbane, Australia; son of Eric (a steam engine driver) and Phyllis (a milliner; maiden name, Winch) Crew; married Christine Joy Willis (a teacher), April 4, 1970; children: Rachel, Sarah, Joel. *Education:* Attended Queensland Institute of Technology; University of Queensland, Diploma of Civil Engineering Drafting, 1970, B.A., 1979, M.A., 1984.

■ Addresses

Home—Green Mansions, 66 Picnic St., Enoggera, Queensland 4051, Australia. *Agent*—c/o Reed Australia, P.O. Box 460, Port Melbourne, Victoria 3027, Australia.

■ Career

McDonald, Wapner, and Priddle, Brisbane, Queensland, Australia, senior draftsman and drafting consultant, 1962-72; Everton Park State High School, Brisbane, English teacher, 1974-78; Mitchelton State High School, Brisbane, English teacher, 1978-81; Aspley High School, Brisbane, subject master in English, 1982; Albany Creek High School, Brisbane, subject master in English and head of English Department, 1983-88; Queensland University of Technology, creative writing lecturer, 1989—; Heinemann Octopus, series editor, 1990—. *Member:* Australian Society of Authors.

■ Awards, Honors

Book of the Year Award, Children's Book Council of Australia, awards for literature from states of Victoria and New South Wales, and Alan Marshall Prize for Children's Literature, all 1991, all for *Strange Objects; Lucy's Bay* was short listed for the Children's Book Council of Australia's picture book of the year, 1993.

■ Writings

NOVELS

The Inner Circle, Heinemann Octopus, 1985.
The House of Tomorrow, Heinemann Octopus, 1988.
Strange Objects, Heinemann Octopus, 1990, Simon & Schuster, 1993.
No Such Country, Heinemann Octopus, 1991, Simon & Schuster, 1994.

Among Others, Heinemann Octopus, 1993.
Angel's Gate, Heinemann, 1993.

CHILDREN'S STORY BOOKS

Tracks, illustrated by Gregory Rogers, Lothian, 1992.

Lucy's Bay, illustrated by Rogers, Jam Roll Press, 1992.

The Figures of Julian Ashcroft, illustrated by Hans DeHaas, Jam Roll Press, 1993.

First Light, illustrated by Peter Gouldthorpe, Lothian, 1994.

Gulliver in the South Seas, illustrated by John Burge, Lothian, in press.

OTHER

Contributor of short stories to anthologies, including *Hair Raising*, edited by Penny Matthews, Omnibus, 1992, and *The Blue Dress*, edited by Libby Hathorn, Heinemann, 1992. Contributor to books, including *At Least They're Reading! Proceedings of the First National Conference of the Children's Book Council of Australia*, Thorpe, 1992, and *The Second Authors & Illustrators Scrapbook*, Omnibus Books, 1992. Contributor to periodicals, including *Australian Author, Magpies*, and *Reading Time*.

■ Adaptations

The story "Sleeping over at Lola's" was adapted as a radio play by the Australian Broadcasting Commission; a film adaptation of *Strange Objects* is being produced by Zoic Films of Australia.

■ Sidelights

Australian novelist and children's story book author Gary Crew weaves themes of identity, nationalism, history, and regeneration into his young adult novels and picture books. Although many of his widely-praised novels feature troubled youths—Danny Coley in *The House of Tomorrow*, Steven Messenger in *Strange Objects*, Sam in *Lucy's Bay*, and Julia Marriott in *Angel's Gate*, for example—they also look at such characteristically Australian problems as relations between European settlers and their descendants and the Aborigines, and the legacy of Australian colonialism. (The

original settlements were founded as penal colonies to hold convicted criminals expelled from Great Britain in the seventeenth and eighteenth centuries.) Crew contends in his novels that Australians, both Aboriginal and European, must learn to live and learn from each other in order to survive on their island continent.

Crew was born in Brisbane, Australia, in 1947. Although he recalled in a *Magpies* essay that he "spent most of my childhood with the local kids racing around the neighbourhood," Crew suffered from poor health early in life, later describing himself in a speech published in *Australian Author* as "a sickly, puny child." "My mother says that I was a very quiet child, and my earliest memories suggest that she is right," Crew once said. "I was always happiest by myself, reading, drawing, or making models. I never did like crowds or noise." Crew's illness often kept him bedridden at home or in hospitals, but it also influenced his later writing career in several ways. First, it allowed him to become an avid reader. Second, it brought him in close contact with an influential setting that would later be featured in one of his books: his great-grandmother's house in Ipswich, to the west of Brisbane.

Crew's stays in Ipswich had many benefits, although some of them were not immediately visible. "My great-grandmother was bedridden in this house; my widowed grandmother cared for her," Crew related in *Australian Author*. "Because I was always sick, there seemed to be some logic in packing me off to join them." The house, Crew recalled in *The Second Authors & Illustrators Scrapbook*, "was wonderful, with verandas all around, and a great big mango tree growing right up against it. We could climb over the rail and drop onto the branches of the mango. This house gave me the main idea for my second novel, *The House of Tomorrow*." "My first public attempts at writing were letters sent from my great-grandmother's house to my parents," Crew continued in *The Second Authors & Illustrators Scrapbook*, and writing and drawing later became important elements in his life. "Until I went to high school, I never seemed to be especially good at anything," Crew once remarked, "but at fifteen years old, I realized that I could write and draw—but that was about all I could do well!"

While he was still a teenager, Crew put his drawing abilities to work in order to help support his struggling family. "My parents had very little money," he remembered, "so I left school at sixteen to become a cadet draftsman, working for a firm of engineers. I hated this, and at twenty-one I returned to college to matriculate by studying at night; then I went to university. All this time I was earning a living as a draftsman, but had decided to be a teacher of English because I loved books so much." Crew soon proved his abilities as a student, and he valued the opportunity to continue his delayed education. "I don't think anyone was ever more comfortable at uni[versity] than I was," he told *Scan* interviewer Niki Kallenberger, "—it was most wonderful! I would have done all the assignments on the sheets! It was a feeling of being totally at home and I was a changed person." In 1974, after ten years as a

An Australian teenager discovers artifacts from a centuries-old shipwreck and a savage massacre in this 1990 work, recipient of the Book of the Year Award in Australia and the Alan Marshall Prize for Children's Literature.

draftsman, Crew obtained a teaching position at Everton Park High School in Brisbane. For the next fourteen years, he continued to work as a teacher at three other institutions.

Troubled Teenagers and Australian Issues

Crew drew inspiration for his first young adult novels from the students in his English classes. "I guess my first novels came out of my experience as a high school teacher," he once revealed. "I saw so many teenagers who were confused and unhappy—about themselves and the world around them." His first book, *The Inner Circle*, turns on the relationship between a black teenager, Joe, and a white one, Tony, who share a sense of alienation and displacement. Tony comes from a divorced home, and he is torn between his parents, who use him as a weapon in their struggles with each other. Joe, on the other hand, comes from an Aboriginal family in the country, with strong family ties, yet is unable to tell them that he has lost his job through racism. Despite their racial differences, the two boys learn to support and affirm each other. "The theme of personal and racial reintegration and harmony," declared Maurice Saxby in *The Proof of the Pudding*, "is inherent in the plot and reinforced through symbolism."

In *The House of Tomorrow,* Crew tells the story of a teenage boy, Danny Coley, who has difficulty coping with the increased pressures in his life. Danny's problems spring at least in part from his interracial identity: he is half-Asian, the son of a dead Australian soldier, born while his father was fighting in Vietnam. Searching for a means to change and understand the world around him, Danny finds solace in a house that is modeled on the author's family's home in Ipswich. As Crew explained in *Australian Author,* "In *The House of Tomorrow* my great-grandmother's house re-established a sense of place and belonging in a young boy's life."

Crew explains that his interest in the past stems from his childhood. "The origins of *Strange Objects* are founded deep in my memory," he stated in his acceptance speech for the Children's Book Council of Australia Award, later published in *Reading Time.* "During the never ending sunshine of my childhood in the 50's, my parents would regularly take me and my sister Anita to the

Queensland Museum. . . . Here we were able to stare goggle-eyed and open-mouthed at mummies stolen-away from the Torres Strait Islands, bamboo headhunters' knives complete with notches from every head taken and other so-called 'cannibal' artifacts. . . . When I had been made wiser by my studies, I began to understand the colonist's fear of the Indigene [or aborigines] as The Other, and to appreciate fully the fantastical and ever-changing phenomenon we call 'history.'"

The Massacre of the *Batavia*

Strange Objects, which was awarded the Book of the Year Award from the Children's Book Council of Australia and the Alan Marshall Prize for Children's Literature, examines both the personal problems of its protagonist, Steven Messenger, and the historical problems of colonialism. Crew mixes several different literary genres to tell the story, including historical research, letters and documents, horror and fantasy fiction, and adventure and social realism. The sixteen-year-old Messenger discovers a leather-bound journal, a seventeenth-century "cannibal pot," and a mummified human hand wearing a golden ring hidden in a cave. The journal originally belonged to Wouter Loos, a survivor of the *Batavia*, a ship lost off the coast of Australia in 1629. The hand is that of a young white girl—according to Loos' journal, an English girl named Ela—who had been shipwrecked years earlier and was adopted by an Aboriginal tribe. The ring originally belonged to Jan Pelgrom, Loos' companion, the cabin boy of the *Batavia*. Pelgrom and Loos were both criminals—murderers and rapists—who were marooned on the Australian coast rather than being hanged for their crimes. Loos' journal traces Pelgrom's dehumanization from a sickly, rather sadistic boy to a terrifying figure who haunts the Australian night.

By wearing the ring, Messenger begins to identify with the psychopathic killer Pelgrom. Both Pelgrom and Messenger have no respect for the native Aboriginal way of life or for the Australian environment. Messenger comes to believe that Pelgrom, whom he resembles, still exists, possibly in the form of the Hitchhiker, a legendary psychopathic killer who haunts western Australia. At the novel's conclusion both Jan Pelgrom and his twentieth-century avatar, Steven Messenger, disappear into the Outback. Crew declared in *Reading Time* that *Strange Objects* is "a novel of colonial discourse intended to challenge the reader to examine what has happened in our past, to re-assess what forces shaped this nation—and the effect the white invasion has had on the original inhabitants of this country."

Crew continues to look at issues in Australia's past and present in works such as *Tracks, Lucy's Bay, No Such Country,* and *Angel's Gate. Tracks* demonstrates the fascination the world of the nighttime Australian jungle can have when it is approached without fear. In it, a young boy traces the shiny path made by a simple slug, marvelling that such a commonplace thing can create such beauty. *Lucy's Bay* is the story of a boy named Sam, whose sister drowns in the ocean while he is taking care of her. Several years later, Sam returns to the scene of the tragedy in an attempt to come to terms with his feelings. Sam has to face his memories and his pain before he can accept his guilt and move ahead with his life. "For him," wrote Joan Zahnleiter in *Magpies*, "this journey is a rite of passage from childhood into maturity, to scale the dreaded red cliffs, to go over into the bay, to find Lucy's memorial plaque and to go on into the next bay, to carry on with his life." A *Reading Time* reviewer found *Lucy's Bay* to be "a beautiful piece of descriptive writing which places in perspective Sam's grief for his sister against the ceaseless rhythm of nature."

No Such Country takes place in the fictional Australian town of New Canaan and looks at problems of religious fanaticism and genocide. The village is entirely controlled by the White Father, a priest who enjoys a strange power over the residents. Two young residents of the town, Rachel and Sarah, begin to work with Sam Shadows, a university student working on a local Aboriginal site, trying to solve the riddle of the White Father's power. Eventually Sam and the girls discover the town's hidden secret: years before the townspeople destroyed an aboriginal village and buried the Aborigines in a shellfish midden; the White Father used the information to blackmail the inhabitants of the town. As the novel reaches its climax, the Father is immolated in a volcanic eruption. Zahnleiter noted that "the book has deeply religious concepts embedded in it so that a working knowledge of the Bible enriches the reading of it. However it is a story which works well for the reader without that knowledge."

In *Angel's Gate*, the protagonist Julia Marriott serves as both participant in and commentator on the fates of two feral girls—children who have run from civilization and live wild in the bush. Julia lives in the small town of Jericho, which is electrified one day by the murder of a vagrant. In fear of their lives, the vagrant's two children disappear from their wilderness camp. They are not caught until months later, and when they are, they are placed in the custody of Julia's father, Doctor Marriott. "The story maps the process of civilising the girls," wrote Zahnleiter, "and how the girls themselves come to terms with the civilising forces." Marriott locks the girls up in the cellar of his home to protect them from the mysterious "Mister" who killed their father. In the process, however, he dehumanizes them still further, imprisoning them behind bars and finally shipping them off to a welfare home. "By what right is a person deprived of her liberty?," asked Zahnleiter. "There are issues of the limits of freedom and of civilising forces here." "But for Julia there is hope," declared Kevin Steinberger in *Magpies*. "She recognises the forces and conventions that threaten the individuality she cherishes. She fights against them but only succeeds when she takes flight from Jericho." "*Angel's Gate*," Steinberger concluded, "is an exceptional work that further consolidates Gary Crew's reputation."

Looking ahead to future projects, Crew believes that his personal experiences will continue to play a large role in his books. "As a writer, I am not done with looking inward," he explained in *Australian Author*. "There is much for me still to find in my house of fiction, in those fantastical inner rooms of childhood from which, I imagine, some choose never to emerge." In each book he writes, Crew has definite aims regarding his young audience. "My main objective in writing is to open the minds of my readers," he told *SATA*, "to say 'the world can be a wonderful place—its possibilities are open to you and your imagination.'"

■ Works Cited

Crew, Gary, essay on *Strange Objects*, *Reading Time*, Volume 35, Number 3, 1991, pp. 11-12.

Crew, Gary, "Awards: The Children's Book Council of Australia Awards, 1991 Acceptance Speeches," *Reading Time*, Volume 35, Number 4, 1991, p. 45.

Crew, Gary, autobiographical essay in *The Second Authors & Illustrators Scrapbook*, Omnibus Books, 1992, pp. 32-35.

Crew, Gary, "New Directions in Fiction," *Magpies*, July, 1992, pp. 5-8.

Crew, Gary, "The Architecture of Memory," *Australian Author*, autumn, 1992, pp. 24-27.

Kallenberger, Niki, "An Interview with Gary Crew," *Scan*, November, 1990, pp. 9-11.

Review of *Lucy's Bay*, *Reading Time*, May, 1992, p. 20.

Saxby, Maurice, *The Proof of the Pudding*, Ashton, 1993, pp. 455, 699-700.

Steinberger, Kevin, review of *Angel's Gate*, *Magpies*, September, 1993, p. 4.

Zahnleiter, Joan, "Know the Author: Gary Crew," *Magpies*, September, 1991, pp. 17-19.

■ For More Information See

BOOKS

Crew, Gary, "What's Next," *At Least They're Reading! Proceedings of the First National Conference of the Children's Book Council of Australia, 1992*, Thorpe, 1992.

PERIODICALS

Magpies, May, 1991, p. 22; July, 1991, p. 37; March, 1992, p. 34.

Papers: Explorations in Children's Literature, August, 1990, pp. 51-58; April, 1992, pp. 18-26.

—*Sketch by Kenneth R. Shepherd*

Ossie Davis

■ Personal

Born December 18, 1917, in Cogdell, GA; son of Kince Charles (a railway construction worker) and Laura (Cooper) Davis; married Ruby Ann Wallace (an actress; professional name Ruby Dee), December 9, 1948; children: Nora, Guy, La Verne (some sources say Hassan); seven grandchildren. *Education:* Attended Howard University, 1935-39, and Columbia University, 1948.

■ Addresses

Agent—Artists Agency, 10000 Santa Monica Blvd., Suite 305, Los Angeles, CA 90067.

■ Career

Actor, playwright, screenwriter, novelist, director, producer, and civil rights activist. Worked as janitor, shipping clerk, and stock clerk in New York City, 1938-41. Actor in numerous stage productions, 1941—, including *Joy Exceeding Glory, Jeb, No Time for Sergeants, A Raisin in the Sun, Anna Lucasta, Jamaica, The Green Pastures, Wisteria Tree,* and *I'm Not Rappaport.* Actor in motion pictures, including *No Way Out, Fourteen Hours, The Joe Louis Story, Gone Are the Days, The Cardinal, Shock Treatment, The Hill, Man Called Adam, The Scalphunters, Sam Whiskey, Slaves, Let's Do It Again, Hot Stuff, House of God, Harry and Son, Avenging Angel, School Daze, Do the Right Thing, Joe Versus the Volcano, Jungle Fever, Gladiator, Malcolm X, Grumpy Old Men,* and *The Client.* Actor in television movies and miniseries, including *The Emperor Jones, All God's Children, Don't Look Back, Roots: The Next Generation, King, Teacher, Teacher, The Ernest Green Story, Ray Alexander: A Taste for Justice, Queen,* and *The Stand.* Actor in television series, including *Name of the Game, Night Gallery, Bonanza, B. L. Stryker, Evening Shade,* and *John Grisham's The Client.*

Producer of stage production *Ballad for Bimshire,* 1963. Director of motion pictures *Black Girl,* 1972, and *Gordon's War,* 1973. Founder, Institute of Cinema Artists, 1973. Co-host of radio program *Ossie Davis and Ruby Dee Story Hour,* 1974-78, and of television series *With Ossie and Ruby,* Public Broadcasting System (PBS-TV), 1981. Narrator of motion picture *From Dreams to Reality: A Tribute to Minority Inventors,* 1986, and of television movie *The American Experience: Goin' Back to T'Town,* 1993. *Military service:* U.S. Army, 1942-45; served as surgical technician in Liberia, West Africa, and with Special Services Department. *Member:* NAACP, Grace Baptist Church.

■ Awards, Honors

Emmy Award nomination for outstanding leading performance by an actor in a leading role, Academy of Television Arts and Sciences, 1969, for *Teacher, Teacher*; Frederick Douglass Award, New York Urban League, 1970 (with wife, Ruby Dee); Paul Robeson Citation for "outstanding creative contributions both in the performing arts and society at large," Actors' Equity Association, 1975; Father of the Year Award, 1987; NAACP Image Award for best performance by a supporting actor, 1989, for *Do the Right Thing*; NAACP Image Awards Hall of Fame, 1989; Monarch Award, 1990.

■ Writings

PLAYS

(And director) *Goldbrickers of 1944*, first produced in Liberia, West Africa, 1944.

Alice in Wonder (one-act), first produced in New York at Elks Community Theatre, 1952, revised and expanded version produced as *The Big Deal* in New York at New Playwrights Theatre, 1953.

Purlie Victorious (first produced in New York at Cort Theatre, 1961; also see below), French, 1961.

Curtain Call, Mr. Aldridge, Sir (first produced in Santa Barbara at the University of California, 1968), published in *The Black Teacher and the Dramatic Arts: A Dialogue, Bibliography, and Anthology*, edited by William R. Reardon and Thomas D. Pawley, Negro Universities Press, 1970.

(With Philip Rose, Peter Udell, and Gary Geld) *Purlie* (musical adaptation of *Purlie Victorious*; first produced on Broadway at Broadway Theatre, 1970), French, 1971.

Escape to Freedom: A Play about Young Frederick Douglass (for young adults; first produced in New York at the Town Hall, 1976), Viking, 1978.

Langston: A Play, Delacorte, 1982.

(With Hy Gilbert; and director) *Bingo* (baseball musical based on novel *The Bingo Long Traveling All-Stars and Motor Kings* by William Brashler), first produced in New York at AMAS Repertory Theater, 1985.

Also author of *Last Dance for Sybil*.

SCREENPLAYS AND TELEPLAYS

Gone Are the Days (film adaptation of *Purlie Victorious*; also released as *Purlie Victorious* and *The Man from C.O.T.T.O.N.*), Trans Lux, 1963.

(With Arnold Perl; and director) *Cotton Comes to Harlem*, United Artists, 1970.

(And director) *Kongi's Harvest* (adapted from work by Wole Soyinka), Calpenny Films Nigeria Ltd., 1970.

Today Is Ours, Columbia Broadcasting System (CBS-TV), 1974.

Also author of teleplay *Just Say the Word*, 1969, and author of screenplay, director, co-producer, and star of *Countdown at Kusini*, 1976. Also author of scripts for television series, including *Bonanza*, *N.Y.P.D.*, *East Side/West Side*, and *The Eleventh Hour*.

YOUNG ADULT NOVEL

Just Like Martin, Simon & Schuster, 1992.

OTHER

(Contributor) Herbert Hill, editor, *Anger, and Beyond: The Negro Writer in the United States*, Harper, 1966.

(Contributor) Hill, editor, *Soon, One Morning: New Writing by American Negroes, 1940-1962*, Knopf, 1968.

(With others) *The Black Cinema: Foremost Representatives of the Black Film World Air Their Views* (sound recording), Center for Cassette Studies 30983, 1975.

(Contributor) Nora D. Day, editor, *Purlie Victorious: A Commemorative*, Emmalyn Enterprises, 1993.

(With Ruby Dee) *Hands upon the Heart* (two-volume videotape), Emmalyn Enterprises, 1994.

Contributor to periodicals, including *Negro History Bulletin*, *Negro Digest*, *Nation*, and *Freedomways*.

■ Sidelights

"The most immediate responsibility faced by African-Americans is the restoration to black youth of their self-esteem and sense of place in a world so cruelly snatched from them every single day, and to encourage within them a visionary view," states actor, director, playwright, novelist, and social activist Ossie Davis in the *Nation*. "A second great responsibility is that of teaching the nation, so that white Americans cannot continue to hide so grotesquely behind the myth of national equality while the relentless quiet and unquiet eradication of millions of their fellow citizens proceeds.

The twentieth century has made such innocence obscene."

Although Davis is perhaps best known as an actor—with appearances on the stage as well as in movies such as *Do the Right Thing, The Client,* and *The Stand*—he is also the author of numerous plays and the 1992 young-adult novel *Just Like Martin.* What ties his various accomplishments together, according to Jayne F. Mulvaney in the *Dictionary of Literary Biography (DLB)* is Davis's commitment to "creating works that would truthfully portray the black man's experience." Long active in the cause of racial justice, Davis was a prominent figure in the civil rights movement of the 1960s. He gave the eulogies at the funerals of black leaders Malcolm X and Dr. Martin Luther King, Jr., and he acted as master of ceremonies at the famous March on Washington in 1963—the peaceful demonstration where Dr. King made his famous "I Have a Dream" speech. Throughout his life, Davis has used his many talents to expose wide audiences to his views. As Davis explains to Calvin Reid in *Publishers Weekly,* "I am essentially a storyteller, and the story I want to tell is about black people. Sometimes I sing the story, sometimes I dance it, sometimes I tell tall tales about it, but I always want to share my great satisfaction at being a black man at this time in history."

Develops Early Love of Theater

Ossie Davis was born in Cogdell, Georgia, in 1917. His father was a railroad foreman, so his family moved around a lot while he was growing up. Eventually they settled in the rural community of Waycross, Georgia. Davis did well in many subjects in school, but his first love was the theater. He enjoyed acting in school plays, and he even wrote a play that was produced by his classmates at Center High School in Waycross. After graduating from high school in 1935, Davis hitchhiked to Washington, D.C., to attend Howard University. He continued acting in plays during his college years, and he also met black scholar Alain Locke, who encouraged him to continue his writing. After three years at Howard, however, Davis became anxious to pursue a career in the theater and decided to move to New York City.

When he arrived in New York, Davis joined the Rose McClendon Players, a Harlem-based theater group, and applied himself to learning about all aspects of the theater—including lighting and stage design. He made his first professional stage appearance in 1941 in the group's production of *Joy Exceeding Glory.* His success as an actor did not come quickly, however, and later that year he sometimes ended up eating scraps of food and sleeping in city parks. In 1942, Davis was inducted into the army and sent overseas to help fight World War II. He first served as a medical technician in Liberia, West Africa, and later he was transferred to the army's Special Services division. During these years, he continued writing plays and produced some of them to entertain the troops, including *Goldbrickers of 1944.*

When Davis was discharged from the army in 1945, he initially went home to Georgia. But then Richard Campbell, director of the Rose McClendon Players, encouraged him to come back to New York and audition for the Broadway play *Jeb.*

Racism and the civil rights movement of the 1960s are the focus of this 1992 novel.

Davis won the starring role and earned critical acclaim for his compelling portrayal of a disabled veteran who must cope with racism when he returns home to an office job in Louisiana. It was also while performing in this play that Davis met actress Ruby Dee. In an interview with Khephra Burns for *Essence*, Dee recalls that she made fun of Davis when they first met because he seemed like such a country boy. He bought all his clothes at a secondhand store, for example, so they were always several sizes too big. His charm, talent, and sense of humor eventually won her over, however, and the couple were married in 1948.

Davis's achievements as an actor expanded in the 1950s, when he performed in many successful stage productions—including a long run co-starring with his wife in *Raisin in the Sun* on Broadway—and also accepted roles in the movies and on television. Throughout these years, "Davis consistently refused to play roles that stereotyped blacks for the amusement of white audiences," according to Mulvaney. Davis also began to encounter success as a playwright. The first American production of one of his plays came in 1952, when his one-act play *Alice in Wonder* debuted at a community theater in New York. Davis starred as a black singer who must decide whether to compromise his integrity in order to retain his contract. Dee played his wife, who does not support his decision and finally leaves him. In a review quoted in *DLB*, playwright Loften Mitchell states that the play "roared the truth about the Negro's plight in America." Davis later expanded *Alice in Wonder* into a full-length play, renamed *The Big Deal*, that premiered Off-Broadway.

Becomes a Broadway Playwright

In 1961, Davis became "one of the few black writers to have had a play successfully produced on Broadway," according to Mulvaney, when his comedy *Purlie Victorious* opened. In the play, Purlie Victorious Judson is a black preacher who returns to his native Georgia determined to buy an old barn and convert it into an integrated church. In order to achieve his goal, however, he must somehow trick a bigoted plantation owner, Captain Cotchipee, into giving him the $500 that a wealthy white woman left to his aunt, the captain's former slave. Since Purlie's aunt and cousin have both died, he decides to have his young girlfriend, Lutiebelle, impersonate his cousin in order to get

the money. The action of the play follows Purlie's hilarious, but unsuccessful, efforts to outsmart the captain. Finally, the captain's liberal son, Charlie, simply gives Purlie the old barn. Upon learning of his son's deed, the captain drops dead, and Purlie ends up officiating at his funeral.

During the play's initial run on Broadway, Davis played Purlie and Dee played Lutiebelle. In a review for the *New York Herald-Tribune*, quoted in *DLB*, Walter Kerr calls *Purlie Victorious* "unique in style, rich in its highly individual humor, and most happily performed." Mulvaney goes on to explain that "the brilliance of this comedy derives chiefly from how cliches and stereotypes are blown out of proportion. . . . Although Davis starts by poking fun at the black stereotypes, in the end the black characters are more than cardboard figures. The play provokes much laughter, but it is laughter created out of the injustices endured by a young black growing up in rural Georgia." In a review for the *New York Times*, quoted in *DLB*, Howard Taubman notes further that "While *Purlie Victorious* keeps you chuckling and guffawing, it unrelentingly forces you to feel how it is to inhabit a dark skin in a hostile or, at best, grudgingly benevolent world."

Although many reviewers appreciated Davis's use of humor to shed light on racial issues, a few objected to the play's stereotyped characters. For example, Robert Brustein of the *New Republic*, quoted in *DLB*, says he was startled by the comedy's underlying "hate and violence" and claims that the play "set back inter-racial harmony . . . about fourteen years." But *DLB* contributor Michael E. Greene notes that "Davis himself recognized that his handling of stereotypes would have been offensive had a white writer created them." In *DLB*, Davis describes his motives in writing the play: "If men may really laugh together at something disturbing to them both, it means that for the moment they have overleapt their separateness."

Overall, *Purlie Victorious* enjoyed positive reviews and a seven-and-a-half month run on Broadway. Such luminaries as writer W. E. B. DuBois and civil rights leaders Malcolm X and Dr. Martin Luther King, Jr. came to see it, and it received an endorsement from the National Association for the Advancement of Colored People (NAACP). However, Davis did not earn any money from it as a playwright. "The financial support of the black community was not enough," Mulvaney

Davis and his wife, Ruby Dee, starred in the 1961 production of *Purlie Victorious*, a comedy about a preacher who schemes to outwit a bigoted plantation owner.

explains. "The white audiences did not come." As Davis explains in *DLB*, this experience taught him that "I would never find my manhood by asking the white man to define it for me. That I would never become a man until I stopped measuring my black self by white standards." The play's influence continued despite its disappointing reception by white audiences, as it was later adapted into a movie, *Gone Are the Days*, and a Broadway musical, *Purlie*, which was nominated for a Tony award.

Stays Active in Movies and TV

Davis kept extremely busy throughout the 1960s and 1970s. He acted in numerous stage productions and movies, often co-starring with his wife. The couple also co-hosted the radio program *Ossie Davis and Ruby Dee Story Hour* from 1974 to 1978, and the TV show *With Ossie and Ruby* in 1981. In addition to his work as an actor, Davis wrote, directed, and produced several plays and movies during these years. One notable example of his work is *Countdown at Kusini*, a 1976 movie for which he was author, director, co-producer, and star. Burns describes it as "the first feature film ever to be financed by a black women's organization . . . and the first American production to be shot entirely in Africa by African-American professionals."

Davis continued to appear in prominent movies and television programs into the 1980s and 1990s. In 1989, for example, he co-starred with Burt Reynolds in the TV series *B. L. Stryker*. Reynolds played a retired policeman who solves many strange mysteries as a private investigator, while Davis played his best friend, a wise retired boxer who runs a local gym. Though the series was only modestly successful, John Leonard calls Davis "brilliant" in a *New York* magazine review. In 1990, he appeared in another TV series with Reynolds, the acclaimed situation comedy *Evening Shade*. Reynolds played a football coach in a rural town in Arkansas, and Davis played one of the town's interesting residents. According to Harry F. Waters in *Newsweek*, Davis helped provide the show with "the most high-powered cast ever assembled for a half-hour series."

Also in 1990, Davis appeared in Spike Lee's controversial movie *Do the Right Thing*. As "Da Mayor," a drunken but good-natured gentleman who can always be found walking around the neighborhood, Davis advises Lee's character, Mookie, to "always do the right thing." In several comic scenes, Davis's character also flirts with the neighborhood matriarch Mother Sister (played by Ruby Dee), who wants nothing to do with him. Davis also appeared in several other films directed by Lee, including *Jungle Fever* and *Malcolm X*. Later in 1990 Davis appeared in the wild comedy *Joe Versus the Volcano*. Though the movie was not particularly well-received, Terrence Rafferty of the *New Yorker* calls Davis "commandingly funny" in his role as a chauffeur to Tom Hanks's title character. In 1994, Davis and Dee appeared in the blockbuster TV miniseries *The Stand* as two of the survivors of a deadly plague that wipes out most of the world's population. Davis also drew acclaim for his portrayal of a stern judge in the 1994 hit movie *The Client*, and he reprised the role in the TV series *John Grisham's The Client* in 1995.

Brings Message to Young Audiences

In addition to his work as an actor, director, and writer for adult audiences, Davis has written two books about prominent African Americans for young adults. His play *Escape to Freedom*, published in 1976, "traces the life of the slave Frederick Douglass, a famous orator, adviser to President Lincoln, and the first black to hold a diplomatic post as U.S. ambassador to Haiti," according to Mulvaney. The play's five scenes follow Douglass beginning with his boyhood as a slave, through his youth as a servant in Baltimore where he learns to read, through his return to the farm of his childhood where he is whipped for teaching other slaves to read, to his eventual escape to freedom in New York. In a review for *Five Owls*, Barbara T. Rollock explains that the key to the play is Davis's "emphasis on how the ability to read opened the door to his freedom from slavery."

Davis published his first novel for young adults, *Just Like Martin*, in 1992. "I always intended to write about the civil rights struggles," Davis tells Reid. "I originally hoped it would be a play about Martin [Luther King], but it just wasn't working. So I tried to branch into the deep waters of the novel." Set in a small Alabama town in 1963, the book views the civil rights movement through the eyes of fourteen-year-old boy, Isaac Stone. Isaac belongs to a local black church and wants to follow in the footsteps of Dr. Martin Luther King,

Davis stands with Coretta Scott King, Percy Sutton, and Ruby Dee at a 1984 reception in New York.

Jr., and lead nonviolent protests to draw attention to racial injustices. Isaac's father, however, feels that King's philosophy of passive resistance is cowardly. Isaac's beliefs are tested when his church is bombed and his father is beaten, but he is eventually able to learn and grow from these experiences. Louise Stearns of *MultiCultural Review* calls *Just Like Martin* an "uplifting and realistic look at the Civil Rights movement," claiming that "it gives the reader a deep admiration for the unconquerable spirit of the people involved in this facet of American history."

Expresses Views on American Society

Davis currently lives in New Rochelle, New York, with Ruby Dee, his wife of nearly half a century. In an article about the couple for *Modern Maturity*, Connie Goldman emphasizes that they "have distinguished themselves not only as creative tal-

ents but as social activists with deep-rooted commitments to civil-rights organizations and causes." Burns notes that their accomplishments are "all the more impressive when you consider the consistently high quality of their projects and the pride-inspiring images they have created or helped in other ways to bring to the stage and screen over the last five decades," adding that "numberless lives" have been influenced "through their art and their example."

In addition to his impressive career and his status as a role model, Davis has also been a direct source of encouragement and support for other African American artists. For example, he founded the Institute of Cinema Artists in 1973, which provides black students with training for careers in television and film. In recognition of his achievements in this area, Mulvaney calls Davis "a force in the development of black culture." Davis explains his commitment to nurturing other artists in *DLB:* "For if we can, in fact, create for our own people; work for our own people; belong to our own people; we will no longer be forced into artistic prostitution and self-betrayal in the mad scramble, imposed upon us far too long, to belong to some other people. . . . Only then can we begin to take a truly independent position within the confines of American culture, a black position."

Davis has written many articles detailing his views about the position of African Americans in the United States. Of particular concern to him is the deterioration of black families and the resulting problems faced by black youth. He relates to Burns how the family structure has changed since his childhood: "The dinner table was a place where much more than food was being exchanged. We learned our history, and we learned the values, attitudes and propositions of the past. Definitions are made and the culture passes from one generation to the other around the dinner table. Now the elimination of the dinner table as a fact in how the family conducts its business means that a marketplace for the transfer of very important ideas, ideas relevant to cultural identity, was lost, creating a kind of vacuum. Into that vacuum came television, which looked upon our children as a market where sales could be made. So our children at the most tender phases of their lives are being manipulated. Now they hear things that relate to consumption, to self-gratification and self-indulgence. And children reflect those values—or that lack of values—they get from having their minds misused." "We have young folks who don't believe anymore that there is a future," Davis tells Goldman. "Yet I believe we who are older can still tell them something deeper."

■ Works Cited

Burns, Khephra, "Ruby Dee and Ossie Davis: A Love Supreme," *Essence*, December 1994, p. 76.

Davis, Ossie, "Jobs, Peace, Justice: Challenge for the Year 2000," *Nation*, July 24-31, 1989, pp. 144-48.

Goldman, Connie, "Hume Cronyn and Jessica Tandy, Ossie Davis and Ruby Dee: Poignant Reflections on Living, Loving, and Aging from Two of America's Most Venerable and Cherished Couples," *Modern Maturity*, July-August 1994, p. 64.

Greene, Michael E., "Ossie Davis," *Dictionary of Literary Biography*, Volume 38: *Afro-American Writers after 1955: Dramatists and Prose Writers*, Gale, 1985.

Leonard, John, "The Cop Who Knew Too Much," *New York*, February 13, 1989, p. 71.

Mulvaney, Jayne F., "Ossie Davis," *Dictionary of Literary Biography*, Volume 7: *Twentieth-Century American Dramatists*, Gale, 1981.

Rafferty, Terrence, review of *Joe Versus the Volcano*, *New Yorker*, March 26, 1990, p. 79.

Reid, Calvin, "Ossie Davis," *Publishers Weekly*, December 28, 1992, p. 27.

Rollock, Barbara T., "The Black Experience in Children's Books," *Five Owls*, January/February 1988, p. 47.

Stearns, Louise, review of *Just Like Martin*, *MultiCultural Review*, vol. 2, no. 1, p. 67.

Waters, Harry F., "A Winner Made in the Shade," *Newsweek*, December 17, 1990, p. 64.

■ For More Information See

BOOKS

Funke, Lewis, *The Curtain Rises—The Story of Ossie Davis*, Grosset & Dunlap, 1971.

PERIODICALS

Kirkus Reviews, September 15, 1992, p. 1185.

Library Journal, January 1990, p. 164.

Nation, July 17, 1989, p. 98.

New Yorker, July 24, 1989, p. 78.

People, February 13, 1989, p. 13; September 24, 1990, p. 7; August 1, 1994, p. 16.

Voice of Youth Advocates, April, 1993, p. 24.

—Sketch by Laurie Collier Hillstrom

Thomas M. Disch

■ Personal

Publishes poetry as Tom Disch; has also written under pseudonym Leonie Hargrave and under joint pseudonyms Thom Demijohn and Cassandra Knye; born Thomas Michael Disch February 2, 1940, in Des Moines, IA; son of Felix Henry (a salesperson) and Helen (Gilbertson) Disch. *Education:* Attended architectural college of Cooper Union, New York City; attended New York University in 1960s.

■ Addresses

Office—31 Union Square West, No. 11E, New York, NY 10003. *Agent*—c/o Karpfinger Agency, 500 Fifth Ave., Suite 2800, New York, NY 10110.

■ Career

Writer. Worked as a structural steel draftsman in Minnesota; worked at various jobs in New York City, including part-time checkroom attendant at Majestic Theatre, 1957-62, and copywriter, Doyle Dane Bernbach Inc., 1963-64. Theater critic for *Nation,* 1987—. *Member:* PEN, Writers Guild East, National Book Critics Circle (board member, 1988-91, secretary, 1989-91).

■ Awards, Honors

O. Henry prize, 1975, for story "Getting into Death," and 1979, for story "Xmas"; American Book Award nomination for science fiction, and John W. Campbell Memorial award, both 1980, both for *On Wings of Song; The Brave Little Toaster* was on the final Hugo and Nebula awards' ballots for best novella of 1980; *Locus* award, 1981; British Science-Fiction award, 1981, for *The Brave Little Toaster.*

■ Writings

NOVELS

The Genocides, Berkley Medallion, 1965.
Mankind under the Leash (expanded version of his short story, "White Fang Goes Dingo" [also see below]), Ace, 1966 (published in England as *The Puppies of Terra,* Panther, 1978).
(With John T. Sladek under joint pseudonym Cassandra Knye) *The House that Fear Built,* Paperback Library, 1966.
Echo round His Bones (serialized in *New Worlds,* 1966), Berkley Medallion, 1967.
Camp Concentration (serialized in *New Worlds,* 1967), Hart Davis, 1968.
(With John T. Sladek under joint-pseudonym Thom Demijohn) *Black Alice,* Doubleday, 1968.

The Prisoner (novelization of British television series of same title), Ace, 1969.

334, MacGibbon and Kee, 1972, Avon, 1974.

(Under pseudonym Leonie Hargrave) *Clara Reeve*, Knopf, 1975.

On Wings of Song (serialized in *Magazine of Fantasy and Science Fiction*, 1979), St. Martin's Press, 1979.

Triplicity (omnibus volume), Doubleday, 1980.

(With Charles Naylor) *Neighboring Lives*, Scribner, 1981.

The Businessman: A Tale of Terror, Harper, 1984.

The Silver Pillow: A Tale of Witchcraft, M.V. Ziesing (Willimantic, CT), 1987.

The M.D.: A Horror Story, Knopf, 1991.

The Priest: A Gothic Romance, Knopf, 1995.

STORY COLLECTIONS

One Hundred and Two H-bombs (also see below), Compact Books, 1966, with new arrangement of stories, Berkley, 1971, expanded edition published as *White Fang Goes Dingo and Other Funny S.F. Stories*, Arrow, 1971.

Under Compulsion, Hart Davis, 1968, published as *Fun with Your New Head*, Doubleday, 1971.

Getting into Death: The Best Short Stories of Thomas M. Disch, Hart-Davis MacGibbon, 1973, revised edition published as *Getting into Death and Other Stories*, Knopf, 1976.

The Early Science Fiction Stories of Thomas M. Disch (includes *Mankind under the Leash* and *One Hundred and Two H-bombs*), Gregg Press, 1977.

Fundamental Disch, edited by Samuel R. Delany, Berkley Medallion, 1980.

The Man Who Had No Idea, Bantam, 1982.

CHILDREN'S BOOKS

The Tale of Dan De Lion: A Fable, Coffee House Press (Minneapolis, Minnesota), 1986.

The Brave Little Toaster: A Bedtime Story for Small Appliances, Doubleday, 1986.

The Brave Little Toaster Goes to Mars, Doubleday, 1988.

POETRY; AS TOM DISCH

(With Marilyn Hacker and Charles Platt) *Highway Sandwiches*, privately printed, 1970.

The Right Way to Figure Plumbing, Basilisk Press, 1972.

ABCDEFG HIJKLM NOPQRST UVWXYZ, Anvil Press Poetry, 1981.

Burn This, Hutchinson, 1982.

Order of the Retina, Toothpaste Press, 1982.

Here I Am, There You Are, Where Were We?, Hutchinson, 1984.

Yes, Let's: New and Selected Poems, Johns Hopkins University Press, 1989.

Dark Verses and Light, Johns Hopkins University Press, 1991.

Contributor of numerous poems to periodicals, including *Poetry* and *Isaac Asimov's Science Fiction Magazine*.

EDITOR

The Ruins of the Earth: An Anthology of the Immediate Future, Putnam, 1971.

Bad Moon Rising: An Anthology of Political Foreboding, Harper, 1973.

The New Improved Sun: An Anthology of Utopian Science Fiction, 1975.

(With Charles Naylor) *New Constellations: An Anthology of Tomorrow's Mythologies*, Harper, 1976.

(With Charles Naylor; and contributor) *Strangeness: A Collection of Curious Tales*, Scribner, 1977.

OTHER

(Ghost editor with Robert Arthur) *Alfred Hitchcock Presents: Stories that Scared Even Me*, Random House, 1967.

(Contributor) *Science Fiction at Large*, edited by Peter Nicholls, Harper, 1976.

(Librettist) *The Fall of the House of Usher* (opera; music by Gregory Sandow), first produced in New York City by Bel Canto Opera Company, 1979.

(Librettist) *Frankenstein* (opera; music by Sandow), first produced in Greenvale, NY, at the C. W. Post Center of Long Island University, 1982.

Ringtime: A Story (short story), Toothpaste Press, 1983.

Torturing Mr. Amberwell (short story), Cheap Street (New Castle, VA), 1985.

Amnesia (computer interactive novel), Electronic Arts, 1985.

Ben Hur (play), first produced in New York City, 1989.

The Cardinal Detoxes (verse play), first produced in New York City by RAPP Theater Company, 1990.

Contributor of short stories to science fiction magazines, including *Fantastic, New Worlds,* and *Magazine of Fantasy and Science Fiction;* work has appeared in numerous anthologies. Disch's papers are part of the collections at Yale University's Beinecke Library.

■ Adaptations

The Brave Little Toaster (animated motion picture), Hyperion Pictures, Kushner-Locke Production, 1988.

■ Work in Progress

The Teddy Bear's Tragedy; The Pressure of Time; A Child's Garden of Grammar, for Story Line Press.

■ Sidelights

"Between them, the old Hoover and the toaster knew enough about the basic principles of electricity to be able, very quickly, to wire the battery so that it would serve their needs instead of an automobile's. But before any of the small appliances who may be listening to this tale should begin to think that they might do the same thing, let them be warned: ELECTRICITY IS VERY DANGEROUS. *Never* play with old batteries! *Never* put your plug in a strange socket! And if you are in any doubt about the voltage of the current where you are living, *ask a major appliance.*"

If the idea of a toaster and a vacuum cleaner wiring a battery seems improbable, you should read some of Thomas M. Disch's science fiction tales for even more incredible images. How about a future world where a speakeasy is a place where people who are licensed to talk go to practice? Or a world where you can fly away from your physical body by simply singing? Even so, the image of the toaster is important to Disch. The appliance in the excerpt above is the title character of his most famous piece of fiction—at least in its musical feature film adaptation—*The Brave Little Toaster.* Unfortunately, while many people associate the name Disney with the film—the Walt Disney Company released the home video version—not many people associate Disch's name

with it or with the award-winning novella upon which it was based. There also seems to be some confusion among critics about just for which audience *The Brave Little Toaster* was intended. While it was marketed for children, several critics noted that its style was literate enough to appeal to adults.

Hard to pigeon-hole, Disch's versatility has made both marketing his work and developing a loyal following of readers difficult. Is he a science fiction writer, a poet, a writer for children, or a playwright? The answer is, of course, that he is all these and more. In refusing to let critics stamp his work with one or another label, Disch has been granted a relative anonymity out of balance with his enormous talent. He seems destined to be, as *Newsweek's* Walter Clemons claims, "the most formidably gifted unfamous American writer."

While some readers of Disch's pessimistic, and often horrific, science fiction novels and short stories, might find it a bit of a stretch to think that he is also the author of children's fables, Disch finds the connection between science fiction and children's literature quite logical. "As for how I came to write for children," he once commented, "that's an easy question for any sci-fi writer to answer, since a good part of science fiction has always been written for 'kids of all ages.' There's a saying in our field that the golden age of science-fiction is twelve—the age you start to read it." In a speech given at London's Institute of Contemporary Arts, published in *Science Fiction at Large* as "The Embarrassments of Science Fiction," he went as far as to declare that science fiction was a branch of children's literature. But much of Disch's science fiction is decidedly not for children. Indeed, as he notes in his *Something about the Author Autobiography Series* entry, from the very beginning of his career he has purposely chosen to avoid those aspects of science fiction, such as "robots and spaceships and other forms of future hardware," that would be more likely to appeal to children. Instead, Disch is interested in producing a highly intelligent, socially aware science fiction, more often than not a witty satire of the present.

While as a mature writer Disch might have chosen to avoid writing about mechanical men and space vehicles, the young Disch who discovered science fiction in the early 1950s found them fascinating. He was drawn from the pages of his favorite horror comic books, such as *The Vault of Horror* and *The Crypt of Terror*, to those of the most influential of all science fiction magazines, *Astounding Science Fiction.* Since 1938, the magazine's legendary editor, John W. Campbell, had been encouraging the writing of a stellar group of authors, including Robert A. Heinlein, Isaac Asimov, and others who would go on to become the most prominent writers of modern science fiction. Disch learned his craft reading and re-reading the work of these great authors in the pages of *Astounding* or in cheap paperbacks. Although he didn't sell his first science fiction story until July 1962, in his autobiographical sketch he recalls having written his first story ten years before that under the influence of those early stories, especially those of Asimov. His first effort has long since disappeared, but Disch observes "the mental muscles I began to exercise in that tablet [containing his first story] are still busy with the same work forty years later."

Published at Last!

Disch's first published story, "The Double Timer," appeared in another popular science fiction magazine, *Fantastic Stories.* Between that periodical and another one called *Amazing Stories* he would publish nine more stories that year and the next. Although Disch admits to not thinking that highly of his first publishing success, he found his second effort at writing a full-length story more satisfactory. This story, entitled "White Fang Goes Dingo," was first published in its short form, then in an expanded version as Disch's second novel, *Mankind under the Leash* (later published under the title Disch prefers, *The Puppies of Terra*). While continuing to publish stories in science fiction magazines during this time, Disch was forced to support himself with a variety of jobs, including bank teller, insurance claims adjuster, and advertising copywriter, until nearly the end of 1964. Then, thanks to the efforts of a friend who showed one of Disch's plot outlines for a novel to a receptive editor, Disch received an advance from Berkley Books. He completed his first novel while living in Mexico, in the spring of 1965. From then on, writing has remained his full-time occupation.

The second half of the sixties were times of great growth for the young writer: he published a new novel every year from 1965 to 1968 and published two collections of short stories during the same period. The success came even though he himself

admits in his autobiographical essay to an ambivalence about his vocation. "Until I was actually a published writer," Disch recalls, "no one, including myself, thought that that was what I ought to do for a living—for the very good reason that it is not a realistic goal for a career." Back in New York City during the summer of 1965, he returned briefly to his advertising job, but was also able to sell outlines to five books. Confident of his continued success as a writer, Disch would soon find himself near the center of an upheaval in the world of science fiction. The previous year influential editor Michael Moorcock had taken over the reins of the British science fiction magazine, *New Worlds.* "Moorcock's *New Worlds*," notes science

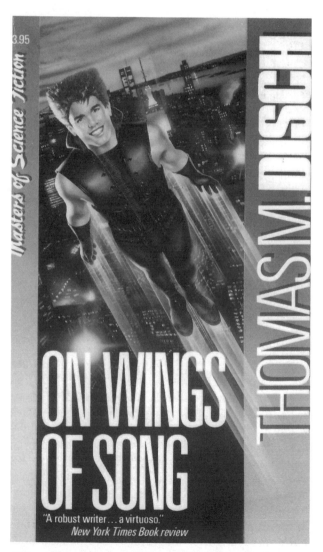

This 1979 science fiction work posits a repressive future America in which people can gain freedom by departing their physical bodies through singing.

fiction novelist and critic Brian Aldiss in his *Trillion Year Spree: The History of Science Fiction,* "had few taboos—something that often got it into trouble with distributors. It encouraged rather than rejected literary experimentation and steadily became the focus for a re-evaluation of genre standards." With the face of science fiction beginning to change, Disch moved to England to be near the center of innovation.

Disch and other writers whose works were published in *New Worlds* were said to belong to the New Wave of science fiction. According to Aldiss, "At the heart of *New Worlds*'s New Wave—never mind the froth at the edges—was a hard and unpalatable core of message, an attitude to life, a scepticism about the benefits of society or any future society." More specifically, the New Wave was interested in new forms of expression and new themes never dreamed of by the older generation of science fiction writers. "In a broad sense," write Robert Scholes and Eric S. Rabkin in *Science Fiction: History, Science, Vision,* "the New Wave represents an attempt to find a language and a social perspective for science fiction that is as adventurous and progressive as its technological vision." The skepticism of its writers made their works on a whole pessimistic and Disch was no exception. Although the New Wave has been followed by succeeding generations of writers, its impact on Disch's work—and the reverse—is undeniable.

While Brian M. Stableford describes Disch's early short stories as "playfully ironic," in *Science Fiction Writers: Critical Studies of the Major Authors from the Early Nineteenth Century to the Present Day* Disch's early novels reveal a darker vision of reality. In *Dictionary of Literary Biography* Erich S. Rupprecht notes that both Disch's first novel, *The Genocides,* and his second, *Mankind under the Leash,* deal with the fight against the destruction of the human spirit. In both books, aliens have control over the Earth, but Disch puts a new twist on this well-worn science fiction theme by focusing not on the aliens but on the reaction of humans to the invading creatures. As Aldiss notes, "People and their strange, alien ways mattered more to Disch than the aliens themselves." In *The Genocides* the Earth is merely a place for a group of unseen aliens to raise a form of gigantic plant essential to their survival. These extraordinary beings view humans as a gardener might a garden pest, as something to be eradicated. Rupprecht finds Disch's depiction of humans in *The Genocides* as typical of his handling of characters in later works. The critic notes: "This becomes Disch's recurrent theme: charting his characters' attempts to keep themselves intact in a world which grows increasingly hostile, irrational, inhuman." *Mankind under the Leash* describes an equally irrational world where aliens domesticate and mate humans in much the same way humans have domesticated and mated dogs for exhibition.

Disch's next two novels, *Echo round His Bones* and *Camp Concentration* were both serialized in *New Worlds.* In *Echo round His Bones,* according to Rupprecht, Disch again places the action of his novel in the future but nevertheless gives us a "disturbing vision of modern life, which he sees as ugly, violent, and inhuman." In the book a "shadow world" is formed as an unexpected result of the use of a matter transmitter. Every time the device is used, whatever is transmitted also appears in duplicate in another world. The inhabitants of this other world can see, but not communicate with, the inhabitants of the real world. Despite being indistinct figures who pass through walls, the dwellers of the shadow world do feel hunger. Since food is rarely transmitted, this hunger leads them to look upon new arrivals as meals rather than companions. The novel ends on an uncharacteristic upbeat, however, as a nuclear disaster is averted by way of a unique plot twist that involves moving the Earth's position in space.

Success with Later Novels

Camp Concentration, 334 and *On Wings of Song* are widely considered Disch's best works. All three appeared in a mid-1980s survey by David Pringle entitled *Science Fiction: The 100 Best Novels.* Scholes and Rabkin call *Camp Concentration* Disch's "first major breakthrough" under the influence of the New Wave, while Stableford is convinced "the novel is a *tour de force* in which Disch shows off his true brilliance to spectacular effect." *Camp Concentration* is a modern-day retelling of the story of Faust, the legendary figure who sells his soul to the devil in exchange for all the knowledge in the world. Astute readers will find numerous references to the various historical versions of the story, including Christopher Marlowe's *The Tragical History of Dr. Faustus* and Goethe's *Faust* in Disch's novel. Set only a few years into the future from when it was first published, *Camp Concentration* tells the story—in the form of a journal—of Louis Sacchetti. Originally imprisoned for his opposition to a war very similar to the conflict in Vietnam, Sacchetti is later mysteriously taken from prison to a military compound called Camp Archimedes. There he and other prisoners are subjected to experiments designed to increase their intelligence. Unfortunately, Sacchetti's intelligence is boosted by an injection of a lethal strain of syphilis. His survival is secured only when his mind is transferred to the body of a dead man. So, while Sacchetti lives, he is morally outraged by the thought that another man had to die so his own life could continue.

Rupprecht calls *334*, Disch's next novel, his "most brilliant and disturbing work." In a series of intertwining stories Disch focuses on the Welfare Department apartment building at 334 East 11th Street in the New York City of the early twenty-first century. The lives of the inhabitants are dull and desperate, each trying to cope with life in the over-crowded urban area. One of the stories, entitled "Bodies," concerns Ab and Chapel, two mortuary attendants who work at a hospital. Ab sometimes smuggles a body out of the hospital for someone who requests one for illicit purposes. *Times Literary Supplement* reviewer William Boyd calls the story "a fascinating study of two deprived lives, the politics of survival and the austere terrors of dissociation." In another episode from the book, "Everyday Life in the Later Roman Empire," the lead character uses the drug Morbehanine to create another self who does historical research in the year 334. Disch paints a world different, yet remarkably similar to our own, with familiar brand names, familiar problems, and all too familiar unworkable solutions to those problems. Reading *334*, we end up feeling, as M. John Harrison points out in his introduction to the work, that it "is a novel about *us* and our precarious relationship with the real, narrated as a series of collisions between what the world is and what we would like it to be, between the kind of life we have now and the kind of life it may lead to."

Like *334*, *On Wings of Song* deals with a future time that resembles our own. Describing the general atmosphere of the novel in the *New York Times Book Review*, Gerald Jonas notes, "Politically and economically, things seem to be going downhill, but in between crises, people can still assure themselves that they are living in 'normal' times." The setting is Iowa, but the United States has been taken over by a police state controlled by a group known as the "undergoders." An im-

A six-year-old boy is given a life-transforming caduceus—the symbol of medicine—by the god Mercury in this 1991 horror novel.

portant technological advance has come in the form of a "flight apparatus" that allows people to be set free from their physical bodies, but only if they can "lose themselves" while singing. Disch's protagonist, Daniel Weinreb and his wife, Boadicea Whiting, attempt to fly on the eve of their honeymoon. Boadicea flies on her first try, but Daniel does not. He is left to care for her comatose body. In *Village Voice*, John Calvin Batchelor calls *On Wings of Song* Disch's "grandest work." The critic maintains that the novel links Disch with other great social critics of the past, including H. G. Wells and George Orwell. "Disch," he writes, "is an unapologetic political writer, a high-minded liberal democrat, who sees doom in

Western Civilization and says so, often with bizarre, bleak scenarios."

Along with his novels, Disch has also contributed numerous short stories to periodicals. These have been gathered in several well-received short story collections and appeared in anthologies, including several volumes of *The Best from Fantasy & Science Fiction*. Reviewers of his short stories have just a hard time as critics of his longer works with classifying Disch as "merely" a science fiction writer. Critics or readers who turn the pages of his short story collections are often surprised at what they find there. *Time* reviewer Paul Gray, observes that in Disch's collection *Getting into Death and Other Stories* there is only one story that is traditional space-oriented science fiction, while the others are deemed comparable to the work of *Alice's Adventures in Wonderland* creator Lewis Carroll or American short story writer John Collier. In "The Asian Shore," one of Disch's most critically acclaimed short stories, an American living in Istanbul finds himself becoming someone else. In "Let Us Hasten Quickly to the Gates of Ivory," another story included in the collection, a pair of bereaved siblings visiting their parents' graves discover they have somehow entered a vast infinite cemetery. Finding yet another notable forebear to whom to compare Disch, *Voice of Youth Advocates* reviewer Wain Saeger refers to the stories in *Fundamental Disch*, as "somber, even eerie, more like Edgar Allen Poe than today's space opera."

Continuing to explore many literary avenues, in the eighties and nineties Disch published novels, stories, poetry, a libretto and an interactive computer novel. Three novels published during this time period further the social criticism seen in earlier works. In *The Businessman: A Tale of Terror*, *The M.D.: A Horror Story*, and *The Priest: A Gothic Romance* Disch combines goosebumps with a critical look at the corruption he sees in the three professions mentioned in the titles. The plots are replete with the type of strange occurrences Disch's readers have grown to expect, including: the story of the after-death experiences of a murdered wife, the giving of a caduceus (the symbol of medicine) to a child by the god Mercury, and a priest who exchanges personalities with a thirteenth-century bishop. And, as usual, the works are a blend of styles. Writing about *The M.D.: A Horror Story* in *Kliatt* Larry W. Prater notes, "The novel combines elements of the macabre, of fantasy and of SF." Evidently, in life as well as in literature, catego-

ries aren't important to Disch. In a *Publishers Weekly* interview with David Finkle, Disch refuses to see *The M.D.* as just a horror novel and with equal fervor defends his right to remain unburdened by a convenient label. "Every book has its own slightly different ground rules from the others. . ." he maintains. "As long as the book plays by its own rules and those are clear, I don't think genre borderlines are especially helpful. I don't spend my life trying to determine what category I'm in."

■ Works Cited

Aldiss, Brian W., *Trillion Year Spree: The History of Science Fiction*, Atheneum, 1986.

Batchelor, John Calvin, "The Weird Worlds of Thomas Disch," *Village Voice*, August 27-September 2, 1980, pp. 35-36.

Boyd, William, "The Freedoms of Futurism," *Times Literary Supplement*, June 12, 1981, p. 659.

Clemons, Walter, "The Joyously Versatile Thomas Disch," *Newsweek*, July 11, 1988, pp. 66-67.

Disch, Thomas M., "The Brave Little Toaster: A Bedtime Story for Small Appliances," *The Best from Science & Science Fiction*, 24th series, edited by Edward L. Ferman, Scribners, 1982, pp. 272-311.

Disch, Thomas M., interview with David Finkle, *Publishers Weekly*, April 19, 1991, pp. 48-49.

Disch, Thomas M., "My Life as a Child: A Mini-Autobiography," *Something about the Author Autobiography Series*, Volume 15, Gale, 1993, pp. 107-123.

Gray, Paul, "Imaginary Toads," *Time*, February 9, 1976, pp. 83-84.

Harrison, M. John, in his introduction to *334* by Thomas M. Disch, Gregg Press, 1976, pp. v-xiii.

Jonas, Gerald, review of "On Wings of Song," *New York Times Book Review*, October 28, 1979, p. 15-18.

Prater, Larry W., review of *The M.D.: A Horror Story*, *Kliatt*, September 1992, p. 20.

Rupprecht, Erich S., "Thomas M. Disch," *Dictionary of Literary Biography*, Volume 8, *Twentieth-Century American Science-Fiction Writers*, Part 1, Gale, 1981, pp. 148-154.

Saeger, Wain, review of *Fundamental Disch*, *Voice of Youth Advocates*, April 1981, p. 39.

Scholes, Robert and Eric S. Rabkin, *Science Fiction: History, Science, Vision*, Oxford University Press, 1977, pp. 88, 96.

Stableford, Brian, "Thomas M. Disch," *Science Fiction Writers: Critical Studies of the Major Authors from the Early Nineteenth Century to the Present Day*, edited by E. F. Bleiler, Scribner, 1982, pp. 351-356.

■ **For More Information See**

BOOKS

Children's Literature Review, Volume 18, Gale, 1989, pp. 114-116.

Contemporary Literary Criticism, Volume 7, Gale, 1977, pp. 86-87; Volume 36, 1986, pp. 123-128.

Delany, Samuel R., *The Jeweled-Hinged Jaw: Notes on the Language of Science Fiction*, Dragon Press, 1977.

Delany, Samuel R., *The American Shore: Meditations on a Tale of Science Fiction by Thomas M. Disch*, Dragon Press, 1978.

Nicholls, Peter, editor, *Science Fiction at Large*, Harper, 1976, pp. 141-155.

Pringle, David, *Science Fiction: The One Hundred Best Novels*, [London], 1985.

PERIODICALS

Los Angeles Times Book Review, November 21, 1982, p. 13.

New Statesman, July 13, 1984, p. 28.

New York Times Book Review, March 21, 1976, p. 6; August 26, 1984, p. 31.

Publishers Weekly, January 7, 1974, p. 56; January 5, 1976, p. 59; August 29, 1980, p. 363.

Science Fiction Chronicle, February 1993, p. 35.

Spectator, May 1, 1982, p. 23.

Time, July 9, 1984, pp. 85-86.

Times Literary Supplement, February 15, 1974, p. 163; November 11, 1994, p. 19.

Washington Post Book World, September 23, 1979, p. 7; July 26, 1981, pp. 6-7.

—Sketch by Marian C. Gonsior

Carole Nelson Douglas

■ Personal

Born November 5, 1944, in Everett, WA; daughter of Arnold Peter (a fisherman) and Agnes Olga (a teacher; maiden name, Lovchik) Nelson; married Sam Douglas (an artist), November 25, 1967. *Education:* College of St. Catherine, B.A., 1966.

■ Addresses

Home—3920 Singleleaf Lane, Fort Worth, TX 76113. *Agent*—Howard Morhaim, 175 Fifth Ave., 14th Floor, New York, NY 10010.

■ Career

St. Paul Pioneer Press & Dispatch (now *St. Paul Pioneer Press*), St. Paul, MN, various writing and editorial positions, 1967-84; full-time novelist, 1984—. Member of board of directors, Twin Cities Local of The Newspaper Guild, 1970-72; first woman show chair of annual Gridiron, 1971; honorary member of board of directors of St. Paul Public Library Centennial, 1981. *Member:* Mystery Writers of America, Science Fiction and Fantasy Writers of America, Romance Writers of America, Sisters in Crime.

■ Awards, Honors

Silver Medal, Sixth Annual West Coast Review of Books, 1982, for *Fair Wind, Fiery Star*; Science Fiction/Fantasy Award, 1984, Popular Fiction Award, Science Fiction, 1987, and Lifetime Achievement Award for Versatility, 1991, all from *Romantic Times*; Nebula Award nomination, Science Fiction Writers of America, 1986, for *Probe*; Best Novel of Romantic Suspense citation, American Mystery Awards, 1990, and *New York Times Book Review* notable book citation, 1991, both for *Good Night, Mr. Holmes*.

■ Writings

"SWORD AND CIRCLET" FANTASY SERIES

Six of Swords, Del Rey, 1982.
Exiles of the Rynth, Del Rey, 1984.
Keepers of Edanvant, Tor Books, 1987.
Heir of Rengarth, Tor Books, 1988.
Seven of Swords, Tor Books, 1989.

"IRENE ADLER" SERIES

Good Night, Mr. Holmes, Tor Books, 1990.
Good Morning, Irene, Tor Books, 1991.
Irene at Large, Tor Books, 1992.
Irene's Last Waltz, Forge, 1994.

"TALISWOMAN" FANTASY SERIES

Cup of Clay, Tor Books, 1991.
Seed upon the Wind, Tor Books, 1992.

"MIDNIGHT LOUIE" MYSTERY SERIES

Catnap, Tor Books, 1992.
Pussyfoot, Tor Books, 1993.
Cat on a Blue Monday, Forge, 1994.
Cat in a Crimson Haze, Forge, 1995.

OTHER

Amberleigh, Jove, 1980.
Fair Wind, Fiery Star, Jove, 1981.
The Best Man, Ballantine, 1983.
Lady Rogue, Ballantine, 1983.
Azure Days and Quicksilver Nights, Bantam, 1985.
Probe, Tor Books, 1985.
The Exclusive, Ballantine, 1986.
Counterprobe, Tor Books, 1988.
Crystal Days and Crystal Nights, two volumes, Bantam, 1990.

Also author of *In Her Prime* and *Her Own Person*, both 1982. Editorial writer for the *Fort Worth Star-Telegram*, 1985—; columnist for *Mystery Scene* magazine, 1991.

■ Sidelights

"An only child who often had to amuse myself, I used to think that everybody made up poems and descriptive sentences when lying on the grass and looking up at the clouds," Carole Nelson Douglas told *Something about the Author* (*SATA*). From this childhood creativity, Douglas went on to take up journalism in college, then turned from that to writing fiction. It was a difficult choice, because her job as a journalist was steady and she was good at it. Since 1980, she has written twenty-four novels in a variety of genres, proving that her creativity goes hand-in-hand with productivity.

In college, Douglas majored in theater and English literature. Upon graduating, she took "a lowly merchandising position with the local newspaper," she recalled in *SATA*, then tried her hand at writing, eventually becoming a reporter. From 1967 to 1984 she worked as a reporter for the *St. Paul Pioneer Press & Dispatch* in St. Paul, Minnesota. Douglas covered "social changes, particularly as they apply to women and family life, and the spectrum of the arts—performing, visual, and literary," she told *Contemporary Authors* (*CA*).

Although journalism was a satisfying career for Douglas in many ways, it began to turn sour. She

Douglas contributed illustrations to her early works, including maps of strange fantasy worlds.

confessed to *SATA* that "I loved newspaper reporting and feature writing, but truly creative writers are not appreciated in a journalism-dominated atmosphere. My work was recognized everywhere but where I was employed. Women weren't made reviewers or given columns or often promoted to editor positions in newspapers then (and now)."

Frustrated with her role at the newspaper, Douglas began looking for other ways to deal with her creative energy. "When a particularly good story of mine was radically cut," she told *SATA*, "I took a YMCA writing class (everybody thought a published journalist was crazy to take a writing course) to learn the mechanics of submitting national-level nonfiction." When it was her turn to read work in front of the class, she didn't choose any of her journalistic pieces. Instead, Douglas "dug out a novel I had begun in college and read from it," she related to *SATA*. "The enthusiastic instructor, the well-known children's author Judy Delton, shooed me out of class with the irresistible injunction to 'write that book and sell it.'"

Douglas took the advice of her teacher seriously and started working diligently on her fiction ideas. The skills she had learned as a newspaper journalist came in handy. She related in *SATA* that a "professional novelist needs many of the skills learned in writing for a newspaper: you must write day in and day out, often under time constraints, and still meet your own standards of quality. You must be tenacious and you must believe in what you are doing, that the 'story' needs to be told, and that you are the only one to tell it." In addition, her reporting of the news for years had given her a great deal of information to use. "Our society has weathered major political, moral, and philosophical watersheds during my years as a reporter, and in 1976 I began to explore, in fiction, these contemporary issues—particularly as they affect past, current, and potential attitudes toward women," she told *CA*.

Writes Women's Gothic

In 1980 Douglas's first novel was published. "*Amberleigh* [1980]," she told *CA*, "was my Victorian-set update of what has been a model for so-called women's fiction since *Jane Eyre*—the Gothic. I call mine a 'feminist' Gothic. Submitting *Amberleigh* to publishers unsolicited resulted in getting it returned unread (because it was considered 'off market'—no sex) until playwright-author Garson Kanin volunteered to take it to his publisher." Douglas and Kanin continued their friendship and it turned out to be a nurturing one for Douglas. "I interviewed Kanin on two separate occasions," she explained to *CA*, "and it was his enduring enthusiasm for my writing style that was the key to opening the door to publishing for me."

Her second novel, *Fair Wind, Fiery Star* (1981), was also an historical in the same vein as *Amberleigh*. After writing these, Douglas decided to turn to a different genre. She told *CA* that "although fiction directed at a woman's audience is extremely lucrative to publishers right now, this very popularity, I discovered, hampers writers who want to expand on the publishers' current limitations of formula. Frustrated by the fact that 'tran-

scending a genre,' as my books do, is considered a handicap rather than an advantage, I turned to applying my same themes in a more veiled and symbolic manner with *Six of Swords* [1982], a fantasy which showed up on national science fiction/fantasy top-ten-bestseller lists its first week out and is now in its twelfth printing. . . . I find [that] both fantasy and science fiction encourage originality and imagination, while so much of commercial fiction does not."

Douglas has written five novels in the "Sword and Circlet" fantasy series that began with the publication of *Six of Swords*. She explained to *SATA* that these books "document the [protagonists'] magical adventures, a means of exploring relationships and the search for self. I describe the series as a 'domestic epic,' because it examines how men and women can form lasting alliances without losing their individuality and independence. By the fifth book, Irissa and Kendric's children are teenagers confronting the same relationship quandaries as their parents. One child is magically gifted; the other not. Each has a special bond with the opposite parent. Fantasy novels offer a writer a subtle means of dealing with contemporary issues like gender role reversal, animal rights and ecology without getting on a soapbox."

With the publication of *Probe* (1985) and *Counterprobe* (1988), Douglas entered the science fiction market. "I want my books to appeal to a wide variety of readers on different levels, and to contain enough levels that they bear re-reading," Douglas told *SATA*. "Although labeled as science fiction novels, *Probe* and *Counterprobe* are contemporary-set suspense/psychological adventure stories with a strong feminist sub-text, the kind that husbands recommend to wives, and vice versa; teenagers to parents, and vice versa. To write books that cross common ground between the sexes and span the generation gap is rewarding, especially in this pigeon-holed publishing world."

Up to this point, Douglas had been writing all her novels as adult novels; she was pleasantly surprised when she found them being reviewed as young adult novels. "I get many charming fan letters from young readers, who absorb my fantasy worlds and themes more readily than many adult reviewers and readers . . ." she told *SATA*. "Magic in fantasy is a metaphor for personal power and self-realization, a word that many young readers may not be able to define, but they grasp the concepts instinctively when they read it."

Elementary, My Dear

With *Good Night, Mr. Holmes* (1990), Douglas launched a new series of books entirely unrelated to any topic she had previously covered. Douglas expands upon the character Irene Adler, the only woman to outwit Sherlock Holmes, an event which took place in Arthur Conan Doyle's *A Scandal in Bohemia.* "This book evolved the way most of my ideas come to me: I realized that all the recent novels set in the Sherlock Holmes world were written by men," pointed out Douglas in *SATA.* "Yet I had loved the stories as a youngster. My years as a newspaper reporter taught me that when men monopolize anything it's time for women to examine it from a female point of view."

Douglas wrote three more novels in this series, including *Good Morning, Irene* (1991), *Irene at Large* (1992), and *Irene's Last Waltz* (1993). "My Irene Adler is as intelligent, self-sufficient and serious about her professional and personal integrity as Sherlock Holmes, and far too independent to be anyone's mistress but her own," Douglas told *SATA.* "She also moonlights as an inquiry agent while building her performing career, so she is a professional rival of Holmes's rather than a romantic interest. Her adventures intertwine with Holmes's, but she is definitely her own woman in these novels."

Good Night, Mr. Holmes takes place a short time after Irene bests Holmes at detective work. Irene finds herself becoming romantically interested in the king of Bohemia. But all is not well with that union, and, in the end, she has to outwit him as well as Holmes. By her side, Irene has assistant Nell Huxleigh, who is as steady and stable as Holmes's friend Watson. Critic Cynthia Ogorek wrote in *Booklist* that *Good Night, Mr. Holmes* is "guaranteed to please Holmes fans or anyone who likes period mysteries."

In *Irene at Large,* Irene and Nell find themselves exiled in Paris when they happen upon an acquaintance who has been poisoned. Nell falls in love with the man, and they spend the rest of the book trying to untangle the intrigue around his murder attempt. Writing in the *New York Times Book Review,* Marilyn Stasio claimed that in *Irene at Large* "the action never loses its jaunty, high-heeled pace."

Irene ventures to Prague to check on strange happenings there in *Irene's Last Waltz,* as well as to

A physician encounters an amnesiac patient who turns out to be a deadly alien spy in this 1988 thriller.

meet up with her former boyfriend, the king of Bohemia. While examining the evidence, they investigate the murder of a young girl that seems to connect to the other happenings. The king is found in the arms of his mistress, Tatyana, as they explore the haunting of the city by the Golem, a mythical monster. A *Kirkus Reviews* contributor called the book "the best . . . of Irene's adventures to date."

In the "Taliswoman Trilogy" Douglas again tried her hand at fantasy writing. The first novel, *Cup of Clay* (1991) focuses on Alison Carver, a journalist who lives in Minnesota. Needing a break after working on a scandalous child-abuse trial, Carver goes to her own island in a mountain lake. Her vacation away from it all takes a strange twist as she finds herself transported into another world, where she wins the Cup of Earth. She becomes the Taliswoman, empowered with skills to save the world. But she doesn't know if she wants to save such a depraved and unfair world. Laura Staley commented in *Voice of Youth Advocates* that "the more serious themes of this book seem to have produced an even better story than usual."

The second book of the trilogy, *Seed upon the Wind* (1992), finds Carver back in the world called Veil. Her friend Rowan Firemayne blames Carver for the mysterious blight that has come over Veil. The two begin to work out their differences, and form a deeper relationship as they set out to make a powerful talisman from the ashes of Rowan's brother. They

CAROLE NELSON DOUGLAS

SEED UPON the WIND

"Douglas is
the intelligent reader's
delight."
—R*A*V*E Reviews

BOOK II
OF THE
TALISWOMAN

"Douglas is the master of the well-told tale and far and away the most successful combiner of fantasy and romance currently writing...[SEED UPON THE WIND is] a rousing, romantic fantasy."
—*Booklist*

In this 1992 romantic fantasy, the sequel to *Cup of Clay*, journalist Alison Carver reassumes her role as the Taliswoman to save the dying parallel world of Veil.

find the danger to the world of Veil, and Alison becomes scared because it is too similar to the evils in our own world. A *Publishers Weekly* reviewer commented that "Douglas's increasingly intricate fantasy raises disturbing issues about environmental depredations."

Of Cats and Crime

In *SATA,* Douglas wrote that "another favorite character of mine is Midnight Louie, an 18-pound, crime-solving black tomcat who is the part-time narrator of a new mystery series. . . . Like many of my creations, Louie goes way back. He was a real if somewhat larger-than-life stray cat I wrote a feature story about for my newspaper in 1973." *Catnap*, published in 1992, follows the adventures of Temple Barr, a public relations person at an American Booksellers Association meeting in Las Vegas. Feline Midnight Louie is able to assist Barr in finding out more information on the killing of Chester Royal, a big time publisher. A *Publishers Weekly* contributor related that "Douglas's fine-tuned sense of humor gives her tame plot enough of a spin to keep readers entertained."

In *Pussyfoot* (1993), Temple Barr finds herself once again in a murder investigation. This time, she has been employed to do publicity for a stripper competition. When one of the contestants is killed, Barr goes into action, and Louie helps her find the sleazy characters involved in the scheme. A *Kirkus Reviews* contributor criticized the story, saying "dog lovers, and lovers of well-made plots and prose, need not apply." A *Publishers Weekly* reviewer, however, praised the character development of the main character, noting that Barr is "a reasonably modern and liberated female."

Douglas commented to *CA* about the body of her work: "Because of my undergraduate major in theater, I'm especially interested in fiction that captures and affects an audience with the immediacy of a stage play. For this reason, I prefer working in 'popular' fiction forms and find nothing unusual in the idea of fiction being 'entertaining' as well as enlightening. . . . I like to say that what I write is principally entertainment, but that the best entertainment always has principles." She went on to point out that "in effect, I write on a fine line between 'serious' fiction on one hand and sneered-at 'popular' fiction on the other. It is not a particularly comfortable position, but somebody has to do it; otherwise we will have nothing but seri-

"One of my favorite hep cats... Several thumbs up!"
–*Mystery News*

Author of
Good Night, Mr. Holmes

CAROLE NELSON DOUGLAS

CATNAP

A MIDNIGHT LOUIE MYSTERY

"Douglas has hit the jackpot again with her nifty new sleuth!"
–*Romantic Times*

This 1992 mystery, the first in the "Midnight Louie" series, introduces Temple Barr, a public relations expert, and Midnight Louie, a crime-solving black tomcat.

ous writers that nobody knows how to read and popular writers that nobody ought to read." Regarding the classification of her work, Douglas also told *SATA* that "my books are classified as fantasy or science fiction, romance, mystery, women's mainstream fiction and historical novels. But many of these elements blend in each book, and none of my novels fits any category formula. Being different is satisfying, though it is frustrating when your work needs to be put into a category for marketing reasons."

Although writing has often been a difficult career to have, Douglas does not regret her decision. She told *SATA*, "If I had known how many setbacks awaited the career novelist I might not have tried doing it. But ignorance is sometimes motivation."

She finds that following her inner guidance has paid off for her. "I've never gone wrong following my talents and my interests. I've survived because I took risks and followed my instincts. When I majored in theater everybody (including me) thought I'd never get a well-paying job. I found myself a well-paid newspaper reporter within a year of graduation. When I left that substantial job security, everybody feared that I'd be unable to replace that salary with book income. When I began to write novels in a variety of so-called genres under my own name, everybody said that wasn't smart marketing. There have been handicaps and setbacks, but I survived. The same Everybody discouraged my novel writing by saying I was too young, but I later discovered that there were a lot of other Everybodies out there more worth heeding: the readers one's work reaches. Their enthusiastic reactions to my writing and my books has kept me going for years. Now all those Everybodies are growing up or developing wider reading tastes, and they're finding my books in different sections of the bookstore."

■ Works Cited

Review of *Catnap, Publishers Weekly*, January 20, 1992, pp. 49-50.

Douglas, Carol Nelson, author comments, *Contemporary Authors, New Revision Series*, Volume 26, Gale, 1989, pp. 122-23.

Douglas, author comments, *Something about the Author*, Volume 73, Gale, 1993, pp. 46-49.

Review of *Irene's Last Waltz, Kirkus Reviews*, December 15, 1993, p. 1553.

Ogorek, Cynthia, review of *Good Night, Mr. Holmes, Booklist*, October 15, 1990, p. 419.

Review of *Pussyfoot, Kirkus Reviews*, February 1, 1993, p. 101.

Review of *Pussyfoot, Publishers Weekly*, January 25, 1993, p. 81.

Review of *Seed upon the Wind, Publishers Weekly*, October 19, 1992, p. 62.

Staley, Laura, review of *Cup of Clay, Voice of Youth Advocates*, February, 1992, pp. 380-81.

Stasio, Marilyn, review of *Irene at Large, New York Times Book Review*, August 9, 1992, p. 20.

■ For More Information See

PERIODICALS

Locus, August, 1982.
Minneapolis/St. Paul Magazine, November, 1981.

St. Paul Sunday Pioneer Press, September 14, 1980.
West Coast Review of Books, December, 1981.

—*Sketch by Nancy E. Rampson*

David Eddings

■ Personal

Full name, David Carroll Eddings. Born July 7, 1931, in Spokane, WA; son of George Wayne and Theone (Berge) Eddings; married Judith Leigh Schall, October 27, 1962. *Education:* Reed College, B.A., 1954; University of Washington, Seattle, M.A., 1961. *Politics:* "Unaffiliated." *Religion:* "Unaffiliated."

■ Addresses

Agent—Eleanor Wood, Blasingame, McCauley, and Wood, 111 Eighth Avenue, Suite 1501, New York, NY 10011.

■ Career

Writer; worked variously for Boeing Co., Seattle, WA, as a buyer; for a grocery store as a manager; and as a college English teacher. *Military service:* U.S. Army, 1954-56.

■ Writings

"BELGARIAD" FANTASY SERIES

Pawn of Prophecy, Del Rey, 1982.
Queen of Sorcery, Del Rey, 1982.
Magician's Gambit, Del Rey, 1984.
Castle of Wizardry, Del Rey, 1984.
Enchanter's Endgame, Del Rey, 1984.

"MALLOREON" FANTASY SERIES

Guardians of the West, Del Rey, 1987.
King of the Murgos, Del Rey, 1988.
Demon Lord of Karanda, Del Rey, 1988.
Sorceress of Darshiva, Del Rey, 1989.
The Seeress of Kell, Del Rey, 1991.

"ELENIUM" FANTASY SERIES

The Diamond Throne, Del Rey, 1989.
The Ruby Knight, Del Rey, 1990.
The Sapphire Rose, Del Rey, 1991.

"TAMULI" FANTASY SERIES

Domes of Fire, Del Rey, 1993.
The Shining Ones, Del Rey, 1993.
The Hidden City, Del Rey, 1994.

OTHER

High Hunt, Putnam, 1973.
The Losers, Fawcett Columbine, 1992.

(With wife, Leigh Eddings) *Belgarath the Sorcerer*, Ballantine Books, 1995.

■ Sidelights

David Eddings is a prolific and widely read fantasy writer whose books offer winning characters, persuasive dialogue, and plenty of humor. Though he has occasionally been taken to task for lacking originality, his well-plotted stories that feature war, politics, and intriguing situations have earned him a loyal readership. Eddings once stated that "I have devoted the majority of my life to writing," and noted that his approach to fiction has been "broadly ecumenical."

Born in Spokane, Washington, Eddings graduated from Reed College and got his M.A. at the University of Washington. Eddings's first book was *High Hunt*, an adventure set in the present. While working at a series of jobs that included teaching college English, working in a grocery store and a stint at the Boeing aircraft company, Eddings continued to write. As he once commented, "I have tried my hand at a wide variety of subgenres with more interest in the technical problems presented by each type than in commercial success." His advice to aspiring writers is blunt: "Never be afraid to discard a day's work—or a month's, or even a year's. Attachment to one's own brilliance is the worst form of juvenile self-indulgence."

Eddings's second novel, *Pawn of Prophecy*, which appeared nine years after *High Hunt*, was the first to have a fantasy setting. Its success allowed him to write full-time and launched both the "Belgariad" and "Malloreon" series. These series chronicle the adventures of Garion, a young orphan, who gradually recognizes his own magic abilities as extraordinary events begin to overtake the ordinary occurrences of his world. By accepting his own powers, Garion is able to enlist the aid of warriors and sorcerers to combat the followers of the evil god Torak. A *Publishers Weekly* reviewer remarked that *Pawn of Prophecy* was "obviously part of a longer work," and noted that Eddings's ability to avoid getting "bogged down in cliches and archaic language" made this first volume "a promising start."

The first book in the "Malloreon" series, *Guardians of the West*, was given a similarly positive reception. In the "Malloreon" books, the adult

This 1984 fantasy, part of the "Belgariad" series, follows the adventures of young Garion and an Imperial Princess as they confront the evil god Torak.

Garion is a king locked in battle with the sorceress Zandramas. Dale F. Martin of *Fantasy Review* found "the real interest is in the characters, who are skillfully presented and deftly developed," making particular note of the "wry humor and . . . credible dialogue." A *Publishers Weekly* reviewer concurred, stating about the fourth book, *Sorceress of Darshiva*, "Eddings depicts a complex, believable and colorful society filled with nobles, rogues, and common people, the latter characters ringing particularly true." Michael Cule, however, reviewing the series in *Twentieth-Century Science-Fiction Writers*, found that "there are few fresh characters," and "both plot and incident repeat themselves."

Mixing Myths and Ordinary Life

Critics have pointed out that Eddings's fantasy worlds and plots are fairly standard: parallels to Imperial Romans, ancient Egyptians, and Vikings are readily apparent, for example. For his part, Eddings stresses the credibility factor in any story. His "basic formula" for believable fantasy, as he once stated, is to "take a bit of magic, mix well with a few open-ended Jungian archetypal myths, make your people sweat and smell and get hungry at inopportune moments, throw in a ponderous prehistory, and let nature take its course."

His third series, the "Elenium" books, was hailed by *Booklist*'s Roland Green for its "well-wrought world" and "originality." The trilogy depicts the adventures of Sparhawk, a knight on the quest for the jewel Bhelliom, whose powers will save the Queen Ehlana from prison. Reviewing *The Sapphire Rose*, the last book in the series, a *Publishers Weekly* critic noted that Eddings "adroitly mixes the exalted with the mundane in a tale that should satisfy his many fans." Cule notes that this series "is designed to be shorter . . . and is written with a greater emphasis on action. . . . Again the nature of magic and of the gods is a focus of interest, and destiny hangs heavy in the background, waiting to guide events."

Rather than embarking on another series, Eddings took a different direction with his next novel, *The Losers*. The novel's protagonist, Raphael Taylor, is a present-day senior at Reed College in Portland, Oregon. Under the influence of his wealthy, reckless roommate, Damon Flood, Taylor plummets from the summit of academic and athletic success to an unhappy affair with an older woman and a lot of drinking. Taylor winds up crashing his car, resulting in an amputated leg. Dropping out of school and moving to Spokane, Taylor recuperates and watches the "losers" of his economically depressed neighborhood, passing judgment on them. Flood comes back into his life, but this time his former roommate's destructiveness is clear to Taylor, who recognizes Flood for the "loser" he is. He becomes a source of redemption for Taylor.

Eddings found little favor among critics for his foray into realistic fiction. Writing in *Voice of Youth Advocates*, Cecilia Swanson warned that readers looking for more of Eddings's "wonderful fantasies" would be disappointed and that the book was "basically a variation on good vs. evil,"

though she praised *The Losers* for being "well written." *Library Journal*'s Jackie Cassada said that "stripped of their fantasy trappings, the author's opinions assume a heavy-handedness that verges on the polemic" and a critic in *Publishers Weekly* found that the "simplistic, fable-like quality. . . patronizes its audiences."

Absurdities with Good Explanations

The writer returned to fantasy for his next series, which he titled "Tamuli." The first of these books was *Domes of Fire*, which reprised the characters of Sir Sparhawk and Queen Ehlana from the

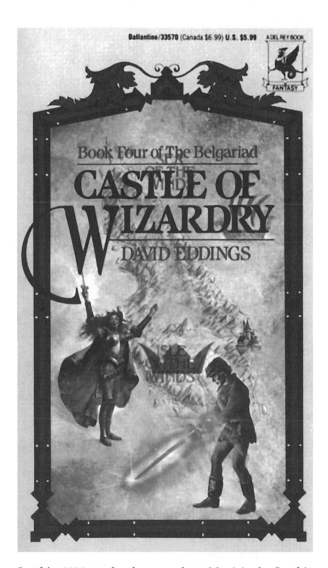

In this 1984 work, the sequel to *Magician's Gambit*, Garion and the princess Ce'Nedra must safely return the Orb, a source of power and security, to its rightful place.

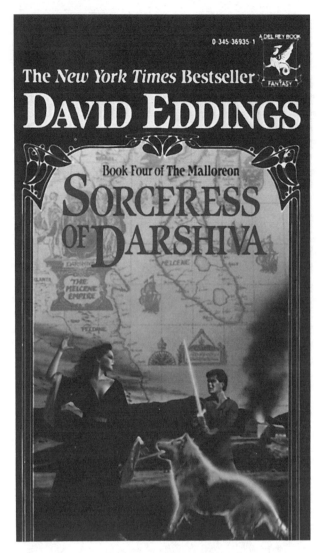

An adult Garion combats the treacherous sorceress Zandramas in this 1989 work from the "Malloreon" series.

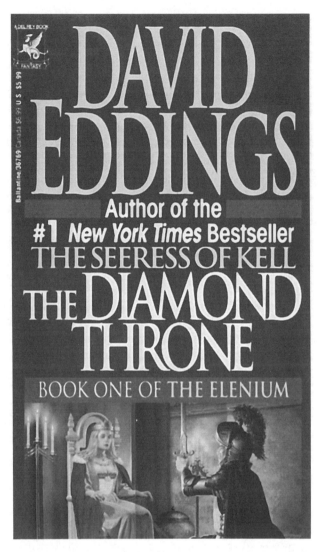

An exiled knight named Sparhawk and the sorceress Sephrenia search for a way to rescue their queen, entombed in a crystal prison, in this 1989 novel.

"Elenium" series. The far-away Tamul Empire pleads with Sparhawk to help them and he sets off with his wife Ehlana and their daughter in tow. They encounter several incidents that lead Sparhawk to suspect magical or godly opposition to his cause. *Publishers Weekly* welcomed the writer's "likable, spirited characters," which "reflect his original touch."

In the second book of the series, *The Shining Ones*, Eddings threw yet another obstacle in the way of Sparhawk and his entourage. The Shining Ones of the title seem human and friendly, but the knight strongly suspects that they are true to the Bhelliom stone rather than to him and his cause. *Booklist*'s Candace Smith highlighted the "well-

drawn, likable characters" and "complex but not unwieldy plots" of the story. In *Library Journal,* Cassada made note of Eddings's "talent for creating appealing, erudite characters and vivid cultures" in this second installment of the trilogy and a reviewer in *Publishers Weekly* termed it "vintage Eddings." The final installment of the "Tamuli" books is entitled *The Hidden City.* In it, Sir Sparhawk must rescue Queen Ehlana, now captive of the followers of the demented god Cyrgon. A *Publishers Weekly* reviewer remarked on a "new note of introspection" which gives "a fuller dimension to Eddings's rousing adventure."

Eddings has emphasized the need for total credibility in fantasy writing. As he once explained,

"My magic is at best a kind of pragmatic cop-out. Many of my explanations of how magic is supposed to work are absurdities—*but* my characters all accept these explanations . . . and if the characters believe, then the readers seem also to believe." By mixing the facts of the everyday world with a "world that never was," Eddings appears to have hit on a magic formula to keep his readers turning pages and asking for more.

■ Works Cited

Cassada, Jackie, review of *The Losers*, *Library Journal*, June 15, 1992, p. 100.

Cassada, Jackie, review of *The Hidden City*, *Library Journal*, September 15, 1993, p. 109.

Cule, Michael, "David Eddings," *Twentieth-Century Science-Fiction Writers*, edited by Noelle Watson and Paul E. Schellinger, St. James, 1991.

Review of *Domes of Fire*, *Publishers Weekly*, October 19, 1992, p. 62.

Green, Ronald, review of *The Sapphire Rose*, *Booklist*, December 1, 1991, p. 659.

Review of *The Hidden City*, *Publishers Weekly*, August 29, 1994, p. 65.

Review of *The Losers*, *Publishers Weekly*, May 18, 1992, pp. 59-60.

Martin, Dale F., "New Series Begins," *Fantasy Review*, June, 1987, pp. 35-36.

Review of *Pawn of Prophecy*, *Publishers Weekly*, March 19, 1982, p. 69.

Review of *The Sapphire Rose*, *Publishers Weekly*, October 25, 1991, p. 49.

Review of *The Shining Ones*, *Publishers Weekly*, August 2, 1993, p. 66.

Smith, Candace, review of *Domes of Fire*, *Booklist*, October 15, 1992, p. 379.

Smith, Candace, review of *The Shining Ones*, *Booklist*, August, 1993, p. 2012.

Review of *The Sorceress of Darshiva*, *Publishers Weekly*, October 27, 1989.

Swanson, Cecilia, review of *The Losers*, *Voice of Youth Advocates*, February, 1993, p. 348.

■ For More Information See

BOOKS

Bestsellers 90, Issue 2, Gale, 1990, pp. 31-32.

PERIODICALS

Library Journal, August, 1994, p. 139.
Voice of Youth Advocates, February, 1994, p. 380.
WB, May/June, 1989.

—Sketch by Megan Ratner

Clyde Edgerton

■ Personal

Born May 20, 1944, in Durham, NC; son of Ernest Carlyle (an insurance salesman) and Susan Truma (a homemaker; maiden name, Warren) Edgerton; married Susan Ketchin (a writer, editor, and teacher), June 21, 1975; children: Catherine. *Education:* University of North Carolina—Chapel Hill, B.A., 1966, M.A.T., 1972, Ph.D., 1977.

■ Addresses

Home—1104 North Mangnum St., Durham, NC 27701. *Office*—c/o Dusty's Air Taxi, 714 Ninth St., G-7, Durham, NC 27705. *Agent*—Liz Darhansoff, 1220 Park Ave., New York, NY 10128.

■ Career

Writer. Southern High School, Durham, NC, English teacher, 1972-73; English Teaching Institute, Chapel Hill, NC, codirector, 1976; Campbell University, Buies Creek, NC, associate professor of English, 1977-81, associate professor of education

and psychology, 1981-85; St. Andrews Presbyterian College, Laurinburg, NC, associate professor of English and education, 1985-89. Visiting lecturer in English at North Carolina Central University, spring, 1977; visiting writer in residence at Agnes Scott College, 1990; lecturer at conferences and workshops. Guest on television and radio programs, including *Today,* National Broadcasting Company, Inc. (NBC-TV), and National Public Radio's *Sunday Weekend Edition, Morning Edition,* and *Good Evening with Noah Adams.* Member (with wife, Susan Ketchin) of Tarwater Band. *Military service:* U.S. Air Force, 1966-71, piloted reconnaissance and forward air control missions in Southeast Asia during Vietnam War; received Distinguished Flying Cross.

■ Awards, Honors

Publishers Weekly named *The Floatplane Notebooks* one of the best books of 1988; Guggenheim fellow, 1989; Lyndhurst fellow, 1991.

■ Writings

NOVELS

Raney, Algonquin Books, 1985.
Walking across Egypt, Algonquin Books, 1987.
The Floatplane Notebooks, Algonquin Books, 1988.
Killer Diller, Algonquin Books, 1991.

In Memory of Junior, Algonquin Books, 1992.
Redeye: A Western, Algonquin Books, 1995.

CHAPBOOKS

Understanding the Floatplane, Mud Puppy Press (Chapel Hill), 1987.
Cold Black Peas, Mud Puppy Press, 1990.

RECORDINGS

(With members of the Tarwater Band) *Walking across Egypt: Songs and Readings from the Books "Raney" and "Walking across Egypt,"* Flying Fish Records, 1987.
Clyde Edgerton Reads "The Floatplane Notebooks," Random House Audiobooks, 1989.
The "Killer Diller" Tapes, Dusty's Air Taxi, 1991.
(With Lee Smith and the Tarwater Band) *The Devil's Dream*, Dusty's Air Taxi, 1993.

OTHER

Contributor to *Family Portraits: Remembrances by Twenty Distinguished Writers*, edited by Carolyn Anthony, Doubleday, 1989. Work represented in anthologies, including *Weymouth: An Anthology of Poetry*, edited by Sam Ragan, St. Andrews Press (Laurinburg, NC), 1987, and *New Stories from the South: The Year's Best, 1990*, edited by Shannon Ravenel, Algonquin Books, 1990. Also contributor to periodicals, including *Chattahoochee Review, Descant, Daily Tar Heel, Journal and Constitution* (Atlanta), *Just Pulp, Leader, Lyricist, Mid-Atlantic Country, Old Hickory Review, Pembroke Magazine, Southern Exposure, Southern Living, Southern Magazine, Southern Review*, and *Southern Style*.

■ Adaptations

Walking across Egypt was adapted as a play of the same title by John Justice, first produced in 1989; *Raney* was adapted as a play by Justice, first produced in Fayetteville, NC, 1990; *The Floatplane Notebooks* was adapted as a play by Jason Moore and Paul Fitzgerald and produced in Chicago, 1992.

■ Sidelights

Clyde Edgerton is widely considered one of the premier novelists working in the Southern tradition today, often compared with such masters as Eudora Welty and Flannery O'Connor. Although most of his books deal with adult concerns—marriage, aging, birth and death—Edgerton's work is most profoundly about family. In books such as *Raney, Walking across Egypt, The Floatplane Notebooks*, and *Killer Diller*, Edgerton explores the dimensions of family life, using an endearing (if eccentric) cast of characters. "Edgerton's characters," writes Mary Lystad in *Twentieth-Century Young Adult Writers*, "have more faults than most, but they also have considerable virtues, and they are so likable that you want to invite them over for a cup of coffee, a piece of homemade apple pie, and a nice long chat."

Raised in the small towns of the North Carolina Piedmont, Edgerton draws heavily on the storytelling traditions of the rural south in his novels. Without the distractions of big-city life and the communications revolution of the late twentieth century, many rural Americans stayed in close touch with their relatives, and often shared stories about family members with each other for entertainment. "I had twenty-three aunts and uncles," Edgerton remarks to Jean W. Ross in an interview for *Contemporary Authors*. "On Sunday afternoons the men would sit around and say three words every hour about the weather, and the women would be in the kitchen going ninety miles an hour telling great stories, often something they remembered about someone in the family. . . . And there were always little sayings repeated at the dinner table that had been passed down from fifty, sixty, seventy years ago. This was a norm in my family, and I didn't realize until I started writing fiction that all of that was important to me as a fiction writer and a person."

Edgerton originally had no intention of becoming a writer. He wrote a few short stories and poems while working on his bachelor's degree at the University of North Carolina at Chapel Hill, but he was more interested in flying. After graduating in 1966, he enlisted in the U.S. Air Force, became a pilot, and flew reconnaissance and air control missions over Vietnam. Although Edgerton had been a supporter of the war before his service, his experiences overseas changed his attitude. He returned to the United States, began to work on his graduate degrees, and took a teaching position at a high school in Durham, North Carolina. In 1975, Edgerton married a fellow teacher, Susan Ketchin, who also shared his passion for bluegrass music. In 1977, the author joined the faculty of Campbell University, a conservative Baptist institution in the small town of Buies Creek, and settled down with Susan to raise a family.

Stories about Everyday Life

In December of 1977, Edgerton was working on his house when he discovered an old well in the crawlspace below his kitchen floor. The event inspired him to start a short story about a boy called Meredith who falls through his kitchen floor into an old well beneath. Inspired by the examples of writers like Eudora Welty, Edgerton realized that stories about everyday people—like the tales

This 1985 work examines a troubled marriage between a provincial southerner and her liberal-minded husband.

he had grown up hearing—were worth telling. "I loved the characters and wanted to come back and write more about them," he tells Ross. "Along with Meredith and his cousin Mark, I also had my Vietnam experience that I wanted to work in, and this family history." For four years, he tried to interest publishers in his fiction. By 1983, Edgerton had sold six stories and come up with one really strong recurring character. Her name was Raney Bell Shepherd, and she was a small-town, narrow-minded, Free Will Baptist. Raney was limited in experience, but she had an unapologetic, energetic personality, a family loyalty, and a strong streak of common sense that endeared her to readers. The novel that Edgerton wrote, using her voice as the narrator, was called *Raney*.

Raney incorporates many elements from Edgerton's own life, including his small-town North Carolina upbringing, his love of country music, and his strong reliance on the bonds that hold families together. The novel begins with Raney's marriage to Charles Shepherd, a librarian from Atlanta, Georgia, whose values are very different than those of his fiancee. The couple share a love of bluegrass music but very little else. Raney is shocked by Charles's liberalism—his lack of racial self-consciousness, his mother's vegetarianism, and his attitude toward pornography and sex. Charles, for his part, is irritated by Raney's provincialism: her attitude toward her North Carolina hometown, her strong family ties, and her religious fundamentalism. The two of them go through some difficult times during their first two years of marriage. At one point, Raney leaves both home and Charles. She matures and returns, however, and the book concludes with the birth of their first child.

Reviewers celebrated Edgerton's accomplishment in his first novel. The conflict between Raney and Charles, according to George Core in the *Washington Post Book World*, derives from their family histories. "Raney comes from a matriarchy," Core states. "Charles is not worldly enough or advanced enough to see women as the equals of men. . . . The result is a playful and humorous war of the sexes, what James Thurber might have written had he lived in North Carolina rather than Connecticut." Edgerton, states Gene Lyons in *Newsweek*, is "in perfect command of Raney's voice, provides wonderful small surprises throughout, and by the night of their sweet reconciliation . . .

has made us care for his characters and wish them well." "Like Charles," writes Carol Verderese in the *New York Times Book Review*, "we are both appalled by Raney's provincial attitudes and awed by her simple wisdom. . . . [Utterly] beguiling, Raney lives beyond the pages of this short novel."

Edgerton left his position at Campbell University in 1985, partly as a result of his depiction of Christian fundamentalism in *Raney*. The administration of the school objected to his characterization of the Baptist church and refused the author the customary raise to accompany his renewed contract. Edgerton, claiming that his academic free-

doms had been violated, left the University and secured another position with St. Andrews Presbyterian College. The author also presented a cynical view of fundamentalist institutions in *Killer Diller*, where the president and provost of Baptist-affiliated Ballard University, Ned and Ted Sears, are shown to be more interested in expanding University institutions than in spreading the word of God. "Edgerton," writes Carol Clark in *School Library Journal*, "humorously chides the Christian college establishment for its judgmental attitudes and opportunistic behavior."

Further Family Adventures

Walking across Egypt, Edgerton's second novel, was inspired by the author's family life and its storytelling tradition. "The first scene in the book came from real life," Edgerton explains to Ross. "My mother actually sat in a chair without a bottom and got stuck for about fifteen minutes, and her sisters and I thought it was the funniest thing we'd ever heard." The woman stuck in the chair evolved into Mattie Rigsbee, a warmhearted seventy-eight-year-old Christian widow with grown children who feels deserted because she no longer has anyone to love and to cook her excellent meals for. Mattie is rescued from her position by the local dogcatcher, who introduces her to his nephew Wesley Benfield, a juvenile delinquent on his way to a career in auto theft. Mattie takes charge of Wesley's life and begins the process of reforming him despite the objections of her friends and children. "This one act of kindness," writes Pam Spencer in *School Library Journal*, "fills her life with laughter and love." "With a touch here of Samuel Clemens, there of *Lucky Jim*," declares a critic in *Kirkus Reviews*, "Edgerton takes on the pieties of church, family, and goodness, and . . . inspires them with a laughable comedy that hits the mark and lingers."

For *The Floatplane Notebooks*, Edgerton drew not only on his family but also on his personal history. It tells the intergenerational story of the Copelands, a Southern family who deal with the tumultuous events of the twentieth century on their own terms and develop their own native means of survival. Albert Copeland, the patriarch of the family, finds purpose in his life through his experimental water-launched aircraft—the floatplane of the title. Albert and his descendants

CLYDE EDGERTON
Author of KILLER DILLER

WALKING ACROSS EGYPT

The story of a spunky woman, a stray dog, a teenage delinquent, and the best home-cooking in Listre, North Carolina

"Reading this book is like sitting down to a big round table full of the best food you ever put in your mouth, you can't quit eating for a minute, this is just so good."
Lee Smith

An juvenile delinquent's life is changed through his contact with a feisty seventy-eight-year-old widow in this 1987 novel.

are faced with their most severe challenges during the 1960s, with the coming of the Vietnam War and the cultural upheaval of the counterculture. The younger Copelands react to these challenges in their own ways: Noralee Copeland becomes a hippie with interracial friendships, while Mark and Meredith Copeland both serve in Vietnam. Mark, like Edgerton himself, is a pilot who emerges from the War physically unharmed, but Meredith, who served in the infantry, is so badly wounded that he can neither walk nor speak. Despite his injuries, Meredith serves as the narrator of the final pages of the novel, making a powerful statement about the impact of the War on American life. "I had tried—unsuccessfully—to write about those experiences [in Vietnam]," Edgerton tells Ross. "The writing was always bad. I think a fiction writer needs a certain kind of distance between his characters and subject matter and himself."

One of Edgerton's major themes, which he addresses in all of his works, is the importance of family and the impact, both positive and negative, of family traditions. Raney is very close to her mother; one of her big arguments with Charles comes after her mother enters their home while the couple is dining out. Mattie Rigsbee in *Walking across Egypt* ignores the objections of her grown children to devote her attentions to Wesley, giving her an outlet for her maternal instincts, and giving Wesley in turn the strong parenting he needs in order to reform. In *The Floatplane Notebooks*, however, family is more central than in either of his two earlier novels. One of the Copeland family's main activities is the cleaning of the family graveyard plots, which connects them both to their ancestors and to each other. "It used to be that the family was buried together," Edgerton tells Ross. "That was true on my mother's side, and all my life I've gone to this little graveyard every year and helped clean it. Many of the people helping clean I see only once a year, because they're from other places. There are usually anywhere from eight to twenty people at the cleaning, and I hear these stories and have heard them over and over."

Family continues to be a central issue in Edgerton's more recent fiction. *Killer Diller* revisits the characters from *Walking through Egypt*. Mattie Rigsbee has been sent to a nursing home, while Wesley has moved into a Baptist-sponsored halfway house called "Back on Track Again."

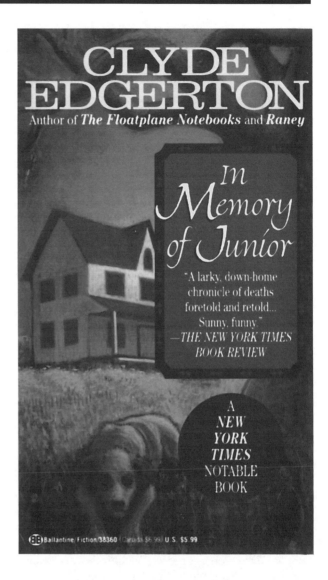

In this 1992 novel, a husband and wife question who will inherit their land—the children from his first or second marriage?

Wesley wrestles with the Christian sense of responsibility that Mattie has passed on to him through her loving example. He tries to teach Vernon Jackson, a mentally-handicapped youth, the art of bricklaying, while at the same time trying to subdue his lust for Phoebe Trent, a resident of the Nutrition House, sponsored by the same church that runs the halfway house. At the climax of the novel Wesley faces difficult choices about his future. "There's an affecting story, authenticity of voice and moral complexity here," declares Lisa Koger in the *New York Times Book Review*. "As Mattie tells Wesley, 'You can't judge your own life by what you don't like in somebody else's.'"

In Memory of Junior also looks at family issues, although in a less comic way than most of Edgerton's previous novels. It introduces two related families, the McCords and the Bales, three of whose members are waiting for death. Glenn Bales and his second wife Laura are both expecting to die shortly, and their children (Glenn's sons by his first wife, Faison and Tate, and Glenn and Laura's daughter Faye) are waiting to divide up the inheritance: the North Carolina ancestral home and property, worth thousands of dollars. In addition, there are questions of why Glenn's first wife deserted her husband and their two boys, and of what to put on the tombstone of Faison's deceased stepson. Commenting and philosophizing on the action is Grove McCord, brother to Glenn's first wife, who is the third person expecting to die. He even attempts suicide, but the gun he had pointed at his head misses, and he decides he'd rather go fishing.

Despite the conflicts between the different narrators of the novel, Edgerton depicts family life as a uniting force in the lives and deaths of the Bales and the McCords. "I think hate and love hold families together," the author tells Ross, "and I think families can be both strengthening and destructive and everything in between. . . . In my fiction I tend to think of family as strengthening and good. I spend a lot of time thinking about family stories and talking to my daughter about them." In *In Memory of Junior*, Grove McCord echoes Edgerton's opinion, according to Shelby Hearon in the *New York Times Book Review*, when he declares that "'whatever you leave behind is your history, and it better be good, because you're history longer than you're fact.'"

■ Works Cited

Clark, Carol, review of *Killer Diller*, *School Library Journal*, May, 1991, p. 126.

Core, George, "Tall Tales, Guffaws, and Sly Southern Humor," *Washington Post Book World*, June 30, 1985, p. 11.

Edgerton, Clyde, in an interview with Jean W. Ross, *Contemporary Authors*, Volume 134, Gale, 1992, pp. 147-55.

Hearon, Shelby, "As They Lay Dying," *New York Times Book Review*, October 11, 1992, p. 9.

Koger, Lisa, "Other People's Cars," *New York Times Book Review*, February 10, 1991, p. 11.

Lystad, Mary, "Clyde Edgerton," *Twentieth-Century Young Adult Writers*, 3rd edition, St. James Press, 1989, pp. 197-98.

Spencer, Pam, review of *Walking across Egypt*, *School Library Journal*, March, 1992, p. 165.

Verderese, Carol, review of *Raney*, *New York Times Book Review*, June 23, 1985, pp. 20-21.

Review of *Walking across Egypt*, *Kirkus Reviews*, February 1, 1987, p. 155.

■ For More Information See

BOOKS

Contemporary Literary Criticism, Volume 39, Gale, 1986.

PERIODICALS

Arts Journal, November, 1988, p. 36.

Detroit News, March 31, 1985; June 14, 1987.

Journal (Atlanta, GA), May 10, 1985; May 12, 1987; October 23, 1988.

Kirkus Reviews, December 15, 1990, p. 1693.

Library Journal, September 1, 1992, p. 213.

Los Angeles Times, March 30, 1987.

Los Angeles Times Book Review, June 23, 1985, p. 3; November 6, 1988, p. 3.

Newsweek, February 25, 1985, p. 86.

New York Times Book Review, March 29, 1987, p. 17; October 9, 1988, p. 10.

Oxford Review, February, 1991, p. 1.

Poets and Writers, November-December, 1987, p. 8.

Publishers Weekly, September 16, 1988, p. 58.

Rocky Mountain News, February 20, 1991.

Sewanee Review, spring, 1985, p. xxxix.

Tribune Books (Chicago), November 6, 1988, p. 5.

Washington Post, June 2, 1987.

Washington Post Book World, November 20, 1988, p. 6; February 24, 1991, pp. 3, 15; November 22, 1992, p. 6.

Washington Times, February 13, 1991, p. E1.

—Sketch by Kenneth R. Shepherd

Esther Forbes

Personal

Born June 28, 1891, in Westborough, MA; died August 12, 1967; daughter of William Trowbridge (a judge) and Harriette (Marrifield) Forbes; married Albert Learned Hoskins, 1926 (divorced, 1933). *Education:* Attended Bradford Junior College (graduated, 1912) and University of Wisconsin—Madison, 1916-18.

Career

Author. Houghton Mifflin Co., Boston, MA, staff member, 1920-26, 1942-46. *Member:* American Academy of Arts and Sciences, American Antiquarian Society, Society of American Historians.

Awards, Honors

Pulitzer Prize for history, 1943, for *Paul Revere and the World He Lived In*; Newbery Medal, 1944, for *Johnny Tremain*; Litt.D. degrees from Clark University, Worcester, MA, 1943, University of Maine, Orono, 1943, University of Wisconsin, 1949, North-eastern University, Boston, 1949, and Wellesley College, Wellesley, MA, 1959; LL.D. degrees from Tufts University, Medford, MA.

Writings

O Genteel Lady!, Houghton, 1926.
Anne Douglas Sedgwick: An Interview, Houghton, 1928.
A Mirror for Witches, in Which Is Reflected the Life, Machinations, and Death of Famous Doll Bilby, Who, with a More than Feminine Perversity, Preferred a Demon to a Mortal Lover, illustrated by Robert Gibbings, Houghton, 1928.
Miss Marvel, Houghton, 1935.
Paradise, Harcourt, 1937.
The General's Lady, Harcourt, 1938.
Paul Revere and the World He Lived In, Houghton, 1942.
Johnny Tremain: A Novel for Old and Young, illustrated by Lynd Ward, Houghton, 1943.
(With Arthur Griffin) *The Boston Book*, Houghton, 1947.
The Running of the Tide, Houghton, 1948.
America's Paul Revere, illustrated by Lynd Ward, Houghton, 1948.
Rainbow on the Road, Houghton, 1954.

Forbes's manuscripts are held in the collections of the American Antiquarian Society in Worcester, MA, and in the Richard Hutchings Goddard Library at Clark University in the same town.

■ Adaptations

The Walt Disney Company made a movie of *Johnny Tremain,* which was released in 1957. The story has also been adapted as an audiobook, by Caedmon in 1974, and again by the Center for Literary Review, 1978. A musical, "Come Summer," based on Forbes's book, *Rainbow on the Road,* opened at the Lunt-Fontanne Theatre on Broadway, March 11, 1969. *A Mirror for Witches* was adapted for Broadway and produced under the title *Bilby's Doll* in 1976. *The Running of the Tide* was also filmed, and the Sadler Wells Ballet of London performed a ballet based on *A Mirror for Witches.*

■ Sidelights

Although she is best known for *Johnny Tremain,* her only novel directed specifically at a younger audience, Esther Forbes was both a writer and a historian whose works offer insight into the colonial and early republic periods of American history. In books ranging in subject from the witchcraft trials of late seventeenth-century Massachusetts to the changes brought about by the transportation revolution of the early nineteenth century, Forbes presents a colorful picture of life in the New England region. Her work is also often praised for the fresh, honest approach her stories take, her historical accuracy, and her moving evocation of her protagonists' feelings. With a reference to the Muses of epic poetry and history, Edith Olivier critiqued Forbes's *A Mirror for Witches* in the *Saturday Review of Literature:* "The 'historical novel' is, as a rule, but a hybrid artistic form, and is commonly neither historical nor a novel; but Miss Forbes could, without misgiving, have dedicated this book, with its rare subtlety and insight, to Calliope and Clio for their joint acceptance."

Forbes's interest in American history, and specifically in the history of the New England region, grew out of her own family's past and traditions. Her father, William Trowbridge Forbes, was a judge in Massachusetts, and her mother was a respected New England antiquarian who had published many works on local history, including *Gravestones of Early New England and the Men Who Made Them* (1927). "As a child," declared Edward J. Jennerich in the *Dictionary of Literary Biography,* "[Esther Forbes] spent hours delving through family manuscripts and reading books of a bygone era. This love of the past, later reflected in her many books, was certainly due in part to the interest of her mother, Harriette Marrifield Forbes, in similar subjects." Esther Forbes's fascination with history took her in 1916 to the University of Wisconsin, where she worked with the noted American historian Frederick Jackson Turner. However, she abandoned her studies during World War I, choosing instead to work as a farmhand in Harper's Ferry, Virginia, to help in the war effort.

Forbes did not return to college after the war ended. Instead, she moved to New York to work for the publisher Houghton Mifflin. For the next six years she served on the company's editorial staff, where she helped supervise the publication of popular historical romance novelists such as Rafael Sabatini, the author of *Scaramouche* and *Captain Blood.* At the same time, Forbes began working on a historical romance of her own, which was published in 1926 as *O Genteel Lady!* The success of this work (A critic writing in the *Saturday Review of Literature* said of the novel: "It might easily in less skillful hands, have become a pretty, sentimental story. . . . Instead of this it has a robustness of theme and of characterization."), combined with her marriage to Albert Learned Hoskins, allowed her to concentrate on her writing. Between 1927 and 1938, she published four more novels that also won critical acclaim. "Her thorough research and writing skills as a novelist," Jennerich explained, "clearly established Forbes as a major force in the writing of historical fiction."

Stories Reclaimed from History

In some ways *O Genteel Lady!* reflects Forbes's own life. It tells the story of a young Boston socialite named Lanice Bardeen, who chooses to forsake the high society world in which she was born for the life of an independent author and illustrator. Forbes demonstrates her familiarity with the culture of late nineteenth-century Massachusetts, with finely-drawn pictures of such literary giants as Oliver Wendell Holmes, Jr., Ralph Waldo Emerson, and the Alcotts. A later novel, *Miss Marvel,* is set during the same period, but it takes the story of its unmarried heroine up to the First World War. *Paradise,* on the other hand, looks at early colonial Puritan culture, telling a story of

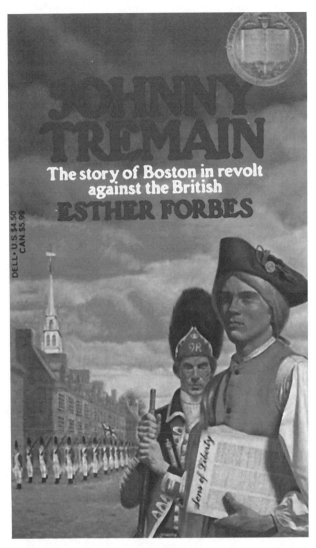

This 1943 work, a Newbery Medal winner, concerns a silversmith's apprentice who becomes involved in the early stages of the American Revolution.

interfamily adultery and persecution against the backdrop of the seventeen-century Indian wars, while *The General's Lady* is about a Revolutionary War-period woman who is executed when she translates her Loyalist sympathies into action against the Patriot cause. In each case, reviewers praised Forbes's command of language, her exhaustive historical research, and her presentation. "To my way of thinking," stated Walter D. Edmonds in the *New York Herald Tribune Book Review*, "books like [*The General's Lady*] express the essence of what historical writing should be."

Forbes's second novel, *A Mirror for Witches*, was originally intended as a novel for adult readers, but confronts many issues that are important to young adults. The story begins in the seventeenth-century French village of Mount Hoel, in which over two hundred people were burned together after being accused of practicing witchcraft. One child escapes the massacre through the aid of an English ship-captain named Jared Bilby. She is given the name of Doll Bilby, and moves into Bilby's house as his foster-daughter. Doll almost at once acquires an unsavory reputation; within a few months of her arrival she is accused of having blighted her foster-mother Hannah's child so that it shrivelled and vanished from her womb. Doll develops into a comely, if somewhat wild, young woman but, because of her birth to parents executed for witchcraft, her fellows suspect her of possessing unearthly powers. Titus Thumb, the son of Bilby's neighbor, falls in love with Doll, but fears her reputation.

As Doll matures, she becomes more and more feared by the local populace, who see that she has a special relationship with some animals, such as the Thumbs' bull Ahab. Soon Doll comes to believe in the diabolic origins of her own powers, taking a demon lover and blaspheming against the Christian religion. When the twin daughters of the Thumb family, Labour and Sorrow, fall ill, they accuse Doll of bewitching them and she is brought to trial. Doll is judged guilty, but she dies in her jail cell while in labor.

Doll's experiences are interpreted one way by her contemporaries, but quite another way by current readers. Doll is, by modern standards, an abused child, condemned to live in an atmosphere of spite and jealousy. The violent death of her parents scarred her and made her cling to Jared Bilby. Bilby in his turn, Forbes explains, treated Doll as if he were her lover. Hannah Bilby hated Doll in turn, partly for her own fears of Doll's reputed power, but also because Doll took her husband's attention. Doll's lover was in fact Shadrach Greene, the pirate son of the wife of the local tinker, although Doll herself later claimed that he returned in true demonic form while she was imprisoned. "As one reads the story," stated Olivier, "one sees that all its events are entirely normal. But . . . so completely does Miss Forbes identify herself with the mental attitude of the period that one realizes how the fantastic beliefs generated in a soil of ignorance and fanaticism can permeate everywhere."

Biography versus Fiction

In 1943, Forbes won the Pulitzer Prize for her biography *Paul Revere and the World He Lived In*, in which she credited her mother as a researcher. Like her novels, the biography presents a panorama of life in colonial America and through the years of the early republic. It begins with the midwinter arrival of a young French refugee named Apollos Rivoire in Boston in 1715, his training as an artisan, his marriage, and the birth of his children, including his son Paul in 1734. It traces the progress of Paul Revere's own life, including his education in his trade of silversmithing, his service in the French and Indian War, and his involvement in early American politics. The book concludes with his death in 1818 at the age of eighty-three, respected by his community. "All agreed that his outstanding characteristics were his generosity and integrity, and had much to say about his willingness to help both publicly and privately," Forbes concluded in her biography. But "the legend had not as yet risen up to swallow the actual man. They, who had so recently seen the stocky, benevolent old gentleman, walking the streets of Boston, could hardly have guessed that he was destined forever to ride a foaming charger, his face enveloped in the blackness of a famous night of almost half a century before, to become in time hardly a man at all—only a hurry of hooves in a village street, a voice in the dark, a knock on a door, a disembodied spirit crying the alarm."

Critics agreed that *Paul Revere* demonstrated the same strengths that characterized her historical novels—vivid character portraits combined with accurate historical details of place and time. "Not every historical novelist can write a good biography," stated Carl Van Doren in the *New York Herald Tribune Book Review*, "but the right kind of historical novelist has some of the qualities most needed in a good biographer. Esther Forbes is that kind of novelist, and her biography of Paul Revere takes at once a high and lasting place in American literature." "In the broader political and military aspects [of Paul Revere's time] there is little [in the book] that is new," said *Saturday Review of Literature* contributor James Truslow Adams. "A good deal of it is rather antiquarian than historical, but it is so well done that one does get a new sense of what those days were like and what their problems were for our ancestors." "Under her hand," declared Allen French

in the *New England Quarterly*, "old Boston becomes a personality. No one else has so mastered and shown the intricacies of relationship and neighborhood in the town of that day."

Forbes used some of the material for *Paul Revere and the World He Lived In* when she wrote her only novel directed specifically at young readers. Forbes commented in her Newbery Medal acceptance speech that she became interested in "the life of the apprentices in and about the shops and wharves of Boston during the eighteenth century" while working on her Revere biography. "I found that whenever these boys (and the much-more-rarely-mentioned girls) appeared in the material I was working on . . . , it was hard for me to keep my resolve to make up nothing," the author explained. "As a sort of reward for the Spartan virtue I was practicing, I promised myself that sometime I would write a story and make up anything I wanted as long as I kept it typical of the period." The result was *Johnny Tremain*.

Growing Up in Revolutionary Times

Like Revere (who appears as a character in the novel), Jonathan Lyte Tremain is training to be a silversmith. However, he is an orphan—his father died before he was born, and his mother a few years later. He has been apprenticed to the Lapham family to learn his trade. Johnny is good at silversmithing—so good, in fact, that he is proud enough to do work that his master cannot do. This leads to his undoing: Johnny, in his pride, bullies the other apprentices, and one of them, named Dove, retaliates by causing him to burn his hand severely. The injury ends Johnny's dream of working as a skilled artisan. It also scars him internally, changing him from a popular boy to an asocial fugitive from society.

Johnny's self-esteem, tied to his abilities as a silversmith, sinks very low. He even seeks help from rich Mr. Lyte, whom he believes is a relative of his dead mother. Lyte, however, treats Johnny as a criminal, ordering the sheriff to arrest the boy and confiscating the silver cup Johnny had produced as proof of his claim. Rejected by his old friends, Johnny turns to a new job: he becomes a courier for a Boston printer named Lorne, and finds a friend in the person of the printer's boy, Rab Silsbee. Rab is one of the Sons of Liberty, a loose group of patriots with the aim of resisting unjust British authority. Johnny and Rab are caught up in the excitement of the opening shots of the American Revolution. Both of them are involved in the Boston Tea Party, helping to dump loads of taxed tea into Boston Harbor. Johnny also serves as a courier for the Americans and as a spy in the British camp. He makes the acquaintance of many of the prominent Boston patriots, including John Hancock, Sam Adams, James Otis, and Dr. Joseph Warren. Finally, after Rab is killed at Lexington, Johnny undergoes surgery to free his scarred hand, shoulders a gun, and marches off to fight for his country. "His maturation from adolescence to manhood, amid personal tragedy and tumultuous events," stated Jennerich, "is the cornerstone of Forbes's novel."

Johnny Tremain was awarded the Newbery Medal in 1944, and was celebrated by reviewers for its depiction of Revolutionary times. Part of its enthusiastic reception may have come from the fact that when it was published, America was once again in a revolutionary struggle: World War II. "Originally," declared Jennerich, "Forbes's idea was to have a central character who wished to

The classic historical novel *Johnny Tremain* was adapted for film in 1957.

remain neutral during the Revolution. However, the Japanese attack on Pearl Harbor convinced Forbes that in war, there is no such thing as neutrality." When American attitudes toward war changed in the period after Vietnam, so did some assessments of *Johnny Tremain.* Christopher Collier, writing in the *Horn Book* magazine in 1976, stated that "*Johnny Tremain,* with its message of ideologically motivated war, is so much the product of World War II that one who grew up in the 1940's must honor its clear one-sidedness. . . . To present history in simple, one-sided—almost moralistic—terms, is to teach nothing worth learning and to falsify the past in a way that provides worse than no help in understanding the present or in meeting the future."

Forbes herself recognized that she had a definite agenda in producing the novel. "One thing I knew I wanted to do," Forbes continued in her Newbery speech "was to show the boys and girls of today how difficult were those other children's lives by modern standards; how early they were asked to take on the responsibilities of men and women. They were not allowed to be children very long. Then came Pearl Harbor and once again we were at war." Forbes concluded: "I also wanted to show that these earlier boys were conscious of what they were fighting for and that it was something which they believed was worth more than their own lives. And to show that many of the issues at stake in this war are the same as in the earlier one. We are still fighting for simple things 'that a man may stand up.'"

Reviewers, whatever their beliefs about the author's political ideology, recognized Forbes's command of place and character. "Miss Forbes brings Boston awake at the same time that the reader plunges into a sense of place—smelling, breathing, hearing, seeing," stated Carolyn Horovitz in the *Horn Book.* "The novel has base in this way, from start to finish; never is skillful use of place merely a garnish or a layer in a sandwich. . . . Life can be as different in the homes of the Silsbees or the Lytes or the Laphams as it can be in Bel-Air or Aliso Village." M. Sarah Smedman, writing in *Touchstones,* declared that "although Forbes' central fictional character is unquestionably partisan and indubitably embodies the author's own vision of the historical period . . . , she does dramatize the character's personal problems, internal struggles, and growth through the interaction of his personal and public

Forbes poses with her dog Sir Tristam in this 1937 photograph.

lives." "If any book can be called a prototype of all that historical fiction should be," Horovitz concluded, "this book merits that appellation."

The Love of New England

Forbes wrote several more novels and another book for children—*America's Paul Revere,* a biography that, according to Jennerich, "maintains the lively style and historical veracity of its distinguished predecessors"—before her death in 1967. Her final novel, *Rainbow on the Road,* was not intended for young readers, but it does feature a juvenile narrator. Young Eddy spends the last summer of his youth in the early 1800s, travelling through New England with Jude Rebough, an itinerant limner, or painter. The book recounts their adventures on the road, but its theme is about the passage of time in Forbes's beloved

New England, and the changes that time brings to the land. The story tells how Eddy and Jude set out on the road looking for work. In the process, they hear stories about a Robin Hood-like bandit named Ruby Lambkin, who seems to resemble Jude. Jude, who occasionally relieves his boredom by pretending to be Lambkin—although never to the point of actually robbing people—is finally arrested and held by a local sheriff, who had been humiliated by Lambkin and consequently brutalizes Jude.

Lambkin is finally caught by the same sheriff, but he escapes, kills his captor, and cruelly mutilates the man's body. This costs him the public esteem he had once enjoyed, and he becomes known as Lamb the Murderer. On their journey home, Jude and Eddy finally encounter Lambkin themselves, and the meeting marks the end of their travels together. Their journey's end terminates the easy relationship between the two. Jude returns home to live quietly on his wife's farm, while Eddy goes to his uncle's shop to be apprenticed, with the aim of heading west once his apprenticeship is over.

In her final novel, Forbes concentrates less on plot and on famous historical happenings, and more on evoking the atmosphere of New England. While in *A Mirror for Witches* and *Johnny Tremain* New England is a setting for events that happen to the protagonists, in *Rainbow on the Road* the setting is in many ways itself the protagonist. The spirit of the novel is one of memory and reminiscence, looking back through time at a country in the process of losing its colonial past, and looking toward a future that seemed to be centered on lands much further west. James Thomas Flexner, himself a distinguished biographer and historian of the colonial and early republic eras, declared in the *Saturday Review* that "the mood of Esther Forbes's charming novel *Rainbow on the Road* is that of a sunlit summer day, variegated with thunderstorms which pass quickly, leaving behind them an ever brighter landscape." "Miss Forbes is in love with New England," asserted *New York Herald Tribune Book Review* contributor Henry Commager, and *Rainbow on the Road* "is her confession and her declaration."

Much of Forbes's work retains its worth to modern readers. "*America's Paul Revere* is still a standard juvenile biography," Jennerich declared, "and *Johnny Tremain* has become a modern children's classic. The constant popularity of her work is statement enough of her audiences' appraisal of her work." Forbes's contributions to American history and literature were recognized when she became the first woman to join the prestigious American Antiquarian Society. She also joined the Society of American Historians and was elected to the American Academy of Arts and Sciences. Her obituary, which appeared in the *New York Times*, declared that Forbes was "a novelist who wrote like a historian and a historian who wrote like a novelist, [who] achieved a reputation as one of the most exciting and knowledgeable authors on the Revolutionary War."

■ Works Cited

Adams, James Truslow, "A New Paul Revere," *Saturday Review of Literature,* July 11, 1942, p. 7.

Collier, Christopher, "Johnny and Sam: Old and New Approaches to the American Revolution," *Horn Book,* April, 1976, pp. 132-38.

Commager, Henry, "A Picaresque Tale Laid among New England's Hills and Streams," *New York Herald Tribune Book Review,* January 31, 1954, p. 3.

Edmonds, Walter D., "A Noble Historical Novel," *New York Herald Tribune Book Review,* October 2, 1938, p. 5.

Flexner, James Thomas, "New England Traveler," *Saturday Review,* January 30, 1954, p. 19.

Forbes, Esther, *Paul Revere and the World He Lived In,* Houghton, 1942.

Forbes, Esther, "The Newbery Medal Acceptance," *Horn Book,* July-August, 1944, pp. 261-67.

French, Allen, review of *Paul Revere and the World He Lived In, New England Quarterly,* September, 1942, pp. 521-22.

Horovitz, Carolyn, "Dimensions in Time: A Critical View of Historical Fiction for Children," *Horn Book,* June, 1962, pp. 255-67.

Jennerich, Edward J., "Esther Forbes," *Dictionary of Literary Biography,* Volume 22: *American Writers for Children, 1900-1960,* Gale, 1983, pp. 176-78.

Obituary of Esther Forbes, *New York Times,* August 13, 1967.

Olivier, Edith, "Witchcraft at Work," *Saturday Review of Literature,* June 2, 1928, p. 930.

"A Romantic Woman" (review of *O Genteel Lady!*), *Saturday Review of Literature,* May 29, 1926, p. 823.

Smedman, M. Sarah, "Esther Forbes' 'Johnny Tremain': Authentic History, Classic Fiction," *Touchstones: Reflections on the Best in Children's Literature, Volume I,* edited by Perry Nodelman, Children's Literature Association, 1985, pp. 83-95.

Van Doren, Carl, "Paul Revere, Mechanic, and His Moonlit Ride," *New York Herald Tribune Book Review,* June 28, 1942, pp. 1-2.

■ For More Information See

BOOKS

Arbuthnot, May Hill, *Children and Books,* 3rd edition, Scott, Foresman, 1964.

Carlsen, G. Robert, *Books and the Teen-Age Reader,* Harper, 1967.

Children's Bookshelf, Child Study Association of America, Bantam, 1965.

Children's Literature Review, Volume 27, Gale, 1992.

Contemporary Literary Criticism, Volume 12, Gale, 1980.

Erskine, Margaret, *Esther Forbes,* Worcester Bicentennial Committee (Worcester, Massachusetts), 1976.

Huck and Young, *Children's Literature in the Elementary School,* Holt, 1961.

Larrick, Nancy, *A Teacher's Guide to Children's Books,* Merrill, 1966.

Larrick, Nancy, *A Parent's Guide to Children's Reading,* 3rd edition, Doubleday, 1969.

Newbery Medal Books: 1922-1955, edited by Berth Mahony Miller and Elinor Whitney Field, Horn Book, 1955.

Twentieth-Century Young Adult Writers, first edition, St. James, 1994, pp. 218-19.

Twentieth-Century Romance and Historical Writers, 3rd edition, St. James, 1994, pp. 242-43.

■ Obituaries

PERIODICALS

Antiquarian Bookman, August 28, 1967.
Newsweek, August 21, 1967.
Publishers Weekly, August 21, 1967.
Time, August 25, 1967.*

—Sketch by Kenneth R. Shepherd

James Douglas Forman

■ Personal

Born November 12, 1932, in Mineola, Long Island, NY; son of Leo Erwin (a lawyer) and Kathryn (Stewart) Forman; married Marcia Fore, September 3, 1956; children: Karli Elizabeth. *Education:* Princeton University, A.B., 1954; Columbia University, LL.B., 1957. *Hobbies and other interests:* Travel, photography, sailing, collecting antique arms from the eighteenth century.

■ Addresses

Home—2 Glen Rd., Sands Point, Port Washington, NY 11050. *Office*—290 Old Country Rd., Mineola, Long Island, NY 11501. *Agent*—Theron Raines, Raines & Raines, 71 Fourth Ave., New York, NY 10016.

■ Career

Writer. Attorney, 1957—. *Member:* Lightning Fleet 142 (sailboats; past president).

■ Awards, Honors

Book World Children's Spring Book Festival Award, 1965, for *Ring the Judas Bell*, and 1969, for *My Enemy, My Brother;* Lewis Carroll Shelf Award, 1972, for *Ceremony of Innocence;* American Library Association Best Book citation, 1979, for *A Ballad for Hogskin Hill.*

■ Writings

NOVELS

The Skies of Crete, Farrar, Straus, 1963.
Ring the Judas Bell, Farrar, Straus, 1965.
The Shield of Achilles, Farrar, Straus, 1966.
Horses of Anger, Farrar, Straus, 1967.
The Traitors, Farrar, Straus, 1968.
The Cow Neck Rebels, Farrar, Straus, 1969.
My Enemy, My Brother, Meredith, 1969.
Ceremony of Innocence, Hawthorn, 1970.
So Ends This Day, Farrar, Straus, 1970.
Song of Jubilee, Farrar, Straus, 1970.
People of the Dream, Farrar, Straus, 1972.
The Life and Death of Yellow Bird, Farrar, Straus, 1973.
Follow the River, Farrar, Straus, 1975.
The Survivor, Farrar, Straus, 1975.
A Fine, Soft Day, Farrar, Straus, 1978.
Freedom's Blood, F. Watts, 1979.
A Ballad for Hogskin Hill, Farrar, Straus, 1979.
That Mad Game: War and the Chances for Peace, Scribner, 1980.

The Pumpkin Shell, Farrar, Straus, 1981.
Call Back Yesterday, Scribner, 1983.
Doomsday Plus Twelve, Scribner, 1984.
Cry Havoc, Scribner, 1988.
The Big Bang, Scribner, 1989.
Prince Charlie's Year, Scribner, 1991.
Becca's Story, Scribner, 1992.

NONFICTION

(With wife, Marcia Forman) *Islands of the Eastern Mediterranean* (booklet), Doubleday, 1960.
Law and Disorder, Thomas Nelson, 1971.
Capitalism: Economic Individualism to Today's Welfare State, F. Watts, 1972.
Communism: From Marx's Manifesto to Twentieth-Century Reality, F. Watts, 1972.
Socialism: Its Theoretical Roots and Present-Day Development, F. Watts, 1972.
Code Name Valkyrie: Count Claus von Stauffenberg and the Plot to Kill Hitler, S. G. Phillips, 1973.
Fascism: The Meaning and Experience of Reactionary Revolution, F. Watts, 1974.
Anarchism: Political Innocence or Social Violence?, F. Watts, 1975.
The White Crow, Farrar, Straus, 1976.
Inflation, F. Watts, 1977.
Nazism, F. Watts, 1978.
Self-Determination: An Examination of the Question and Its Application to African-American People, Open Hand Publishing, 1984.
The Making of Black Revolutionaries, Open Hand Publishing, 1985.
Sammy Younge, Jr.: The First Black College Student to Die in the Black Liberation Movement, Open Hand Publishing, 1986.

■ **Sidelights**

Whether dealing with civil war-torn Greece, the Rebel yells and gunfire of a Virginia battlefield, or a kibbutz in Palestine, a James Douglas Forman novel brings readers side-by-side with a young person trying to negotiate a wartime path through another time and another place. Reviewing recent world history for some of its most notable conflicts, Forman attempts to personalize and make real for readers war's grim realities through vivid characters and dramatic, suspenseful plots. In an essay for the *Third Book of Junior Authors*, the author comments: "If there is a common theme in the books I've written . . . it is the individual responding to the more savage impositions of the

larger world . . . with the salvation of some dignity and love."

Forman was born on New York's Long Island "during the Depression on a bright autumn Monday, twelve hours late for Armistice Day," the author notes in his essay. Except for time away for schooling and travel, Forman has never left Long Island, maintaining a home there on Sands Point. The author grew up in a household full of books where reading was a routine activity (in fact, his parents held book discussion groups every other week). Inspired by an English teacher, Forman tried his hand at creative writing while still a youngster; unfortunately, the appeal of extracurricular activities put the budding writer's further attempts on hold until after college.

After graduating from high school, Forman went to Princeton University, where he "forgot writing, becoming passionate about Freudian psychology, Ernest Hemingway, sailboats, and cameras," the author notes in *Junior Library Guild*. Forman thought about becoming a psychiatrist, but found himself unsuited to certain aspects of medical school. Eventually, he changed course and enrolled in law school at Columbia University. While at Columbia, the author married Marcia Fore, a fashion illustrator. After passing the state bar examinations, Forman joined the family law firm.

"My primary creative outlet at that time was photography and I entertained fantasies of becoming a dashing world wandering photographer," Forman once recalled. The author got his chance in 1959, when he and his wife spent the summer photographing the Eastern Mediterranean islands for the American Geographic Society (a tour which was further highlighted for Forman by a meeting with Ernest Hemingway in Pamplona, Spain). The couple's photos were later published—along with text by Forman—as a travel booklet. Inspired by the success of this project, Forman decided to give creative writing another chance.

The "Crete" Trilogy

Drawing on his recent experiences in Greece—as well as extensive research—Forman began a book about the Nazi occupation of Crete during World War II. After countless revisions, the manuscript became *The Skies of Crete*. *The Skies of Crete* invokes the mythic nature of the island's history and the passions and bravery of its people in the story of their confrontation with Nazi invaders. Madeleine L'Engle, commenting in the *New York Times Book Review*, terms *The Skies of Crete* "an unusually challenging and beautiful book."

Forman received his first real acclaim from readers and critics alike, however, with the second book in his "Crete" trilogy, *Ring the Judas Bell*. The story takes place in the late 1940s during the Greek civil war that followed World War II, and is based on the actual kidnapping of 30,000 Greek children by militant Communist partisans. The protagonist of the novel is Nicholos Lanaras, a shepherd boy whose mother is killed by the Nazis and whose father is the village's peace-loving priest. Nicholos and his sister Angela find themselves among a group of children taken from their villages and marched to Albania. The centuries-old Judas bell—which supposedly has fused in its metal a coin belonging to the biblical traitor Judas Iscariot—falls from the village's chapel tower on the terrible day of the kidnapping. This act later becomes an inspirational symbol of Father Lanaras' pacifist convictions. Nicholos draws upon that inspiration and his courage to escape his captors. *The Judas Bell* "has more depth, bite and stark realism than most of what is written for young readers," writes Edmund Fuller in the *New York Times Book Review*. Fuller continues that the novel "is a worthwhile tale of courage, faith and patriotism with the characters well drawn and the wild Greek terrain excellently evoked."

The Shield of Achilles completes Forman's Greek trilogy. In *The Shield of Achilles*, young art student Eleni Lambros returns from school in Athens to Cyprus, where she must learn to rise above the complicated mix of personal and civil strife that awaits her. Drawn to the "Shield of Achilles," a depiction of war painted for the church by a patriotic priest, Eleni paints a new shield which glorifies the beauty of her culture rather than the conflicts which have threatened to tear it apart. "This is undoubtedly a message book, but the messge has nothing directly to do with growing up. It deals with more basic things: good and evil, courage, loyalty, the value of frindship and of human life, the effects of war," notes reviewer Sandra Schmidt in the *Christian Science Monitor*.

Fifteen-year-old Nicholos encounters many obstacles—including bad weather, enemy forces and hungry predators—when he tries to save some children kidnapped by communist guerrillas.

Seeking Answers to Questions of War

The events and effects of World War II—particularly the Holocaust—are predominant aspects of Forman's fiction. *Horses of Anger*, described by Lore Segal in the *New York Times Book Review* as "uncompromising in the difficulty of its vocabulary, the integrity and complexity of its historical facts, and the gruesomeness of its detail," is about a German schoolboy recruited for indoctrination by the Nazis to fight for the Third Reich. *The Traitors* is another argument against fascism set in Nazi-era Germany. The book tells the story of three "traitors": young Paul, his foster father, who is a clergyman, and Paul's Jewish friend, Noah, who Paul and his foster father hide in a church tower. Forman details the trio's attempts to defy the Nazis—Paul's foster brother among them—and to assist the advancing American forces.

"A number of my books have concerned themselves with World War II," Forman once explained. "I was an impressionable child at that time and had a great many older friends who were in the service. . . . Before the war I had become acquainted with a Jewish family of refugees from Vienna, and through them I got a head start on the war. . . . I have met a number of people who fought on the other side—good friends now—but of course monsters then, which has left me with a number of unresolved questions about the nature of war and I suppose I go on writing about it in the hopes that I may stumble on the answers."

Forman's seventh novel, *My Enemy, My Brother*, features a protagonist who also hopes to stumble upon answers to the questions raised by war. Daniel Baratz is a Polish Jew whose family dies fighting the Nazis in Warsaw's ghetto sewers. Daniel and his grandfather Joseph have survived life in a concentration camp, largely due to Joseph's watchmaking skills (talents put to use making bomb timing devices for their captors). After liberation, the Baratzes make their way back to Jacob's hometown, where Dan befriends several young politically idealistic Jews planning to emigrate to a kibbutz—a communal farm settlement—in British-occupied Palestine. Daniel eventually joins the group in Palestine; he also becomes a shepherd and befriends an Arab shepherd named Said. But when Israel's official independence is announced and war breaks out between the Arabs and Jews over land claims, the young men's friendship becomes first dangerous, then impossible. "Taking history for his source and a lean narrative technique for his method, James Forman has written a convincing contemporary novel that probably will better inform many of today's 16-year-olds about a slice of the recent past than miles of microfilm on spools in the school library," writes Mitchel Levitas in the *New York Times Book Review*.

Some critics found the book flawed by the abruptness of its ending, remarking that Forman abandoned his main character in favor of history's turn of events in the region and their impact on a lesser character, the Arab Said. Other reviewers, however, felt that the lack of resolution merely reflected the ongoing nature of the Arab/Israeli conflict: "The uninitiated may feel cheated at the lack of neat plot resolution, but the mark James Forman's story-telling leaves on them is nevertheless likely to last," Jean C. Thomson notes in *School Library Journal*. Other Forman novels related to World War II include *Ceremony of Innocence*, a

In this tale from 1973, Forman explores a number of themes, including the effects of war, the allure of power, and spirituality.

story about Hans and Sophie Scholl, who are imprisoned and sentenced to death for standing against Nazism in their native Germany; *Follow the River*, which focuses on the son of a Nazi war criminal whose quest takes him from Germany to Israel to post-independence India; and *The Survivor*, the story of a Dutch Jew who survives his time in Auschwitz and sets out for Palestine in search of family members and a new life.

Closer to Home

Forman also has written extensively about historical conflicts closer to home. A lifelong resident of Long Island, the author delved into local history to produce *The Cow Neck Rebels,* a novel about one Long Island family's involvement in the Revolutionary War. Sixteen-year-old Bruce Cameron leaves the family grist mill on the Cow Neck

Peninsula to follow his Scottish grandfather and older brother into war. Bruce returns from the Battle of Long Island with a true understanding of war's violent horrors, including his brother's death. "One message comes through . . . all must decide on what course to take when the drums begin to roll, for there can be no bystanders when war is a flame on the doorstep," a reviewer for the *Christian Science Monitor* comments.

Forman attempted a different perspective on a war in *Song of Jubilee*, in which the author's narrator is Jim Chase, a self-educated black slave raised as a companion to his white master's children. Repeatedly compared to *The Confessions of Nat Turner* by William Styron, *Song of Jubilee* raised the ire of some critics who found the book rife with cliches and flawed by a hero whose actions did not follow the motivations provided by Forman. Dorothy M. Broderick remarks in the *New York Times Book Review* that Forman's "constant apologies and rationalizations for remaining loyal [to his white masters] throughout the war are sickening." Broderick continues that "*Song of Jubilee* can only add fuel to the argument that white men cannot, indeed should not, write about black people." A *Horn Book* reviewer also notes problematic character stereotypes, but credits the book with managing "to convey the debilitating influence which the institution of slavery had on white and black alike and, using material cankered by strong emotion, produces a balanced and solid adventure story."

Other noteworthy Forman books concerned with American history include two devoted to the Native American experience. *People of the Dream* is the story of the defeat of the Nez Perce as told from the perspective of Chief Joseph, a story which a *Kirkus Reviews* contributor describes as "permeated by a single emotion—overwhelming sadness. . . . This [novel] isn't intended to be read for the battles, but for the ambiguities of Joseph's character and the epic dignity of the Indians' defeat." *The Life and Death of Yellow Bird* focuses on the years leading up to the Battle of Wounded Knee and the struggles of the Cheyenne people and other area tribes to retain their land and independence. Though a reviewer for *Kirkus Reviews* finds the book "more ambitious" but "somehow less moving than Forman's more modest, gentle *People of the Dream*," a *Horn Book* critic calls *Yellow Bird* "a deeply stirring historical novel . . . [whose] real impact . . . comes from its out-

pouring of details about the characters and about the life of Indians."

Forman took up the civil rights struggles of the 1960s in *Freedom's Blood*, a fictionalized account of the murders of three civil rights workers in Mississippi by a mob that included Klan members and local law enforcement officers. Robert Unsworth, writing in the *School Library Journal*, comments: "Coming at a time when the fires of idealism have cooled considerably, Forman's moving recall of that summer's events commands our attention." *Freedom's Blood* was followed by *The Ballad for Hogskin Hill*, the story of young David and his family, whose country way of life in the Kentucky hills is threatened by an encroaching strip-mining operation. Though more than one critic cited *Ballad* as heavy with stereotyped characters, it nevertheless earned a American Library Association's 1979 Best Book citation. "This is a good

After a pack of genetically-engineered dogs begin attacking people in her town, a young teen and her friend begin a campaign to stop them.

book for young adult collections because it offers a new setting and problem based on an old theme whose idea and question of traditional versus modern remains to be solved," writes Karen Merguerian in a review for the *Young Adult Co-operative Book Review Group of Massachusetts.*

Forman's later books take a decidedly different turn in that they focus more particularly on teen relationships and problems. In *Call Back Yesterday*, a revolution in Saudi Arabia—where the protagonist's father is serving as American ambassador—leads to events that touch off a nuclear world war. *Doomsday Plus Twelve* is a sequel of sorts, taking place twelve years after a nuclear war, when groups of survivors along the West Coast of the United States are trying to rebuild their collapsed society. When a militaristic group in California sets out to destroy Japan—the only nation unaffected by the war—a fourteen-year-old girl named Valerie organizes a 500-mile peace march to stop them. In *Cry Havoc*, a genetically engineered killer dog, created as part of an aborted top-secret government plot, is on the loose and threatening lives in a small Long Island town. In the midst of this horror story is a subplot about troubled family relationships between the main character, fifteen-year-old Cathy, her lawyer father and her mentally ill mother. Roger Sutton remarks in the *Bulletin of the Center for Children's Books* that "the straight-ahead horror of the genetically altered dogs is far more controlled and compelling than the family story. . . . Still, the intensity of the situations and the writing is effectively frightening, especially when the story lines do find each other."

A Family Story

Forman returned to historical war fiction in one of his most recent efforts. *Becca's Story* was based on hundreds of family letters and numerous diaries that detailed the Civil War-era romance between the author's great grandparents. It became something of a family project, with Marcia Forman deciphering and typing up the hard-to-read diaries and letters and creating the book's jacket, which shows a collage of letters, photos and family keepsakes. Becca Case is fourteen years old in 1859, when the novel begins. She is a typical teenager, oblivious of the politics of the day. In fact, most of Becca's early musings surround attending social gatherings with her two suitors: Alex Forman, a responsible and serious young man,

and Charlie Gregory, a light-hearted adventurer. Both young men join Michigan's Seventh Regiment when the Civil War breaks out, but only one comes back alive. Critics note that what sets the novel apart is its basis on fact and the use of correspondence to help bring its characters and events to life. "Unfortunately, the informational properties of the primary sources and background material often seem at war with the plot, as when the the main characters' experiences of a battle or home situation are interrupted by generalized descriptions of the war's progress . . . however, the characters' own words . . . are often vivid and reveal a firsthand glimpse of ordinary people caught up in forces beyond their control or understanding," writes Betsy Hearne in the *Bulletin of the Center for Children's Books.* Colleen Macklin, in a *Voice of Youth Advocates* review, agrees. She states that although the correspondence sometimes slowed the pace, "both girls and boys will gain insight into the Civil War, both on the battlefield and at home."

Forman has indicated that he may write another family book, this one to feature the old house where four generations of the Forman family have lived and "the psychological dynamics of all the relationships involved. [The book is] only a gleam at the moment, but all parties seem interested and eager." Forman is no doubt at work on other ideas as well. "As a result of my enthusiasm for writing," he explains in his *Junior Library Guild* article, "the sailboat is on the verge of becoming a flower box. Law has been neglected as well, though a benevolent family firm has not yet locked me out. Without doubt writing is a nasty habit, but one which I am not prepared to break."

■ Works Cited

Broderick, Dorothy M., review of *Song of Jubilee,* *New York Times Book Review,* May 2, 1971.

Review of *The Cow Neck Rebels, Christian Science Monitor,* November 6, 1969.

Forman, James Douglas, article in *Junior Library Guild,* May-September, 1965.

Forman, James Douglas, essay in *Third Book of Junior Authors,* edited by Doris de Montreville and Donna Hill, Wilson, 1972, pp. 89-90.

Fuller, Edmund, review of *Ring the Judas Bell, New York Times Book Review,* April 4, 1965.

Hearne, Betsy, review of *Becca's Story, Bulletin of the Center for Children's Books,* February, 1993, p. 175.

L'Engle, Madeleine, review of *The Skies of Crete, New York Times Book Review,* November 10, 1963.

Levitas, Mitchel, review of *My Enemy, My Brother, New York Times Book Review,* May 25, 1969, p. 70.

Review of *The Life and Death of Yellow Bird, Horn Book,* February, 1974.

Review of *The Life and Death of Yellow Bird, Kirkus Reviews,* November 15, 1973.

Macklin, Colleen, review of *Becca's Story, Voice of Youth Advocates,* February, 1993, p. 339.

Merguerian, Karen, review of *A Ballad for Hogskin Hill, Young Adult Cooperative Book Review Group of Massachusetts,* December, 1979.

Review of *People of the Dream, Kirkus Reviews,* May 15, 1972.

Schmidt, Sandra, "Object Lessons for Intrepid Girls," *Christian Science Monitor,* May 5, 1966.

Segal, Lore, "The Education of Hans," *New York Times Book Review,* May 7, 1967.

Review of *Song of Jubilee, Horn Book,* August, 1971.

Sutton, Roger, review of *Cry Havoc, Bulletin of the Center for Children's Books,* July/August, 1988.

Thomson, Jean C., review of *My Enemy, My Brother, School Library Journal,* May, 1969.

Unsworth, Robert, review of *Freedom's Blood, School Library Journal,* September 1979.

■ For More Information See

BOOKS

Contemporary Literary Criticism, Volume 21, Gale, 1982, pp. 115-123.

—Sketch by Tracy J. Sukraw

Athol Fugard

Sophiatown, cofounder, 1958-59; New Africa Group, Brussels, cofounder, 1960; Serpent Players, Port Elizabeth, cofounder, director, and actor, 1963—; Ijinle Company, London, cofounder, 1966; The Space Experimental Theatre, Cape Town, cofounder, 1972.

Director of most of his plays produced in South Africa; also directed *The Cure* (adapted from Machiavelli's *Mandragola*), Grahamstown, 1963; *Woyzeck*, Georg Büchner, South Africa, 1964; *Antigone*, Sophocles, Cape Town, 1965; and *The Trials of Brother Jero*, Wole Soyinka, London, 1966. Actor in most of his plays produced in South Africa; also played the part of Okkie the Greek in *A Kakamas Greek*, David Herbert, Brussels, 1960; played Morrie in *The Blood Knot*, New York City, 1962, 1985, London, 1966; played Pavel in *A Place with the Pigs*, New Haven, CT, 1987; and played in *The Road to Mecca*, New York City, 1988. Actor in television films, including *The Blood Knot*, BBC-TV, 1968; and *The Guest at Steenkampskraal*, 1977. Actor in motion pictures, including *Boesman and Lena*, 1973, *Meetings with Remarkable Men*, 1979, *Marigolds in August*, 1980, *Gandhi*, 1982, and *The Killing Fields*, 1984.

Port Elizabeth Evening Post, Port Elizabeth, journalist, 1954; South African Broadcasting Corporation, Port Elizabeth and Cape Town, reporter, 1955-57. Worked variously as a crew member on the *S. S. Graigaur*, a tramp steamer bound from Port Sudan, Sudan, to the Far East, 1953-54, as a

■ Personal

Full name, Harold Athol Lannigan Fugard; born June 11, 1932, in Middelburg, Cape Province, South Africa; son of Harold David (a general store owner) and Elizabeth Magdalena (a cafe manager) Fugard; married Sheila Meiring (a novelist, poet, and former actress), 1956; children: Lisa. *Education:* Attended Marist Brothers College, 1938-45, Port Elizabeth Technical College, 1946-50, and University of Cape Town, 1950-53. *Hobbies and other interests:* Jogging, music, poetry.

■ Addresses

Home—P.O. Box 5090, Port Elizabeth, South Africa. *Agent*—Esther Sherman, William Morris Agency, 1350 Avenue of the Americas, New York, NY 10019.

■ Career

Playwright, director, and actor. Circle Players Theatre Workshop, Cape Town, cofounder, 1957; National Theatre Organization, stage manager and publicity agent, 1958; African Theatre Workshop, clerk for Fordsburg Native Commissioner's Court, Johannesburg, South Africa, 1958, and as a cleaner in London, 1960.

■ Awards, Honors

New York Times Award, 1965; Obie Award, Distinguished Foreign Play, *Village Voice*, 1971, for *Boesman and Lena;* Award for Best New Play, *Plays & Players*, 1973, for *Sizwe Banzi Is Dead;* London Theatre Critics Award, 1974; Ernest Artaria Award, Locarno Film Festival, 1977; Golden Bear, Berlin Film Festival, 1980; Fellowship, Yale University, 1980; Award for Best Play, New York Critics Circle, 1981, for *A Lesson from Aloes;* Drama Desk Award, and Award for Best Play, Critics Circle, both 1983, and *Evening Standard* of London Award, 1984, all for *"Master Harold" . . . and the Boys;* Commonwealth Award, 1984, for contribution to the American theater; Drama League Award, 1986; Circle Award, New York Drama Critics, 1988; Helen Hayes Award, 1990, for direction; honorary degrees from Yale University, Georgetown University, Natal University, Rhodes University, and University of Cape Town.

■ Writings

PLAYS

No-Good Friday, first produced in Cape Town, South Africa, 1956; produced in Johannesburg, 1958; produced in Sheffield, 1974.

Nongogo, first produced in Cape Town, 1957; produced in Sheffield, 1974; produced in New York City, 1978.

The Blood Knot (produced in Johannesburg, South Africa, and London, 1961; produced Off-Broadway, 1964), Simondium, 1963, Odyssey, 1964; published with other plays as *Blood Knot and Other Plays*, Theatre Communications Group, 1991.

Hello and Goodbye (first produced in Johannesburg, 1965; produced Off-Broadway at Sheridan Square Playhouse, 1969; produced in Leicester, 1971; produced in London, 1973), A. A. Balkema, 1966, Samuel French, 1971.

The Occupation: A Script for Camera, published in *Ten One-Act Plays*, edited by Cosmos Pieterse, Heinemann, 1968.

Boesman and Lena (first produced in Grahamstown, South Africa, 1969; produced Off-Broadway at Circle in the Square, 1970; produced on the West End at Royal Court Theatre Upstairs, 1971), Buren, 1969, revised edition, Samuel French, 1971; published with *The Blood Knot, People Are Living There,* and *Hello and Goodbye* as *Boesman and Lena, and Other Plays*, Oxford University Press, 1978.

People Are Living There (first produced in Cape Town at Hofmeyr Theatre, 1969; produced on Broadway at Forum Theatre, Lincoln Center, 1971), Oxford University Press, 1970, Samuel French, 1976.

(With Don MacLennan) *The Coat* [and] *Third Degree* (the former by Fugard, the latter by MacLennan), A. A. Balkema, 1971.

Orestes (produced in Cape Town, 1971), published in *Theatre One: New South African Drama*, edited by Stephen Gray, Donker, 1978.

Statements (contains three one-act plays: [With John Kani and Winston Ntshona] *Sizwe Banzi Is Dead*, first produced in Cape Town, 1972, produced in New York City, 1974; [With Kani and Ntshona] *The Island*, first produced in South Africa, 1972, produced on the West End at Royal Court Theatre, 1973, produced in New York City at Edison Theatre, 1974; and *Statements after an Arrest under the Immortality Act*, first produced in Cape Town, 1972, produced in London, 1974), Oxford University Press, 1974.

Three Port Elizabeth Plays: The Blood Knot, Hello and Goodbye, Boesman and Lena, Viking, Oxford University Press, 1974.

Dimetos (first produced in Edinburgh, 1975; produced in London and New York City, 1976), published with *No-Good Friday* and *Nongogo* as *Dimetos and Two Early Plays*, Oxford University Press, 1977.

(With Ross Devenish) *The Guest: An Episode in the Life of Eugene Marais* (screenplay), Donker, 1977.

A Lesson from Aloes (first produced in Johannesburg, 1978; produced in New York City, 1980), Oxford University Press, 1981.

The Drummer, produced in Louisville, 1980.

(With Devenish) *Marigolds in August* (screenplay), Donker, 1982; published with *The Guest* as *Marigolds in August and The Guest: Two Screenplays*, Theatre Communications Group, 1992.

"Master Harold" . . . and the Boys (first produced in New Haven, CT, 1982; produced on Broadway at Lyceum Theatre, 1982), Oxford University Press, 1983; published with *The Blood Knot, Hello and Goodbye,* and *Boesman and Lena* as *Selected Plays*, Oxford University Press, 1987.

The Road to Mecca (first produced in New Haven, CT, 1984; produced in London at Lyttelton Theatre, 1985; produced in New York City at Promenade Theatre, 1988), Faber, 1985.

A Place with the Pigs (first produced in New Haven, CT, 1987; produced in London, 1988), Faber, 1988.

My Children! My Africa! (produced in Johannesburg and New York City, 1989; produced in London, 1990), Faber, Theatre Communications Group, 1990.

Playland (first produced in Cape Town, 1992), published with *A Place with the Pigs* as *Playland and A Place with the Pigs*, Theatre Communications Group, 1993.

Valley Song, produced in Market Theater, Johannesburg, South Africa, and McCarter Theater, Princeton, NJ, 1995.

OTHER

Tsotsi (novel), Donker, Collings, 1980, Random House, 1981.

Notebooks, 1960-1977, edited by Mary Benson, Donker, Faber, 1983, Knopf, 1984, Theatre Communications Group, 1990.

Writer and Region: Athol Fugard (essay), Anson Phelps Stokes Institute, 1987.

Also author of screenplays *Boesman and Lena* (based on the play of the same name), 1972, and *Meetings with Remarkable Men*, 1979. Teleplays include *Mille Miglia* and *The Guest at Steenkampskraal*. Plays and essays reprinted in various anthologies, including *Text & Teaching: The Search for Excellence*, edited by Michael Collins, Georgetown University Press, 1991.

■ Sidelights

As a white child growing up in segregated South Africa, Athol Fugard resisted the racist upbringing society offered him. Nevertheless, the boy who would become, in the words of Gillian MacKay of *Maclean's*, "perhaps South Africa's most renowned literary figure, and its most eloquent anti-apartheid crusader abroad" did not completely escape apartheid's influence—he insisted that the family's black servants call him Master Harold, and he even spat at one of them. Fugard told MacKay that the servant, an "extraordinary" man who had always treated him as a close friend, "grieved for the state" of Fugard's soul and forgave him "instead of beating" him "to a pulp."

Fugard will never forget this incident, which he transformed into a powerful scene in the play, *"Master Harold" . . . and the Boys*. As he commented to Lloyd Richards in *Paris Review*, it is like a deep stain which has "soaked into the fabric" of his life. In Fugard's career as a playwright, director, and actor, he has forced himself and his audiences to consider their own "stains." As Frank Rich remarked in a 1985 *New York Times* review of *The Blood Knot*, "Mr. Fugard doesn't allow anyone, least of all himself, to escape without examining the ugliest capabilities of the soul."

Despite Fugard's insistence that he is not a political writer and that he speaks for no one but himself, his controversial works featuring black and white characters have found favor with critics of apartheid. According to Brendan Gill of the *New Yorker*, *The Blood Knot*, the play that made Fugard famous, "altered the history of twentieth-century theatre throughout the world" as well as the world's "political history." Not all critics of apartheid, however, have appreciated Fugard's works. Some "see a white man being a spokesman for what has happened to black people and they are naturally intolerant," Fugard explained to Paul Allen in *New Statesman and Society*.

Whether Fugard's theatrical explorations of passion, violence, and guilt played a role in undermining apartheid or not, it is clear that he was involved in breaking physical and symbolic barriers to integration. He defied the apartheid system by founding the first enduring black theater company in South Africa, by collaborating with black writers, and by presenting black and white actors on stage together for integrated audiences. He insisted upon performing plays for local audiences in South Africa as well as for those in New York City and London; his plays carried messages that he believed people around the world deserved to hear. Even after the government took Fugard's passport and banned his plays, he refused to consider himself an exile or to renounce his country. Love, and not hate for South Africa, Fugard maintained, would help it break the chains of apartheid. "Wouldn't be ironic if South Africa could teach the world something about harmony?," he asked MacKay in *Maclean's*.

Fugard is highly regarded by literary and theater critics. As Stephen Gray, writing in *New Theatre Quarterly*, noted, Fugard has been called "the greatest active playwright in English." His plays are noted for their multifaceted, marginalized characters, realistic yet lyrical dialogue, and carefully crafted, symbolic plots. Critics have also appreciated Fugard's ability to write scenes which elicit emotion without declining into melodrama. Fugard has forged new paths in theater by directing and acting in many of his own plays, and by writing and composing plays with the actors who perform in them.

Growing Up in South Africa

Fugard credits his parents with shaping his insights about South African society. As a child, he developed close relationships with both his English- speaking South African father, Harold, and his mother, Elizabeth, the daughter of Dutch-speaking Afrikaners. Harold, a jazz musician and amputee who spent a great deal of time in bed, amused the boy with fantastic stories and confused him with his unabashed bigotry. Fugard's mother Elizabeth supported the family by efficiently managing their tea room. In an interview with Jamaica Kincaid for *Interview,* Fugard described his mother as "an extraordinary woman" who could "barely read and write." In Fugard's words, she was "a *monument* of decency and principle and just anger" who encouraged Fugard to view South African society with a thoughtful and critical eye.

If Fugard learned the power of words from his father, and if he discovered how to question society from his mother, he gained an understanding of the complexity of human nature from both parents. Like Fugard's characters, his parents were neither entirely good or evil. Nevertheless, as Fugard explained to Kincaid in *Interview,* "I think at a fairly early age I became suspicious of what the system was trying to do to me. . . . I became conscious of what attitudes it was trying to implant in me and what *prejudices* it was trying to pass on to me." Fugard fed his intellectual appetite with conversations with his mother and daily trips to the local library. By the time he began college, he knew he wanted to be a writer. He accepted a scholarship at the University of Cape Town and studied philosophy, but he left school before graduating to journey around the Far East on a steamer ship.

At this time in his life, Fugard entertained notions of writing a great South African novel. Yet his first attempt at writing a novel, as he saw it, was a failure, and he destroyed it. After Fugard met and married Sheila Meiring, an out-of-work South African actress, in 1956, he developed an interest in writing plays. *The Cell* and *Klaas and the Devil* were the first results of this ambition.

It wasn't until after Fugard began to keep company with a community of black writers and actors near Johannesburg and worked as a clerk in a registration bureau that he experienced a revelation in his work. During this time, he witnessed the frustration of the black writers and learned the intricacies of a system which shrewdly and cruelly thwarted their efforts to live and work freely. The plays he penned at this time, *No-Good Friday* and *Nongogo,* were performed by Fugard and his black actor friends for private audiences.

This 1982 drama, Fugard's best-known work, is an somewhat autobiographical look at a young boy's relationship with his black servants.

Tsotsi

In 1959 Fugard moved to England to write. His work received little attention there, and Fugard began to realize that he needed to be in South Africa to follow his muse. Upon his return home in 1961, Fugard wrote a second novel. Although he tried to destroy this work, a pair of graduate students later found the only surviving copy, and it was published in 1981. Critics have noticed the presence of many of the elements which would re-emerge in Fugard's more famous plays in this novel, *Tsotsi*.

Tsotsi portrays the life of David, a young black man whose nickname, "Tsotsi," means "hoodlum." Tsotsi spends his time with his gang of thieving, murderous friends. He has no family and cannot remember his childhood. It is not until a woman he is about to attack gives him a box with a baby in it, and David gives the baby his name, that he begins to experience sympathy and compassion, and to recall his childhood. When David is about to kill a crippled old man he has been pursuing, he suddenly remembers how his mother was arrested and never came home, and how he began to rove with a pack of abandoned children. It is not long before he recalls the trauma that led to his violent life on the streets. Fugard does not allow David's character to revel in his newly discovered emotions or to continue his search for God: at the novel's end, David is crushed under a bulldozer in an attempt to save David, the baby. Critics appreciated *Tsotsi* for the fact that it provides insight into the lives of even minor characters. Fugard did not allow his readers to categorize characters as "good" or "bad"; instead, he forced them to understand their complexity. In a 1981 review of the book in the *New York Times Book Review*, Ivan Gold found *Tsotsi* to be "a moving and untendentious book" which demonstrates Fugard's ability to "uncannily insinuate himself into the skins of the oppressed majority and articulate its rage and misery and hope." Although Barbara A. Bannon of *Publishers Weekly* commented that *Tsotsi* is "altogether different in tone" from some of his plays, she observed that the "milieu is much the same as the one that has made Fugard . . . the literary conscience of South Africa."

While Fugard generally works on one project at a time (typically writing with pens instead of word processors), he wrote *Tsotsi* and *The Blood Knot* at the same time. Fugard explained the in-

An elderly black teacher and his radical young student argue over the means to end apartheid in this 1989 drama.

spiration for *The Blood Knot* to Richards in *Paris Review*. Fugard walked in a room and saw his brother was asleep in bed one night; Fugard's brother had lived a difficult life, and his pain was apparent in his face and body. Fugard realized that there was nothing he could do to save his brother from suffering so, and he experienced guilt. By writing *The Blood Knot*, Fugard recalled, he "was trying to examine a guilt more profound than racial guilt—the existential guilt that I feel when another person suffers, is victimized, and I can do nothing about it. South Africa afforded me the most perfect device for examining this guilt. . . ."

The Blood Knot Shocks South Africa

The Blood Knot is the story of two brothers born to the same mother. Morris, who has light-skin, can "pass" for white; he confronts the truth about his identity when he returns home to live with his dark-skinned brother, Zachariah. Although the opening scene of the play finds Morris preparing a bath for hard-working Zachariah's feet, it soon becomes clear that the brothers' relationship is a tenuous one. The tension between the brothers is heightened when Zach's white pen pal (a woman who thinks Zach is white) wants to meet him, and Morris must pretend to be the white man with whom she has been corresponding.

Morris's attempts to look and sound white are painful for both brothers: to convincingly portray a white man, Morris must treat his black brother with the cruelty of a racist. In his role as a white man, Morris sits in the park and calls insults at his brother, who chases black children from the presence of his "white" brother. By the last scene, the "game" is out of control, and Zach tries to kill Morris. According to Robert M. Post in *Ariel: A Review of International English Literature*, the brothers in *The Blood Knot* "are typical victims of the system of apartheid and bigotry" and "personify the racial conflict of South Africa."

Fugard had little support in producing the play; it was not until actor Zakes Mokae joined the project that the production emerged. As a result of this collaboration, the first production of *The Blood Knot* in Johannesburg, in 1961, was controversial not only for its content, but because it featured a black actor and a white actor on stage together. Fugard played the light-skinned brother who "passes" for a white man, while Mokae played the darker-skinned brother. *The Blood Knot* opened in front of a mixed-race, invitation-only audience in a run-down theatre. As Derek Cohen wrote in *Canadian Drama*, this first production of *The Blood Knot* "sent shock waves through" South Africa. "Those who saw the initial performance knew instinctively that something of a revolution had taken place in the stodgily Angloid cultural world of South Africa. . . . Whites, faced baldly with some inescapable truths about what their repressive culture and history had wrought, were compelled to take notice."

Responses to *The Blood Knot* varied. As Cohen noted, some Afrikaners asserted that the play's message was that blacks and whites could not live together in peace, and some black critics called the work racist. Many critics now accept the interpretation of the play as a sad commentary on the way racism has twisted and tangled our understanding of brotherhood and humanity. More specifically, Cohen has insisted, *The Blood Knot* is "about the hatred which South African life feeds on."

According to Dennis Walder in his book, *Athol Fugard*, Fugard's plays "approximate . . . the same basic model established by *The Blood Knot*: a small cast of 'marginal' characters is presented in a passionately close relationship embodying the tensions current in their society, the whole first performed by actors directly involved in its creation, in a makeshift, 'fringe' or 'unofficial' venue." In other words, since the first production of *The Blood Knot*, the substance of Fugard's plays as well as the means of their production reflect the historical circumstances in which they evolved. Fugard insists that the actual performance, or rather each performance, of his plays is the legitimate play; he selects the actors to perform in his plays and continues to direct and act in them.

Voicing Discontent

Boesman and Lena, produced in 1969, was Fugard's next great success; in the words of Cohen, it is "possibly the finest of Fugard's plays." This work develops around the image of an old, homeless woman Fugard once saw, presenting a homeless couple (both "colored") who wander without respite. According to Cohen, it is a "drama of unrelieved and immitigable suffering" which becomes "more intense as the characters, impotent against the civilization of which they are outcasts, turn their fury against each other." Fugard suffered from writer's block after he wrote *Boesman and Lena*, but went on to work in collaboration with actors to create *Orestes* in 1971. *Orestes* developed as a collection of images which, wrote Walder, "defies translation into a script" and explores "the effect of violence upon those who carry it out."

Fugard's next project began after two amateur actors, John Kani and Winston Ntshona, asked Fugard to help them become professional actors. As Fugard explained to Richards in his *Paris Review* interview, "At that point in South Africa's theater history . . . the notion that a black man could earn a living being an actor in South Africa was just the height of conceit." Nevertheless, the trio searched for a project and decided to create their own play. The three plays that emerged from this plan in 1972 are known as *The Statements Trilogy* or *The Political Trilogy*, and include *The Island*, *Sizwe Banzi Is Dead*, and *Statements after an Arrest under the Immortality Act*.

In these plays, personal experiences, along with the direction of Fugard, combine to provoke audiences. Post commented that *The Island* and *Statements* share "the basic conflict of the individual versus the government." In *The Island*, prisoners (portrayed by Kani and Ntshona) in a South African jail stage Sophocles's *Antigone*; the play within the play suggests that, according to Post, the "conflict between individual conscience and individual rights . . . and governmental decrees . . . corresponds to the conflict between the individual conscience and the rights of black prisoners and white government." *Statements* follows the relationship between a white librarian and a black teacher who become lovers despite their fear of being caught and castigated; eventually, their "illegal" love is uncovered by the police.

The development of *Sizwe Banzi Is Dead* began with an image of a black man in a new suit, seated and smiling, that Fugard saw in a photographer's store. Speculation about why the man was smiling led to a story about the passbook that blacks had to carry around to travel or to get a job and, as a consequence, to live. Before Sizwe Banzi can get his passbook in order, he must trade his identity for another and, symbolically, die. This play was performed "underground" until, as Fugard told Richards, it "had played in London and New York" and earned a reputation that "protected" its writers and cast. In 1974, Kani won a Tony Award for his New York performance in *Sizwe Banzi Is Dead*.

After another long and traumatic bout of writer's block in the late 1970s, Fugard penned a play based on the story of an Afrikaner who tries to work for justice but fails when he is suspected of informing the police. Fugard unveiled *A Lesson from Aloes* in 1978. Like his other works, this play demonstrates the extent to which apartheid effects everyone in South African society. Piet, a Dutch Afrikaner living in Port Elizabeth in 1963, tends his collection of hardy, bitter aloe plants and joins a group of political activists. When the group's bus boycott is disrupted by the police and Piet's only friend Steve is found to have mixed blood and sent away, Piet is blamed. Even Piet's wife,

whose diaries have been read by the police, believes he betrayed Steve.

Instead of defending himself, Piet isolates himself in his quiet aloe garden, and even the audience is unsure of his innocence. At the same time, Gladys, his wife, laments the violation of her diaries and goes insane. Fugard has related that he wanted to demonstrate the "complexity" of the Afrikaner in *A Lesson from Aloes*. He explained to Richards in his *Paris Review* interview that we will "never understand how we landed in the present situation or what's going to come out of it" if we "simply dispose of the Afrikaner as the villain in the South African situation."

Earning Fame Abroad with *"Master Harold"*

"Master Harold" . . . *and the Boys* (a play which, according to many critics, is one of Fugard's best) communicates similar notions. Hallie, whose childhood parallels Fugard's, is troubled by his father's thoughtless and unthinking attitude. Although he has a close relationship with his family's black servants, Sam and Willie, even he is not immune to the evil of apartheid; at one point in the play, the boy spits in Willie's face. Fugard told Richards how the relationship shared by Hallie, Sam, and Willie is autobiographical, and how he really did spit in Willie's face. He felt that it was "necessary" to deal with what he'd done by writing *"Master Harold"* . . . *and the Boys*.

"Master Harold" . . . *and the Boys* (1982) was the second of Fugard's plays to open in the United States, and it earned critical acclaim. Despite this success in the United States, the play provoked criticism from individuals and groups who, as Jeanne Colleran noted in *Modern Drama*, either asserted that characters like Sam exhibit "Uncle Tom-ism," or demanded that Fugard present his plays in South Africa instead of abroad, in "languages of the black majority." Colleran suggested that because of this criticism, "Fugard cannot write of Johannesburg or of township suffering without incurring the wrath of Black South Africans who regard him as a self-appointed and presumptuous spokesman; nor can he claim value for the position previously held by white liberals without being assailed by the more powerful and vociferous radical left. . . . Ironically . . . Fugard has been forced to practice a kind of self-censorship by those whose cause he shared."

"Master Harold" . . . and the Boys also received negative attention from the South African Government, which claimed that it was subversive. The government proclaimed it illegal to import or distribute copies of the play. Fugard later managed to present *"Master Harold" . . . and the Boys* in Johannesburg anyway, because the government did not forbid the play's performance.

The publication of *Notebooks 1960-1977* reinforced Fugard's growing popularity in the United States. This book provides his students and fans with what Pico Iyer of *Time* magazine called "the random scraps out of which Fugard fashioned his plays" and "a trail of haunting questions." Richard Eder of the *Los Angeles Times Book Review* asserted that, in addition to providing "the most vivid possible picture of an artist striving to shape his material even as it was detonating all around him," the *Notebooks* are "an illuminating, painful and beguiling record of a life lived in one of those tortured societies where everything refers back, sooner or later, to the situation that torments it."

When *The Road to Mecca* opened in 1984 at the Yale Repertory Theatre, American audiences were captivated by Fugard's mastery once again. Nevertheless, this play reinforced Fugard's reputation as a regional writer by reconstructing the character and life of a woman who lived in Karoo, where Fugard kept his South African home. Unable to take comfort from the Karoo community, the woman, Helen Martins, isolated herself at home; there, she produced sculpture after sculpture from cement and wire. As Benedict Nightingale noted in *New Statesman*, Helen Martins actually committed suicide by "burning out her stomach with caustic soda," Fugard recreates her as "a docile old widow" with a beautiful life; "that paranoia, that suicide are ignored" in *The Road to Mecca*.

The central problem in the play consists of the local pastor's attempts to get Helen to enter a home for the elderly to hide his secret love for her. As Jack Kroll observed in *Newsweek*, though, *The Road to Mecca* "doesn't seem to be a political play at all," it "concerns love and freedom, and for Fugard that is the germ cell of the South African problem." According to Fugard in his interview with Richards, the play "focuses on the possibility that creative energy can exhaust itself," a fear that is very real for Fugard. "[I]n describ-

ing the end of Helen Martins's creative energy, I was in fact writing my own epitaph."

With some exceptions, *The Road to Mecca* was lauded by critics. While Nightingale appreciated the presentation of the Afrikaner pastor "in the round, from his own point of view as much as that from the liberal outsider," he also found the play to be "exasperatingly uneven, as unreal and real a play as Fugard has ever yet penned." According to Colleran, *The Road to Mecca* was "extraordinarily well received," playing at Britain's National Theatre and on Broadway. Graham Leach asserted in *Listener* that *The Road to Mecca* is "universal" and "a major piece of theatre. . . . Many

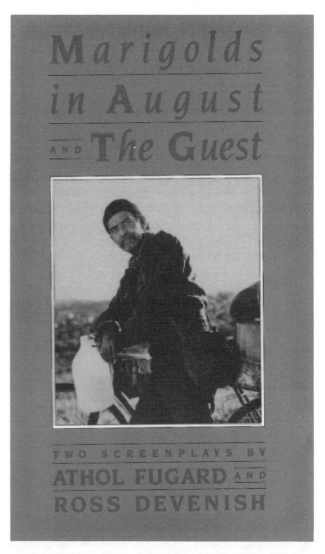

Fugard and director Ross Devenish collaborated on two original screenplays about South African life, both found in this 1992 publication.

people here believe it may well end up being judged Fugard's finest work."

A Place with the Pigs, as Colleran recounted in *Modern Drama,* is a personal parable "concerning the forty years spent in a pigsty" by a "Red Army deserter." It premiered at the Yale Repertory Theatre in 1987 with Fugard in the leading role. Unlike *The Road to Mecca, A Place with the Pigs* did not receive critical acclaim. Colleran suggested that the play may have failed to gain positive attention because it "simply does not conform to the audience's expectations of what a work by Athol Fugard should be like." In her opinion, the "dismissal" of *A Place with the Pigs* is unfortunate, in part because this "parable of one segment of South African society—the white South African who is committed both to dismantling apartheid and to remaining in his homeland—it adds a new voice, an authentic one, to those clamoring to decide the future of South Africa."

Describing South Africa's Future

My Children! My Africa! was the first of Fugard's plays to premiere in South Africa in years. According to Gray in *New Theatre Quarterly,* Fugard believed that "South African audiences should have this play first." Fugard ensured that many audiences were exposed to this work: after a long run at the Market Theatre in Johannesburg, *My Children! My Africa!* was performed for six weeks in a tour of black townships in South Africa in 1989 with Lisa Fugard, Fugard's daughter, and John Kani in starring roles.

Like *"Master Harold"* . . . *and the Boys, My Children! My Africa!* portrays the struggles of youths to live with or confront the division between races in South Africa. Yet, as Allen of *New Statesman and Society* observed, the play marks "the first time Fugard . . . put the struggle itself on stage." Fugard was inspired by the story of a black teacher who refused to participate in a school boycott and was later murdered in Port Elizabeth by a group that believed he was a police informer.

The protagonist of *My Children! My Africa!,* an elderly black teacher, challenges his radical students to eschew violence as a means of procuring justice. "Choose!" he tells one of his best pu-

pils at a critical moment in the play. "I'm holding a stone! In this hand I'm holding the whole English language!" According to Fugard in his interview with Kincaid, the scene is his "literary testament."

Playland (1992) was the first of Fugard's plays to appear after the fall of apartheid. It is set on New Year's Eve in a traveling amusement park in Karroo. Here, a black night watchman painting a bumper car and a white South African whose car has broken down meet, discuss their lives, and reveal their darkest secrets: the white man tells how he killed blacks in a border war, and the black man confesses that he killed a white man who tried to force his fiancee (who was working as the white man's servant) to have sexual intercourse with him.

John Simon of *New York* criticized the play when it later opened in New York: "There is hardly a situation, a snatch of dialogue, an object that isn't, or doesn't become, a symbol." According to Edith Oliver in a *New Yorker* review of the play, the spell cast by the actors' performances "is rooted in Mr. Fugard's moral passion." "I have rarely seen an audience so mesmerized, or been so mesmerized myself."

Set after Nelson Mandela's election as South Africa's new president, *Valley Song* portrays four "colored" characters as they prepare to face the challenges of the future. Fugard was happy to premiere *Valley Song* at the Market Theatre in Johannesburg. As Dohald G. McNeil, Jr., of the *New York Times* reported, Fugard was also optimistic about the future of South Africa, and quoted him as saying "We're pulling off a political miracle here." Fugard believed that South Africa's government was "turning into a genuine democracy."

If Fugard's plays have actually influenced history by undermining apartheid, the author may credit his native land and the power of art. "I come from a country which is so highly politicized that there is no act, even the most private you can think of, which does not resonate politically," Fugard told Richards in *Paris Review.* "Art is at work in South Africa. . . . Art goes underground into people's dreams and surfaces months later in strange, unexpected actions."

■ Works Cited

Bannon, Barbara A., review of *Tsotsi, Publishers Weekly,* December 19, 1980, p. 38.

Cohen, Derek, "Drama and the Police State: Athol Fugard's South Africa," *Canadian Drama/L'Art dramatique canadien,* spring, 1980, pp. 151-61.

Colleran, Jeanne, "'A Place with the Pigs': Athol Fugard's Afrikaner Parable," *Modern Drama,* March, 1990, pp. 82-92.

Eder, Richard, "Delving beneath the Cruelty and Bitterness in South Africa," *Los Angeles Times Book Review,* April 8, 1984, pp. 3, 5.

Fugard, Athol, in an interview with Lloyd Richards, *Paris Review,* summer, 1989, pp. 128-51.

Fugard, Athol, in an interview with Jamaica Kincaid, *Interview,* August, 1990, pp. 64-69.

Fugard, Athol, in an interview with Paul Allen, *New Statesman and Society,* September 7, 1990, p. 38.

Gill, Brendan, *New Yorker,* December 23, 1985, pp. 78, 80.

Gold, Ivan, review of *Tsotsi, New York Times Book Review,* February 1, 1981, pp. 8, 27.

Gray, Stephen, "'Between Me and My Country': Fugard's 'My Children! My Africa!' at the Market Theatre, Johannesburg," *New Theatre Quarterly,* February, 1990, pp. 25-30.

Iyer, Pico, review of *Notebooks, 1960-1977, Time,* April 30, 1984, pp. 76-77.

Kroll, Jack, "Love and Freedom in the Karoo," *Newsweek,* May 28, 1984, pp. 85-86.

Leach, Graham, "Finding Mecca in the Outback," *Listener,* December 13, 1984, p. 20.

MacKay, Gillian, "Drama of Dissent," *Maclean's,* June 18, 1990, pp. 58-59.

McNeil, Dohald G., Jr., "Fugard, after Apartheid," *New York Times,* January 13, 1995, p. C2.

Nightingale, Benedict, "Sweetmeat," *New Statesman,* March 8, 1985, pp. 30-31.

Oliver, Edith, review of *Playland, New Yorker,* June 28, 1993, p. 95.

Post, Robert M., "Victims in the Writing of Athol Fugard," *Ariel: A Review of International English Literature,* July, 1985, pp. 3-17.

Rich, Frank, "'Blood Knot,' with Fugard and Mokae," *New York Times,* December 11, 1985, p. C23.

Simon, John, "Invasion of the One-Actors," review of *Playland, New York,* June 21, 1993, pp. 71-72.

Walder, Dennis, *Athol Fugard,* Macmillan, 1984.

■ For More Information See

BOOKS

Contemporary Literary Criticism, Volume 80, pp. 59-89, Gale, 1994.

Gray, Stephen, *Athol Fugard,* McGraw Hill, 1982.

Hauptfleisch, Temple, *Athol Fugard: A Source Guide,* Donker, 1982.

Vandenbroucke, Russell, *Athol Fugard: A Bibliography, Biography, Playography,* TQ Publications, 1977.

Vandenbroucke, *Truths the Hand Can Touch: The Theatre of Athol Fugard,* Theatre Communications Group, 1985.

Wells, Ronald A., editor, *Writer and Region: Athol Fugard,* Anson Phelps Stokes Institute for African, Afro-American, and American Indian Affairs, 1987.

PERIODICALS

America, March 21, 1992, pp. 250-51.

Booklist, December 1, 1982, p. 478.

Chicago, March, 1989, p. 34.

Commonweal, June 3, 1988, pp. 342-43.

Kirkus Reviews, December 1, 1980, p. 1530.

Los Angeles Times, March 13, 1982.

New Republic, July 25, 1970.

Newsweek, May 2, 1988, p. 73.

Theater, fall-winter, 1984, pp. 40-42.

Times Literary Supplement, May 2, 1980.

Travel and Leisure, December, 1992, pp. 118-22.

Variety, March 15, 1993, p. 70.

Washington Post, April 3, 1985.

World Literature Today, summer, 1983, pp. 369-71.

—Sketch by R. Garcia-Johnson

Robert Heinlein

■ Personal

Full name: Robert Anson Heinlein (surname rhymes with "fine line"); also writes under pseudonyms Anson Macdonald, Lyle Monroe, John Riverside, Caleb Saunders, and Simon York; born July 7, 1907, in Butler, MO; son of Rex Ivar (an accountant) and Bam (Lyle) Heinlein; died May 8, 1988, of heart failure in Carmel, CA; cremated and ashes scattered at sea with military honors; married Leslyn Macdonald (divorced, 1947); married Virginia Doris Gerstenfeld, October 21, 1948. *Education*: Attended University of Missouri, 1925; U. S. Naval Academy, graduated 1929; University of California, Los Angeles, graduate study in physics and mathematics, 1934. *Hobbies and other interests*: Ballistics, cats, fencing, figure skating, fiscal theory, stone masonry and sculpture, and "an expert rifleman and pistol shot, both right and left-handed."

■ Career

Writer. Commissioned ensign, U.S. Navy, 1929, became lieutenant (junior grade), retired due to physical disability, 1934; Shively and Sophie Lodes silver mine, Silver Plume, CO, owner, 1934-35; candidate for California State Assembly, 1938; also worked as a real estate agent during 1930s; Naval Air Experimental Station, Philadelphia, PA, aviation engineer, 1942-45. James V. Forrestal Memorial Lecturer, U.S. Naval Academy, 1973; guest commentator for Apollo lunar landing, Columbia Broadcasting System. 1969.

■ Awards, Honors

Guest of Honor, World Science Fiction Convention, 1941, 1961, and 1976; Hugo Award, World Science Fiction Convention, 1956, for *Double Star*, 1960, for *Starship Troopers*, 1962, for *Stranger in a Strange Land*, 1967, for *The Moon Is a Harsh Mistress*; Boys' Clubs of America Best Liked Book Award, 1959; Sequoyah Children's Book Award of Oklahoma, Oklahoma Library Association, 1961, for *Have Space Suit—Will Travel*; named best all-time author, *Locus* magazine readers' poll, 1973, 1975; Humanitarian of the Year, National Rare Blood Club, 1974; Nebula Grand Master Award, Science Fiction Writers of America, 1975; Council of Community Blood Centers Award, 1977; American Association of Blood Banks Award, 1977; Inkpot Award, 1977; L.H.D., Eastern Michigan University, 1977; Distinguished Public Service Medal, National Aeronautics and Space Administration, 1988 (posthumously awarded), "in recognition of his meritorious service to the nation and mankind in advocating and promoting the exploration of space"; the Rhysling Award of the Science Fiction Poetry Association is named after a character in Heinlein's short story, "The Green Hills of Earth"; Tomorrow Starts Here Award, Delta Vee Society; numerous other awards for his work with blood drives.

■ Writings

SCIENCE FICTION NOVELS

Rocket Ship Galileo, Scribner, 1947.

Beyond This Horizon (originally serialized under pseudonym Anson Macdonald in *Astounding Science Fiction*, April and May, 1942), Fantasy Press, 1948.

Space Cadet, Scribner, 1948.

Red Planet, Scribner, 1949, new paperback edition including previously unpublished passages, Del Rey, 1989.

Sixth Column, Gnome Press, 1949, published as *The Day After Tomorrow*, New American Library, 1951.

Farmer in the Sky (originally serialized as "Satellite Scout" in *Boy's Life*, August, September, October, and November, 1950), Scribner, 1950.

Waldo [and] *Magic, Inc.*, Doubleday, 1950, published as *Waldo: Genius in Orbit*, Avon, 1958.

Between Planets (originally serialized as "Planets in Combat" in *Blue Book*, September and October, 1951), Putnam, 1951.

Universe, Dell, 1951, published as *Orphans of the Sky*, Gollancz, 1963, Putnam, 1964.

The Puppet Masters (originally serialized in *Galaxy Science Fiction*, September, October, and November, 1951), Doubleday, 1951.

The Rolling Stones (originally serialized as "Tramp Space Ship," in *Boy's Life*, September, October, November, and December, 1952), Scribner, 1952, published in England as *Space Family Stone*, Gollancz, 1969.

Revolt in 2100, Shasta, 1953.

Starman Jones, Scribner, 1953.

The Star Beast (originally serialized as "The Lummox Star" in *Magazine of Fantasy and Science Fiction*, May, June, and July, 1954) Scribner, 1954.

Tunnel in the Sky, Scribner, 1955.

Double Star (originally serialized in *Astounding Science Fiction*, February, March, and April, 1956), Doubleday, 1956.

Time for the Stars, Scribner, 1956.

The Door into Summer (originally serialized in *Magazine of Fantasy and Science Fiction*, October, November, and December, 1956), Doubleday, 1957.

Citizen of the Galaxy (originally serialized in *Astounding Science Fiction*, September, October, November, and December, 1957), Scribner, 1957.

Methuselah's Children (originally serialized in *Astounding Science Fiction*, July, August, and September, 1941), revised, Gnome Press, 1958.

Have Space Suit—Will Travel (originally serialized in *Magazine of Fantasy and Science Fiction*, August, September, and October, 1958), Scribner, 1958.

Starship Troopers (originally serialized as "Starship Soldier" in *Magazine of Fantasy and Science Fiction*, October and November, 1959), Putnam, 1959.

Stranger in a Strange Land, Putnam, 1961, revised and uncut edition with preface by wife, Virginia Heinlein, 1990.

Podkayne of Mars: Her Life and Times (originally serialized in *Worlds of If*, November, 1962, January and March, 1963), Putnam, 1963.

Glory Road (originally serialized in *Magazine of Fantasy and Science Fiction*, July, August, and September, 1963), Putnam, 1963.

Farnham's Freehold (originally serialized in *If*, July, August, and October, 1964), Putnam, 1964.

Three by Heinlein (contains *The Puppet Masters*, *Waldo*, and *Magic, Inc.*), Doubleday, 1965, published in England as *A Heinlein Triad*, Gollancz, 1966.

A Robert Heinlein Omnibus, Sidgwick & Jackson, 1966.

The Moon Is a Harsh Mistress (originally serialized in *If*, December, 1965, January, February, March, and April, 1966), Putnam, 1966.

I Will Fear No Evil (originally serialized in *Galaxy*, July, August, October, and December, 1970), Putnam, 1973.

Time Enough for Love: The Lives of Lazarus Long, Putnam, 1973.

The Notebooks of Lazarus Long (excerpted from *Time Enough for Love*), Putnam, 1978.

The Number of the Beast, Fawcett, 1980.

Friday, Holt, 1982.

Job: A Comedy of Justice, Ballantine, 1984.

The Cat Who Walks through Walls: A Comedy of Manners, Putnam, 1985.

To Sail beyond the Sunset: The Life and Loves of Maureen Johnson, Being the Memoirs of a Somewhat Irregular Lady, Putnam, 1987.

SHORT STORY COLLECTIONS

The Man Who Sold the Moon, Shasta, 1950.

The Green Hills of Earth, Shasta, 1951.

Assignment in Eternity, Fantasy Press, 1953.

The Menace from Earth, Gnome Press, 1959.

The Unpleasant Profession of Jonathon Hoag, Gnome Press, 1959, published as *6 x H,* Pyramid Publications, 1962.

The Worlds of Robert A. Heinlein, Ace Books, 1966.

The Past through Tomorrow: Future History Stories, Putnam, 1967.

The Best of Robert Heinlein, 1939-1959, two volumes, edited by Angus Wells, Sidgwick & Jackson, 1973.

Destination Moon, Gregg, 1979.

Expanded Universe: The New Worlds of Robert A. Heinlein, Ace Books, 1980.

SCREENPLAYS

(With Rip Van Ronkel and James O'Hanlon) *Destination Moon* (based on *Rocket Ship Galileo;* produced by George Pal/Eagle Lion, 1950), edited by David G. Hartwell, Gregg Press, 1979.

(With Jack Seaman) *Project Moonbase,* Galaxy Pictures/Lippert Productions, 1953.

Also author of scripts for television and radio programs.

OTHER

(Contributor) Lloyd Arthur English, editor, *Of Worlds Beyond: The Science of Science Fiction,* Fantasy Press, 1947.

(Author of preface) *Tomorrow, the Stars* (anthology), Doubleday, 1952.

(With others) *The Science Fiction Novel: Imagination and Social Criticism,* edited by Basil Davenport, Advent, 1959.

(Author of preface) Daniel O. Graham, *High Frontier: A Strategy for National Survival,* Pinnacle Books, 1983.

Grumbles from the Grave (letters), edited by V. Heinlein, Ballantine, 1989.

Robert A. Heinlein Requiem (collection of fiction and nonfiction), edited by Yoji Kondo, Tor Books, 1992.

Take Back Your Government: A Practical Handbook for the Private Citizen Who Wants Democracy to Work, Baen, 1992.

Trump Royale (travel), Putnam, 1992.

Also author of engineering report, *Test Procedures for Plastic Materials Intended for Strucural and*

Semi-Structural Aircraft Uses, 1944. Contributor to anthologies and to the *Encyclopaedia Britannica.* Contributor of over 150 short stories and articles, some under pseudonyms, to *Saturday Evening Post, Analog, Galaxy, Vertex, Astounding Science Fiction,* and others.

Heinlein's manuscripts are kept at the University of California, Santa Cruz.

■ Adaptations

The television series *Tom Corbett: Space Cadet,* which aired between 1951 and 1956, was based on Heinlein's novel, *Space Cadet;* television, radio, and film rights to many of Heinlein's works have been sold; *Starship Troopers* was the basis for a military simulation board game.

■ Sidelights

Robert Heinlein was a major figure in science fiction from the late 1930s until his death in 1988. Heinlein's innovative ideas and stylistic approach earned him great popularity with both his readers and his peers, yet perhaps his most significant contribution to the genre was, according to Peter R. Weston in *Contemporary Novelists,* "in *attitudes.* In this respect he is responsible more than any other for establishing the methods and traditions of modern science fiction." Alfred Bester voiced similar feelings in *Publishers Weekly,* stating, "The one author who has raised science fiction from the gutter of pulp space opera . . . to the altitude of original and breathtaking concepts is Robert A. Heinlein."

Heinlein's childhood was spent in Missouri. He was born in the small town of Butler, but he grew up in Kansas City, along with six brothers and sisters. Heinlein credits his grandfather, whom he once called "a horse and buggy doctor," with strongly influencing him. According to Heinlein, other influences were his "parents and six siblings and everything I have seen, touched, eaten, endured, heard, and read." Heinlein's interest in science fiction began early, when as a youngster he read authors such as Jules Verne, H. G. Wells, and Edgar Rice Burroughs, as well as stories in *Argosy* magazine.

Heinlein graduated from high school in 1924 and attended the University of Missouri for one year before he joined the military. Heinlein was accepted by the U.S. Naval Academy in Annapolis, Maryland, where he was given an appointment with the help of Senator James Reed. So, in 1925, Heinlein followed in one of his older brother's footsteps and began a career in the Navy. He graduated from the Academy in 1929 and was commissioned aboard the *U.S.S. Lexington*, eventually becoming a gunnery specialist. Heinlein also served on the *U.S.S. Roper* as a gunnery officer. When he developed tuberculosis, however, the Navy insisted that he retire from active duty, which he did in 1934. Heinlein was bitterly disappointed, and told Curt Suplee in the *Washington Post*: "I write stories for money. What I wanted to be was an admiral."

Heinlein then attended the University of California, Los Angeles, to study mathematics and physics, but his health prevented him from completing his courses. To augment his small pension, Heinlein tried various careers, including silver mining, selling real estate, and politics. None of these were successful, however, and he was forced to find another way to pay the bills.

The Heinlein-Campbell Collaboration

In fact, Heinlein's first storywriting experience was motivated by the simple reason that he needed to pay the mortgage on his house. As his widow, Virginia Heinlein, explained in *Grumbles from the Grave*, Heinlein found an ad for a story contest in a science fiction magazine and thought it would be a good way to make some money quickly. After he had written "Lifeline" in 1939, about a man who invented a machine that could tell the exact moment of a person's death, he felt it was better than pulp magazine fiction and tried to sell it to a popular mainstream magazine, *Colliers*. When *Colliers* rejected the story, he sent it to John W. Campbell, the editor of *Astounding Science Fiction*. Campbell paid Heinlein seventy dollars for "Lifeline," more than the original magazine, *Thrilling Wonder Stories*, had offered as the prize for the contest.

Heinlein would enjoy a long, fruitful association with *Astounding Science Fiction*. The working relationship between Campbell and Heinlein developed into an excellent and profitable one for Heinlein. Heinlein sent so many stories to Campbell that were accepted for *Astounding Science Fiction* that he was asked to create several pseudonyms, so his byline would not appear twice in one issue. In fact, over a three year period Heinlein published twenty-eight stories, all but four of them appearing in *Astounding Science Fiction* or *Unknown Worlds*, another periodical edited by Campbell. Joseph Patrouch, writing in the *Dictionary of Literary Biography*, commented on the relationship between writer and editor: "Through Campbell's editorship and Heinlein's innovation, the face of science fiction was changed radically." Frank Robinson, in a *Locus* obituary, stated that Heinlein's two-part serial "If This Goes On—," published in 1940, "was to go a long way

A native of Mars uncovers a plot that threatens the planet's human colonists in this 1949 thriller.

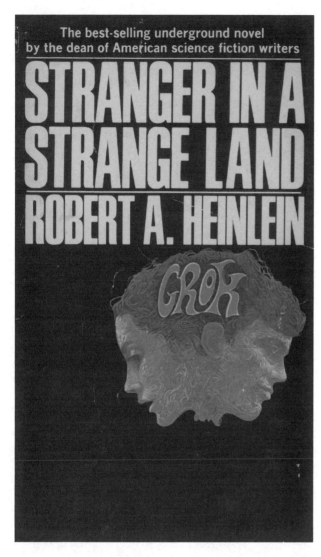

This controversial, Hugo Award-winning 1961 novel concerns Valentine Michael Smith, a human born and educated on Mars, who returns to Earth and finds himself an alien among men.

in establishing Heinlein's reputation. By now, it was apparent that no other writer in the history of science fiction had written about the future in such a way as to make it as believable as the present." In the *Los Angeles Times Book Review,* Theodore Sturgeon declared that Heinlein's "knowledge of the hard sciences and his gift for logical extrapolation inspired many beginning writers—and a good many already established hands—to knit fact and conjecture with a little more care and a great deal more literary quality than previously." Mainstream acceptance of Heinlein's work, and the science fiction genre, came when the *Saturday Evening Post* published several of his stories in the late 1940s.

In these stories, Heinlein centered on a particular type of science fiction—logically extrapolating current science into the near-future. Suplee declared that he "pioneered the extrapolative story format, in which present trends are projected into a plausible future [,and] couched his scientific problems in human terms." Some of Heinlein's stories predict developments years before they became fact, including the atom bomb, nuclear power plants, moving sidewalks, and the waterbed. Patrouch found that Heinlein used his scientific knowledge "to make the future believable, plausible, possible. . . . Heinlein's stories convinced a whole generation that man will really be able to do things he can only imagine now—and that generation grew up and sent Apollo to the moon."

When the United States entered World War II, Heinlein stopped writing. Instead, he worked as an aviation engineer in Philadelphia. The time spent working at the naval yards interrupted Heinlein's writing until 1947, a total of three years. It was during this time that Heinlein met his second wife, Virginia Gerstenfeld, in Philadelphia. After the war ended, Heinlein divorced his then-wife, Leslyn Macdonald, married Virginia, and began writing again, taking his work a step further by publishing novels.

Adventures in Space

Heinlein's earliest novels explored the conquest of space. His debut novel, *Rocket Ship Galileo,* (1947) concerns a trip to the moon, and others such as *Red Planet* (1949) and *Farmer in the Sky* (1950) address colonizing nearby planets. Succeeding works like *Have Space Suit—Will Travel* (1958) and *Tunnel in the Sky* (1955) take readers deeper into the galaxy. Robinson believed that Heinlein's most significant work during these early years was *Methuselah's Children.* The novel was serialized in *Astounding Science Fiction* in 1941, republished in 1958, and introduced a number of memorable characters who would appear in later works, such as the Howard Families and Lazarus Long. According to Robinson, "the themes of *Methuselah's Children* foreshadowed all his later philosophical novels."

Heinlein's popularity can be traced in some measure to the optimism his works displayed about humankind's ability to settle the galaxy. Williamson described Heinlein's attitude toward

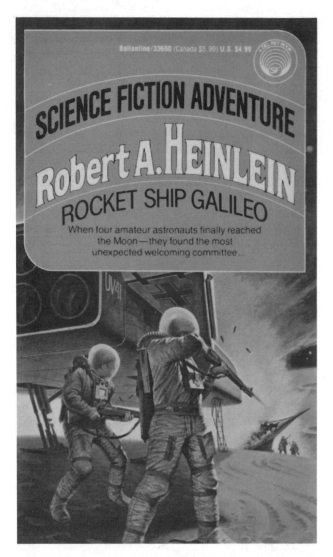

After building their own rocket ship, four men travel to the moon, unaware of the dangers that await them, in this 1947 adventure.

humanity as "dogged faith." Williamson also wrote that Heinlein was "no blind optimist, he is very much aware of evil days to come. His future worlds are often oppressively misruled, pinched by hunger, and wasted by war. Yet his heroes are always using science and reason to solve problems, to escape the prison of Earth, to seek and build better worlds."

At the time, Heinlein's novels were considered suitable for juvenile audiences, although H. Bruce Franklin, writing in *Robert A. Heinlein: America as Science Fiction*, claimed that "there is no clear demarcation of Heinlein's 'juvenile' fiction" from his adult fiction. One successful aspect of Heinlein's writing for young people, as for adults,

is the care he takes to not underrate his readers. Heinlein once explained: "When an editor assigned me the task of writing a juvenile novel, I entered the field with determination not to 'write down' to children." Jack Williamson found that Heinlein managed to meet this goal. Williamson stated in *Robert A. Heinlein* that the author's "main characters are young, the plots move fast, and the style is limpidly clear; but he never insults the reader's intelligence." The fact that many of Heinlein's novels were republished for an adult audience further shows that his work cannot be easily categorized. H. H. Holmes in the *New York Herald Tribune Book Review* observed that Heinlein's juvenile novels "stand so far apart from even their best competitors as to deserve a separate classification."

While Heinlein was busy publishing novels and short stories, he also worked on a television series, *Tom Corbett: Space Cadet,* based on his novel, *Space Cadet* (1948). He also wrote the screenplay and served as technical advisor for the film *Destination Moon,* which Weston described as "the first serious *and* commercially successful space flight film."

A New Direction

During the late 1950s, Heinlein's work changed direction, and he began writing more for adult audiences. His novels began to focus on ideas, on changes in society, and how individuals are affected by society, rather than on heroic adventures in alien places. The turning point was his novel *Starship Troopers* (1959), about a militaristic society; Patrouch noted the author's "intellectual kinship with H.G. Wells appears in the theme of the novel: the idea that common men must be guided and guarded by a competent elite." *Starship Troopers* was considered so controversial at the time that Scribner's rejected it, even though they had published many of Heinlein's works. Critics accused the novel of being fascistic, but Dennis E. Showalter in *Extrapolation* argued that the society portrayed lacked the "common benchmarks of fascism." The military society, engaged in constant war with the Bugs, a spider-like alien race, had no "ruling party, [no] secret police, [no] charismatic leader, [nor] an official ideology," explained Showalter. Despite the controversy, *Starship Troopers* won Heinlein his second Hugo Award.

Heinlein's next novel was no less controversial and became his best known work. *Stranger in a Strange Land* (1961) won Heinlein another Hugo Award, in part because Heinlein took science fiction into new territory. As Richard E. Nicholls in the *New York Times Book Review* reported, Heinlein explained to his agent, Lurton Blassingame, "I believe that I have dreamed up a really new S-F idea, a hard thing to do these days." The story of a human raised on Mars by Martians, then brought to Earth, *Stranger in a Strange Land* provided Heinlein the opportunity to examine and critique contemporary society. He described Valentine Michael Smith, the main character, in this way: "Absolutely everything about Earth is strange to him . . . its orientations, motives, pleasures,

A case of mistaken identity forces a former military man to travel through other dimensions in this 1985 work.

evaluations. On the other hand, he himself has received the education of a wise and subtle and very advanced—but completely nonhuman—race." recalled Heinlein's statement that the work attacked "the two biggest, fattest sacred cows" of Western society, "monotheism and monogamy."

David N. Samuelson wrote in *Critical Encounters: Writers and Themes in Science Fiction* that *Stranger in a Strange Land* was "in some ways emblematic of the Sixties. . . . It fit the iconoclastic mood of the time, attacking human folly under several guises, especially in the person or persons of the Establishment: government, the military, organized religion. By many of its readers, too, it was taken to advocate a religion of love, and of incalculable power, which could revolutionize human affairs and bring about an apocalyptic change, presumably for the better." Kurt Vonnegut, writing in the *New York Times Book Review,* defended the book, saying that detractors and critics disliked it because of "social prejudices, and that intellectual and esthetic standards have nothing to do with it."

An uncut version of *Stranger in a Strange Land,* the version Heinlein preferred, was released in 1990 by Virginia Heinlein. As his widow said, the 1961 edition was edited because it was "so different from what was being sold to the general public" at that time. Much of what was cut was sexual in nature. Reviewers generally believed that the original version was better, including Greg Frost of the *Washington Post Book Review* who stated that after making a page-by-page comparison of the two editions, "what's clear is that most of the editing was done to trim the fat." Other critics agreed, including science fiction writer Rudy Rucker, who wrote in the *Los Angeles Times Book Review,* "I always remembered *Stranger in a Strange Land* as a reasonably good science-fiction book. . . ." However, he did not praise the enlarged edition, commenting, "Ace/Putnam and Virginia Heinlein should have let the book be."

The Later Years

Much of Heinlein's writing after *Stranger in a Strange Land* also challenged societal mores. *The Moon Is a Harsh Mistress* portrays a lunar colony that revolts against its Terran Federation rulers. *I Will Fear No Evil* (1971) and *Time Enough for Love* (1973) examine ideas about love, marriage,

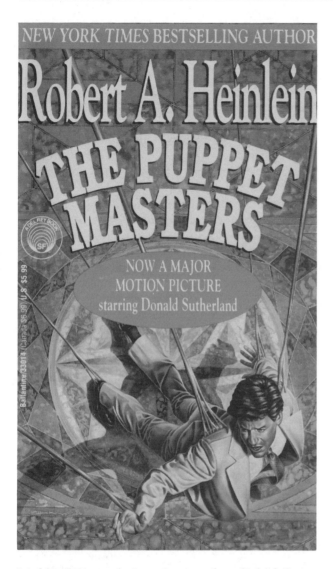

NEW YORK TIMES BESTSELLING AUTHOR

Robert A. Heinlein

THE PUPPET MASTERS

NOW A MAJOR
MOTION PICTURE
starring Donald Sutherland

In this 1951 novel, Sam Cavanaugh, a United States intelligence officer, finds himself at the center of a nationwide invasion by unknown forces.

and sex. In *I Will Fear No Evil* a dying man's brain is transferred into a woman's body, and he impregnates himself with his own sperm, which had been stored in a sperm bank. *Time Enough for Love* chronicles the adventures of the immortal Lazarus Long, including his numerous sexual affairs with members of his extended family. *To Sail beyond the Sunset: The Life and Loves of Maureen Johnson, Being the Memoirs of a Somewhat Irregular Lady*, Heinlein's final novel, was deemed "a perfect example of the 'new Heinlein,'" by a critic in the *West Coast Review of Books*. *To Sail beyond the Sunset*, which details the life--notably the sexual adventures--of Lazarus Long's mother, received decidedly mixed reviews. Tom Easton, in *Analog*, found the opening chapter ap-

pealing, then stated "the story quickly became a bore." However, the critic in the *West Coast Review of Books* called the work "a family reunion of sorts," and added "it is one of Heinlein's gifts to make such an event romp. . . ."

Several critics maintain that Heinlein's later works do not live up to the standards set by his novels from the 1940s and 1950s. "In science-fiction circles it is a truism that the early Heinlein was a much better writer than the late Heinlein," Rucker noted. One often-voiced complaint is that Heinlein's writing became contentious, preachy, even self-indulgent. Fred Lerner, writing in *Voice of Youth Advocates*, stated that Heinlein's "value as a prophet of libertarianism was diminished by the way he stacked the deck: Lazarus Long's immortality and Valentine Michael Smith's Martian superpowers made their actions and opinions irrelevant to the merely human condition."

After his death, Heinlein's *Grumbles from the Grave* was edited by his wife and published in 1989. It consists mostly of letters between him and his editors and agents, and reveals little about the private life of the writer. This does not diminish the book's value, wrote Gregory Feeley in the *Washington Post Book World,* because "Heinlein was never the kind of writer whose persona lay invisible behind his work. . . . Readers will turn to these letters confident that they already know the man who wrote them." Though Charles Solomon in the *Los Angeles Times Book Review* found the letters to show Heinlein as "a censorious arch-conservative," Feeley discovered a "sensitive, easily hurt man." Feeley adds, *"Grumbles from the Grave* is fascinating for anyone who reads science fiction, and essential for anyone interested in the genre's history."

Heinlein was plagued with various health problems in his later years, and spent less and less time writing. He spent his time travelling with his wife, including trips to Antarctica and China. Shortly after his death, in 1988, his wife journeyed to Washington, D. C. to receive the Distinguished Public Service Award on his behalf. She commented in *Grumbles from the Grave*, "My greatest regret is that he could not have known of that."

Heinlein's long career changed the entire genre of science fiction. Over forty million copies of his books in thirty different languages had sold at the time of his death. James Gunn, in his *Locus* obituary of Heinlein, said, "He pioneered the techniques of modern sf writing, the matter-of-fact acceptance of change and the economical ways of evoking that change in his stories, and he pioneered new fields in which sf could present itself: the slick magazine, books, the juvenile, film, and finally the bestseller. Like Moses he led sf into the promised land." Robert Silverberg, in a *Locus* obituary, called Heinlein "a great writer, an extraordinary man, a figure of high nobility; there was no one else remotely like him in our field. Within the science fiction field there were many who disagreed with him about many things, but there was no one who did not respect him, and there were a good many, myself included, who came close to revering him."

■ Works Cited

Bester, Alfred, "Robert Heinlein," *Publishers Weekly*, July 2, 1973, pp. 44-45.

Easton, Tom, review of *To Sail beyond the Sunset: The Life and Loves of Maureen Johnson, Being the Memoirs of a Somewhat Irregular Lady*, *Analog*, April, 1988, p. 177.

Feeley, Gregory, "Citizen of the Galaxy," *Washington Post Book World*, December 31, 1989, p. 4.

Franklin, H. Bruce, *Robert A. Heinlein: America as Science Fiction*, Oxford University Press, 1980, pp. 73-124.

Frost, Gregory, "Strangers from Paradise," *Washington Post Book World*, December 30, 1990.

Gunn, James, obituary of Robert A. Heinlein, *Locus*, June, 1988, p. 42.

Heinlein, Robert A., *Grumbles from the Grave*, edited by V. Heinlein, Ballantine, 1989.

Holmes, H. H., "Journey into Outer Space," *New York Herald Tribune Book Review*, Part II, November 18, 1956, pp. 3-4.

Lerner, Fred, "The Posthumous Heinlein," *Voice of Youth Advocates*, April, 1994, pp. 15-16.

Nicholls, Richard E., "The Biggest, Fattest, Sacred Cows," *New York Times Book Review*, December 9, 1990, p. 13.

Patrouch, Joseph, "Robert A. Heinlein," *Dictionary of Literary Biography*, Volume 8: *Twentieth Century American Science Fiction Writers*, Gale, 1981, pp. 208-28.

Robinson, Frank, "Robert A. Heinlein Dies," *Locus*, June, 1988, pp. B78-81.

Rucker, Rudy, "Grok and the World Groks with You," *Los Angeles Times Book Review*, December 23, 1990, p. 7.

Samuelson, David N., "'Stranger' in the Sixties: Model or Mirror?," *Critical Encounters: Writers and Themes in Science Fiction*, edited by Dick Riley, Ungar, 1978, pp. 144-75.

Showalter, Dennis E., "Heinlein's 'Starship Troopers': An Exercise in Rehabilitation," *Extrapolation*, May, 1975, pp. 113-24.

Silverberg, Robert, obituary of Robert A. Heinlein, *Locus*, June, 1988, p. 82.

Solomon, Charles, review of *Grumbles from the Grave*, *Los Angeles Times Book Review*, December 30, 1990, p. 10.

Sturgeon, Theodore, "Heinlein with a Capital S for Story," *Los Angeles Times Book Review*, June 20, 1982, p. 4.

Suplee, Curt, *Washington Post*, September 5, 1984.

Review of *To Sail beyond the Sunset: The Life and Loves of Maureen Johnson, Being the Memoirs of a Somewhat Irregular Lady*, West Coast Review of Books, Number 3, 1987, p. 30.

Vonnegut, Kurt, review of *Stranger in a Strange Land*, *New York Times Book Review*, December 9, 1990, p. 13.

Weston, Peter R., "Robert A(nson) Heinlein," *Contemporary Novelists*, 4th edition, edited by D. L. Kirkpatrick, St. Martin's, 1986, pp. 403-05.

Williamson, Jack, "Youth Against Space: Heinlein's Juveniles Revisited," *Robert A. Heinlein*, edited by Joseph D. Olander and Martin Harry Greenberg, Taplinger, 1978, pp. 15-31.

■ For More Information See

BOOKS

Aldiss, Brian W., *Billion Year Spree: The True History of Science Fiction*, Doubleday, 1973, pp. 269-74.

Atheling, William, Jr., *The Issue at Hand*, Advent, 1964, pp. 68-79.

Atheling, William, Jr., *More Issues at Hand*, Advent, 1970, pp. 51-58.

Contemporary Literary Criticism, Gale, Volume 1, 1973, Volume 3, 1975, Volume 8, 1978, Volume 14, 1980, Volume 26, 1983, Volume 55, 1989.

Downing, Nancy Bailey, *A Robert Heinlein Encyclopedia: A Complete Guide to the People, Places, and Things in the Fiction of Robert A. Heinlein*, Borgo Press, 1989.

Gunn, James, *Alternate Worlds: The Illustrated History of Science Fiction*, Prentice-Hall, 1975.

Gunn, James, *The Road to Science Fiction: From Heinlein to the Present*, New American Library, 1979.

Knight, Damon, *In Search of Wonder: Critical Essays on Science Fiction*, Advent, 1956, pp. 76-89.

Moskowitz, Sam, *Seekers of Tomorrow: Masters of Modern Science Fiction*, Ballantine, 1967, pp. 191-214.

Panshin, Alexei, *Heinlein in Dimension: A Critical Analysis*, Advent, 1968.

Rose, Lois, and Stephen Rose, *The Shattered Ring: Science Fiction and the Quest for Meaning*, John Knox, 1970.

Scholes, Robert, and Eric S. Rabkin, *Science Fiction: History, Science, Vision*, Oxford University Press, 1977, pp. 52-58.

Slusser, George Edgar, *Robert A. Heinlein: Stranger in His Own Land*, Borgo, 1976.

Slusser, George Edgar, *The Classic Years of Robert A. Heinlein*, Borgo, 1977.

Wollheim, Donald A., *The Universe Makers: Science Fiction Today*, Harper, 1971, pp. 99-102.

PERIODICALS

American Mercury, October, 1960.

Analog, May, 1954; September, 1964.

Author and Journalist, January, 1963.

CEA Critic, March, 1968.

Chicago Tribune, August 6, 1961.

Chicago Tribune Book World, August 17, 1980; January 7, 1984.

Christian Science Monitor, November 7, 1957.

Detroit News, July 25, 1982.

Extrapolation, December, 1970; spring, 1979; fall, 1979; fall, 1982.

Galaxy, February, 1952; December, 1966.

Journal of Popular Culture, spring, 1972.

Los Angeles Times, December 19, 1985.

Los Angeles Times Book Review, June 20, 1982; October 21, 1984.

Magazine of Fantasy and Science Fiction, June, 1956; November, 1961; March, 1971; October, 1980.

Modern Fiction Studies, spring, 1986.

National Observer, November 16, 1970.

National Review, March 26, 1963; November 16, 1970; December 12, 1980.

New Statesman, July 30, 1965.

New Worlds, June, 1962.

New Yorker, July, 1974.

New York Herald Tribune Book Review, November 28, 1954; November 13, 1955; May 12, 1962.

New York Times Book Review, October 23, 1949; November 14, 1954; December 29, 1957; December 14, 1958; January 31, 1960; March 23, 1975; August 24, 1980; September 14, 1980; July 4, 1982; November, 1984; December 22, 1985.

Observer, December 23, 1984.

Punch, August 25, 1965; November 22, 1967.

San Francisco Chronicle, November 8, 1959.

Saturday Review, November, 1958.

Science Fiction Review, November, 1970.

SF Commentary, May, 1976.

Spectator, June 3, 1966; July 3, 1977.

Speculation, August, 1969.

Times Literary Supplement, October 6, 1969; December 1, 1970; April 2, 1971; June 14, 1974.

Washington Post Book World, May 11, 1975; June 27, 1982.

■ Obituaries

Chicago Tribune, May 11, 1988.

Detroit News, May 10, 1988.

New York Times, May 10, 1988.

Time, May 23, 1988.

Times (London), May 11, 1988.

Washington Post, May 10, 1988.*

—Sketch by Hollis E. Helmeci

David Hockney

■ Personal

Born July 9, 1937, in Bradford, Yorkshire, England; son of Kenneth and Laura Hockney. *Education:* Attended Bradford College of Art, 1953-57; Royal College of Art, graduate (gold medal), 1962.

■ Addresses

Office—7508 Santa Monica Blvd., West Hollywood, CA 90046-6407.

■ Career

Artist. *Teaching appointments:* Maidstone College of Art, England, instructor, 1962; University of Iowa, Iowa City, lecturer, 1964; University of Colorado, Boulder, lecturer, 1965; University of California at Berkeley, lecturer, 1967; University of California at Los Angeles, lecturer, 1966, honorary chairman of drawing, 1980.

Exhibitions: (One-man shows) Kasmin Gallery, Ltd., London, 1963-89; Museum of Modern Art, New York City, 1964, 1968; Alan Gallery, New York City, 1964-67; Stedlijk Museum, Amsterdam,

1966; Whitworth Gallery, Manchester, England, 1969; (retrospective) Whitechapel Art Gallery, London, 1970; Andre Emmerich Gallery, New York City, 1970, 1972—; Galerie Springer, Berlin, 1970; Kunsthalle Bielefeld, 1971; Musée des Arts Decoratifs, Paris, 1974; Michael Walls Gallery, New York City, 1974; Galerie Claude Bernard, Paris, 1975; "Paper Pools," Andre Emmrich Gallery, and Warehouse Gallery, London, 1979; "Travels with Pen, Pencil, and Ink," Touring U.S.A., 1978-80, and Tate Gallery, London, 1980; (retrospective) Hayward Gallery, London, 1983; Museo Tamayo, Mexico City, 1984; L.A. Louver, 1986, 1989-90; Nishimura Gallery, Tokyo, 1986, 1989; Metropolitan Museum of Art, New York City, 1988; Los Angeles County Museum of Art, 1988; Tate Gallery, 1988.

Stage designs: Ubu Roi, Royal Court, London, 1966; *Rake's Progress,* Glyndebourne, England, 1975; *Magic Flute,* Glyndebourne, 1978; Parade Triple Bill, Stravinsky Triple Bill, Metropolitan Opera House, New York City, 1980-81; *Tristan and Isolde,* Los Angeles Music Center Opera, 1987; *Turandot,* Chicago Lyric Opera, 1992; *Die Frau ohne Schatten,* Covent Garden, 1992, and Los Angeles Music Center Opera 1993; San Francisco Opera, 1993.

■ Awards, Honors

Guiness award and first prize for etching, 1961; Gold Medal for drawing, Royal College of Art, 1962; Graphic prize, Paris Biennale, 1963; First prize, 8th International Exhibition of Drawings, Lugano, Italy, 1964; First prize, John Moores Exhibition, Liverpool,

England, 1967; German award of excellence, 1983; Kodak photography book award, 1984, for *Cameraworks;* First prize, International Center of Photography, New York City, 1985; Honorary degree, University of Aberdeen, 1988; Praemium Imperiale, Japan Art Association, 1989.

■ Writings

David Hockney by David Hockney, edited by Nikos Stangos, Thames & Hudson, 1976, 2nd edition, with introduction by Henry Geldzahler, Abrams, 1977.

Paper Pools, edited by Stangos, Abrams, 1980.

David Hockney: Looking at Pictures in a Book, Petersburg Press, 1981.

Cameraworks, including essay "True to Life," by Lawrence Weschler, Knopf, 1984.

Martha's Vineyard: My Third Sketchbook from the Summer of 1982 (facsimile reproduction), Abrams, 1985.

Hockney on Photography: Conversations with Paul Joyce, Harmony Books, 1988.

Picasso, Hanuman Books, 1990.

Hockney's Alphabet, written contributions edited by Stephen Spender, Faber & Faber, 1991, Random House, 1991.

That's The Way I See It, Chronicle Books, 1993.

Also author of introduction for *Draw: How to Master the Art,* by Jeffery Camp, Dorling Kindersley, 1994, and *Making It New: Collected Essays and Writings of Henry Geldzahler,* by Henry Geldzahler, Turtle Point Press, 1994.

ILLUSTRATOR

David Posner, *A Rake's Progress: A Poem in Five Sections,* Lion & Unicorn Press (London), 1962.

Six Fairy Tales from the Brothers Grimm, Petersburg Press (in association with the Kasmin Gallery; London), 1970.

William Hogarth, *A Rake's Progress,* translated into German by Alfred Hrdlicka, Oesterreichisches Museum fuer Angewandte Kunst (Vienna), 1971.

Wallace Stephens, *The Man with the Blue Guitar,* Petersburg Press, 1977.

Tor Seidler, *The Dulcimer Boy,* Viking, 1979.

Stephen Spender, *China Diary,* Abrams, 1982.

Horst Bienek, *Selected Poems: 1958-1988,* Unicorn Press, 1989.

COLLECTIONS

72 Drawings Chosen by the Artist, Cape, 1971.

18 Portraits by David Hockney, photographs by Malcolm Lubliner and Sidney B. Felsen, Gemini G.E.L. (Los Angeles), 1977.

David Hockney Prints, 1954-77, Petersburg Press, 1979.

Pictures by David Hockney, selected and edited by Stangos, Thames & Hudson, 1979, 2nd edition, Abrams, 1979.

David Hockney, 23 Lithographs, Tyler Graphics (New York), 1980.

David Hockney Photographs, Petersburg Press, 1982.

Hockney's Photographs, Arts Council of Great Britain, 1983.

Kasmin's Hockneys: 45 Drawings, Knoedler Gallery (London), 1983.

David Hockney fotografo, Alinari (Florence), 1983.

David Hockney in America, introduction by Christopher Finch, W. Beadleston (New York), 1983.

Hockney Posters, Harmony Books, 1983.

Photographs by David Hockney, edited by B. J. Bradley, Art Services International, 1986.

David Hockney: Etchings and Lithographs, text by Marco Livingstone, Thames & Hudson, 1988.

David Hockney: Graphics, Distributed Art Publishers, 1992.

Off the Wall, Pavilion Books (London), 1994, published in the United States as *David Hockney: Poster Art,* Chronicle Books, 1994.

EXHIBIT CATALOGS

Paintings, Prints, and Drawings, 1960-1970 (Whitechapel Art Gallery exhibit, 1970), Boston Book and Art, 1970.

David Hockney: tableau et dessins: Musée des arts decoratifs, Palais du Louvre, Pavillon de Marsan, 11 Octobre-9 Decembre 1974, Petersburg Press, 1974.

David Hockney: dessins et gravures, Galerie Claude Bernard, Paris, Avril 1975, introduction by Marc Fumaroli, Galerie Claude Bernard, 1975.

David Hockney: Prints and Drawings Circulated by the International Exhibits Foundation, Washington, D.C., 1978-1980, International Exhibits Foundation, 1978.

Travels with Pen, Pencil, and Ink (first major Hockney exhibition to tour North America), introduction by Edmund Pillsbury, Petersburg Press, 1978.

David Hockney: Sources and Experiments: An Exhibition Held at the Sewall Gallery, Rice University, September 7 to October 15, 1982, text by Esther de Vecsey, Sewall Art Gallery, 1982.

David Hockney: Frankfurter Kunstverein, Steinernes Haus am Romerberg, Frankfurt am Main, 15.3.-24.4. 1983, introduction by Peter Weiermair, Der Verein (Frankfurt), 1983.

Hockney Paints the Stage, text by Martin Friedman with contributions by John Cox and others, Walker Art Center (Minneapolis), 1983.

Photographs by David Hockney: Organized and Circulated by the International Exhibitions Foundation, Washington, D.C., 1986-88, introduction by Mark Haworth-Booth and essay by Hockney, International Exhibits Foundation, 1986.

David Hockney: A Retrospective, Organized by Maurice Tuchman and Stephanie Barron, Los Angeles County Museum of Art, 1988.

David Hockney: Fax Cuadros, Centro Cultural/ Arte Contemporaneo (Mexico), 1990.

■ Sidelights

"No other English artist has ever been as popular in his own time, with as many people, in as many places, as David Hockney," Robert Hughes asserted in *Time.* Throughout Hockney's career his reputation as a serious artist has depended on the attention of critics, but his versatility and willingness to reveal his artistic processes have earned him admirers around the world. Like Picasso, Hockney refuses to limit himself to a single discipline or style, and has continually expanded his practice to include engraving, painting, illustration, photography, graphic design, and stage design. Hockney has also filled the role of critic and theorist, and his writings have found a significant readership. It is Hockney's desire to engage his audience in narrative, both as a visual artist and writer, that underscores his success. Unlike the work of many of his counterparts, Hockney's art is primarily figurative (that is, representational). Hockney's narratives, then, begin in pictures which tell stories, and are continued in the artist's ready explanation of his intentions. The demonstrative relationship between image and narrative is characteristic of Hockney's most highly regarded work. Hockney, the artist, captures his viewer's imagination as a storyteller.

David Hockney was born in Bradford, Yorkshire, England. He attended Bradford Grammar School and as a teenager entered the Bradford College of Art. When

Hockney completed this work, entitled *Iowa,* during his tenure as a lecturer at the University of Iowa.

he became a student at the progressive Royal College of Art in London in 1959, Hockney's skills as a draftsman were already firmly established. During these student years, Hockney experimented with the most visible styles of the time, Abstract Expressionism (which demanded non-representational, purely visual expression) and Pop (which appropriated the imagery and reproduction techniques of mass media). In 1960 Hockney viewed his first Picasso retrospective, and in the same year, according to Kay Larson in *New York,* invented his singular manner of drawing. Larson described the typical Hockney drawing as "a cross between Saul Steinberg and Dr. Seuss, though the more common references are Francis Bacon, English Pop, and modern magazine illustration." Hockney's early influences also included classmates from the Royal College who later gained considerable reputations, including the American painter R. B. Kitaj.

First Major Exhibit

In 1961 Hockney was chosen to participate in an exhibit titled "Young Contemporaries." The show was immediately recognized as a turning point in contemporary British art, and is today viewed as something of a landmark. Remarkably, Hockney

Hockney's interest in the interplay between light and dark is seen in this 1967 work, *A Lawn Being Sprinkled.*

and several of the artists selected were still students when the show was mounted. Nearly thirty years later, *Nation* critic Arthur C. Danto opened his review of a major Hockney retrospective with an analysis of a painting included in "Young Contemporaries." *The Most Beautiful Boy* combines obscure imagery at the canvas margins, such as an Alka Seltzer label, with a rough portrait of a figure wearing what appear to be a woman's nightclothes. As is usual in early Hockney, text is also forced into the space surrounding the figure, adding an articulate layer of meaning to the work. Danto noted that in 1961 British critic Lawrence Alloway declared that Hockney's imagery was fundamentally urban and likened his use of text to graffiti. *The Most Beautiful Boy* and its companion paintings were presumed to demonstrate a new concern for the depiction of the city.

Without denying the presence of the urban environment in these works, Danto contended that *The Most Beautiful Boy*, and Hockey's art in general, is more personal. The sexual ambiguity of the boy is taken as reference to Hockney's homosexuality (an issue which the artist has dealt with frankly in other works), while the symbolism and the alternating crude and delicate aspects of the portrait are understood as expressions of desire. "It is a witty and confessional piece of work," Danto proclaimed, "a declaration of love, and sexually explicit, . . . and it engages the viewer in the artist's own emotional affairs, as if he wore his heart on his canvas." This was unique in 1961, according to Danto, because Hockney's work was neither abstract nor pop, but full of people he had actually seen, interiors he observed, and landscapes that might be located on a map. As a result, Hockney communicated something about the world, as well as something about his relationship to the objects of his affection. "Hockney's art is to be found between the work and its viewers," Danto declared, "a space curiously filled by the artist himself."

Upon graduating from the Royal College in 1962, Hockney became a popular personality, sporting large round-rimmed glasses and playboy clothes. In 1963 Hockney traveled to Los Angeles; he became a resident of the city a year later. During this period Hockney turned his attention to his new surroundings, and his paintings of the L.A. landscape are often credited with establishing the iconography of the city. While Hockney's observation of the intense light of Southern California was not always accurate, wrote Hughes, "he fixed other things—those pastel planes, insouciant scraggy palms, blank panes of glass, and blue pools full of wreathing reflections and brown bodies." Hockney's most frequently seen works from this period are paintings of swimming pools, where the surface of the water is treated as if it held spiritual implications for the culture of Los Angeles. Hockney evoked meaning from these oases of water in the middle of the desert, using the swimming pool as a representation of the California lifestyle.

Los Angeles Paintings

A Bigger Splash, painted in 1967, utilizes the pool and the pool deck as a landscape. A diving board cantilevers from the front of the picture into the scene and out over the pool, where the surface of the water has just been broken, the splash and spray frozen in the air. With the exception of the taught energy of the splash, the scene is curiously still: the light is intense and uninflected, an empty deck chair faces the pool, and the diving board is flat, without indication of the shock of the implied dive. Noting the importance of this work, *Time*'s Hughes called *A Bigger Splash* "the quintessential L.A, painting . . . a radiant acceptance of Now—an eye blink, picture perfect."

Portrait of an Artist (Pool with Two Figures) painted in 1972, is among the most naturalistic of the pool paintings. In addition to the quality of the rendering, the ten foot by seven foot canvas lends a certain life-size authority to the figures. In the painting a man swims underwater, from left to right, arms ahead of him and body fully extended, toward the edge of a pool. The second figure, also male, stands at the pool edge fully clothed, facing the swimmer and peering down into the pool. In the background the green hillsides of Southern California momentarily frame the scene, then overlap into the distance. In a *Film Comment* article, David Thomson asserted that the painting's power springs from the visual relationship of the figures: the standing figure waits unnoticed, that is, unseen. The painting depicts the moment before the revelatory moment when the swimmer surfaces and confronts the watcher. "That is how it is such a study of yearning," Thomson concluded, "that is why there is a feeling of fragility or danger in this secluded Eden up above L.A."

American Collectors (Fred and Marcia Weisman), from 1968, presents another facet of Hockney's study of Los Angeles. Here two figures stand on opposite sides of a courtyard containing a few outdoor pieces from their art collection. Fred is presented in profile, staring intently in the direction of Marcia, who faces the viewer. Thomson pointed out the similarity of this situation to the setup in *Portrait of an Artist (Pool with Two Figures)*, but here "one figure has turned to look at the other, while the other resolutely fails to notice the attention." In his comments on *American Collectors*, Hughes noted that Marcia's features are slightly distorted to resemble a totem in the background and that paint is dribbling from Fred's hand, as if the couple have actually become artifacts in the process of collecting art.

Experiments with Photography

Hockney continued to paint into the 1970s, but in the second half of the decade his production

This 1973 still-life, entitled *Sun,* is part of Hockney's "The Weather" series.

dropped precipitously. During this period Hockney was approached by the Glyndebourne Opera about doing stage design for a production of Igor Stravinsky's *The Rake's Progress*. "To begin with, the music seemed very difficult," Hockney recalled in *That's the Way I See It*. "I listened and there was probably very little I got.... But slowly the music came to me. The more I listened, the more beautiful it became, and I saw how exciting it was." Hockney proposed a sequence of sets inspired by the engravings of William Hogarth, the eighteenth-century originator of *The Rake's Progress*, and a series of prints with the same title that Hockney had done in the early sixties. Cross-hatching became the central motif of the designs, a stylized version of the technique Hogarth employed in his engravings. The production received wide acclaim, and Hockney has continued to design sets for a variety of opera companies in England and the United States.

It was during his reprieve from painting that Hockney began to explore photography as a vehicle for his art. In Lawrence Weschler's essay "True to Life" (orginally published in *New Yorker* and later as a preface to Hockney's *Cameraworks*), Weschler illuminated Hockney's practice of using photographs as an aid to memory while painting. Some of these photographs had even been assembled for an exhibition at the Pompidou Center in Paris in 1982. Despite its value as a recording device, Hockney maintained what he characterized as an ambivalent relationship to photography. "It's not that I despised photography *ever*," Hockney told Weschler, "it's just that I distrusted the claims that were made on its behalf—claims as to its greater reality or authenticity." That suspicion of the limitations of photography launched Hockney on a series of photographic experiments that resulted in the photocollages presented in *Cameraworks*.

Initially, Hockney combined dozens of polaroid photos in a grid; the individual photos created a composite image, with several points of view and locations in time represented. As the work progressed, the grids gave way to compositions which adapted to the forms of the subject matter: sprawling collages of the Grand Canyon, strongly vertical arrangements showing a telephone pole bursting from the ground in L.A., portraits which present several views and facial expressions. "There is, in some of these collages, as in some of Hockney's finest pencil drawings, a remarkable psychological acuity at work," Weschler declared. "In the [Stephen] Spender combine, for example,

the face itself develops out of six squares—three tall and two wide—those aspects to the left are alert, inquisitive and probing; to the right, they are tired, weary, resigned. Spender, Hockney seems to be suggesting, is both." In another collage, *The Scrabble Game* from 1983, Hockney incorporates an element from his earlier work, creating a fragmented narrative with the words played on the scrabble board.

According to Larson in *New York*, Hockney's photography allowed him to resume painting with a new sense of perspective that avoided the "claustrophobic intimacy" of some of his earlier paintings. Larson found Hockney's narratives more "systematic" following the photographic experiments as well, and pointed to the mural *Mulholland Drive: The Road to the Studio* as evidence. The intense colors used to depict the vegetation of the California hills are reminiscent of the Fauvist landscapes painted by Derain and Matisse, while the road is sinuous line running up the center of the composition. In *That's the Way I See It* Hockney offered this insight on the painting: "When you look at *Mulholland Drive*—and drive is not the name of the road, but the act of driving—your eye moves around the painting at about the same speed as a car drives along the road." Despite the stylization of images in the painting, Hockney maintained that the work is the result of intense observation, and that the presentation of the vegetation and color, especially, are more realistic than they might initially seen.

Publication of *That's the Way I See It*

Since he resumed painting, Hockney has continued to experiment with perception and has explored Cubism as well as other styles. While his concerns have changed since the early days of his celebrity, most notably with respect to naturalism, Hockney continues to challenge audiences with work of dedicated craftsmanship. Hockney's reflections on his work and his interests in new technology, such as photo reproduction, are collected in *That's the Way I See It*. This "lively, unpretentious memoir," as a *Publishers Weekly* reviewer described it, presents the text of recorded and unrecorded conversations between David Hockney and Nikos Stangos. Much of this book is devoted to Hockney's "break with naturalism," as well as his explorations of spatial perception and new printing or reproduction techniques, which include faxing and laser color printing. During the five

Hockney examines complex emotional relationships in this 1975 work, *My Parents and Myself*.

years of discussions between Stangos and Hockney presented in *That's the Way I See It*, Hockney recalls his travels through China and Egypt, reflects about the death of his father, and expresses his thoughts about his own loss of hearing. Hockney also explains the production of his acclaimed opera sets for *Tristan and Isolde* and *The Magic Flute*. Throughout the book, drawings, paintings, and collages illustrate Hockney's creative process.

While Stephen Galloway in the *Los Angeles Times Book Review* found the work to be repetitive at times, he felt that "it is impossible not to be drawn" to Hockney and concluded that the artist's "endless questioning and genuine delight in all the processes of creation make it difficult not to admire him." In the *Times Literary Supplement*, Rosemary Hill asserted that *That's the Way I See It* is "the friendliest and most enjoyable book about art since *David Hockney by David Hockney* appeared in 1976." "Readers are in for an insightful journey," exclaimed *Booklist*'s Alice Joyce. In *That's the Way I See It*, Hockney touches the subject of AIDS as he discusses death." The first friend of mine to die was Joe MacDonald. . . . He was the first person I knew to become ill with AIDS, just after 1981." Hockney went on to describe MacDonald's death of pneumonia and related, "Then there were more deaths, each person dying in a different way."

In the early 1990s, Hockney contributed his talent and reputation to an AIDS fundraising project with editor Stephen Spender. The result, *Hockney's Alphabet*, is a "picture book for adults of the highest order" as Ray Olson in *Booklist* described it. Each of the twenty-six letters of the alphabet is rendered in Hockney's unique style and accompanied by short literary pieces written by respected contemporary writers, including Joyce Carol Oates, John Updike, Patrick Leigh Fermor, Susan Sontag, and Ian McEwan. Hockney's letters, according to David Bryant in *Library Journal*, are "bright, cheery, surprising mini-artworks." One hundred percent of the net proceeds of *Hockney's Alphabet* were promised to the fight against AIDS.

While Hockney continues to live in the Los Angeles area, his reputation as an artist reaches around the world. He has also worked in variety of locations, particularly as a stage designer, and his travels are a source of inspiration and influence. Hockney's willingness to experiment, his craftsmanship, and his unfailing ability to evoke narrative through the image, have expanded the importance of the figure, especially the human figure, in contemporary art. Hockney expressed his commitment to the figure in the form of a question posed to Weschler: ". . . Cezanne's apples are lovely and very special," Hockney confessed, "but what finally can compare to the image of another human being?"

■ Works Cited

Bryant, David, review of *Hockney's Alphabet*, *Library Journal*, March 15, 1992, p. 86.

Danto, Arthur C., "Art: David Hockney," *Nation*, July 30/August 6, 1988, pp. 104-7.

Galloway, Stephen, review of *That's the Way I See It*, *Los Angeles Times Book Review*, December 26, 1993, p. 9.

Hill, Rosemary, review of *That's the Way I See It*, *Times Literary Supplement*, November 19, 1993, p. 8.

Hockney, David, *That's the Way I See It*, Chronicle Books, 1993.

Hughes, Robert, "Giving Success a Good Name," *Time*, June 20, 1988, pp. 76-79.

Joyce, Alice, review of *That's the Way I See It*, *Booklist*, January 1, 1994, p. 799.

Larson, Kay, "Art: The Fine Line," *New York*, June 20, 1988, pp. 62-63.

Olson, Ray, review of *Hockney's Alphabet*, *Booklist*, February 1, 1992, p. 1001.

Review of *That's the Way I See It*, *Publishers Weekly*, October 11, 1993, p. 76.

Thomson, David, "Hockney's Hollywood," *Film Comment*, July-August 1989, pp. 53-65.

Weschler, Lawrence, "True to Life," introductory essay in *Cameraworks*, Knopf, 1984.

■ For More Information See

PERIODICALS

Library Journal, September 15, 1993, p. 38.

Publishers Weekly, February 5, 1988, p. 80.

Times Literary Supplement, November 22, 1991, p. 19.

U.S. News and World Report, September 25, 1989, p. 18.

—*Sketch by David P. Johnson*

Felice Holman

book citation, 1979, for *The Murderer*; best book for young adults citation, 1985, for *The Wild Children*; Child Study Association Book Award, 1991, for *Secret City, U.S.A.*

■ Personal

Born October 24, 1919, in New York, NY; daughter of Jac C. (an engineering consultant) and Celia (an artist; maiden name, Hotchner) Holman; married Herbert Valen, April 13, 1941; children: Nanine Elizabeth. *Education:* Syracuse University, B.A., 1941.

■ Addresses

Home—Del Mar, CA. *Office*—c/o Charles Scribner's Sons, 866 Third Ave., New York, NY, 10022.

■ Career

Poet and writer of books for children and young adults, 1960—. Worked as an advertising copywriter in New York City, 1944–50.

■ Awards, Honors

Austrian Book Prize, Lewis Carroll Shelf Award, best book for young adults citation, and American Library Association (ALA) notable book citation, all 1978, all for *Slake's Limbo*; ALA notable

■ Writings

YOUNG ADULT NOVELS

Slake's Limbo, Scribner, 1974.
The Murderer, Scribner, 1978.
The Wild Children, Scribner, 1983.
Secret City, U.S.A., Scribner, 1990.

JUVENILE NOVELS

Elisabeth, The Birdwatcher, illustrated by Erik Blegvad, Macmillan, 1963.
Elisabeth, The Treasure Hunter, illustrated by Erik Blegvad, Macmillan, 1964.
Silently, the Cat and Miss Theodosia, illustrated by Harvey Dinnerstein, Macmillan, 1965.
Victoria's Castle, illustrated by Lillian Hoban, Norton, 1966.
Elisabeth and the Marsh Mystery, illustrated by Erik Blegvad, Macmillan, 1966.
Professor Diggins' Dragons, illustrated by Ib Ohlsson, Macmillan, 1966.
The Witch on the Corner, illustrated by Arnold Lobel, Norton, 1966.
The Cricket Winter, illustrated by Ralph Pinto, Norton, 1967.

The Blackmail Machine, illustrated by Victoria DeLarrea, Macmillan, 1968.

A Year to Grow, illustrated by Emily McCully, Norton, 1968.

The Holiday Rat and the Utmost Mouse, illustrated by Wallace Tripp, Norton, 1969.

Solomon's Search, illustrated by Mischa Richter, Norton, 1970.

The Future of Hooper Toote, illustrated by Gahan Wilson, Scribner, 1972.

The Escape of the Giant Hogstalk, illustrated by Ben Schecter, Scribner, 1974.

(With Nanine Valen) *The Drac: French Tales of Dragons and Demons,* illustrated by Stephen Walker, Scribner, 1975.

Terrible Jane, illustrated by Irene Trivas, Scribner, 1987.

POETRY

At the Top of My Voice and Other Poems, illustrated by Edward Gorey, Scribner, 1970.

I Hear You Smiling and Other Poems, illustrated by Lazlo Kubinyi, Scribner, 1973.

The Song in My Head, illustrated by James Spanfeller, Scribner, 1985.

■ **Adaptations**

Elisabeth and the Marsh Mystery was made into a short film; *Slake's Limbo* was produced as a TV movie under the title *The Runaway,* PBS.

■ **Sidelights**

It may be that Felice Holman is living her second life as a writer. That, at least, was the opinion expressed by Holman's aunt—a psychic—when Felice was born. Aunt Marie informed the author's family that she had had a message from "the other side" regarding young Felice. She was the reincarnation of Florence Marryat, a prolific if little-known novelist who lived in the 1800s.

Holman isn't sure whether she knew, when she first began to write as a child, that she was allegedly a reincarnated writer, and so turned to writing in a sort of self-fulfilling prophecy. And she's never been sure whether or not to believe the story, even though her Aunt Marie was well-regarded enough as a psychic to be a personal consultant to many of the movie stars of her day. Regardless of the truth, Holman grew up to be a respected—if less prolific author—in her own

right. While Marryat wrote some ninety novels as well as short stories and plays, Holman has published twenty novels for children and young adults and three books of poetry. "If I don't think of Florence," Holman writes in an autobiographical essay for the *Something About the Author Autobiography Series* (*SAAS*), "I usually feel quite satisfied with my work. Sometimes I think the reward for (Marryat's) industry and accomplishment may be the relatively easy pace her soul may be enjoying in her present incarnation—*if* that's the case."

Whether Holman was invested with the reincarnated soul of a writer or simply came to writing of her own account, she began practicing her life's work when she was only eight years old. Her first completed work was a book of poetry that was illustrated by her mother, an artist who had ex-

After his family is taken away by the police, teen-aged Alex joins a gang of other young people who forage the streets for survival.

hibited her work in galleries in New York and Washington. Even at this tender age the signs of her talent were evident. "My poems," Holman writes in her *SAAS* entry, "were strongly influenced by Robert Louis Stevenson, and not bad."

Holman's childhood was a happy one filled with love, laughter, and poetry. She grew up in a comfortable colonial-style house in Flushing, Long Island, then a small, quiet suburb. Quite by accident, the house provided Holman with her first writing studio. It was a tiny sun room that sat above the porticoed front stoop of the house, overlooking a street lined with maple trees. Because it was freezing in the winter and hot in the summer, none of the other family members cared to spend much time there. More or less by default, it became Holman's special place, a place to sit and stare out the window, fall into reverie, and write poetry. "Poetry sang in my head all the time," the author writes in her *SAAS* entry. "There was never any question of my feelings being suppressed: they were all spread out there on lined paper between covers of black and white marbled notebooks."

While Holman wrote poetry, the adults in her family undoubtedly worried about the Great Depression and its effects on her father's construction business. Times were hard, but her family made it through the Depression relatively unscathed. While others stood in soup lines and sold pencils on the street corners, Holman's family always had a roof over their heads and enough to eat.

Tall Tales: A Family Legacy

And always, in spite of the Depression, there was laughter. In her *SAAS* entry Holman notes that one of her earliest memories is of standing at the banister outside her bedroom, listening to the adults laugh until they were helpless. Their laughter stemmed from an apparently inborn ability on her mother's side to embellish stories until they passed from the realm of the factual into pure fantasy. "The story would start out to be the presentation of fact—something that had happened to the teller that day, something he or she had observed or overheard. The story, which might begin mildly, would then take off in directions that would enhance it, until it passed belief. It was the moment when everyone recognized that inven-

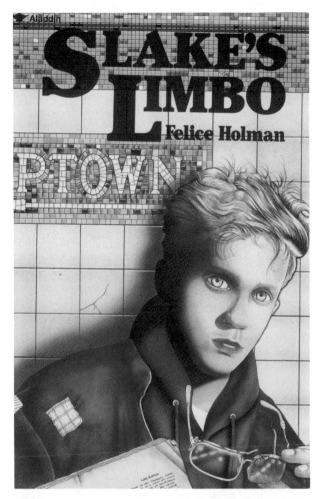

Slake tries to find a sense of balance in his life by running away and hiding in the New York subway system.

tion had taken over that the laughter would start to build," Holman writes in her *SAAS* entry. The process was called "Hotchenizing," after her mother's maiden name, Hotchner. For Holman, the freedom to invent "facts" was a joyous and liberating quality, and one that would eventually serve her well in her career as a novelist.

Holman attended both public and private schools as a child, and even spent one year at boarding school, when she was fifteen. Boarding school, it was thought, would help her overcome her shyness and uneasiness around strangers. Her parents also believed boarding school would accustom her to living away from home before attending college. It was, unfortunately, an unpleasant experience. In her *SAAS* entry, Holman describes the institution as "the exact opposite of a progressive school . . . (where) ninety girls uniformed in green poplin were kept to a strict regimen of nearly unrelenting dullness." As much as she disliked the school, though, the author's year there did serve two purposes. First, she met a teacher who was a poet who informed her of a poetry competition that could lead to publication in an anthology. Holman entered it and won, earning the distinction of being a published poet even before entering college. Second, the year provided her with material for a novella she wrote more than thirty years later, *A Year to Grow.*

Although her father hoped she would attend his university, Cornell, Holman opted to go to Syracuse University, a smaller school that she thought would better suit her shy personality. Knowing that she would eventually become some kind of writer, Holman at first majored in journalism. Before long, though, Holman realized that she did not have the drive, stamina, or thick skin that was required to become a successful newspaper reporter, and changed her major to English with a minor in journalism.

At Syracuse Holman met and fell in love with Herbert Valen, a journalism student. They were married the year Holman graduated. Shortly afterward, World War II began, and Herbert, who was in the army, was sent to England and then France. Holman moved to Washington D.C. and took a job as at the Office of War Information, hoping they could use her talents as a writer. Instead, she became a clerk-typist, a job for which she was not particularly well suited, being a poor typist and a terrible file clerk. After a year Holman moved to New York City and took a job as a fashion copywriter. Although she was successful enough to win several awards for her work, the author was still not satisfied with her job. "I had the feeling," she remembers in her *SAAS* entry, "that I was trying to make people long for things they might not be able to afford."

Holman continued to work as a fashion copywriter after Herbert returned from the war. The couple rented a tiny flat in New York City, and Herbert worked as a freelance journalist. To make ends meet, the couple did odd jobs, including putting together a neighborhood newspaper and writing promotional booklets for an advertising agency. Though their New York years were lean ones, Holman remembers them fondly. "For entertainment, we walked a lot—New York was one great show all the time—and went to museums,

the public library, five-cent cruises on the Staten Island Ferry. There was no fancy dining out, and we sat in the top balcony at the theater, but it was a wonderful time," she comments in her *SAAS* entry.

A Two-Typewriter Family

When their daughter Nanine was born, Holman and Valen moved from New York to Westport, Connecticut, where they spent many years, both working as writers. Valen eventually hooked up with the *New Yorker,* for whom he devised cartoon ideas, among other things. Holman and Valen were a two-typewriter family, with writing so much a part of their existence that when she was young, their daughter Nanine believed that typewriters were necessary to earn a living. (Nanine eventually carried on the family tradition, writing two books for children before settling into a career as a psychotherapist.)

The house in Westport was a small converted barn that was close to a mill pond and a marsh. The surrounding property was an excellent spot for bird watching, and the author and her daughter became so engrossed in the hobby that they considered themselves "bird people." Their attempts to feed the birds without also feeding all the neighborhood squirrels led to the invention of a bird feeder which, in turn, led to Holman's first book for children, *Elisabeth, the Birdwatcher.* Two more Elisabeth books followed, one of which, *Elisabeth and the Marsh Mystery,* was made into a short film.

With the Elisabeth books, Holman apparently found the perfect outlet for her talents. She continued to write children's novels over the next thirty years, sometimes taking her inspiration from personal experiences, sometimes from newspaper stories, and sometimes from ideas "that just seem to come out of my head like daydreams that settle themselves onto pages of a book," as she once commented.

Her earliest books are directed to younger children and middle-grade readers. *The Witch on the Corner*, like *A Year to Grow*, is one that was inspired by personal experience. The main character is based on a neighbor of Holman's in Westport. In her *SAAS* entry, the author describes the woman as "a mean, snappish person that didn't want you to admire her garden and certainly would not let you in." Holman took it from there, inventing a character named Miss Pinchon who has trouble relating to people but works wonders with the plants in her garden. After overhearing some neighborhood children refer to her as "a witch," Miss Pinchon decides that she must really be a witch, and that is the reason she has such terrible luck with people. She sets out to learn to fly and cast spells like a proper witch. One of the neighborhood children spies her trying to fly and is soon helping with the effort. Miss Pinchon never does learn to fly, and her shape-changing spells are doomed, too. Nevertheless, she manages to make friends with the neighborhood children, and all ends happily when it is decided that this witch works her magic on her wonderful garden. She is a witch after all—a flower witch.

Benno and Moon realize their dream of adventure by fixing up an abandoned house, only to have gangs and the police threaten what they have built.

Survival Stories and the Homeless

In later years Holman turned to writing "survival stories." The first of these was *Slake's Limbo,* the story of a boy who runs away from a bad home to live in the New York subway. He stays for three months, surviving through ingenuity and a little bit of luck. Slake makes his home in a small "room" in one of the subway tunnels and sets up a small "business" selling used newspapers that he collects. He finds friendship of a sort from his customers, one of whom brings him her son's cast-off clothes, and a waitress at a lunch counter, who gives him food in exchange for sweeping the floor. By the end of the story Slake's circumstances are no better, but he has learned that he has the ability to survive by his own wits.

To make the details of *Slake's Limbo* convincing, Holman did thorough research on the subway. In addition to learning the history and layout of the entire system, she had to research the ways in which Slake might survive: how he could get water, food, a place to sleep, and manage to stay hidden. Her husband helped with some of the difficult details, and served as a cheering squad. Their efforts were rewarded when the book was met with widespread acclaim. It was later produced as a TV movie (*The Runaway*) by PBS, although Holman has said that she was not happy with the film version.

The Wild Children is another survival story that required the author to do thorough research. The novel takes place in the 1920s in Russia, after the Russian revolution. Groups of children (the "bozpizonrni") who were made homeless by the revolution banded together and ran wild, squeezing out a meager existence through crime. *The Wild Children* tells the story of a boy who, after his parents and sister are taken away by the police, joins one such group of children. *The Wild Children* was also praised by reviewers. According to Carolyn Noah of *School Library Journal,* "the strength of the human spirit shines through as a powerful beacon of optimism" in *The Wild Children.*

More recently, Holman published *Secret City, U.S.A.,* another novel in which children learn to fend for themselves because adults cannot or will not take care of them. The hero of the story, Benno, lives in a crowded, rundown tenement in an squalid inner city neighborhood. Under his leadership, a group of boys—some homeless, some merely downtrodden by poverty—begin to convert space in an abandoned building into a home of sorts. Working together, the boys clean up the building, plant a garden, and begin to create a community unlike any they have experienced before. Ultimately, their work is threatened by a dispute with gang members, and the cops arrive. With the help of a social worker who has become a friend, the boys publicize their story and inspire adults to continue what they have begun. In *Horn Book* magazine, reviewer Ethel R. Twichell commented that "While the . . . ending (may be) more hopeful than reality might allow, the author paints an uncompromising picture of the misery and squalor of our cities and sends an unmistakable cry for help." Barbara Chatton also praised the book in *School Library Journal,* citing its "strong characterization," and noting that "Benno and Moon's vision of a better world and the careful steps they take to try to create it will captivate those readers who enjoy survival stories." The novel also impressed Cathi MacRae of the *Wilson Library Journal,* who claimed the book "is both an eloquent portrait of Hispanic youth in a New York barrio and a bold manifesto on homelessness."

Helping the homeless is a cause Holman feels strongly about, and she hopes books like *Slake's Limbo, The Wild Children,* and *Secret City, U.S.A.* will make her readers understand how important it is to reach out to those in need. After all, the people who are reading her books today may be tomorrow's leaders. As Holman once noted, "It gives me a lot of satisfaction to be talking to the most important people around—the people who are going to help fix up a lot of the things we know are wrong." Maybe, just maybe, she will touch someone who will find a way to make the world a better place. As she notes in her *SAAS* entry, "If something I write connects with just one person, *just one,* I will have done *something.*" And that, she concludes, will be enough.

■ Works Cited

Chatton, Barbara, review of *Secret City, U.S.A.,* *School Library Journal,* April, 1990, p. 141.

Holman, Felice, essay in *Something about the Author Autobiography Series,* Volume 17, Gale, 1994, p. 121.

MacRae, Cathi, review of *Secret City, U.S.A., Wilson Library Journal,* April, 1991, p. 103.

Noah, Carolyn "Tightrope Walking: Children on Their Own," *School Library Journal,* April, 1992, p. 42.

Twichell, Ethel R., review of *Secret City, U.S.A., Horn Book,* May/June, 1990, p. 335.

■ For More Information See:

BOOKS

Fourth Book of Junior Authors and Illustrators, edited by Doris de Montreville and Elizabeth Crawford, Wilson, 1978, p. 182.

Twentieth-Century Children's Writers, edited by D. L. Kirkpatrick, St. Martin's, 1983, p. 386.

—Sketch by Sarah Verney

Gale Anne Hurd

■ Personal

Born October 25, 1955, in Los Angeles, CA; daughter of Frank E. and Lolita (Espiau) Hurd; married James Cameron (a director), 1985 (divorced, 1989). *Education:* Stanford University, B.A., 1977. *Hobbies and other interests:* Scuba diving and paso fino horses.

■ Addresses

Office—Pacific Western Productions, 270 North Canon Drive, #1195, Beverly Hills, CA 90210-5323.

■ Career

Producer and writer. New World Pictures, Los Angeles, CA, executive assistant, director of advertising and publicity, 1977; Pacific Western Productions, founder and owner, 1982—; founder and owner of No Frills Productions; creator of Gale Anne Hurd production grants for American Film Institute's Directing Workshop for Women. Television work includes: creative consultant, *Alien Nation*, 1989-90; *The Whole World*

Is Watching, 1992; and executive producer, *Witch Hunt*, 1994. Juror, U.S. Film Festival, Salt Lake City, UT, 1988, and Focus Student Awards, 1989. Appeared on television special *The New Hollywood.* Member: American Film Institute (trustee 1989—), American Motion Picture Arts and Sciences (producer's executive committee, 1990—), Women in Film (board of directors, 1989-90), Hollywood Women's Political Committee, Feminist Majority, Phi Beta Kappa.

■ Awards, Honors

Grand Prix, Avoriaz Film Festival, 1984, for *The Terminator*; National Association of Theater Owners Special Merit Award, and Hugo Award, best dramatic presentation, World Science Fiction Society, 1987, both for *Aliens*; Saturn nomination, 1988, for *Alien Nation*; Stanford Entrepreneur of the Year Award, Business School Alumni, Los Angeles, 1990.

■ Films

PRODUCER

(With Roger Corman) *Smokey Bites the Dust*, New World Pictures, 1981.
The Terminator, Orion Pictures, 1984.
Aliens, Twentieth Century-Fox, 1986.
(With Richard Kobritz) *Alien Nation*, Twentieth Century-Fox, 1988.
Bad Dreams, Twentieth Century-Fox, 1988.

The Abyss, Twentieth Century-Fox, 1989.
Raising Cain, Universal, 1992.
(With Marie Cantin) *The Waterdance*, Samuel Goldwyn, 1992.
No Escape, Savoy Pictures, 1994.

SCREENPLAYS

(With James Cameron and William Wisher, Jr.) *The Terminator*, Orion Pictures, 1984.

OTHER

Other film work includes production assistant, *Humanoids from the Deep*, New World Pictures, 1980; executive producer of *Tremors*, 1990, *Downtown*, 1990, and *Terminator 2: Judgment Day*, 1991; *Cast a Deadly Spell*, 1991; and *Safe Passage*, New Line Cinema, 1994.

■ Sidelights

Movie producer Gale Anne Hurd makes great stories: a privileged, well-educated young woman, she has produced some of the most monstrous and monstrously successful sci-fi hits Hollywood—and anyone else—has ever seen. In the male dominated action/sci-fi arena, she has introduced gritty, determined heroines, taking the genre in a new direction. "Male heroes have been done to death, whereas with women you can be like Lewis and Clark," is how she explained it in an interview with Marjorie Rosen for *Ms.* Hurd is known as a tough, budget-conscious professional whose lady-like demeanor and dress belie a boundless enthusiasm, fierce intelligence, and indefatigable persistence.

Hurd cites a combination of good luck and hard work as the key to her success. "Getting the break and then maximizing the opportunity" is how she summed up her strategy for *Savvy*'s Michael J. Bandler. She began with a few marks in her favor. She was the only child of a Palm Springs real estate entrepreneur who had semi-retired by the time she turned ten; she attended Palm Valley High School and lived in relative luxury, which included owning a horse that she rode every day after school. In her interview with Rosen, Hurd described herself as an overachieving child who "read fourteen books a week" and took great pains to impress her father. She majored in economics at Stanford University, adding communications as a second major after a two-quarter stay at the university's

London campus. Because the economics courses included communications at the British location, Hurd had come into contact with filmmakers. Their excitement and commitment left a strong impression on her and determined the course she would eventually take.

In the meantime, Hurd excelled academically, rarely dipping below an "A" average. She was elected to Phi Beta Kappa in her junior year. Eagerly informing her father of this achievement, she thought he would be satisfied. As she told Rosen, "I called up my father. I was so thrilled that finally he would say, 'This is enough.' But he said, 'I would have been disappointed if you hadn't made it.' I didn't talk to him for six months."

When she graduated in 1977, Hurd knew she wanted to make films but not exactly how she would go about it. She received a letter from a former professor, who had gone to Hollywood to work with B-movie producer/director Roger Corman, well-known for his high productivity and low budgets. The framed "Please contact us . . . concerning employment" letter from Corman's New World Pictures hangs in her office. As Corman's assistant, she did everything from advertising and publicity to fetching coffee and emptying chemical toilets. The studio that produced fare such as *Humanoids from the Deep*, on which Hurd worked as a production assistant, perfectly suited her need to break away from academia. Her first co-production work was on *Smokey Bites the Dust*. In an interview in *People Weekly*, she described working for Corman with affection: "Every day was full of challenges. It was never just drudge work."

Success Triggered by *The Terminator*

Another member of Corman's crew was Hurd's future creative partner and husband, director James Cameron. He was as unknown as she was when they teamed up to write what would become *The Terminator* in 1982. They planned to use it as a "calling card" (a means to interest backers in other projects). Having made an agreement not to sell each other out, they presented themselves as a producer/director team. No studio wanted the script, but they stuck to their guns. Finally, the project attracted Arnold Schwarzenegger, whose box-office draw was enough to interest Hemdale films in backing the picture.

The relatively low-budget *Terminator* became a sleeper hit when it was released in 1984. Set in present-day Los Angeles, it tells the story of a mercenary, human-looking robot who has been sent from the post-nuclear Los Angeles of 2029 to kill a young woman who will eventually give birth to the leader of the rebel humans that are the robot's enemies. He is unswerving in his mission and is only thwarted by the far less powerful woman because she can out-think him. Film critic Richard Corliss, quoted by Beverly Walker in *American Film*, dubbed *The Terminator* a "hip retelling of the Annunciation."

Working on *The Terminator*, Hurd showed herself to be budget-conscious and persuasive. She insisted on weapons rehearsals for *The Terminator*, leading Schwarzenegger to comment in his interview with Walker that "she was adamant. . . . Even before shooting started, she set up practice sessions, aware of how much time could be lost if, for example, a gun jammed on the set. More than most producers, she's concerned about cost." On the other hand, he also found her "supportive" and "upbeat" and recalled agreeing to some additional shooting time because her request wasn't "mean or sleazy."

After their unexpected hit, newlyweds Cameron and Hurd teamed up on *Aliens*, the sequel to the 1979 hit, *Alien*. Cameron scripted the story, which revolves around Ripley, the cool survivor of the first episode, who has been in suspended animation for 57 years. She awakes to find out that the horrible creatures she successfully combatted are still around and now threaten a little girl, the only one to survive their attack on her planet. By pitting the maternally-inspired Ripley against the mother of the creatures, the film becomes a fight between a good mother and an evil one. The film was awarded two Academy Awards. Both *The Terminator* and *Aliens* show a strong moral basis, which Hurd felt came from her upbringing. "My father was Jewish, and my mother Roman Catholic, and I got guilt from both," she revealed in her interview with Walker.

Hurd recalled that the only strident sexism she has encountered was during the filming of *Aliens*, which took place in England. "I'm not sure what they said behind my back, but to my face they called me 'ruthless' . . . ," she told Rosen. "I am compassionate and kind but I have a budget and a schedule." Hurd also had to balance her personal and professional relationship with Cameron. Speaking with Walker, Sigourney Weaver, who played Ripley, commented that "as

a couple, they shared a united vision and a work ethic that was unstoppable. They worked very independently. She was the troubleshooter."

For her part, Hurd has had to face a more subtle form of discrimination in Hollywood, where her low-key but focused style misled some studio executives. As she told Rosen, "Since I don't scream and yell, people here thought that they could dismiss me. But I'm very persistent. I won't be intimidated, I don't give up when I believe in something." Her concentration extends to all her relationships, and Michael Biehn, an actor who appeared in both *The Terminator* and *Aliens* noted in his interview with Rosen that "it's very hard to know Gale . . . she just kind of keeps on a business level with people."

In the meantime, Hurd also founded two production companies, Pacific Western Productions and No Frills. She has said that the first is limited to "studio-driven" projects. No Frills, on the other hand, is meant to take on riskier prospects with less substantial bankrolls. She appears to thrive on multiple projects in process (two or more in pre-production is not unusual), living proof of her remark to Rosen that "producing means constant 'crisis management.'"

Following *Aliens*, Hurd produced two films in 1988, *Alien Nation* and *Bad Dreams*. The first is a sci-fi story that looks at how the United States might assimilate 100,000 outer space aliens and was co-produced with Richard Kobritz. *Bad Dreams* is a horror picture that looks at the lone female survivor of a Jim Jones-style cult massacre/suicide. Neither of these pictures enjoyed the success of *The Terminator* or *Aliens* and eventually Hurd collaborated with Cameron once more.

Taking a Dive on *The Abyss* and Moving On

With two large successes to their names, Hurd and Cameron tackled what would be their Waterloo. They had begun to consider *The Abyss* while they were at work on *Aliens*. The screenplay, by Cameron, was based on a short story he had written in high school. They got a tentative go-ahead from Twentieth Century-Fox studios at the end of 1987, which was also when they separated. The couple at the center of *The Abyss* are in deep marital trouble, their problems precipitated by their class and professional differences: she is an engineer, he is an oil rigger foreman. Their con-

A team of divers sent to rescue a marooned submarine discovers an alien lifeform in the 1989 film *The Abyss*.

flicts erupt when a nuclear submarine picks up an alien "form" on its sonar. In the resulting panic, the crew loses control of the submarine and it becomes marooned at the edge of an abyss. A team of oil riggers led by the foreman are told to rescue the submarine and to destroy the "form." They are joined by the engineer and several navy underwater experts, whose secret mission involves the 150 nuclear warheads on the sub.

Many reviewers and journalists commented on the similarities of the two main characters in the story to Hurd and Cameron, leading to speculation about how much of the story was based on their situation. Hurd told Rosen, "I think when you work together for as long as we did and then develop a romantic relationship you sometimes find that when you're not working, you have very little in common."

Unlike Hurd's previous projects, which were within their budgets and on time, *The Abyss* suffered one setback after another. Hurd and Cameron elected to shoot in a tank in order to avoid the less predictable aspects of open water. Even with the supposedly controlled environment, they frequently had to ask the actors to wait, nearly always in full costume, sometimes in a submersible, for hours until they were ready to shoot. There were numerous leaks and electrical blackouts; the toll on cast and crew was huge. "No one had ever worked in that amount of water before," she told Walker. "We had problems with chlorine and tremendous ones with clarity . . . within a couple of hours it could become so murky we couldn't shoot."

The film made a disappointing showing at the box office and received little praise from critics. One exception was *Rolling Stone*'s Peter Travers, who found the film "relentlessly unnerving." Acknowledging the technical proficiency of the film, he nonetheless declared that it is "the human drama of *The Abyss* that carries the show." Its sophisticated visual effects, some of which relied on underwater technology that was adapted to shooting film and some of which were invented for the project, won the film an Academy Award.

Hurd's next studio production was *Raising Cain*, heralded as the comeback for writer/director Brian De Palma. The psychological thriller about an out-of-control child psychologist marked Hurd's first excursion into this genre and met with mixed results. Her No Frills company produced *The Waterdance*, the directorial debut for writer Neal Jimenez. The comedy/drama took on the difficult subject of a recently disabled paraplegic trying to put his life together after a hiking accident. She continued to expand beyond the sci-fi/action genre with *No Escape*, which is set in a prison, and *Safe Passage*, a family drama.

Recognizing the low number of women who occupy positions such as hers in the film world, Hurd has made efforts to expand opportunities for other women. She established the Gale Anne Hurd production grants for the American Film Institute's Directing Workshop for Women. In addition, ten of the 23 staff members of *Tremors* were women.

The producer also tries to avoid some of the pitfalls of buying into "the Hollywood power elite, that your self-worth is measured by your box office potential," as she related in her *People* interview. One way she tries to keep her wits about her and get some perspective is through horseback riding. She owns several paso fino horses and rides often. She also enjoys scuba diving, particularly in unusual locations such as New Guinea.

Hurd is fond of noting that movies are "a product-driven industry," as she described to Rosen, and appears to attribute her success to lots of good luck. But actors and production staff who have worked with her use terms like "singleminded" and "tough." She admits that she wants to be liked and respected but has said that the latter is far more important—"otherwise, in the end, you'll lose on both counts," she told Rosen.

No matter how far success has taken her, Hurd still focuses on the nuts and bolts of every project. It's not uncommon for her to discuss costume changes, the composition of the chemical used in fake blood, or the time to set up shots during a preliminary script read-through. In her interview with Rosen, Hurd traced her technique to an initial thoroughness that she maintains: "I started out by learning everything I could so that if I looked at a budget or a screenplay, I could tell what the costs would be, what the problems were. I still do my homework—always. Detail work is boring, but it has to be done."

■ Works Cited

Bandler, Michael J., "Sci-Fi's Superwoman Takes the Plunge," *Savvy,* August, 1989, p. 14.

"A Phi Beta Kappa Gets Her Kicks Making Sci-Fi Flicks," *People Weekly,* spring, 1991, p. 49.

Rosen, Marjorie, "The Hurd Instinct," *Ms.,* September, 1989, pp. 66-71.

Travers, Peter, "Sunken Treasure," *Rolling Stone,* August 24, 1989, p. 37.

Walker, Beverly, "Teetering over 'The Abyss,'" *American Film,* June, 1989, pp. 34-39.

—Sketch by Megan Ratner

Belinda Hurmence

■ Personal

Surname pronounced *her*-mense; born August 20, 1921, in Oklahoma; daughter of Warren Coleman (an electrician) and Eula (a homemaker; maiden name, Bonnell) Watson; married Howard Henry Hurmence (a chemical engineer), March 10, 1948; children: Leslie Hurmence Abrams. *Education:* University of Texas, B.A., 1942; attended Columbia University, 1945-47. *Politics:* "Moderate to liberal." *Religion:* Episcopalian. *Hobbies and other interests:* Early child development, tennis, gardening, breadmaking.

■ Addresses

Home and office—149 East Water St., Statesville, NC 28677.

■ Career

Writer. *Mademoiselle*, New York City, assistant fiction editor, 1947-48; *Flair*, New York City, executive editor, 1948-49. *Member:* Society of Children's Book Writers and Illustrators, Authors Guild, Authors League of America.

■ Awards, Honors

Work-in-progress grant, Society of Children's Book Writers, 1978-79, for *A Girl Called Boy*; American Library Association (ALA) notable children's book, 1980, and National Council for Social Studies (NCSS) Notable Children's Trade Book in the Field of Social Studies, 1981, both for *Tough Tiffany*; Parents' Choice Award and National Council of Teachers of English Teacher's Choice Award, 1984, for *A Girl Called Boy*; Golden Kite Award, Society of Children's Book Writers, and NCSS Notable Children's Trade Book in the Field of Social Studies, 1984, for *Tancy*; American Association of University Women (NC Division) Award in Juvenile Literature, 1984, for *Tancy*, and 1989, for *The Nightwalker*; North Carolina Writer's Fellowship, 1985; *School Library Journal* Best Adult Book for Young Adults citation, for *My Folks Don't Want Me to Talk about Slavery*.

■ Writings

Tough Tiffany, Doubleday, 1980.
A Girl Called Boy, Clarion, 1982.
Tancy, Clarion, 1984.
The Nightwalker, Clarion, 1988.
Dixie in the Big Pasture (historical novel), Clarion, 1994.

EDITOR

My Folks Don't Want Me to Talk about Slavery (slave narratives), John Blair, 1984.

Before Freedom, When I Just Can Remember: Twenty-Seven Oral Histories of Former South Carolina Slaves (slave narratives), John Blair, 1989.

Before Freedom: Forty-Eight Oral Histories of Former North & South Carolina Slaves (combined edition of *Before Freedom* and *My Folks Don't Want Me to Talk about Slavery*), New American Library-Dutton, 1990.

We Lived in a Little Cabin in the Yard (Virginia slave narratives), John Blair, 1994.

■ Work in Progress

Two nonfiction titles on working days of female airline pilot and sports clothes designer and manufacturer; a historical novel about an oil camp child of the 1930s; a volume of slave narratives geared to the juvenile market.

■ Sidelights

As a white woman writing about black children and slave history, Belinda Hurmence has encountered some controversy. While her books are very popular with children, some black scholars questioned the validity of her work. "Some critics started to say that blacks should have their own writers writing about them," Hurmence recalled in an interview by Scott Gillam for *Something About the Author*. Hurmence has remained undaunted by the criticism and has continued to write about a topic that is of great interest to her and her readers.

Hurmence's roots are in the pioneer territory of Oklahoma. She was born there, and her family had been farming and ranching the lands for decades. She told the *Sixth Book of Junior Authors and Illustrators* that "my parents and both sets of my grandparents homesteaded in the Oklahoma Indian Territory, in the Kiowa-Comanche-Apache lands known among those tribes as the Big Pasture. My mother's people came into the O.T., as it was called, in three covered wagons the year Oklahoma became one of the United States. My father's family also arrived prior to statehood."

Queen of Contests

From an early age, Hurmence found herself writing and enjoying it. Encouraged by her teachers,

Hurmence was awarded the Beatrix Potter book *Peter Rabbit* for a writing competition in first grade. "In it my teacher had inscribed 'I'm very proud of you. You are a good writer,'" Hurmence told *SATA*. "I knew from then on that I was going to be a writer." From that time on, she was also hooked on writing contests. "In high school I was always looking for contests to enter," she recalled, "and I actually won a good many of them. When I was a senior, a national essay contest that I entered won me a week in Washington, D.C., and an invitation to the White House, for tea with Mrs. Roosevelt." Her writing success continued as she decided to pursue it more seriously in college. She took classes from Frank Dobie, considered an excellent western regionalist writer. "He was the advisor on the literary magazine. I wrote and did editing and production for the magazine and learned a lot," she told Gillam.

After graduating from college, Hurmence moved to New York City. "I'd always wanted to live there, and the end of the war seemed like a good breaking point," she said to Gillam. "While I was working on Wall Street, in the insurance industry, I was going to Columbia School of General Studies at night and studying creative writing under Gladys Tabor and George Davis, who was executive editor of *Mademoiselle*. At first I wanted to be a writer of adult fiction, and I did write a couple of short stories that were published, as well as a novel that wasn't. It was George, my teacher, who bought my first story, and almost immediately after that he asked me if I would be interested in a job working on *Mademoiselle*."

Hurmence was thrilled at getting offered such an exciting job in a field that interested her. She grabbed the offer and went to work almost immediately as the assistant fiction editor. "I worked on *Mademoiselle* for a year or so, and then Cowles Publications started a new publication called *Flair*," she related. "It was a bit like *Vanity Fair*, but they didn't get the advertising, so it lasted only a couple of years." At this time, she met her husband-to-be Howard Hurmence. They married in 1948 and soon after had a baby girl.

In 1951, Hurmence and her family moved across the river to New Jersey. "I belonged to a writer's group and was trying to sell adult stories, but in the 1960s I was also working as a volunteer librarian in a neighborhood house in Morristown. I was really struck with how few books there

In this 1982 novel, Blanche Overtha Yancey (or "Boy"), travels back in time to the days of slavery.

were for the black children there. I started to write for these children," she explained in her interview. Hurmence and her husband moved to North Carolina in 1968. She found herself reading stories every day to black children in a day care center there. Her experience with these young children helped her enormously in her writing. "My own knowledge of black dialect I use in my stories comes, I think, because of my close connection with the black community," she related to Gillam. "I didn't sell books for a long time, but I did sell some stories to children's magazines."

As she changed from writing for adults to writing for children, Hurmence found herself hitting a few stumbling blocks. In fact, she found that writing for children was more difficult than writing for adults. She remarked that "you follow the same rules, I suppose—except if you're writing for adults, I think you don't *have* to write as well as

you can. You can get away with writing sloppy. Whereas with children you can't because there are too many people keeping up the standards, like the librarians who choose the books." Still, she kept on working toward her writing goals.

First Novel is Tough

It took her until 1980 to get her first book for young adults published. *Tough Tiffany* is a contemporary story about an eleven-year-old girl named Tiffany who lives in a poor black family. Tiffany is constantly worried about the tensions in her family—her fifteen-year-old sister is pregnant and unmarried, and the family's poverty is a constant threat to their life. Marilyn Kaye, writing in the *School Library Journal* thought that "Tiffany's perspective is apparent and constant, and her naive, candid point of view brings to light sharply defined characters."

Hurmence's first novel received a warm critical reception. Zena Sutherland wrote in *Bulletin of the Center for Children's Books*, that "her characterizations are sharply drawn, and she has—in a fine first novel—used every situation in the book to develop and extend her characters." A *Publishers Weekly* reviewer noted that "no one would guess that this is Hurmence's first novel. . . . [I]t outclasses the works of many seasoned professionals." The American Library Association named *Tough Tiffany* a Notable Children's Book in 1980; the book was also named a Notable Trade Book in Social Studies by the National Council for Social Studies (NCSS).

While researching *Tough Tiffany*, Hurmence decided her next novel should be about the Underground Railroad through a child's viewpoint. She commented in her interview that it was "hard to get materials written from the slave's viewpoint. At that point I didn't know about the WPA [Works Progress Administration] collection of slave narratives." During the Depression, the United States government created jobs for out-of-work writers by assigning them to take down the oral histories of former slaves. Hurmence continued: "I was visiting an historical museum in Savannah, Georgia, and looking for pictures of slaves. While I was going through their picture collection, my husband said he'd found an interesting book. The book was *Slavery Time*, published by the Beehive Press in 1973. It had excerpts from the WPA collection of Georgia slaves, and I immediately thought, 'That's for me!' So I got in touch with the Library of Congress and they provided me with microfilm of all the slave narratives. And believe me, that's a production—10,000 pages' worth!"

While narrowing in on the topic of her next book, Hurmence made a discovery. "The more I read the more I realized that the Underground Railroad didn't really figure with most slaves in the South. Most slaves did not escape north but rather to someplace closer to home. So that's when I came up with the idea for *A Girl Called Boy*." In this book, Blanche Overtha Yancey—Boy for short—despises her family's slave origins until, in this time travel tale, she finds herself fleeing from slave patrols in the 1850s. She experiences deprivation and fear as a runaway, and security, complacency, and self-hatred as a house slave before returning to the present.

"Hurmence can be applauded for breaking new ground here, for she's taken the well-used time-travel fantasy mode and freshened it with black characters and a vivid historical context," wrote Denise M. Wilms of the novel in *Booklist*. Another reviewer, Leila Davenport Pettyjohn, concluded in *Children's Book Review Service* that "the characterizations are excellent, the historical aspects accurate, and it is a non-preachy revelation for all readers." *A Girl Called Boy* received the Parents' Choice Award and the National Council of Teachers of English Teacher's Choice Award in 1984. As Hazel Rochman related in *School Library Journal*, readers will enjoy the story "for its adventure and setting and for the universal nightmare it dramatizes."

Tancy's Fancy

In an author's note appended to her next book, *Tancy*, Hurmence writes that the idea for the novel, like that of *A Girl Called Boy*, "began among the pages of the slave narratives. . . . Tancy is meant to embody the innumerable ex-slaves who set out to find their families after the Civil War. Her yearning and searching parallel what many young people experience even today, looking for some idea, or 'mother,' on the way to discovering themselves." Like Tiffany and Boy, Tancy is a resourceful, adventurous black girl. Tancy is sixteen, a little older than either of her

predecessors, and she has been taught to read and write by the plantation owner's son, Billy. She uses these skills to her advantage after escaping, becoming a worker in a Freedman's Bureau center and later a teacher.

Stephanie Zvirin wrote in *Booklist* that in *Tancy*, "Hurmence conjures up an illuminating and absorbing picture of Civil War-era slavery and the changes freedom brought to southern blacks." Leila Davenport Pettyjohn commented in *Children's Book Review Service* that "*Tancy* is a rich, evocative, detailed novel of the brutality of slavery, the era of Reconstruction, and the Bewilderment of the slaves forced to choose between the security of slavery and the difficulties of freedom." *Tancy* received the Golden Kite Award and was selected as an NCSS Notable Children's Trade Book in the

Based on the experiences of Hurmence's aunt, this 1994 work follows the adventures of a young girl whose family builds their homestead in the Oklahoma Territory in 1907.

Field of Social Studies in 1984. Jeannette Pergam praised the book in *Best Sellers,* writing that "I can heartily recommend this book and feel that it is unobjectionable for all readers who fall in the 11 year and older group."

Hurmence's novel *The Nightwalker* is about the intriguing people living on the Outer Banks of North Carolina. The story focuses on twelve-year-old Savannah and her brother. Savannah's father is a half Coree Indian, like many of the people living on Breach Island. When a series of fires destroy local fishing shanties, the island is in an uproar. There already exists tension between the locals and the rich landowners who have vacation homes on the island. Savannah forms a relationship with one of the vacationers, (or ditdots, as they are called) that is discouraged by her father. Savannah begins to think that her sleepwalking brother is setting the fires, but she later finds out that she is also a sleepwalker. And there is always the spirit of the "nightwalker," a legend told to her by her father, that could be causing trouble.

"Good atmospheric writing and realistic portrayals of island life on the Outer Banks of North Carolina are the highlights of this mystery," noted a *Publishers Weekly* reviewer. Although Marcia Hupp found in *School Library Journal* that "the plot is . . . jumpy and difficult to follow," she indicated the book is a "reasonably diverting mystery and a finely drawn regional portrait." Elizabeth S. Watson, writing in the *Horn Book Magazine* indicated that "the book can be read easily for just a rousing good story, but for the more thoughtful reader the suggestion of the complexity of human thought and action provides substance."

On to Oklahoma

Hurmence returned to a topic closer to her own personal history with *Dixie in the Big Pasture.* Covering the period of early statehood in Oklahoma, Hurmence comented that "the central character in the book is based on my aunt, who is ninety-eight now. She was twelve when Oklahoma became a state. My family is very long-lived. My uncle is still alive at 103. All my relatives were very helpful in writing the book. . . . *Dixie in the Big Pasture* is the first time I have written about my family, and it's taken me a long time."

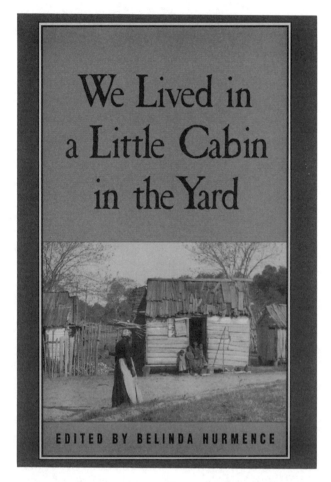

Hurmence collected twenty-one Virginia slave narratives for this 1994 publication.

Ann Welton found problems with *Dixie in the Big Pasture.* Writing in *School Library Journal,* she indicated that the novel was "adequate, though bland."

Several books of slave narratives emerged from Hurmence's research. *My Folks Don't Want Me to Talk About Slavery* is a compilation of oral histories from former North Carolina slaves. Hurmence noted in her introduction to *My Folks:* "But in the sense of the self-sufficiency for which Americans admire their forebears—working the land, building houses, growing and preparing food—slaves were genuine homesteaders. They not only did the work; they endured through bondage to freedom. The idea for *My Folks Don't Want Me to Talk About Slavery* grew out of my admiration of these very real pioneers." Robert C. Bealer wrote in *Science Books & Films* that "The book is a useful instrument to better comprehend and learn from history."

Hurmence continued this work in *Before Freedom, When I Just Can Remember: Twenty-Seven Oral Histories of Former South Carolina Slaves*. In her introduction Hurmence again described her first excitement upon discovering "the treasure that lay in the oral histories." She added: "The concept of bondage has always fascinated free Americans. With slavery more than a century behind us, and beyond the recollection of any living person, the fascination still persists. Perhaps the invisible, traumatic ties that bind us evoke a dread empathy with the physically enslaved." *We Lived in a Little Cabin in the Yard* is Hurmence's collection of slave narratives from the state of Virginia.

Asked about her audience, Hurmence admitted to Gillam: "I like the kids that I'm writing for. The middle grades are my favorite age. They're still unspoiled, and there's an innocence about them as well as a certain sophistication."

■ Works Cited

Bealer, Robert C., review of *My Folks Don't Want Me to Talk about Slavery*, *Science Books & Films*, March-April, 1986, p. 206.

Hurmence, Belinda, introduction to *My Folks Don't Want Me to Talk About Slavery: Twenty-One Oral Histories of Former North Carolina Slaves*, John F. Blair, 1984, pp. ix-xiv.

Hurmence, Belinda, introduction to *Before Freedom, When I Just Can Remember: Twenty-Seven Oral Histories of Former South Carolina Slaves*, John F. Blair, 1989, pp. ix-xvi.

Hurmence, Belinda, interview with Scott Gillam, *Something About the Author*, Volume 77, Gale, 1994, pp. 95-100.

Holtze, Sally Holmes, editor, *Sixth Book of Junior Authors and Illustrators*, H. W. Wilson, 1989, pp. 143-144.

Hupp, Marcia, review of *The Nightwalker*, *School Library Journal*, November, 1988, p. 112.

Kaye, Marilyn, review of *Tough Tiffany*, *School Library Journal*, February, 1980, pp. 56-7.

Review of *The Nightwalker*, *Publishers Weekly*, October 14, 1988, p. 77.

Pergam, Jeannette, review of *Tancy*, *Best Sellers*, September, 1984, pp. 232-33.

Pettyjohn, Leila Davenport, review of *A Girl Called Boy*, *Children's Book Review Service*, spring, 1982, p. 117.

Pettyjohn, Leila Davenport, review of *Tancy*, *Children's Book Review Services*, July, 1984, p. 141.

Rochman, Hazel, review of *A Girl Called Boy*, *School Library Journal*, May, 1982, p. 62.

Sutherland, Zena, review of *Tough Tiffany*, *Bulletin of the Center for Children's Books*, March, 1980, p. 135.

Review of *Tough Tiffany*, *Publishers Weekly*, March 14, 1980, p. 74.

Watson, Elizabeth S., review of *The Nightwalker*, *Horn Book*, January-February, 1989, pp. 70-71.

Welton, Ann, review of *Dixie in the Big Future*, *School Library Journal*, May, 1994, p. 114.

Wilms, Denise M., review of *A Girl Called Boy*, *Booklist*, July, 1982, p. 1445.

Zvirin, Stephanie, review of *Tancy*, *Booklist*, May 15, 1984, p. 1339.

■ For More Information See

BOOKS

Children's Literature Review, Volume 25, Gale, 1991, pp. 92-97.

Killion, Ronald G., compiler, *Slavery Time When I Was Chillun Down on Marster's Farm*, Beehive Press, 1973.

PERIODICALS

Social Education, April, 1981; April, 1985.

—*Sketch by Nancy E. Rampson*

Magic Johnson

■ Personal

Full name, Earvin "Magic" Johnson, Jr.; born August 14, 1959, in Lansing, MI; son of Earvin, Sr. (an auto worker) and Christine (a cafeteria worker) Johnson; married Earletha "Cookie" Kelley, September, 1991; children: (from previous relationship) Andre; Earvin III. *Education:* Attended Michigan State University, 1977–79.

■ Addresses

Home—Los Angeles, CA. *Office*—c/o Los Angeles Lakers, The Forum, 3900 West Manchester Blvd., P.O. Box 32, Inglewood, CA 90312.

■ Career

Los Angeles Lakers, Inglewood, CA, professional basketball player, 1979–91, 1992, and 1996—, head coach, 1994; member, U.S. Olympic basketball "Dream Team", 1992; basketball announcer for National Broadcasting Company, Inc. (NBC-TV). Entrepreneur and philanthropist; owner of a sports apparel company and partner in a soft drink distribution company; holds fundraising dinners and conducts basketball camps; briefly a member of U.S. President George Bush's Council on AIDS.

■ Awards, Honors

Most Valuable Player, Final Four National Collegiate Athletic Association (NCAA) basketball playoff tournament, 1979; member of NCAA Championship Team, 1979; Most Valuable Player, National Basketball Association (NBA) championship series, 1980, 1982, and 1987; selected to NBA All-Star Team, 1980, and 1982–92; member of NBA Championship Team, 1980, 1982, 1985, 1987, and 1988; Schick Pivotal Player Award, 1984; named NBA Most Valuable Player, 1987, 1989, and 1990; named Sporting News Player of the Year, 1987; named American Express/NBA Man of the Year, 1987, for charity and community service work.

■ Writings

(With Richard Levin) *Magic* (autobiography), Viking, 1983.

(With Roy S. Johnson) *Magic's Touch: From Fast Break to Fundamentals with Basketball's Most Exciting Player* (nonfiction), Addison-Wesley, 1989.

(With William Novak) *My Life* (autobiography), Random House, 1992.

(With Novak) *What You Can Do to Avoid AIDS* (nonfiction), Times Books, 1992.

■ Adaptations

My Life has been adapted into an audiocassette, read by Danny Glover, Random House, 1992; *What You Can Do to Avoid AIDS* has been adapted into an audiocassette, read by Robert O'Keefe, Random House, 1992.

■ Sidelights

Magic Johnson, the suave, adept basketball player who led Michigan State University and the Los Angeles Lakers to several championships, is now just as well-known and famous for having contracted HIV, the virus that causes AIDS (acquired immunodeficiency syndrome) as he is for his athletic abilities. Charles Leerhsen, in a *Newsweek* article covering Johnson's stunning 1991 announcement, quoted activists who termed Johnson's revelation "the biggest thing to happen to AIDS since Rock Hudson."

But it was Johnson's extraordinary skills as a player for the Los Angeles Lakers, starting with a spectacular 1979–80 season (his first pro season) during which he drove his team to the National Basketball Association title, that originally garnered the athlete world-wide fame and recognition. Alex Ward, in a *New York Times Magazine* profile, gave this description of the basketball star's astonishing ability to pass and handle a basketball: "Johnson is a point guard, the basketball equivalent of a quarterback. He brings the ball upcourt, sets up the plays, runs the fast breaks. His height gives him an advantage over other guards, and his ability to determine in an instant how a play might develop—by now it's a reflex—allows him to take maximum advantage of his teammates' extraordinary quickness."

Johnson earned the moniker "Magic" while he was still in high school playing basketball at Everett High School in Lansing, Michigan. A local sportswriter who happened to catch the smiling, fluid, high-energy, swift-footed style that was to become Johnson's trademark, could think of no better word to describe his playing than "magic." In later years, though, Lakers coach Pat Riley would say it was too bad he got stuck with the name, because it implied a trick, and Johnson's talent was earned and real, the result of hard work and clear, level-headed playing.

Johnson attended Michigan State in East Lansing (eschewing offers from UCLA, Notre Dame, and

Johnson—pictured here as a senior at Everett High— dreamed of playing basketball from a very young age.

the University of Michigan) and in his freshman year led his school team, the Spartans, to their first Big Ten title in nineteen years. In his sophomore year, the Spartans won the NCAA title. When Johnson received an offer from the Los Angeles Lakers to turn pro at the end of his sophomore year of college, just before his twentieth birthday, he characteristically sought the best counsel he could imagine: he telephoned his idol, Julius Erving ("Dr. J"), whom he did not know, and asked for his advice. Erving not only advised young Johnson, but also invited him to Philadelphia to watch the NBA playoffs. The rest, as they say, is history.

Fairy Tale Career

Johnson wrote his first autobiography at the ripe old age of 22. *Magic,* published in 1983, was written in collaboration with author Richard Levin, combining autobiographical sketches of Johnson's childhood and college days along with a journal recording the events of the 1981–82 NBA season. *Magic* includes glowing reminiscences of Johnson's now-legendary, fairy-tale rookie season with the until-that-time lackluster Los Angeles Lakers, as well as a record of the tensions that developed between Johnson and his teammates when he signed a contract (in 1981) that made him the highest-paid basketball player in the history of the game.

Johnson's teammates feared that his huge salary would give him a say in the management of the team, and this would appear to have been a valid fear. When Lakers coach Paul Westhead tried to change the style of the team's game, Johnson asked to be traded rather than continue to force himself to play in a way that was not working for him or for the team. Westhead quit the day after Johnson's public request, and Johnson took some flak from fans (who thought he was flexing a little too much muscle)—that is until the Lakers started to win again.

In 1989 Johnson wrote his second book, *Magic's Touch: From Fast Break to Fundamentals with Basketball's Most Exciting Player*, in collaboration with *Sports Illustrated* editor Roy S. Johnson. This book, unlike his first, is a guide to the game of basketball—albeit with the occasional autobiographical comment. A *Publishers Weekly* contributor, reviewing the book, noted Johnson's observation that "growing up in a family of 10 children with a father who held two jobs simultaneously instilled in him the work ethic and discipline needed on the court." As far as Johnson is concerned, basketball is an exacting sport that demands of its players hard work and diligence. Defense, Johnson asserts, is the key to the game and great stats are nothing if the team doesn't win. The *Publishers Weekly* reviewer added that the book is "a trove of practical information," and that "those who are merely spectators will also be the wiser for it."

In addition to tributes to his large family, Johnson also took the opportunity in *Magic's Touch* to explore his debt to those who supported his rise to superstardom. Ron Chepesiuk, reviewing the book for the *Library Journal*, observed that it covers "Johnson's career from his boyhood roots in Lansing, Michigan, through his ten-year career as

leader of the Los Angeles Lakers. Johnson discusses his friendship and rivalry with Larry Bird, his NCAA championship at Michigan State, and his five NBA championships with the Lakers. Interesting are the discussions of basketball's finer points, such as dribbling and passing . . . and the key to basketball success—'defense, defense, defense.'"

New Kind of Champion

In 1991 Johnson made the stunning announcement that he had contracted the HIV virus through heterosexual contact and would be retiring from the game of basketball to preserve his health. His much-lamented retirement was short-lived, however, when in 1992 he made an emotional comeback as a member of the 1992 U.S. Olympic "Dream Team," playing alongside such former competitors as Michael Jordan, Larry Bird, Patrick Ewing, and Clyde Drexler. Savoring his return to the sport, Johnson followed his Olympic performance with a partial return to the Lakers during the 1992 pre-season.

In an interview with Jack McCallum for *Sports Illustrated*, Johnson discussed the experience of playing at the Olympics and being a member of the "Dream Team": "We have grabbed the world in a way that won't happen again. The excitement of the fans, the excitement of the other players who don't care how bad you beat them as long as they get a picture." Indeed, Johnson observed, "What happened is that people missed seeing my style, the passes, the fakes and all that. Michael and these guys played for a whole season, but I'm getting welcomed back in a way. And then, you know what else it is? Everybody wants me to smile. Everybody. I'll hear that in my sleep. 'Ma-jeek! Ma-jeek! Please smile for me. Smile for the camera.' And as you know, I've always been able to smile."

Indeed, even in the face of the HIV infection, Johnson has continued to smile, to work, and to make magic. In 1992 he published a new volume of autobiography, *My Life,* which brings the story of his life up to date. Written in collaboration with freelance writer William Novak, the book once again details Johnson's childhood and college experiences, his break into professional basketball, and his years as an NBA star. This time around, however, Johnson also offers a candid account of his role as a "sex object" in his capacity as sports superstar, and explores how that relates to his consequent discovery (during a routine blood test for an insurance policy taken out on him by the Lakers) that he was HIV-positive.

Benjamin Segedin, reviewing *My Life* for *Booklist*, observed: "Readers won't find many revelations here; the question of Magic's future in the NBA is left unanswered. He addresses his promiscuity in a chapter entitled 'Women and Me,' discreetly refusing to name names . . . but making no apologies for his former lifestyle." In addition to "a few well-placed jabs at President Bush for lack of leadership in the fight against the deadly virus" (Johnson briefly served on the former President's Council on AIDS, before resigning in disgust at the committee's lack of power and action), the book concludes with "A Message for Black Teen-

agers," encouraging them to help themselves, to work hard to become what they wish to become.

In a review of *My Life, Publishers Weekly* contributor Genevieve Stuttaford cited "Johnson's straight talk on AIDS" as the source of the book's "thrust and power," adding that "the strongest sections describe his retirement, his coming to terms with his condition and return to play, his role as an AIDS activist. . . ." Harvey Araton, writing in the *New York Times Book Review*, maintained: "As an author, Mr. Johnson is at his best when he shares his insights about his coaches and fellow players, including hilarious exchanges between the Lakers and their stubbornly prideful former teammate Bob McAdoo." Faulting the book now and then, Araton nonetheless concluded that "ultimately the beauty and legacy of Magic Johnson will be as an inspirational athlete and a living symbol of an HIV-infected person attempting to get on with his life." Indeed, Johnson's 1991 diagnosis has served to transform the ever-optimistic, ever-compassionate, ever-smiling champion from a world class athlete to a dedicated champion of the victims of AIDS.

Newsweek's Leerhsen analyzed Johnson's nobility in the face of tragedy: "Part of Magic's appeal no doubt is that he has the courage of his convictions, which in his case means remaining relentlessly upbeat." Mike Dunleavy, a former Lakers coach, lamented to Leerhsen the fact that Johnson, whose legacy was "going to be one of a player" now would be that of "crusader for a cause." Only Johnson keeps smiling in the face of it. Roy S. Johnson, reporting on Johnson's condition for *People*, put the situation most soberly: "No matter how much he smiles, no matter how much he laughs, no matter how much he nearly becomes Magic again in his new role as Lakers head coach, Johnson, 34, can't escape the specter of his announcement on November 7, 1991, that he had tested positive for HIV, the virus that causes AIDS. His greatest challenge, he says, is to make the world understand that HIV and AIDS are not, in themselves, reasons to stop living."

One of Johnson's longest-standing rivalries—and friendships—is with Michael Jordan.

In 1992 Johnson followed *My Life* with *What You Can Do to Avoid AIDS*, another collaboration with Novak, a reflection of his newfound role as AIDS activist. Though the target audience for the book is teenagers, the book contains useful information for parents as well. The language used here is straightforward, and the illustrations depict explicit

MY LIFE

EARVIN "MAGIC" JOHNSON

WITH WILLIAM NOVAK

In this autobiographical work, Johnson talks about his life, career, family, and struggle with the AIDS virus.

instructions for how young people can have safer sex. For this reason, the book became (for a brief period) a matter of controversy when three major booksellers refused to stock it in their stores. Johnson defended the book at an American Booksellers Association meeting, stating that its point was to be "real—about everything" and to save the lives of kids.

A Consummate and Rare Individual

Pico Iyer, in a *Time* profile, described the irresistible Johnson in glowing terms: "Even outside the world of sports, Mr. Showtime's enormous smile and unquenchable grace have become almost ubiquitous—on music video shows, on billboards, at fund-raising dinners. For more than a decade, Earvin 'Magic' Johnson Jr. has commanded the

world of entertainment on the court and off with an irreplaceable blend of poise and surprise." Indeed, over the years Johnson has been a spokesman for countless products (including Converse basketball shoes, Pepsico, and Spalding), performed on a sit-com (he taped three episodes of ABC-TV's *The Pursuit of Happiness* in 1987), started a T-shirt company sanctioned by the NBA (Magic Johnson T's), made public appearances at pop concerts, at businesses willing to pay for his presence (a Spanish meat-packing company once paid him one million dollars, as a promotion for their product, to come to Spain and conduct a few basketball clinics), and on behalf of charities, and even performed (with the rest of the Lakers) on an anti-drug rap record called "Just Say No." He also owns a store catering to his fans in Los Angeles called Magic 32, and has that now-infamous 25-year $25 million contract with the Lakers signed in 1981 and later restructured to Johnson's advantage in 1987, with the gratis help of Laker and Johnson fan Joe Smith, president and CEO of Capitol-EMI Records.

Johnson continues to dream and be inspired, while at the same time inspiring millions of others. Not one to rest on his laurels, he has simply added a new branch to his tree of charitable works and activities, while paring back the physical demands of rigorous professional sports to preserve his strength while he is still healthy and symptomless. In addition to continuing his product endorsements and clinics, Johnson dreams of owning an office building and of achieving the goals he described to Richard Hoffer in a 1990 *Sports Illustrated* interview: "I want to be in the $100-$200 million range," he told Hoffer, "which is what you basically got to have . . . for a franchise. And it doesn't even have to be the Lakers, it doesn't even have to be an NBA team. I'm a sports fan. If baseball became available before basketball, I'd be right there. I want to do big business."

Johnson, Iyer observed, "has become famous for his eagerness to parlay his success into a show-biz career and a $100 million business empire, [but] he has also managed to exemplify the same winning unselfishness off court as on." In 1990, for example, he donated a portion of his salary to his team (to help them acquire another player) and raised $2.65 million for charity. Off court or on, Johnson has always exemplified a consummate talent, a winning determination, and an irrepressible will to transcend all obstacles. In 1996, he

No matter how busy he may be with his career, Johnson tries to find time to work with young people.

announced his return as an active player for the Lakers. "It's now or never," he was quoted as saying in the *Detroit Free Press.* "I'm 36. If this is the last hurrah, so be it. If it's next year, we'll see." In contrast to his previous return, Magic's announcement was greeted with eagerness and understanding from his fellow athletes, most of whom expressed no fear of catching HIV during play because of the awareness Johnson had brought to the issue. Indeed, McCallum observed that "Magic Johnson did no less than force everyone who watched basketball to examine the preconceptions about what constituted the prototypical NBA player."

According to McCallum, Johnson "was neither particularly fast—he moved with a kind of lumbering grace—nor as quick as many others at his position. What he was able to do was get where he wanted to go, not more quickly but more efficiently than anyone else." Hoffer said of Johnson: "Nobody else in this entertainment capital has sustained such purity of effort and enthusiasm for

11 years, not to mention a talent for public performance that has allowed Laker basketball to be celebrated as Showtime." Hoffer, much impressed with his subject, concluded that Johnson may be the ultimate team player, not because he needs a team in order to succeed, but because he "can single-handedly wrest control of a game." In other words, he is a top team player because he chooses to play well with others, not because he has to. "He may be the last great example of selfless play," Hoffer wrote, "but he also has enormous confidence in his own abilities and dreams."

Johnson says his friends and family have always seen him as two people: Magic and Earvin. Magic is the guy everyone knows from the courts, the guy with the easy smile and winning combinations. So who is Earvin Johnson, Jr.? Friend Isiah Thomas, star of the Detroit Pistons, asserted in a *People* interview with Benita Alexander that Johnson is the guy who "woke up this morning. He ate breakfast. He's going to have lunch. We've just lost our friend as a competitor on the basketball court. We haven't lost our friend as a human being."

■ Works Cited

Alexander, Benita, and Lorenzo Benet, "Believe in Magic," *People*, November 25, 1991, pp. 59–61.

Araton, Harvey, "A Point Guard Like No Other," *New York Times Book Review*, November 8, 1992, p. 20.

Chepesiuk, Ron, review of *Magic's Touch: From Fast Break to Fundamentals with Basketball's Most Exciting Player*, *Library Journal*, October 1, 1989, p. 99.

Hoffer, Richard, "Magic's Kingdom," *Sports Illustrated*, December 3, 1990, pp. 106–18.

"'It's Now or Never,'--Johnson Ends Retirement, Rejoins Lakers," *Detroit Free Press*, January 30, 1996, pp. 1D, 3D.

Iyer, Pico, "It Can Happen to Anybody. Even Magic Johnson," *Time*, November 18, 1991, pp. 26–27.

Johnson, Roy S., "Magic and His Shadow," *People*, April 25, 1994, pp. 101–03.

Leerhsen, Charles, and others, "Magic's Message," *Newsweek*, November 18, 1991, pp. 58–62.

Review of *Magic's Touch*, *Publishers Weekly*, September 22, 1989, p. 45.

McCallum, Jack, "Unforgettable," *Sports Illustrated*, November 18, 1991, pp. 29–37.

McCallum, Jack, "I'm Still Strong," *Sports Illustrated*, August 17, 1992, pp. 75–79.

Segedin, Benjamin, review of *My Life*, *Booklist*, October 1, 1992, p. 194.

Stuttaford, Genevieve, review of *My Life*, *Publishers Weekly*, October 12, 1992, p. 57.

Ward, Alex, "The Magic Touch," *New York Times Magazine*, December 6, 1987, pp. 67–73, 77.

■ For More Information See

PERIODICALS

Newsweek, December 23, 1991, pp. 59–60; November 16, 1992, p. 91.

New York, December 2, 1991, pp. 30, 34.

People, December 28, 1987, p. 64; November 25, 1991, p. 61.

Sports Illustrated, December 18, 1989, pp. 45–49.

—*Sketch by Mindi Dickstein*

Stephen King

REVISED ENTRY

■ Personal

Full name, Steven Edwin King; has also written under the pseudonym Richard Bachman; born September 21, 1947, in Portland, ME; son of Donald (a merchant sailor) and Nellie Ruth Pillsbury (a laundry presser and donut maker) King; married Tabitha Jane Spruce (a poet and novelist), January 2, 1971; children: Naomi Rachel, Joseph Hillstrom, Owen Phillip. *Education:* University of Maine at Orono, B.A. (English) and teaching certification, 1970. *Politics:* Democrat.

■ Addresses

Home—Bangor and Center Lovell, ME; and c/o Penguin USA, 375 Hudson St., New York, NY 10014. *Office*—P.O. Box 1186, Bangor, ME 04001. *Agent*—Arthur Greene, 101 Park Ave., New York, NY 10178.

■ Career

Writer. Has also worked as a janitor, gas station attendant, sheet presser in an industrial laundry and in a knitting mill. Hampden Academy (high school), Hampden, ME, English teacher, 1971-1973; University of Maine, Orono, writer in residence, 1978-79. Philtrum Press (publishing house), and WZON-AM (rock 'n' roll radio station), both in Bangor, ME, owner. Co-executive producer of television series, *Stephen King's "Golden Years,"* Columbia Broadcasting Systems, Inc. (CBS-TV), and of movie, *The Stand,* American Broadcasting Companies, Inc. (ABC-TV), 1994; made cameo appearances in films *Knightriders,* as himself, 1980, *Creepshow,* 1982, *Maximum Overdrive,* 1986, and *Pet Sematary,* 1989; played Teddy Weizak in *The Stand,* ABC-TV, 1994, and Tom Holby in *The Langoliers,* ABC-TV, 1995; appeared in television special, *Fear in the Dark,* Arts & Entertainment, 1991, and on an American Express television commercial. Served as judge of 1977 World Fantasy Awards, 1978. Participated in radio honor panel with George A. Romero, Peter Straub, and Ira Levin, moderated by Dick Cavett on WNET in New York, October 30-31, 1980. *Member:* Authors Guild, Authors League of America, Writers Guild, Screen Artists Guild, Screen Writers of America.

■ Awards, Honors

World Fantasy Award nominations, 1976, for *'Salem's Lot,* 1979, for *The Stand* and *Night Shift,*

1980, for *The Dead Zone,* 1981, for "The Mist," and 1983, for "The Breathing Method: A Winter's Tale" in *Different Seasons;* two Hugo Award nominations, World Science Fiction Convention, 1978, for *The Shining;* Balrog Award runner-up, 1979, for novel *The Stand,* and for collection *Night Shift;* American Library Association (ALA), best books for young adults list, 1979, for *The Long Walk;* World Fantasy Award, 1980, for contributions to the field, and 1982, for "Do the Dead Sing?"; Career Alumni Award, University of Maine at Orono, 1981; ALA best books for young adults list, 1981, for *Firestarter;* Nebula Award nomination, Science Fiction Writers of America, 1981, for "The Way Station"; special British Fantasy Award for outstanding contribution to the genre, British Fantasy Society, 1982, for *Cujo;* Hugo Award for nonfiction, 1982, for *Stephen King's Danse Macabre;* Best Fiction Writer of the Year, *Us* Magazine, 1982; *Locus* Award for best collection, 1986, for *Stephen King's Skeleton Crew.*

■ Writings

NOVELS

Carrie, Doubleday, 1974, movie edition, New American Library, 1976.

'Salem's Lot, Doubleday, 1975, television edition, New American Library, 1979.

The Shining, Doubleday, 1977, movie edition, New American Library, 1980.

The Stand, Doubleday, 1978, revised edition published as *The Stand: The Complete and Uncut Edition,* 1990.

The Dead Zone, Viking, 1979, movie edition published as *The Dead Zone: Movie Tie-In,* New American Library, 1980.

Firestarter, Viking, 1980.

Cujo, Viking, 1981.

The Dark Tower: The Gunslinger, Donald M. Grant, 1982.

Pet Sematary, Doubleday, 1983.

Christine, Viking, 1983.

(With Peter Straub) *The Talisman,* Viking/Putnam, 1984.

Cycle of the Werewolf, illustrated by David Wrightson, New American Library, 1985, new edition including the complete screenplay from the movie adaptation and with a new foreword by King published as *Silver Bullet,* New American Library, 1985.

It, Viking, 1986.

Misery, Viking, 1987.

The Tommyknockers, Putnam, 1987.

The Dark Tower: The Drawing of the Three, illustrated by Phil Hale, Donald M. Grant, 1987.

Night Visions, Dark Harvest, 1988.

The Dark Half, Viking, 1989.

Needful Things: The Last Castle Rock Story, Viking, 1991.

Gerald's Game, Viking, 1992.

The Dark Tower: The Waste Lands, illustrations by Ned Dameron, Donald M. Grant, 1992.

The Dark Tower Trilogy: The Gunslinger; The Drawing of the Three; The Waste Lands, New American Library/Dutton, 1993.

Dolores Claiborne, Viking, 1993.

Insomnia, Viking, 1994.

Rose Madder, Viking, 1995.

NOVELS; UNDER PSEUDONYM RICHARD BACHMAN

Rage, New American Library/Signet, 1977.

The Long Walk, New American Library/Signet, 1979.

Roadwork: A Novel of the First Energy Crisis, New American Library/Signet, 1982.

The Running Man, New American Library/Signet, 1982.

Thinner, New American Library, 1984.

SHORT STORY AND NOVELLA COLLECTIONS

Night Shift: Excursions into Horror (stories), Doubleday, 1978.

Different Seasons (contains novellas *Rita Hayworth and the Shawshank Redemption, Apt Pupil, The Body,* and *The Breathing Method*), Viking, 1982.

Skeleton Crew, Viking, 1985, published as *Stephen King's Skeleton Crew,* illustrations by J. K. Potter, Scream Press (Santa Cruz, CA), 1985.

Four Past Midnight (contains *The Langoliers, The Sun Dog, The Library Policeman,* and *Secret Window, Secret Garden*), Viking, 1990.

Nightmares and Dreamscapes, Viking, 1993.

OMNIBUS EDITIONS

Stephen King (contains *The Shining, 'Salem's Lot, Night Shift,* and *Carrie*), W. S. Heinemann/Octopus Books, 1981.

The Bachman Books: Four Early Novels by Stephen King (contains *Rage, The Long Walk, Roadwork* and *The Running Man*), with introduction "Why I Was Richard Bachman," New American Library, 1985.

FOR CHILDREN

The Eyes of the Dragon: A Story (fantasy novel), illustrations by David Palladini, G. K. Hall, 1987.
(With Barbara Kruger) *My Pretty Pony*, Knopf, 1989.

NONFICTION

Stephen King's Danse Macabre, Everest House, 1981.
Black Magic and Music: A Novelist's Perspective on Bangor (pamphlet), Bangor Historical Society, 1983.
Bare Bones: Conversations on Terror with Stephen King, edited by Tim Underwood and Chuck Miller, McGraw-Hill, 1988.
Nightmares in the Sky: Gargoyles and Grotesques (on architecture), photographs by f-Stop Fitzgerald, Viking, 1988.
Feast of Fear: Conversations with Stephen King, edited by Tim Underwood and Chuck Miller, McGraw-Hill, 1989.

SCREENPLAYS

Stephen King's Creepshow: A George Romero Film, New American Library, 1982.
Cat's Eye, Metro-Goldwyn-Mayer/United Artists, 1984.
Silver Bullet, Paramount, 1985.
(Also director) *Maximum Overdrive* (based on the short story, "Trucks"), Dino De Laurentiis Entertainment Group, 1986.
Pet Sematary, Laurel Productions, 1989.
Stephen King's Golden Years (television series), CBS-TV, 1991.
Stephen King's Sleepwalkers, Columbia, 1992.

OTHER

(Under name Steve King) *The Star Invaders*, Gaslight Books, 1964.
Another Quarter Mile (poetry), Dorrance, 1979.
The Plant, Parts I-III, Philtrum, 1982-1985.
Stephen King's Year of Fear 1986 Calendar, New American Library, 1986.

Also author of several early unpublished novels, a teleplay "Sorry, Right Number" for *Tales from the Darkside* television series, numerous unproduced screenplays, short fiction, poetry, book reviews and articles in several magazines, and a newspaper column for *Maine Campus* during his college years. Wrote song, "Baby Can U Dig Your Man," for television movie, *The Stand*.

Also contributor of short stories to numerous anthologies, including *The Year's Finest Fantasy*, 1978; *Shadows*, Volume 1, 1978, Volume 4, 1981; *Nightmares*, 1979; *More Tales of Unknown Horror*, 1979; *New Tales of the Cthulhu Mythos*, 1980; *The 17th Fontana Book of Great Ghost Stories*, 1981; *New Terrors*, 1982; *The Year's Best Horror Stories*, Series XII, 1984; *The Dark Descent*, 1987; *Masques II: All New Stories of Horror and the Supernatural*, 1987; *The New Adventures of Sherlock Holmes: Original Stories by Eminent Mystery Writers*, 1987; *Prime Evil: New Stories by the Masters of Modern Horror*, 1989. Contributor of essays to *Murderess Ink: The Better Half of the Mystery*, 1979; *Grand Illusions*, 1983; *Shadowings: The Reader's Guide to Horror Fiction, 1981-82*, Starmont House, 1983; *The Writer's Handbook*, 1984; *Stephen King Goes to Hollywood*, 1987. Author of forewords and introductions for numerous fiction collections, special editions, and nonfiction works.

■ Adaptations

Films based on King's work include: *Carrie*, United Artists, 1976; *The Shining*, Warner Bros., 1980; *Cujo*, Warner Bros., 1983; *Christine*, Columbia, 1983; *The Dead Zone*, Paramount, 1983; *Children of the Corn* (based on the short story from *Night Shift*), New World Pictures, 1984; (directed by King) *Firestarter*, Universal, 1984; *Cat's Eye* (based on three short stories, "Quitters, Inc.," "The General," and "The Ledge"), Metro-Goldwyn-Mayer, 1985; *Stand by Me* (from his novella "The Body"), Columbia, 1986; *The Running Man*, Tri-Star, 1987; *Misery*, Columbia, 1990; *Graveyard Shift*, Paramount, 1990; *Tales from the Darkside: The Movie* (based on stories by Stephen King, Michael McDowell, and Arthur Conan Doyle), Paramount, 1990; *The Dark Half*, Orion, 1993; *Needful Things*, Columbia, 1993; *The Shawshank Redemption* (from the novella *Rita Hayworth and the Shawshank Redemption*), Columbia, 1994; *Dolores Claiborne*, Columbia, 1995; and *The Mangler* (from a short story), New Line Cinema, 1995. Television movies based on King's writings include: *'Salem's Lot*, CBS-TV, 1979; *It*, ABC-TV, 1990; *Sometimes They Come Back* (from a short story), CBS-TV, 1991; *The Tommyknockers*, ABC-TV, 1993; *The Stand*, ABC-TV, 1994; and *The Langoliers*, ABC-TV, 1995.

Carrie was adapted for the stage by Lawrence Cohen and first produced May 12, 1988, at Virginia Theater, closing after only five performances.

Rights to *The Talisman* have been sold for television. The films *Creepshow II*, New World Pictures, 1987, *A Return to 'Salem's Lot*, 1987, *The Lawnmower Man*, New Line, 1992, and *Children of the Corn II: The Final Sacrifice*, Miramax, 1993, are not based on King's writings. Many of King's works have been adapted for audiotape cassette by Recorded Books, Warner Audio, Listen for Pleasure, and New American Library.

■ Work in Progress

Wizard and Glass, the fourth book in the "Dark Tower" series.

■ Overview

"I don't think I ever will be taken seriously," horror novelist Stephen King told Jack Matthews in the *Detroit Free Press.* "People write to me and say how much they enjoy my books, but when someone walks by with a book by John Barth in their hands, they hide me so they won't get caught." King, whose books have sold millions of copies worldwide and have nearly all been adapted into movie or television releases—making him a millionaire several times over—readily admits that his chilling tales will never earn him critical plaudits, though he doesn't deny that it would be nice to win some coveted award or other. "I'd like to win the National Book Award, the Pulitzer Prize, the Nobel Prize," he admitted to *Publishers Weekly* writer Bill Goldstein. "I'd like to have someone write a *New York Times Book Review* piece that says, 'Hey, wait a minute guys, we made a mistake—this guy is one of the great writers of the 20th century.' But it's not going to happen, for two reasons. One is I'm not the greatest writer of the 20th century, and the other is that once you sell a certain number of books, the people who think about 'literature' stop thinking about you and assume that any writer who is popular across a wide spectrum has nothing to say."

But King does have something to say. His novels and short stories delve into the hidden terrors harbored deep within all of us, and, most especially, in himself. "Just about everything frightens me, in one way or another," he once said at a presentation at the Massachusetts Public Library. "I can see something frightening in most things. And I think about getting all of this out—you

know, there are people who are full of fear in our society who pay psychiatrists $75 or $80 an hour and it's not even a full hour. . . . And I get rid of all of this stuff by writing and people pay me. It's great. I love it." Mark Harris, writing in the *Dictionary of Literary Biography: 1980,* pointed out the psychological routes of King's stories: "In a way, King is less concerned with the events of his fiction than with the fear these events produce in his characters. For him, all fear moves us toward the comprehension of death, and he sees a parallel between fear and sexual desire: 'As we become capable of having sexual relationships, our interest in those relationships awakens. . . . As we become aware of our own unavoidable termination, we become aware of the fear-emotion.' King's growth as a writer can in part be measured by his progress as he develops a rhetoric of fear."

King's less-than-ideal childhood would have provided most other "serious" authors with plenty of angst-ridden fodder for dozens of books. Born September 21, 1947, in Portland, Maine, he was the second child of Donald and Nellie Ruth Pillsbury King. His father, a merchant marine, abandoned his family when King was only two years old. Overweight and awkward as a child, King sometimes felt alienated from his peers, but he compensated for his perceived inadequacies with an active imagination, which led him to a lifelong love of science fiction and horror movies. Like his father—who the author later learned had submitted stories to men's magazines—King developed a desire to write, which he quickly twisted into something awful: a satiric high school newspaper he called *The Village Vomit.* One day he got himself into trouble for writing unflattering things about his teachers. This turned out to be an unexpected opportunity for the young King when his school counselor, who believed the student needed some way to express himself, helped him to get a job writing about sports in the Lisbon, Maine, *Enterprise.*

King was further encouraged by his mother, who insisted that he submit his writing to magazines. King subsequently sold his first tales to *Startling Mystery Stories* for $35 each. "Even then he had the power to terrify," according to Harris: "A story he published in the student literary magazine continues to horrify a classmate who remembers it." Attending the University of Maine at Orono, where his mentor was a teacher named Burton

Hatlen, King decided to major in English. He earned a bachelor's degree and teaching certificate and, only a year after graduation, married Tabitha Jane Bruce ("The only important thing I ever did in my life for a conscious reason," he confessed in his introduction to *The Bachman Books*). King got a job teaching English at Hampden Academy high school, and soon his family included a daughter, Naomi, and son, Joseph.

But King wasn't completely satisfied with his life—he wanted to become a published writer. He wrote four novels, none of which sold, a failure that naturally caused him to become somewhat depressed. Then, drawing on some ideas he got from a grade-B movie called *The Brain from Planet Arous*, he began to write *Carrie*. At first, King didn't believe the story had much potential, but his wife convinced him that it had merit. She was right. Doubleday published *Carrie* in 1973, and the author received his first advance of $2,500. Although according to Goldstein, "*Carrie* probably lies lowest in King's estimation of his works," it jumpstarted his career. He received $400,000 for the paperback rights, and the book sold over a million copies in its first year.

Like many of his books, *Carrie* presents characters which are based upon people King has known in his life. The story's protagonist, Carrie White, was inspired by a poor girl in one of King's classes who was made fun of by her peers because she owned only one change of clothes. Like this student, Carrie is a misfit whose alienation from her peers is made even more pronounced by her frightening telekinetic powers. The novel comes to a climax when the other kids at Carrie's high school go too far. At the prom, they name Carrie queen only to humiliate her by dousing the teen and her date in pig's blood. Pushed past her limit, Carrie uses her supernatural powers to wreak a final, lethal revenge on all those who have hurt her. *Journal of Popular Culture* writer Alex E. Alexander noted the mix of horror and sexual overtones in King's first novel, describing *Carrie* as "an adult fairy tale explicit in matters of sex, killing and revenge."

King quickly followed the success of *Carrie* with *'Salem's Lot* ('Salem is short for Jerusalem), about a vampire who begins to prey on the residents of a small New England town. *'Salem's Lot* was even more popular than *Carrie*, selling over two million copies in only

six months. King had clearly made it as a professional writer, and, with some of the royalties he received, he took his family on a Colorado vacation. Because they were there toward the end of the summer season, one of the resorts where they stayed was nearly deserted, giving King the idea for the setting of his next book, *The Shining*.

In *The Shining*, a recovering alcoholic and down-on-his-luck writer named Jack Torrance takes a job as winter caretaker of an isolated hotel called The Overlook, bringing along his wife and son. The Overlook has a sinister history of murder, madness, and suicide, and the evil spirits of the place slowly take hold of Jack's mind, driving him to a

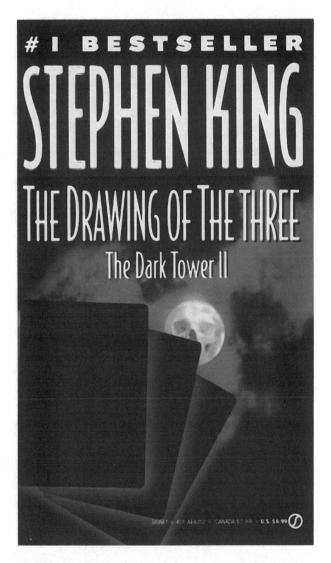

In the second installment in the "Dark Tower" series, a lone crusader continues his magical quest for knowledge and revenge.

The Stand, King's novel about survival in a post-apocalyptic world, was made into a successful ABC-TV miniseries in 1994.

madness that leads him to stalk his own family with murderous intent. According to Harris, *The Shining* garnered King "his first wide acclaim, and also his first sharp criticism." *New York Times Book Review* critic Jack Sullivan, for example, called the horror scenes "derivative" and lacking in atmosphere. But while Frederick Patten agreed in an article in *Delap's Fantasy and Science Fiction Review* that the novel "has flaws," he concluded that "the novel works!" By this time, for good or ill, King had established his own unique writing style, which Harris described this way: "His predilection for approximate alliteration . . . and exotic punctuation . . . can be cloying, but on the whole his prose serves its purpose well. And the use of brand names, popular songs, and other accoutrements of modern culture can be seen as part of King's strategy for making the bizarre seem familiar, possible, actual." King had become so prolific by the late 1970s and early 1980s that his publisher suggested he write under a pseudonym to help assuage any criticism that he was writing too quickly to produce quality stories. While agreeing to write under the pen name of Richard Bachman, King didn't do so for that reason. "I didn't think I was overpublishing the market," the author asserted in his *Bachman Books* introduction. "I think I did it to turn the heat down a little bit; to do something as someone other than Stephen King. . . . I think all novelists are inveterate role-players and it was fun to be someone else for a while." By 1984, however, King's little ruse was discovered. Remarkably, it took seven years for people to figure out the ploy, even though King's name appears on all of the copyright pages to the Bachman books, and the novels are dedicated to his family and friends.

A couple of the books published under the Bachman name, *Rage* (which was originally titled *Getting It On*) and *The Long Walk*, were written in 1966 and 1967, when King was a senior in high school and freshman in college. Another work that the author had begun before *Carrie* is *The Gunslinger*, which was inspired by King's college reading of Robert Browning's poem, "Childe Roland to the Dark Tower Came." *The Gunslinger* later became the first part of his "Dark Tower" trilogy, which also includes *The Drawing of the Three* and *The Waste Lands*, a series of connected stories about an errant gunslinger living in a postapocalyptic world who is chasing after a sinister "man in black." King also relies on the apocalypse theme in his ambitious novel, *The Stand*. In this work, the apocalypse comes about when a deadly virus is accidentally released, killing most of the world's population. Those few who survive converge into two sects: the wicked people gather around the "dark man," who makes his base in Las Vegas, while the good people are drawn to Mother Abagail, who eventually settles in Boulder, Colorado. Although those who follow Mother Abagail try to defeat the dark man and his cronies themselves, it takes the intervention of God to finally destroy the forces of evil and open the way to a more hopeful future for the plague survivors.

The same year that *The Stand* was published, the Kings' third child, Owen, was born. It was about this time that King bought a large Victorian home outside of Bangor, Maine, complete with indoor swimming pool and wrought-iron fence with big black spiders on the gates (he also owns a lakefront home in Center Lovell near the border of New Hampshire). The 1980s saw a string of novels, including *Firestarter*, *Cujo*, *Pet Sematary*, *Christine*, *It*, *Misery*, and *The Tommyknockers*. The author had become so popular by this time, observed *Writer's Digest* contributor W. C. Stroby, that even "the books on which King has taken a critical drubbing—notably 1983's haunted-car opus *Christine* and 1987's *The Tommyknockers* [about sinister aliens]—became bestsellers almost as soon as they hit the stores. Likewise, even King's most relentlessly grim and pessimistic novels—like 1983's *Pet Sematary* and 1981's *Cujo* . . . have sold millions of copies, proving there was a willing and eager audience for even his darkest visions."

■ Update

While still a prolific author, Stephen King has learned to slow down a little in recent years. For example, according to Stroby, the author spent the summer of 1991 playing baseball and goofing off. "I remember working on *Eyes of the Dragon* [a fantasy that King wrote for his daughter] and *Misery* at the same time," the author reflected in his interview with Stroby, "one in the morning and one at night. But I was younger then and I can't seem to do that anymore." King has also spent some time jamming with an unusual group called the Rock Bottom Remainders, which includes authors like Dave Barry and Amy Tan, who perform for charity. Nevertheless, King has remained prolific by most standards, producing on average a novel a year, as well as short stories and screenplays.

Some of the author's novels in the last few years have been in the typical King tradition. *The Dark Half,* for one, echoes the psychological horror in *Misery* in that the protagonist is an author facing his worst nightmare. While in *Misery,* Paul Sheldon faces a very real nemesis in the form of psychotic fan and terrifying health care worker Annie Wilkes, Thad Beaumont must face down his own evil side in *The Dark Half.* Both Paul and Thad suffer from the dilemma that audiences don't seem to care for sophisticated writing as much as they do for tawdry romances and bloodthirsty horror novels. When Annie, Paul's "biggest fan," discovers that the writer has killed off the heroine of his romance novels, she makes him a prisoner in her home and deliberately cripples him; similarly, when Thad tries to put his horror novelist alter ego to rest in order to concentrate on his more literary work, his evil side—in the form of George Stark, the living ghost of Thad's long-dead twin, whose vestigial remains were surgically removed from Thad's brain when he was a child—strikes back with a vengeance. Stark begins to hunt down all those he considers responsible for his "death," including Thad's editor and literary agent, until he discovers that his body is slowly deteriorating. The only cure is for a new George Stark horror novel to be written. Just as Annie forces Paul to write a new "Misery" novel, George makes Thad write a horror story, only in this case the evil alter ego kidnaps one of Thad's twin eight-month-old children for leverage. The novel concludes when Thad finally confronts the evil in himself—as represented by George—and destroys his dark half.

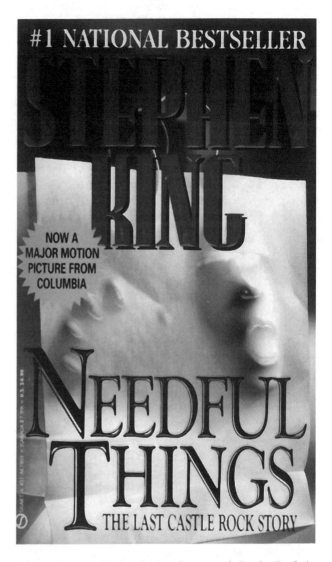

King "destroyed" the fictional town of Castle Rock in this 1991 novel about a strange man and his "little shop of horrors."

Breaking with the Dark Half

"*The Dark Half* is arguably King's most personal work," according to Peter Travers in *Rolling Stone.* "Thad grows up an outsider with a repressed hostility he can let out only through writing. King has admitted to a similar background. The workaholic monster in him can't stop recycling the same revenge plot. His work is alive with dark halves." Just as Thad does, King killed his alter ego, Richard Bachman (who King once said died of a brain tumor), and even went so far as to dedicate *The Dark Half* to Bachman. "It's a typical King joke," remarked Travers. "For all his success, he can't get respect." Both *Misery* and *The Dark Half* are reflective of some of the inner doubts that their author harbors inside himself. These two books "can be read as grimly ironic parables on King's own success," John Sutherland proposed in the *Times Literary Supplement.* "They suggest that once he rids himself of old formulas—however remunerative—he may yet write a book which will make his enemies, the critics, think twice about him." But King is understandably hesitant to take steps to change the course of his career. "I don't want there to be a time when I think that Steve King should be exclusively a horror writer," King confessed to Edward Gross in *Fangoria.* "The temptation is great, though. You say to yourself, if I don't produce horror stories, I won't have any more Number Ones—and it's very satisfying to have Number Ones."

With the publication of *Needful Things*, however, King made a symbolic break with his past work by destroying the town of Castle Rock, Maine, the fictional setting of many of his stories, including *Cujo*, *The Dead Zone*, *The Dark Half*, and the novella, *The Body*, which was later adapted as the successful film, *Stand by Me*. Readers might notice how the beginning of *Needful Things* is similar to *'Salem's Lot*, in that it all starts with the arrival in a small town of a stranger who, because of his very sinister nature, is set on destroying the lives of all who live there. In *'Salem's Lot*, the evil visitor was a vampire, while in *Needful Things* it is Leland Gaunt, ostensibly an entrepreneur who has just opened a curio shop in Castle Rock with the same name as the book's title. Gaunt specializes in selling his customers the objects of their greatest desires—for a price. To young Brian Rusk, for example, the most special item in the world is a rare Sandy Koufax baseball card. Gaunt gives it to him in exchange for an unusual request: he asks Brian to throw mud onto a woman's clean sheets while they're hanging out to dry. While strangely mischievous, the request seems fair enough to Brian, who, from this small misdeed, unwittingly begins a feud between the woman and her friend that will eventually lead to both of their deaths.

As the story progresses, Sheriff Alan Pangborn slowly comes to realize that Gaunt is more than he seems. Somehow the merchant knows everything about the lives of the people of Castle Rock, and he knows just what buttons to push to bring out the worst in each of them. Murder and mayhem proliferates throughout the town, while Gaunt works behind the scenes, devilishly orchestrating each horrible event until Pangborn is finally able to convince the townspeople that Gaunt is behind it all. In the book's climax, however, the town is destroyed, and Gaunt, whose nature is clearly not human, manages to escape. *Needful Things* did not get the best reviews from critics, and perhaps it works better as a catharsis than an important novel in itself for King. *New York Times Book Review* contributor Joe Queenan, for example, said that the novel "is not the sort of book that one can readily recommend to the dilettante, to the dabbler or to anyone with a reasonable-sized brain." However, a *Los Angeles Times Book Review* critic felt that *Needful Things* demonstrates that King is a "tremendous storyteller . . . and that is what makes even this very long, and secondary, novel a rapid read."

Hollywood King

If King sometimes struggles with the side of his literary self that wants to write cheap-thrill bestsellers, he also has another love/hate relationship with Hollywood. Almost from the beginning of his writing career, with the release of Brian De Palma's adaptation of *Carrie*, King's name has been as omnipresent in movie theaters as it has been in the horror section of book stores. With only a couple of exceptions—most notably the "Dark Tower" books—King's works have been transmogrified to various degrees of success from the page to celluloid, so that any discussion of the author's works would be incomplete without mentioning their corresponding films. Some of these adaptations, including *Carrie*, *The Shining*, *Stand by Me*, *Misery*, and *The Shawshank Redemption* have been very successful, while others like *Maximum Overdrive* and *Graveyard Shift* have been bombs. The blame for these cinematic failures lies with both King and the studios, according to Travers. "Hollywood traditionally kongs King by playing him safe, meaning crude," he observed. But while remarking that films like *Pet Sematary* have been ruined by their directors, Travers added that "King often colludes in his own undoing: He wrote the script for *Pet Sematary* and wrote and directed the wretched *Maximum Overdrive*."

Still more problematic for the author, however, is that filmmakers have also been buying the titles to stories for which King no longer owns the copyrights and turning them into schlock films, such as *Children of the Corn II* and *The Return to 'Salem's Lot*. Some of these movies, such as *The Lawnmower Man*, have absolutely nothing in common with the story from which the title was stolen. "The prospect of all these sequels is one thing that can make King sick," said Richard Corliss in a *Time* article. "'I don't want them to make any more movies from my stuff!'" King exclaimed to Corliss. Despite his troublesome relationship with Hollywood, however, King has become increasingly involved with film adaptations, sometimes even directing, producing, and acting in them. Still, he told Corliss, "Writing a novel is like swimming. . . . You plunge in. Making a movie is like ice skating; everything's on the surface."

Sleepless in Maine

Three of the novels that have followed *Needful Things*—*Gerald's Game*, *Dolores Claiborne*, and *Rose*

Madder—show some signs of a turn in the course of King's career that was hinted at in *Misery.* These books feature characters facing often frightening situations, but there is very little paranormal about their experiences. However, initial examination of the author's 1994 novel, *Insomnia,* appears to reveal an interruption in this trend. It is difficult to say whether *Insomnia,* which was published after *Dolores Claiborne* and harks back to his typical horror formulas, is any indication of whether or not King is pulling away from the genre for which he is best known. This is because *Insomnia* was actually begun in 1990 and abandoned temporarily by the author. In his 1992 interview with Stroby, King said, "I spent about four months of 1990 writing . . . *Insomnia.* It's a long piece of work, it's about 550 pages long. It's no good. I know it's not publishable. And I've been writing and publishing books for a long time. Taken piece by piece and chapter by chapter, it is [good]. But I didn't get this one out of the ground." Later in the interview, King added, "The thing that hurts is that the last 80 or 90 pages are wonderful. . . . But things just don't connect; it doesn't have that novelistic roundness that it should have."

King did finish *Insomnia,* however, and it was published two years after he spoke with Stroby. The protagonist of the story is Ralph Roberts, a resident of Derry, Maine, who is in his seventies, recently widowed, and suffering from an inability to sleep. A side effect, or so Ralph at first believes, of his worsening insomnia is that he begins to see auras around people and objects, and he begins to experience reality more intensely than ever before. But then his visions become even more eerie when he begins to see four-foot-tall ghouls, who look like bald doctors in white coats, whose job it is to cut off the aura balloons from people who have died. Other phantoms begin to appear, and Ralph fears for his sanity until he learns that his friend, Lois Chase, who is also a widower, is experiencing the same visions. Together they learn that they have become involved in a struggle between the forces of good and evil that exist on a higher plain of existence, and that the fate of reality itself is teetering upon the life of a small child, whose life has been placed in peril in a town torn in two by an upcoming abortion rights rally.

Insomnia is one of King's more complex and ambitious novels. As Chris Bohjalian wrote in the *New York Times Book Review,* the book is "about God, the Devil, birth, abortion, wife abuse, why aliens always look alike on the covers of tabloid newspapers, hyper-reality, Connie Chung, and how important it is to get a good night's sleep." Although King touches on some serious issues in the novel, Bohjalian pointed out that the anti-abortion versus abortion rights debate is a central concern for only about the first quarter of the story. "I was disappointed to see Mr. King again shy away from tougher, more complex issues," Bohjalian lamented. "There are some truly haunting scenes in the book about wife abuse and fanaticism, as well as touching observations about growing up and growing old, but they're quickly consumed by more predictable sensationalism." Other critics, evaluating *Insomnia* purely on its effectiveness as a horror tale, were kinder in their reviews. While acknowledging that King doesn't resolve the issues he brings up, *People* contributor Ralph Novak said that "King keeps up readers' curiosity . . . [so that] you're anxious to know what will happen next." In her *Washington Post Book World* review, Kinky Friedman called *Insomnia* "an exceptionally chilling tale," adding that, although the novel is 781 pages long, those who "make the effort . . . will find it long on insight, charm, magic and excitement."

Moving away from Traditional Horror?

Gerald's Game, Dolores Claiborne, and *Rose Madder* further develop the more serious themes seen in *Insomnia,* especially with regard to spouse abuse. All three of these books deal with husbands who physically attack their wives in one way or another, but King approaches this theme from different angles in each. In *Gerald's Game,* the subject is sexual abuse. King quickly sets up the premise in this story within the first chapter of the book: Jessie Burlingame's husband, Gerald, has a taste for handcuffing his wife to the bed when he makes love to her. Jessie, however, isn't too fond of the game, and one day, while they are at an isolated Maine summer house playing Gerald's game, Jessie decides she doesn't want to do this again. When Gerald doesn't listen to her protests, thinking that she's just role playing, Jessie kicks him out of desperation. The kick is more serious than she intended, though, and Gerald has a heart attack and dies.

Now, handcuffed to the bed and miles from the earshot of anyone who might help her, Jessie realizes that she's in desperate trouble. Jessie faces the very real possibility that she will starve or die of thirst. As she contemplates this fate, a mangy stray dog enters the room and begins chewing on

Kathy Bates (right)—who won an Oscar for her portrayal of Annie Wilkes in *Misery*—played the lead character in the 1995 film adaptation of *Dolores Claiborne*, which also starred Jennifer Jason Leigh.

Gerald's face—will Jessie be next? But King doesn't stop there. Soon Jessie's mind begins to weave in and out of madness and she starts to hear voices. As darkness approaches, an even more frightening specter appears, a ghoulish figure with a face like a skull, who could be a real madman entering the house or merely a figment of her panicked imagination. "The interaction of these phantoms of the heroine's past tells another, older story of sexual exploitation and terror, the molestation of Jessie when she was just 10 years old," reported Kathryn Harrison in a *Washington Post Book World* review.

Criticism of *Gerald's Game* has particularly focused on debate as to whether King is successful in balancing the realities and fantasies that swirl through Jessie's mind to illustrate his apparent themes of child and spouse abuse. Harrison believed that King is not entirely convincing in his attempt: "The wild,

exaggerated horror of Jessie's ordeal becomes burlesque at points, and [King's] talent for the absurd inclusion of pop culture . . . overwhelms the horror of child abuse." Harrison later added that the author's "purpose is undone by his method. In comparison with the finely detailed unraveling of Jessie's mind and the horror show of the dog and the flies and the fiend in the corner, the usual crimes committed against women and children seem mundane, unremarkable, boring." *New York Times Book Review* critic Wendy Doniger, on the other hand, felt that King's attempt to connect Jessie's current abuse by her husband with the past abuse by her father when she was a girl is "masterfully interwoven." Nevertheless, Doniger added that the "two genres cancel each other out: the horror makes us distrust the serious theme, and the serious theme stops us from suspending our disbelief to savor the horror. Mr. King seems to be handcuffed to his old technique, the tried-and-true formula, but perhaps it is now time for him to break loose from his own past. To do this he would have to confront what may well be his own personal horror: to try (perchance to fail) to write a good novel without any horror scenes."

Dolores Claiborne was written as a companion piece to *Gerald's Game,* and King originally planned to publish them in a single volume, until their lengths made it clear that this wasn't possible. Interestingly, the protagonists in these two books are linked together during a total eclipse over Maine during the summer of 1963. As with its predecessor, *Dolores Claiborne* is about spouse abuse. At the beginning of the novel, the heroine of the title is accused of murdering her aged employer by pushing her down the stairs. Early in the book, however, it becomes clear that Dolores did not commit this crime, but she did commit another one thirty years earlier: she killed her abusive husband by taunting him into beating her one last time, then running from him and tricking him into falling down an unused well. She planned his death to end the torture he inflicted upon her, but, more importantly, to keep him from further sexual molestation of his own teenage daughter. It is while she is committing the murder during the eclipse that Dolores is mysteriously linked to Jessie, actually seeing Jessie as a small girl just after her father has molested her, while Jessie, in turn, sees Dolores sitting beside the well. In this way King "implies a psychic sisterhood of abused women," according to Bill Kent in the *New York Times Book Review,* a development the critic labelled "gimmicky."

Dolores's narrative of how these events came to pass takes up most of the novel and forms what, in the opinion of several critics, becomes a sensitive character study. One *Publishers Weekly* reviewer, who asserted that *Dolores Claiborne* surpasses *Gerald's Game,* felt that the novel "shows that King, even without the trappings of horror and suspense, is a magnificent storyteller." Kent complained that King "burdens Dolores's dialect with too many obscenities and banalities," but the reviewer also praised the author for his "compassionate observation" of the main character and concluded that *Dolores Claiborne* "proves that [King] can do more than simply frighten readers."

Finally, *Rose Madder* touches upon an issue that has been reported with increasing frequency in the 1990s: stalking. In this story, Rosie Daniels realizes after fourteen years of marriage—as if awakening from a horrible nightmare—that she needs to get away from her husband, Norman, who has been physically abusing her for much of that time. Without giving away her plans, she picks up and leaves one day, stopping only to withdraw money from the ATM machine. Against the odds, Rosie manages to begin a new life for herself; she finds a place to live, a job, and even a new boyfriend named Bill Steiner. But she hasn't really escaped her husband yet. Norman, who is a policeman, begins to stalk her, and with his professional background he knows all the tricks. Using his skills at creating tension from his horror stories, King quickly builds excitement in the story equal to

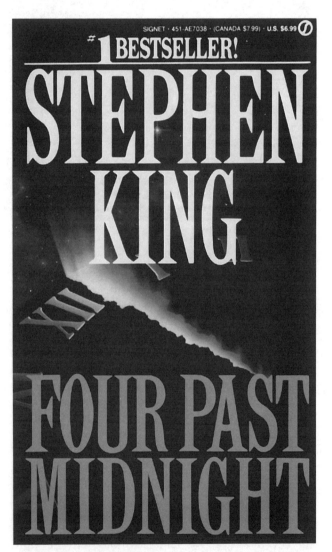

This 1990 novella collection was highlighted by *The Langoliers,* a dark tale about a group of airline passengers on a nightmare flight.

that of any of his books featuring horrible monsters. After all, Norman is indeed a monster, although he lacks fangs or claws.

Judging from his recent books, King indeed has something to say that might satisfy his literary critics: of all the monsters he has written about, the everyday monsters, the ones who might be sleeping right beside you every night, are perhaps the most frightening of all. Yet this doesn't mean that his earlier novels are without value. Many critics believe that King has always been a remarkable storyteller. "Mr. King, however prolific he may be and however fabulously rich, is our premiere and much-to-be-valued storyteller, and that is so because his stories *matter*," declared *Commonweal* contributor Frank McConnell. McConnell concluded, "Neither King's dog-in-the-manger critics nor his oh-boy-we-love-horror fans seem to have noticed the immense current of tenderness and nostalgia that underlies his gothicism. . . . King does this in a prose that is not 'Literature,' maybe. He does it in a more ancient and vastly more sacred form—that of the storyteller."

■ Works Cited

Alexander, Alex E., "Stephen King's 'Carrie'—A Universal Fairy Tale, *Journal of Popular Culture*, fall, 1979, pp. 282-87.

Bohjalian, Chris, "The Ghouls Next Door," *New York Times Book Review*, October 30, 1994, p. 24.

Corliss, Richard, "The King of Creep," *Time*, April 27, 1992, pp. 62-63.

Review of *Dolores Claiborne, Publishers Weekly*, October 12, 1992, pp. 64-65.

Doniger, Wendy, "Shackled to the Past," *New York Times Book Review*, August 16, 1992, p. 3.

Friedman, Kinky, "Things That Go Snip in the Night," *Washington Post Book World*, October 9, 1994, p. 4.

Goldstein, Bill, "King of Horror," *Publishers Weekly*, January 24, 1991, pp. 6-9.

Gross, Edward, "Stephen King Takes a Vacation," *Fangoria*, October, 1986.

Harris, Mark, "Stephen King," *Dictionary of Literary Biography Yearbook: 1980*, edited by Karen L. Roos, Jean W. Ross, and Richard Ziegfeld, Gale, 1981, pp. 226-34.

Harrison, Kathryn, "The Ties That Bind," *Washington Post Book World*, July 19, 1992, p. 7.

Kent, Bill, review of *Dolores Claiborne, New York Times Book Review*, December 27, 1992, p. 15.

King, Stephen, "An Evening with Stephen King at the Billerica, Massachusetts Public Library," Colony Communications, Inc., 1983.

King, Stephen, introduction to *The Bachman Books: Four Early Novels by Stephen King*, New American Library, 1985.

Matthews, Jack, "Novelist Loves His Nightmares," *Detroit Free Press*, November 12, 1982.

McConnell, Frank, "Just Doing It: Stephen King's Craft," *Commonweal*, January 25, 1991, pp. 57-59.

Review of *Needful Things, Los Angeles Times Book Review*, October 20, 1991, p. 6.

Novak, Ralph, review of *Insomnia, People*, October 10, 1994, pp. 32, 34.

Patten, Frederick, review of *The Shining, Delap's Fantasy and Science Fiction Review*, April, 1977, p. 6.

Queenan, Joe, "And Us without Our Spoons," *New York Times Book Review*, September 29, 1991, pp. 13-14.

Stroby, W. C., "Digging Up Stories with Stephen King," *Writer's Digest*, March, 1992, pp. 22-27.

Sullivan, Jack, review of *The Shining, New York Times Book Review*, February 20, 1977, p. 8.

Sutherland, John, review of *Needful Things, Times Literary Supplement*, November 15, 1991, p. 6.

Travers, Peter, "Stephen King Divided," *Rolling Stone*, May 13, 1993, pp. 113-114.

■ For More Information See

BOOKS

Beahm, George W., editor, *The Stephen King Companion*, Andrews and McMeel, 1989.

Beahm, George W., editor, *The Stephen King Story*, revised edition, St. Martin's Press, 1992.

Blue, Tyson, *The Unseen King*, Borgo Press, 1989.

Blue, Tyson, *Observations from the Terminator: Thoughts on Stephen King and Other Modern Masters of Horror Fiction*, Borgo Press, 1995.

Browne, Ray B., and Gary Hoppenstand, editors, *The Gothic World of Stephen King: Landscape and Nightmares*, Bowling Green State University Popular Press, 1987.

Cohen, Daniel, *Masters of Horror*, Clarion, 1984.

Collings, Michael R., and David Engebretson, *The Shorter Works of Stephen King*, Starmont House, 1985.

Collings, Michael R., *The Many Facets of Stephen King*, Starmont House, 1985.

Collings, Michael R., *Stephen King as Richard Bachman*, Starmont House, 1985.

Collings, Michael R., *The Annotated Guide to Stephen King: A Primary and Secondary Bibliography of the Works of America's Premier Horror Writer*, Starmont House, 1986.

Collings, Michael R., *The Films of Stephen King*, Starmont House, 1986.

Collings, Michael R., *The Stephen King Phenomenon*, Starmont House, 1987.

Collings, Michael R., *The Work of Stephen King: An Annotated Bibliography and Guide*, Borgo Press, 1993.

Collings, Michael R., *Scaring Us to Death: The Impact of Stephen King on Popular Culture*, 2nd revised and expanded edition, Borgo Press, 1995.

Connor, Jeff, *Stephen King Goes to Hollywood: A Lavishly Illustrated Guide to All the Films Based on Stephen King's Fiction*, New American Library, 1987.

Contemporary Literary Criticism, Volume 61, Gale, 1990.

Davis, Jonathan P., *Stephen King's America*, Bowling Green State University Popular Press, 1994.

Docherty, Brian, editor, *American Horror Fiction: From Brockden Brown to Stephen King*, St. Martin's Press, 1990.

Gagne, P., *Stephen King Goes to the Movies*, Underwood-Miller (Los Angeles), 1987.

Herron, Don, editor, *Reign of Fear: Fiction and Film of Stephen King*, Underwood-Miller, 1988.

Horsting, Jessie, *Stephen King: At the Movies*, Signet/Starlog, 1986.

Keyishian, Amy and Marjorie, *Stephen King*, Chelsea House, 1995.

Lloyd, Ann, *The Films of Stephen King*, St. Martin's Press, 1994.

Magistrale, Tony, *Landscape of Fear: Stephen King's American Gothic*, Bowling Green State University Press, 1988.

Magistrale, Tony, *The Moral Voyages of Stephen King*, Starmont House, 1989.

Magistrale, Tony, editor, *The Shining Reader*, Starmont House, 1991.

Magistrale, Tony, editor, *A Casebook on The Stand*, Starmont House, 1992.

Magistrale, Tony, *Stephen King, the Second Decade: Danse Macabre to The Dark Half*, Twayne Publishers, 1992.

Magistrale, Tony, editor, *The Dark Descent: Essays Defining Stephen King's Horrorscape*, Greenwood Press, 1992.

Platt, Charles, *Dream Makers: The Uncommon Men & Women Who Write Science Fiction*, Berkeley, 1983.

Reino, Joseph, *Stephen King, the First Decade: Carrie to Pet Sematary*, Twayne, 1988.

Saidman, Anne, *Stephen King, Master of Horror*, Lerner Publications, 1992.

Schweitzer, Darrell, *Discovering Modern Horror Fiction*, Starmont House, 1985.

Schweitzer, Darrell, editor, *Discovering Stephen King*, Starmont House, 1985.

Spignesi, Stephen J., *The Shape under the Sheet: The Complete Stephen King Encyclopedia*, Popular Culture (Ann Arbor, MI), 1991.

Underwood, Tim, and Chuck Miller, editors, *Fear Itself: The Horror Fiction of Stephen King*, foreword by Stephen King, introduction by Peter Straub, Underwood-Miller, 1986

Underwood, Tim and Chuck Miller, editors, *Kingdom of Fear: The World of Stephen King*, Underwood-Miller, 1986.

Winter, Douglas E., editor, *Shadowings: The Reader's Guide to Horror Fiction, 1981-1982*, Starmont House, 1983.

Winter, Douglas E., *Stephen King: The Art of Darkness*, New American Library, 1984.

PERIODICALS

Library Journal, January, 1995, p. 162.

Newsweek, May 9, 1994, p. 70.

New York, May 10, 1993, pp. 64-65; September 26, 1994, pp. 96, 98.

New York Times Book Review, January 8, 1989, pp. 22-23; October 29, 1989, p. 12; July 20, 1990, p. 48; September 2, 1990, p. 21; October 24, 1993, p. 22.

People Weekly, November 7, 1988, p. 38; November 12, 1990, p. 17; April 27, 1992, p. 20.

Publishers Weekly, November 8, 1991, pp. 60-61; August 2, 1993, p. 62.

School Library Journal, January, 1991, p. 121; April, 1993, p. 149.

Time, May 30, 1988, p. 65; November 20, 1989, pp. 105-06; October 15, 1990, p. 86; July 22, 1991, p. 56; November 11, 1991, p. 93; July 13, 1992, p. 81; May 9, 1994, p. 83; March 27, 1995, p. 73.

OTHER

King, Stephen, *The Author Talks* (cassette recording), Recorded Books (Charlotte Hall, MD), 1987.

Subscriptions to *Castle Rock, the Official Stephen King Newsletter*, a monthly newsletter devoted to the news and worlds of King's fiction, are available by writing to: P.O. Box 8183, Bangor, ME 04401.*

—*Sketch by Janet L. Hile*

Julian May

■ Personal

Full name, Julian May Dikty; also writes under pseudonyms Bob Cunningham, Lee N. Falconer, John Feilen, Matthew G. Grant, J. C. May, Ian Thorne, Jean Wright Thorne, and George Zanderbergen; born July 10, 1931, in Chicago, IL; daughter of Matthew M. and Julia (Feilen) May; married Thaddeus "Ted" E. Dikty (a writer and publisher), 1953; children: Alan Samuel, David Bernard, Barbara Ellen. *Education:* Attended Rosary College, 1949–52. *Hobbies and other interests:* Backpacking, canoeing, electronic music, gardening, jewelry making.

■ Addresses

Home and office—P.O. Box 851, Mercer Island, WA 98040.

■ Career

Freelance writer. Booz Allen & Hamilton, Chicago, IL, editor, 1953; Consolidated Book Publishers, Chicago, editor, 1954–57; Publication Associates, editor and co-owner, Chicago, 1957–68, Naperville, IL, 1968–74, West Linn, OR, 1974–80, and Mercer Island, WA, 1980—. Has also worked in art design, art direction, commercial art, and photography.

■ Awards, Honors

Locus Award for Best Science Fiction Novel, 1982, and Hugo and Nebula Award nominations, all for *The Many-Colored Land.*

■ Writings

"THE SAGA OF PLIOCENE EXILE"; SCIENCE FICTION

The Many-Colored Land, Houghton, 1981.
The Golden Torc, Houghton, 1981.
Brede's Tale (short story), Starmont House, 1982.
The Nonborn King, Houghton, 1983.
The Adversary, Houghton, 1984.
A Pliocene Companion: A Reader's Guide to The Many Colored Land, The Golden Torc, The Nonborn King, The Adversary, Houghton, 1984.

"GALACTIC MILIEU" SERIES; SCIENCE FICTION

Intervention: A Root Tale to the Galactic Milieu and a Vinculum between It and the Saga of Pliocene Exile, Houghton, 1987, published in two volumes as *The Surveillance* and *The Metaconcert,* Ballantine, 1989.

Jack the Bodiless, Knopf, 1992.
Diamond Mask, Knopf, 1994.
Magnificat, Knopf, 1996.

FANTASY FICTION

(With Marion Zimmer Bradley and Andre Norton)
Black Trillium, Doubleday, 1990.
Blood Trillium, Bantam Spectra, 1992.

JUVENILE NONFICTION

There's Adventure in Atomic Energy, Popular Mechanics Press, 1957.
There's Adventure in Chemistry, Popular Mechanics Press, 1957.
There's Adventure in Electronics, Popular Mechanics Press, 1957.
There's Adventure in Geology, Popular Mechanics Press, 1958.
There's Adventure in Rockets, Popular Mechanics Press, 1958.
You and the Earth Beneath Us, Children's Press, 1958.
There's Adventure in Jet Aircraft, Popular Mechanics Press, 1959.
There's Adventure in Marine Science, Popular Mechanics Press, 1959.
Show Me the World of Astronomy, Pennington Press, 1959.
Show Me the World of Electronics, Pennington Press, 1959.
Show Me the World of Modern Airplanes, Pennington Press, 1959.
Show Me the World of Space Travel, Pennington Press, 1959.
The Real Book About Robots and Thinking Machines, Doubleday, 1961.
There's Adventure in Astronautics, Hawthorn, 1961.
There's Adventure in Automobiles, Hawthorn, 1961.
Motion, Accelerated Instruction Methods, 1962.
(With husband, T. E. Dikty) *Every Boy's Book of American Heroes*, Fell, 1963.
They Turned to Stone, Holiday House, 1965.
Weather, Follett, 1966.
Rockets, Follett, 1967.
They Lived in the Ice Age, Holiday House, 1968.
Astronautics, Follett, 1968.
The Big Island, Follett, 1968.
The First Men, Holiday House, 1968.

Horses: How They Came to Be, Holiday House, 1968.
Alligator Hole, Follett, 1969.
Before the Indians, Holiday House, 1969.
Climate, Follett, 1969.
How We Are Born, Follett, 1969.
Living Things and Their Young, Follett, 1969.
Man and Woman, Follett, 1969.
Moving Hills of Sand, Follett, 1969.
Why the Earth Quakes, Holiday House, 1969.
Do You Have Your Father's Nose?, Creative Educational Society, 1970.
Dodos and Dinosaurs are Extinct, Creative Educational Society, 1970.
(With others) *The Ecology of North America*, Creative Educational Society, 1970.
The First Living Things, Holiday House, 1970.
How to Build a Body, Creative Educational Society, 1970.
Millions of Years of Eggs, Creative Educational Society, 1970.
A New Baby Comes, Creative Educational Society, 1970.
Tiger Stripes and Zebra Stripes, Creative Educational Society, 1970.
Why Birds Migrate, Holiday House, 1970.
Why Plants Are Green Instead of Pink, Creative Educational Society, 1970.
Wildlife in the City, Creative Educational Society, 1970.
Blue River: The Land Beneath the Sea, Holiday House, 1971.
Cactus Fox, Creative Educational Society, 1971.
These Islands Are Alive, Hawthorn, 1971.
Why People Are Different Colors, Holiday House, 1971.
The Antarctic: Bottom of the World, Creative Educational Society, 1972.
The Arctic: Top of the World, Creative Educational Society, 1972.
Cascade Cougar, Creative Educational Society, 1972.
The Cloud Book, Creative Educational Society, 1972.
Deserts: Hot and Cold, Creative Educational Society, 1972.
Eagles of the Valley, Creative Educational Society, 1972.
Forests That Change Color, Creative Educational Society, 1972.
Giant Condor of California, Creative Educational Society, 1972.
Glacier Grizzly, Creative Educational Society, 1972.
Islands of the Tiny Deer, Young Scott Books, 1972.

The Land is Disappearing, Creative Educational Society, 1972.

Living Blanket on the Land, Creative Educational Society, 1972.

The Mysterious Evergreen Forest, Creative Educational Society, 1972.

Plankton: Drifting Life of the Waters, Holiday House, 1972.

The Prairie Has an Endless Sky, Creative Educational Society, 1972.

Prairie Pronghorn, Creative Educational Society, 1972.

Rainbows, Clouds, and Foggy Dew, Creative Educational Society, 1972.

Sea Lion Island, Creative Educational Society, 1972.

Sea Otter, Creative Educational Society, 1972.

Snowfall!, Creative Educational Society, 1972.

What Will the Weather Be?, Creative Educational Society, 1972.

Birds We Know, Creative Educational Society, 1973.

Fishes We Know, Creative Educational Society, 1973.

Insects We Know, Creative Educational Society, 1973.

The Life Cycle of a Bullfrog, Creative Educational Society, 1973.

The Life Cycle of a Cottontail Rabbit, Creative Educational Society, 1973.

The Life Cycle of a Monarch Butterfly, Creative Educational Society, 1973.

The Life Cycle of an Opossum, Creative Educational Society, 1973.

The Life Cycle of a Polyphemus Moth, Creative Educational Society, 1973.

The Life Cycle of a Raccoon, Creative Educational Society, 1973.

The Life Cycle of a Red Fox, Creative Educational Society, 1973.

The Life Cycle of a Snapping Turtle, Creative Educational Society, 1973.

Mammals We Know, Creative Educational Society, 1973.

Reptiles We Know, Creative Educational Society, 1973.

Wild Turkeys, Holiday House, 1973.

How the Animals Came to North America, Holiday House, 1974.

Cars and Cycles, Bowmar-Noble, 1978.

The Warm-Blooded Dinosaurs, Holiday House, 1978.

JUVENILE BIOGRAPHIES

Captain Cousteau: Undersea Explorer, Creative Educational Society, 1972.

Hank Aaron Clinches the Pennant, Crestwood, 1972.

Jim Brown Runs With the Ball, Crestwood, 1972.

Johnny Unitas and the Long Pass, Crestwood, 1972.

Matthew Henson: Co-Discoverer of the North Pole, Creative Educational Society, 1972.

Mickey Mantle Slugs It Out, Crestwood, 1972.

Sitting Bull: Chief of the Sioux, Creative Educational Society, 1972.

Sojourner Truth: Freedom Fighter, Creative Educational Society, 1972.

Willie Mays: Most Valuable Player, Crestwood, 1972.

Amelia Earhart: Pioneer of Aviation, Creative Educational Society, 1973.

Bobby Orr: Star on Ice, Crestwood, 1973.

Ernie Banks: Home Run Slugger, Crestwood, 1973.

Fran Tarkenton: Scrambling Quarterback, Crestwood, 1973.

Gale Sayers: Star Running Back, Crestwood, 1973.

Hillary and Tenzing: Conquerors of Mount Everest, Creative Educational Society, 1973.

Kareem Abdul Jabbar: Cage Superstar, Crestwood, 1973.

Quanah: Leader of the Comanche, Creative Educational Society, 1973.

Thor Heyerdahl: Modern Viking Adventurer, Creative Educational Society, 1973.

Roberto Clemente and the World Series Upset, Crestwood, 1973.

Billie Jean King: Tennis Champion, Crestwood, 1974.

Bobby Hull: Hockey's Golden Jet, Crestwood, 1974.

Lee Trevino: The Golf Explosion, Crestwood, 1974.

O. J. Simpson: Juice on the Gridiron, Crestwood, 1974.

Roy Campanella: Brave Man of Baseball, Crestwood, 1974.

A. J. Foyt: Championship Auto Racer, Crestwood, 1975.

Arthur Ashe: Dark Star of Tennis, Crestwood, 1975.

Bobby Clarke: Hockey with a Grin, Crestwood, 1975.

Chris Evert: Princess of Tennis, Crestwood, 1975.

Evel Knievel: Daredevil Stuntman, Crestwood, 1975.

Evonne Goolalgong: Smasher from Australia, Crestwood, 1975.

Frank Robinson: Slugging toward Glory, Crestwood, 1975.

Janet Lynn: Figure Skating Star, Crestwood, 1975.

Pele: World Soccer Star, Crestwood, 1975.

Joe Namath: High Flying Quarterback, Crestwood, 1975.

Muhammad Ali: Boxing Superstar, Crestwood, 1975.

Vince Lombardi: The Immortal Coach, Crestwood, 1975.

Phil Esposito: The Big Bruin, Crestwood, 1975.

SPORTS NONFICTION

The Baltimore Colts, Creative Educational Society, 1974.

The Dallas Cowboys, Creative Educational Society, 1974.

The Green Bay Packers, Creative Educational Society, 1974.

The Kansas City Chiefs, Creative Educational Society, 1974.

The Miami Dolphins, Creative Educational Society, 1974.

The New York Jets, Creative Educational Society, 1974.

The Stanley Cup, Creative Educational Society, 1975.

The Super Bowl, Creative Educational Society, 1975.

The Indianapolis 500, Creative Educational Society, 1975.

The Kentucky Derby, Creative Educational Society, 1975.

The Masters Tournament of Golf, Creative Educational Society, 1975.

The U. S. Open Golf Championship, Creative Educational Society, 1975.

Wimbledon: World Tennis Focus, Creative Educational Society, 1975.

The World Series, Creative Educational Society, 1975.

The NBA Playoffs: Basketball's Classic, Creative Educational Society, 1975.

The Olympic Games, Creative Educational Society, 1975.

The PGA Championship, Creative Educational Society, 1976.

The Pittsburgh Steelers, Creative Educational Society, 1976.

The Winter Olympics, Creative Educational Society, 1976.

America's Cup Yacht Race, Creative Educational Society, 1976.

Boxing's Heavyweight Championship Fight, Creative Educational Society, 1976.

Daytona 500, Creative Educational Society, 1976.

Forest Hills and the American Tennis Championship, Creative Educational Society, 1976.

The Grand Prix, Creative Educational Society, 1976.

The Triple Crown, Creative Educational Society, 1976.

The Rose Bowl, Creative Educational Society, 1976.

The Washington Redskins, Creative Educational Society, 1977.

The Los Angeles Rams, Creative Educational Society, 1977.

The Minnesota Vikings, Creative Educational Society, 1977.

The New York Giants, Creative Educational Society, 1977.

The Oakland Raiders, Creative Educational Society, 1977.

The San Francisco 49ers, Creative Educational Society, 1977.

The Oakland Raiders: Superbowl Champions, Creative Educational Society, 1978.

The Baltimore Colts, (different from previous publication of same title), Creative Educational Society, 1980.

The Cincinnati Bengals, Creative Educational Society, 1980.

The Dallas Cowboys, (different from previous publication of same title), Creative Educational Society, 1980.

The Denver Broncos, Creative Educational Society, 1980.

The Green Bay Packers, (different from previous publication of same title), Creative Educational Society, 1980.

The Kansas City Chiefs, (different from previous title of same title), Creative Educational Society), 1980.

The Miami Dolphins, (different from previous publication of same title), Creative Educational Society, 1980.

The New York Jets, (different from previous publication of same title), Creative Educational Society, 1980.

The Pittsburgh Steelers, (different from previous publication of same title), Creative Educational Society, 1980.

The San Diego Chargers, Creative Educational Society, 1980.

NONFICTION; UNDER PSEUDONYM JOHN FEILEN

Air, Follett, 1965.
Deer, Follett, 1967.
Squirrels, Follett, 1967.
Dirt Track Speedsters, Crestwood, 1976.
Racing on the Water, Crestwood, 1976.

Winter Sports, Crestwood, 1976.
Four-Wheel Racing, Crestwood, 1978.
Motocross Racing, Crestwood, 1978.

NONFICTION; UNDER PSEUDONYM MATTHEW G. GRANT

A Walk in the Mountains, Reilly and Lee, 1971.
Buffalo Bill of the Wild West, Creative Educational Society, 1974.
Champlain: Explorer of New France, Creative Educational Society, 1974.
Chief Joseph of the Nez Perce, Creative Educational Society, 1974.
Clara Barton: Red Cross Pioneer, Creative Educational Society, 1974.
Columbus: Discoverer of the New World, Creative Educational Society, 1974.
Coronado: Explorer of the Southwest, Creative Educational Society, 1974.
Crazy Horse: War Chief of the Oglala, Creative Educational Society, 1974.
Daniel Boone in the Wilderness, Creative Educational Society, 1974.
Davy Crockett: Frontier Adventurer, Creative Educational Society, 1974.
DeSoto: Explorer of the Southeast, Creative Educational Society, 1974.
Dolly Madison: First Lady of the Land, Creative Educational Society, 1974.
Elizabeth Blackwell: Pioneer Doctor, Creative Educational Society, 1974.
Francis Marion: Swamp Fox, Creative Educational Society, 1974.
Geronimo: Apache Warrior, Creative Educational Society, 1974.
Harriet Tubman: Black Liberator, Creative Educational Society, 1974.
Jane Addams: Helper of the Poor, Creative Educational Society, 1974.
Jim Bridger: The Mountain Man, Creative Educational Society, 1974.
John Paul Jones: Naval Hero, Creative Educational Society, 1974.
Leif Ericson: Explorer of Vinland, Creative Educational Society, 1974.
Lewis and Clark: Western Trailblazers, Creative Educational Society, 1974.
Kit Carson: Trailblazer of the West, Creative Educational Society, 1974.
Lafayette: Freedom's General, Creative Educational Society, 1974.
Osceola and the Seminole War, Creative Educational Society, 1974.

Paul Revere: Patriot and Craftsman, Creative Educational Society, 1974.
Pontiac: Indian General and Statesman, Creative Educational Society, 1974.
Robert E. Lee: The South's Great General, Creative Educational Society, 1974.
Squanto: The Indian Who Saved the Pilgrims, Creative Educational Society, 1974.
Sam Houston of Texas, Creative Educational Society, 1974.
Susan B. Anthony: Crusader for Women's Rights, Creative Educational Society, 1974.
Ulysses S Grant: General and President, Creative Educational Society, 1974.

NONFICTION; UNDER PSEUDONYM IAN THORNE

Meet the Coaches, Creative Educational Society, 1975.
Meet the Defensive Linemen, Creative Educational Society, 1975.
Meet the Linebackers, Creative Educational Society, 1975.
Meet the Quarterbacks, Creative Educational Society, 1975.
Meet the Receivers, Creative Educational Society, 1975.
Meet the Running Backs, Creative Educational Society, 1975.
The Great Centers, Creative Educational Society, 1976.
The Great Defenseman, Creative Educational Society, 1976.
The Great Goalies, Creative Educational Society, 1976.
The Great Wingmen, Creative Educational Society, 1976.
King Kong, Creative Educational Society, 1976.
Mad Scientists, Crestwood, 1977.
Godzilla, Crestwood, 1977.
Ancient Astronauts, Crestwood, 1977.
Dracula, Crestwood, 1977.
Frankenstein, Crestwood, 1977.
Monster Tales of Native Americans, Crestwood, 1978.
The Bermuda Triangle, Crestwood, 1978.
Bigfoot, Crestwood, 1978.
The Loch Ness Monster, Crestwood, 1978.
UFO's, edited by Howard Schroeder, Crestwood, 1978.

NONFICTION; UNDER PSEUDONYM GEORGE ZANDERBERGEN

The Beatles, Crestwood, 1976.
Made for Music: Elton John, Stevie Wonder, John Denver, Crestwood, 1976.

Laugh It Up: Carol Burnett, Bill Cosby, Mary Tyler Moore, Crestwood, 1976.

Nashville Music: Loretta Lynn, Mac Davis, Charley Pride, Crestwood, 1976.

Stay Tuned: Henry Winkler, Lee Majors, Valerie Harper, Crestwood, 1976.

Sweetly Singing: Cher, Roberta Flack, Olivia Newton John, Crestwood, 1976.

NONFICTION; UNDER PSEUDONYM BOB CUNNINGHAM

Ten-Five: Alaska Skip, Crestwood, 1977.

Ten-Seven for Good Sam, Crestwood, 1977.

Ten-Seventy: Range Fire, Crestwood, 1977.

Ten-Thirty-Three: Emergency, Crestwood, 1977.

Ten-Two Hundred: Come on Smokey!, Crestwood, 1977.

FILM NOVELIZATIONS; UNDER PSEUDONYM IAN THORNE

The Wolf Man, Crestwood House, 1977.

The Creature from the Black Lagoon, Crestwood House, 1981.

Frankenstein Meets the Wolfman, Crestwood House, 1981.

The Blob, Crestwood House, 1982.

The Deadly Mantis, Crestwood House, 1982.

It Came from Outer Space, Crestwood House, 1982.

OTHER

(Under pseudonym Jean Wright Thorne) *Horse and Rider*, Creative Educational Society, 1976.

(Under pseudonym Jean Wright Thorne) *Rodeo*, Creative Educational Society, 1976.

(Under pseudonym Lee N. Falconer) *A Gazetteer of the Hyborian World of Conan*, Starmont House, 1977.

Editor, "Life in God's Love" series, *Franciscan Herald*, 1963. Contributor of stories to periodicals, including *Astounding*.

■ Adaptations

The 1951 novelette *Dune Roller* has been adapted for television and radio.

■ Work in Progress

Sky Trillium, another novel in the "Trillium" fantasy series; the "Rampart Worlds" trilogy.

■ Sidelights

"I love action-filled science fiction. I am a fan. I have been accused of being a fan and I admit to it," Julian May told Darrell Schweitzer in *Science Fiction Review*. After twenty-five years of earning her living by writing juvenile nonfiction works to order, May's love for science fiction led her to return to the field in the 1980s with the four-volume "Saga of the Pliocene Exile." This epic series involving time travel, psychic powers, alien conquerors, and human determination has proved popular with readers who enjoy tales of adventure. As the author told Schweitzer: "To me, SF should not be didactic, but rather a literature of entertainment. . . . I [have always] wanted to give the reader books that would be fun."

Even as a young child, May had a taste for the fantastic. "I was the kid who devoured the Lang fairytale books at the Elmwood Park Public Library back in Illinois," the author said in a Pan Books interview reprinted in *A Pliocene Companion*. "I also cut out and saved the Buck Rogers comic strips and had a stack of Wonder Woman comic books a foot high. In 1947, when I was sixteen, I discovered pulp SF magazines and became hooked." After her introduction to the genre, May briefly became involved in what is known as science fiction "fandom," corresponding with other enthusiasts, editing a science fiction newsletter, and even organizing a convention in her hometown of Chicago. In 1951, her novelette "Dune Roller" was published in *Astounding*, the magazine edited by the legendary John W. Campbell, who had fostered the careers of writers like Isaac Asimov and Robert A. Heinlein. This brought her to the attention of other editors—leading to the publication of her second story—as well as a young publisher named Ted Dikty, whom she married in 1953.

While "Dune Roller" became a minor classic in the field, May left science fiction fandom and writing soon after her marriage. As she explained to Schweitzer, "In the 1950s you couldn't make a living writing science fiction unless you wrote a great volume of work, mostly short pieces for magazines. I am not that sort of writer." Instead, May took a job with a publishing company, where she wrote some 7,000 encyclopedia articles about science and natural history. She discovered a talent for producing nonfiction quickly, and in 1957 she turned freelance, forming an editorial services

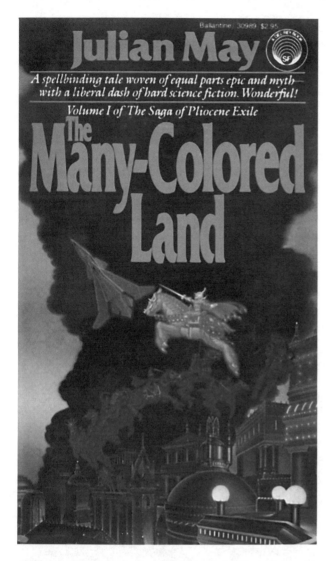

After traveling back in time to six million B.C., the Pliocene Era, a group of humans find it inhabited by two alien races in this 1981 science fiction adventure, part of "The Saga of Pliocene Exile" series.

company with her husband that handled every aspect of book production, from research and writing to printing and binding. Along the way, the couple also cooperated in raising their three children, as May once explained: "From the beginning, my husband and I shared the care of house and children and pursued overlapping careers."

May wrote almost 250 nonfiction books between 1957 and 1982, most of which dealt with science, sports, or famous people. While these books gave her the chance to learn about new subjects and hone her writing skills, they provided little room for creativity—even the subjects were assigned by the publishers. As a result, May said, she had "little emotional involvement in my juvenile books. . . . I did not write my long list of books because of a creative itch, but because I was good at it and it paid the bills." The "itch" to write science fiction always remained, however, and as her children grew up and the royalties from her nonfiction works accumulated she began considering a return to science fiction.

Space Suit Leads to Prehistoric Saga

A homemade "diamond"-studded space suit May created for a science fiction convention provided the inspiration that led to her first novel. "At first I had no notion of writing a novel," the author told Schweitzer, "but then as I was writing my other stuff, the damn costume would come creeping back into my subconscious mind and I would wonder what kind of character would wear something like that." May began jotting down notes and collecting research, and by 1978 had the outline for a series of novels set in what she called the Galactic Milieu, a future in which humans with extraordinary mental powers such as telepathy and telekinesis have led Earth into a galaxy-wide civilization with several alien races. The author recognized that she might have difficulty marketing a story with such complex concepts, however, and decided that first she would create "a more simple type of SF book, a time-travel story using characters from the elaborate future civilization that was worked out." This story became the "Saga of the Pliocene Exile," which is comprised of four volumes: *The Many-Colored Land, The Golden Torc, The Nonborn King,* and *The Adversary.*

Set in the early twenty-second century, *The Many-Colored Land* opens upon a near-utopian Earth where the social problems of previous years have been solved with the cooperation of the alien races that form the Galactic Milieu. For those unsatisfied with the new structure of society, however, there exists an intriguing option: a one-way trip to the past, six million years ago, through an invention called the Guderian field. Travellers have been passing through the timegate in Lyon, France, for over seventy years when a unique group of eight individuals makes the same trip. Once there, they discover that two related but warring races of aliens, the Tanu and the Firvulag, are already inhabiting this area of Europe, which they call the "Many-Colored Land"; the Tanu's advanced metapsychic powers have allowed them to enslave most of the 100,000 humans who have arrived there. The eight members of "Group Green" are witness to the unique relationships between the races that have developed, with some assimilating into the society and others rebelling. *The Many-Colored Land* is "an enjoyable book," Algis Budrys writes in the *Magazine of Fantasy Science Fiction*, adding that this "page-turner on an intelligent level" is "a book which signally rewards" science fiction readers of all stripes. A *Publishers Weekly* critic likewise calls the novel "a most enjoyable entertainment that will have readers eagerly turning pages and awaiting the promised sequel."

The Green Group's increasing involvement in and influence of Pliocene society makes up the action of the series' second volume, *The Golden Torc.* Those humans with latent metapsychic abilities or skills otherwise useful to the Tanu have been fitted with collars, called torcs, that can enhance mental skills and stimulate pain or pleasure centers to ensure compliance. They discover some of the secrets of the Tanu, and one human, Aiken Drum, begins insinuating himself into the Tanu royal family, helping them prepare for ritual combat against the Firvulag. The other members of Green Group, originally consigned to labor camps, have managed to escape, kill a Tanu, and secure the cooperation of the Firvulag in searching for their ancient spaceship. By the end of the volume, the rebel humans have shut down the timegate and one, the half-mad Felice, has caused a giant flood that has killed many prominent Tanu leaders. Like the first volume, *The Golden Torc* is entertaining "as superhero adventure raised to its highest level," a *Publishers Weekly* critic states, adding that "May develops her premises seriously and gives her large cast of characters a surprising amount of life." "May seems to be trying to do everything at once," *Booklist* reviewer Roland Green similarly observes of *The Golden Torc's* many characters, subplots, and themes. "She also seems to succeed most of the time—the book is as powerful and gripping as it is complex."

The third volume of the Pliocene Exile, *The Nonborn King,* relates the sweeping changes that occurred in the wake of the great flood. The human Aiken Drum has assumed kingship of the Tanu, and has forged an uneasy peace with the Firvulag. He is beset by enemies from within and

without, however, including a previously unknown threat: a band of metapsychics led by Marc Remillard, the leader of an unsuccessful rebellion against the Galactic Milieu who escaped through the timegate almost thirty years before. Living in Pliocene Florida, Remillard has been searching the galaxy for another species with advanced mental technology; but many of his children want to give up on that hope of rescue and instead use Felice's powers to create a way to return to the future of the Milieu. *The Nonborn King* "maintains the high standard of entertainment established" in previous volumes, a *Publishers Weekly* reviewer asserts, comparing May's skills in creating "richly plotted,

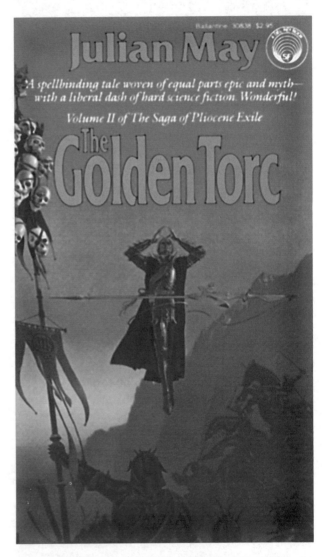

In this 1981 sequel to *The Many-Colored Land,* the Tanu, a powerful race of humanoids, seek to rule over both the earthling community and the Tanu's antagonists, the Firvulag.

extravagant adventures spun from a blend of myth and science" to those of Roger Zelazny. Elton T. Elliott concurs that this third volume "marks May's continued growth and maturity as a novelist," as he writes in *Science Fiction Review*. "There is a surety about her handling of the characters and narrative," he explains, and her writing "is as rich as ever, but more under control."

The saga concludes in *The Adversary*; even as Aiken Drum has emerged victorious if injured from a battle against his Tanu enemies and Felice, he now faces the plotting of Marc Remillard as well as betrayal by his former Firvulag allies. To counter Remillard, Aiken secures the assistance of the Adversary's children by beginning construction of a new, two-way timegate that would allow return to the future. The conflict is consummated in a spectacular mental battle that could destroy the entire civilization of the Many-Colored Land. "In a rousing climax," Pat Royal comments in *School Library Journal*, the author "brings to a glorious and grand conclusion" her "extraordinarily complex and rich science fantasy." While *Fantasy Review* contributor Susan L. Nickerson finds the conclusion somewhat disappointing, noting that "one of the dangers of using time travel as a plot device [is that] sometimes the reader already knows the result," she adds that the series is "still a cracking good story."

While the length and "dizzying scope" of this four-volume series makes for "a tough, complex mix of characters, groups and events to manage," Elliott asserts in *Science Fiction Review*, May "handles it admirably." The critic reserves special praise for the author's characterizations, adding that "Marc Remillard is one of the most memorable personalities to ever appear in science fiction. He's complex, utterly ruthless, . . . yet I found him sympathetic." In addition, Sue Martin remarks in the *Los Angeles Times Book Review*, "May has a delightful sense of the stately and the wickedly rude that works so well with a cast of decidedly pungent personalities. Her handling of dialogue and smooth and spicy." Assessing the author's "rousing, carousing carnival of a saga," Martin concludes: "Good job, May. The Pliocene will never be the same."

While May's epic has won praise and popularity as an exciting read, several reviewers have observed more to the Pliocene Saga than just an adventure story. Todd H. Sammons remarks in

Aiken Drum declares himself king of the Tanu after a great flood kills several of their leaders in this 1983 work.

Twentieth-Century Science-Fiction Writers that the series "is Wagnerian in scope: the principals number in the dozens, the chorus in the hundreds, and . . . May uses Freudian concepts or Jungian archetypes (sometimes both) as musical leitmotifs to characters her human principals, as well as some of the important aliens." The use of these psychological theories was deliberate, May revealed in an interview with Robert A. Collins for *Fantasy Newsletter*. "In my novels, the archetypes, the undercurrents, the different levels of meaning are there. If you're not looking for them, I promise they won't get in the way of the blood and guts and sex and fun. But if you *are* looking, you can find something like six different levels, all deliberately put there. . . . I'm here to entertain us all: the guys looking for a good read as well as the

In this 1984 novel, the finale to "The Saga of Pliocene Exile" series, King Aiken confronts a man capable of overthrowing his reign.

academics who like to find strange things hidden away." Because "The Saga of the Pliocene Exile" contains so much information, May wrote *A Pliocene Companion* in 1984 to help readers enhance their enjoyment of the series. Complete with glossary, characters, maps, chronologies, and genealogies, this work is "a much needed guide," Martin writes in the *Los Angeles Times Book Review*; "I wish I'd had this when I was sailing through the series."

Invents Novels of Intergalactic Intrigue

Since writing the four Pliocene books, May has investigated the origins of the Remillard family's powers and the Galactic Milieu in *Intervention*

(1987) which was republished in 1988 as two books, *The Surveillance* and *The Metaconcert*. Beginning with the explosion of the first atomic bomb in 1945, *Intervention* presents an alternate Earth history which culminates in the telepathic call sent by Denis Remillard and his associates that leads to humanity's first contact with an alien culture. The novel "has the feel of historical fiction," Sammons writes, "and May uses an array of literary techniques to tell the story—memoirs, straight narration, dramatic dialogue, excerpts from actual speeches or reports, a television script," among other "sources." The development of the new intergalactic society is revealed further in the "Galactic Milieu" trilogy, consisting of *Jack the Bodiless* (1992), *Diamond Mask* (1994), and *Magnificat* (1996). These three works concern events that happen before the Pliocene Era books, explaining the events leading to the rebellion led by Marc Remillard.

Jack the Bodiless begins in the twenty-first century, as humanity's fate as a member of the Galactic Milieu is being decided by five alien races. The birth of Jack Remillard, whose extraordinary metapsychic potential indicates an evolutionary leap for humankind, also poses a problem, for his physical genetic defects are unacceptable under Milieu law. At the same time, a malevolent creature known only as Fury also comes into being, killing off many of the Remillards and jeopardizing Earth's entry into the Milieu. "May combines a compelling vision of humanity's future with the drama and political intrigue" of the Remillards' political involvements, Jackie Cassada says in *Library Journal*. While a *Publishers Weekly* reviewer believes May's narrow focus on the Remillard "elites" mars the novel, the critic nonetheless allows that *Jack the Bodiless* "is engaging and May's prose adequate to it."

In *Diamond Mask,* the story of Earth's fate within the Galactic Milieu continues. As Dorothea, or Dee, Macdonald begins to acknowledge her growing metapsychic powers, she assumes the identity of Diamond Mask and confronts the power of Fury and several renegade Remillards. Working in concert with Jack and Marc Remillard, Dee saves an entire planet from a catastrophic earthquake. A *Kirkus Reviews* critic labels *Diamond Mask* as "patchy and irritatingly inconclusive," but finds that May "handles both the psychic complication and the family interactions with pleasing skill." *Library Journal's* Cassada, however, praises May's book and the development of the trilogy, calling them "rich in intrigue and vibrating with creative energy." In *Metaconcert*, the concluding volume of the trilogy, May will detail the rebellion of Marc Remillard and reveal the secrets behind the evil entity known as Fury.

May has also ventured into fantasy writing with a series of novels that began with *Black Trillium*, a volume she coauthored with noted writers Marion Zimmer Bradley and Andre Norton, and continued with the solo effort *Blood Trillium*. The series is set on the World of Three Moons, which has been threatened by various sorcerers who can only be defeated by certain powerful talisman. In *Blood Trillium*, as in the first book, three sisters

must fulfill separate quests; unlike *Black Trillium*, May makes the book more positive by changing "its focus from the absolute destruction of evil to the possibility of its ultimate transformation," according to *Library Journal* reviewer Cassada. A *Publishers Weekly* critic notes that May's *Blood Trillium* is "a superior tale, giving life, character, and emotion to the Three Petals of the Living Trillium." May plans to write another installment in this series, *Sky Trillium*.

Late in her career, May has finally been able to devote her efforts to her first love, science fiction. She has a positive view of humanity's future, which she hopes to communicate in her works. "I am an optimist," she told Collins. "I don't think we are going to die in a mushroom cloud. I think something great will happen. I don't know if there are flying saucers—if there *are* galactic civilizations they're quite sensible in leaving us alone until we have attained suitable enlightenment. But I *am* an optimist and it shows in my novels. I've been accused of being upbeat. I triumph in being upbeat! I don't know how successful I've been, but it's been a lot of fun."

This 1988 work presents an alternate history in which humans with extraordinary mental abilities begin to exercise their powers.

■ **Works Cited**

Review of *Blood Trillium, Publishers Weekly*, May 25, 1992, pp. 42–43.

Budrys, Algis, review of *The Many-Colored Land, Magazine of Fantasy and Science Fiction*, October, 1981, pp. 29–37.

Cassada, Jackie, review of *Jack the Bodiless, Library Journal*, December 1991, p. 202.

Cassada, Jackie, review of *Blood Trillium, Library Journal*, June 15, 1992, p. 105.

Cassada, Jackie, review of *Diamond Mask, Library Journal*, March 15, 1994, pp. 103–04.

Review of *Diamond Mask, Kirkus Reviews*, February 15, 1994, p. 181.

Elliott, Elton T., review of *The Nonborn King, Science Fiction Review*, spring, 1983, p. 25.

Elliott, Elton T., review of *The Adversary, Science Fiction Review*, spring, 1984, p. 36.

Review of *The Golden Torc, Publishers Weekly*, December 11, 1981, p. 53.

Green, Roland, review of *The Golden Torc, Booklist*, March 1, 1982, p. 848.

Review of *Jack the Bodiless, Publishers Weekly*, December 20, 1991, p. 68.

Review of *The Many-Colored Land, Publishers Weekly*, March 6, 1981, p. 91.

Martin, Sue, review of *The Adversary, Los Angeles Times Book Review,* June 3, 1984, p. 6.

Martin, Sue, review of *A Pliocene Companion, Los Angeles Times Book Review,* December 9, 1984, p. 14.

May, Julian, interview with Robert A. Collins, *Fantasy Newsletter,* March, 1983.

May, Julian, "Pan Books Interviews Julian May," in *A Pliocene Companion,* Del Rey, 1984, pp. 249–52.

Nickerson, Susan L., "Great Expectations Dashed," *Fantasy Review,* August, 1984, pp. 16–17.

Review of *The Nonborn King, Publishers Weekly,* December 24, 1982, p. 51.

Royal, Pat, review of *The Adversary, School Library Journal,* November, 1984, p. 146.

Sammons, Todd H., "Julian May," *Twentieth-Century Science Fiction Writers,* 3rd edition, St. James Press, 1991, pp. 534–35.

Schweitzer, Darrell, "Interview: Julian May," *Science Fiction Review,* fall, 1984, pp. 33–36.

■ For More Information See

BOOKS

Dikty, T. E. and R. Reginald, *The Work of Julian May: An Annotated Bibliography and Guide,* Borgo Press, 1985.

PERIODICALS

Analog, August, 1983, pp. 129–30.
Booklist, November 1, 1991, p. 475.
Kliatt, winter, 1984.
Publishers Weekly, March 9, 1984, p. 101; February 14, 1994, p. 83.
Voice of Youth Advocates, February, 1985, p. 339.
Washington Post Book World, March 28, 1982, p. 22.

—*Sketch by Diane Telgen*

Robert McCammon

■ Personal

Born July 11, 1952; son of Jack and Barbara (Bundy) McCammon. *Education:* University of Alabama, B.A., 1974. *Religion:* Methodist. *Hobbies and other interests:* Antique automobile restoration.

■ Addresses

Home—8912 Fourth Ave. S., Birmingham, AL 35206. *Office*—4321 Fifth Ave. S., Birmingham, AL 35214.

■ Career

Writer. Loveman's Department Store, Birmingham, AL, advertising, 1974-75; B. Dalton Booksellers, Birmingham, advertising, 1976; *Birmingham Post-Herald*, Birmingham, copy editor, 1976-78.

■ Awards, Honors

Bram Stoker Awards, best horror novel, 1988, 1991, and 1992.

■ Writings

Baal, Avon, 1978.
Bethany's Sin, Avon, 1979.
Diana's Daughters, Avon, 1979.
The Hungry, Avon, 1980.
The Night Boat, Avon, 1980.
They Thirst, Avon, 1981, illustrated by Wendy and Charles Lang, Dark Harvest, 1991.
Mystery Walk, Holt, 1983.
Usher's Passing, Holt, 1984.
Swan Song, Holt, 1987.
Stinger, Pocket, 1988.
The Wolf's Hour, Pocket, 1989.
Blue World, Grafton Books, 1989, Pocket, 1990.
Mine, Pocket, 1990.
Boy's Life, Pocket, 1991.
Gone South, Pocket, 1992.

Also author of the afterward for *Night Visions 8: All Original Stories*, Dark Harvest, 1990; editor and contributor, *The Horror Writers of America Present: Under the Fang*, Pocket, 1991.

■ Sidelights

Robert McCammon appreciates fear and believes in examining what fear tells us. He once explained that "probing the counterfeit fears, the fun fears, can tell us a lot about how we tick and define the things that really make us afraid." Writing horror fiction has allowed McCammon to do this for more than fifteen years. "Nothing makes me feel better than getting a good scare out of a novel, or putting a good scare *into* a novel," he once commented. According to reviewers, McCammon's writing is successful at scaring readers, whether it is with short stories, novellas, or novels. Lately, however, McCammon has found the modern terrors of day-to-day life as frightening as anything his imagination can create. McCammon told Sam Staggs in a *Publishers Weekly* interview, "Reality has become so horrific, there's no point in trying to compete with the evening news." He also commented on Hollywood's embrace of graphic violence in horror films: "Now writers and moviemakers shove the horror in your face. I don't like that. I think you can do a lot more with a lot less."

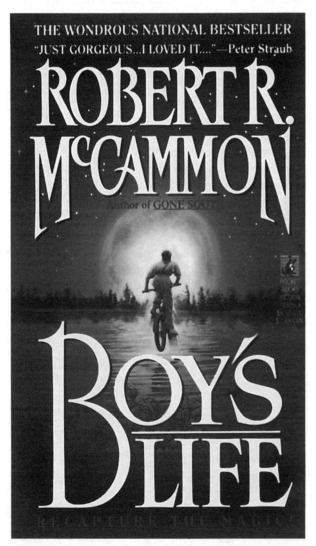

A boy and his father in small-town Alabama discover a murdered man handcuffed to the steering wheel of his car in this 1991 publication.

In the Beginning

Baal, published in 1978, was McCammon's first novel, which he wrote while working as a copy editor for the *Birmingham Post-Herald*. He continued working for the paper while he wrote *Bethany's Sin*, his second book. His early works were published as paperbacks, but he changed publishers in 1983 and began to be published in hardcover with *Mystery Walk*. McCammon's second hardcover work, *Usher's Passing*, inspired by Edgar Allan Poe's story "The Fall of the House of Usher," made a surprising impression on one reader, who came to a book signing with a sword. The reader claimed he was a descendent of Poe, and he was angry that McCammon hadn't asked permission to continue the story of Usher.

McCammon's earliest writings built his reputation as a horror writer. His highly praised *Swan Song* has been compared to Stephen King's work, especially King's *The Stand*. Swan, a girl with special healing powers, is sought by an evil figure, the Man with the Scarlet Eyes, and his brutal Army of Excellence through the post-World War III landscape of the American midwest. Sarah K. Martin writes in her *School Library Journal* review of *Swan Song*: "McCammon makes a powerful statement about the worth and resilience of mankind" by focusing on "good and evil coming from the human condition." A *Publishers Weekly* contributor similarly states that *Swan Song* is a "compelling story of good and evil."

McCammon has moved away from supernatural horror in his more recent writings, and instead he has emphasized psychological horror. In his first novel of this type, *Boy's Life*, published in 1991, McCammon shows how a murder affects the life of a Southern boy from a small town. The protagonist of *Boy's Life*, Cory Jay Mackenson, sees a car crash into a lake, and when Cory and his father examine the wreck, they find a naked man handcuffed to the steering wheel. A *Publishers Weekly* contributor commended the "expertly told episodic tale" that explores the sinister side of human behavior. Brad Hooper, writing in *Booklist*, called *Boy's Life* a "compelling, even haunting yarn," and *Library Journal* contributor David Keymer described the work as "an affecting tale of a young man growing out of childhood. . . ." *Boy's Life* won the 1992 Bram Stoker Award for best horror novel.

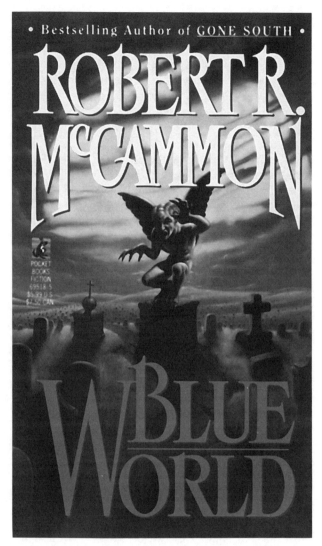

McCammon explores themes of imagination, fear, and violence in this 1989 collection of stories.

The change from horror fiction to psychological fiction for McCammon was not as sudden as it seemed. He explored this territory as early as 1989, in a collection of short stories called *Blue World*. The stories focus on individuals' fears, such as the priest who falls in love with a porn star in the title story, or the Vietnam vet whose nightmares become reality in "Nightcrawlers." The edges of reality, science fiction, and horror meet in these stories. As a result, says Patrick Jones in his *Voice of Youth Advocates* review, *Blue World* "advances McCammon's reputation as one of the finest horror authors."

Not all of McCammon's books are as acclaimed as *Blue World* or *Boy's Life*, though. *Mine* and *Stinger,* for example, were not as well received by some critics. *Mine* focuses on a sixties radical known as Mary Terror and her kidnapping of a young boy. The child's mother, Laura Clayborne, pursues Mary across the country to recover her son. In *Library Journal,* Mark Annichiarico stated that "unlikely coicidences and shabby dialog abound" in *Mine*, and *Booklist* contributor Elliot Swanson believed that the "lead characters are written larger than life," a weakness in psychological horror. In the 1980 thriller *Stinger,* an alien bounty hunter named Stinger traces an alien fugitive to the small town of Inferno, Texas. The townspeople, who are threatened with death by the hunter unless they return his quarry, react in predictable ways, according to a *Publishers Weekly* critic, who described their behavior as "a stale gamut [that runs] from bravery to venality."

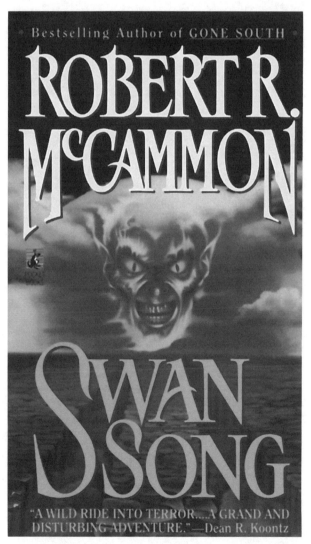

In this 1987 novel, Swan, a child with special powers, is pursued by an ancient evil.

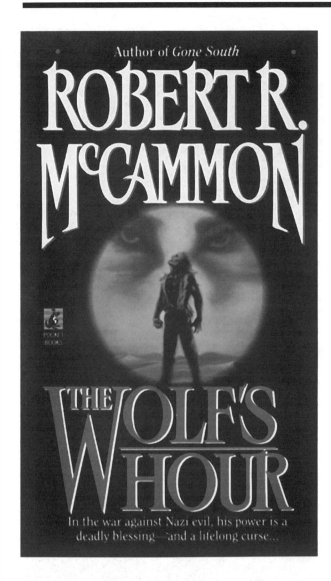

Author of *Gone South*

ROBERT R. McCAMMON

THE WOLF'S HOUR

In the war against Nazi evil, his power is a deadly blessing—and a lifelong curse...

This 1989 work—a combination spy novel and horror story—offers a World War II secret agent who is also a werewolf.

Demons and Monsters

Vampires and werewolves are another part of McCammon's repertoire. The evil and horror of those supernatural creatures provides McCammon with several ways to examine human reactions to fear. In *They Thirst*, first published in 1981, Prince Vulcan brings his vampire army to Los Angeles where he plots to take over the world city by city. A policeman, an Hungarian immigrant, a young boy, a television star, and a priest defend humanity from the leader of the vampires and his hordes. A *Publishers Weekly* contributor, reviewing *They Thirst*, wrote that the author "delivers terror with skillful ferocity . . . and raises the stan-

dards for the craft a notch or two." *The Horror Writers of America Present: Under the Fang* received similar praise for McCammon's editing skill, as well as his writing ability. This anthology of tales about vampires will "disgust, horrify, appall, [and] astound" readers, according to Ray Olson in a *Booklist* review.

McCammon's *The Wolf's Hour*, a historical novel that incorporates elements of horror and espionage, is set during World War II and features a werewolf in a heroic role. The protagonist is Michael Gallatin, a Russian-born British spy whose ability to change from man to wolf is known to only three people. Although a *Publishers Weekly* contributor termed Gallatin's super-spy qualities part of "a familiar genre figure," James Blair Lovell called *The Wolf's Hour* "a genuine triumph" in his *Washington Post Book World* review. He also claimed that "werewolf stories can never be the same" after McCammon's work.

McCammon has only one real fear himself—confinement as a writer. As he told Staggs in his *Publishers Weekly* interview, "I don't want to be limited by anyone's preconceptions." He later added, "My satisfaction is writing by myself, being in control of what I do and having the freedom to write what I want."

■ Works Cited

Annichiarico, Mark, review of *Mine*, *Library Journal*, March 15, 1990, pp. 114-15.

Review of *Boy's Life*, *Publishers Weekly*, May 31, 1991, p. 60.

Hooper, Brad, review of *Boy's Life*, *Booklist*, May 15, 1991, p. 1755.

Jones, Patrick, review of *Blue World*, *Voice of Youth Advocates*, August, 1990, p. 168.

Keymer, David, review of *Boy's Life*, *Library Journal*, July, 1991, p. 136.

Lovell, James Blair, review of *The Wolf's Hour*, *Washington Post Book World*, June 18, 1989, p. 4.

Martin, Sarah K., review of *Swan Song*, *School Library Journal*, October, 1987, p. 146.

Olson, Ray, review of *The Horror Writers of America Present: Under the Fang*, *Booklist*, July, 1991, p. 2032.

Staggs, Sam, "Robert R. McCammon," *Publishers Weekly*, August 2, 1991, pp. 54-55.

Swanson, Elliott, review of *Mine*, *Booklist*, February 15, 1990, p. 1121.

Review of *Stinger, Publishers Weekly,* March 18, 1988, p. 82.

Review of *Swan Song, Publishers Weekly,* May 8, 1987, pp. 65-66.

Review of *They Thirst, Publishers Weekly,* May 10, 1991, p. 272.

Review of *The Wolf's Hour, Publishers Weekly,* February 3, 1989, p. 105.

■ **For More Information See**

BOOKS

Science Fiction and Fantasy Literature 1975-1991, Gale, 1992, pp. 645-46.

PERIODICALS

Booklist, March 15, 1992, p. 1364.

Locus, June, 1992, p. 56.

Publishers Weekly, March 18, 1988, p. 82; March 23, 1990, pp. 67-68; April 13, 1992, p. 56.

School Library Journal, September, 1990, p. 266.

Voice of Youth Advocates, April, 1988, pp. 13-14.

Washington Post Book World, June 14, 1987, p. 12.

—Sketch by Hollis E. Helmeci

Walter Mosley

■ Personal

Born January 12, 1952, in Los Angeles, CA; son of LeRoy (a school custodian) and Ella (a school personnel clerk) Mosley; married Joy Kellman (a dancer and choreographer), 1987. *Education:* Attended Goddard College, 1971; Johnson State College, B.A., 1977; attended writing program at City College of the City University of New York, 1985-89.

■ Addresses

Home—New York, NY. *Agent*—c/o W. W. Norton & Co., 500 Fifth Avenue, New York, NY 10110.

■ Career

Full-time writer, 1986—. Worked variously as a computer programmer, computer consultant for Mobil Oil, potter, and caterer. *Member:* National Book Award Committee, PEN (vice-president, Open Book Committee chairman).

■ Awards, Honors

John Creasey Memorial Award for best first novel, 1990, Shamus Award, Private Eye Writers of America, and Edgar Award nomination for best first mystery, Mystery Writers of America, 1990, all for *Devil in a Blue Dress;* Edgar Award nomination, 1992, for *White Butterfly;* three nominations for Gold Dagger Awards, Crime Writers' Association.

■ Writings

"EASY RAWLINS" MYSTERY NOVELS

Devil in a Blue Dress, Norton, 1990.
A Red Death, Norton, 1991.
White Butterfly, Norton, 1992.
Black Betty, Norton, 1994.

The "Easy Rawlins" mystery series has been published in eighteen countries.

OTHER

R. L.'s Dream (novel), Norton, 1995.

■ Work in Progress

Two more "Easy" Rawlins mysteries for Norton, *A Little Yellow Dog* and *Bad Boy Bobby Brown.*

■ Adaptations

Devil in a Blue Dress was adapted as a motion picture starring Denzel Washington, produced by Jonathan Demme, and directed by Carl Franklin.

■ Sidelights

When LeRoy Mosley, an African American, returned home after fighting in World War II, he was disappointed because he was treated like a second-class citizen instead of like a hero. Almost fifty years later, Mosley's son Walter transformed that bitter experience into a popular series of mystery novels. Although LeRoy Mosley went unrecognized by a society that would have wel-

comed him warmly if he'd been white, Walter Mosley's books have received attention and praise from critics and readers alike, including the President of the United States, Bill Clinton, who claims that Mosley is his favorite mystery novelist. In 1994, as Malcolm Jones, Jr. of *Newsweek* asserted, Mosley was "the hottest mystery writer around." Various aspects of Mosley's work in the "Easy Rawlins" mystery series distinguish him from the great mystery writers with whom he's been compared. Detective Easy Rawlins, first introduced in *Devil in a Blue Dress* in 1990, is black, sensitive, and usually enmeshed in a moral dilemma. The novels are set in the Los Angeles area, with the action taking place in the bars, nightclubs, and streets of Compton and Watts. The dialogue in Mosley's novels features African-American colloquial speech from the late 1940s to the early 1970s, and his colorful narratives resound in a jazz-like rhythm. While readers of any book in the "Easy Rawlins" series escape into an exciting mystery story, they gain startling insight into another world and an entertaining lesson in the recent social history of America as well. According to one *Publishers Weekly* critic, in a review of *A Red Death*, Mosley is an "extraordinary storyteller," who may be "creating a genre classic."

Mosley told Bob McCullough in a *Publishers Weekly* interview that he "wouldn't be unhappy" if, when his name is mentioned in the future, his race is noted as well. "I'd like to think that I'm breaking new ground. . . . I'm using a wide range of black characters and trying to reflect life in America . . . taking the point of view that black people are insiders rather than standing on the outside looking in."

Growing Up Dissatisfied

Mosley grew up in South Central Watts and the Pico-Fairfax districts of Los Angeles. He listened intently to the stories, conversations and dialogue shared among his family and friends. From his African-American father, and his Jewish mother of Eastern European heritage, he heard stories of racism and prejudice. Mosley's father, a World War II veteran, and Mosley's uncles gave the boy an understanding of the kind of disillusionment that plagues the fictional Easy Rawlins.

When LeRoy Mosley realized that the South would not offer him a hero's welcome or even

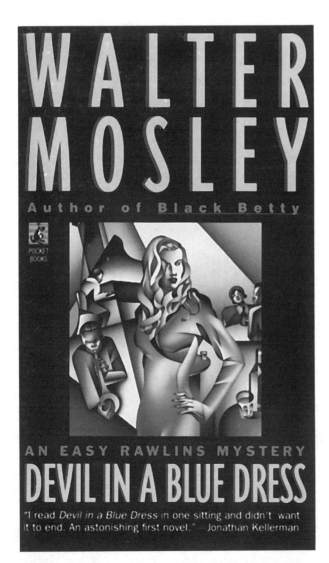

Mosley introduced his popular detective Easy Rawlins in this 1990 novel.

the respect he'd found in Europe, he became enchanted with the tales he heard of the wealth and opportunity available in Los Angeles. Yet once the elder Mosley arrived in Los Angeles, he realized that his dreams of being respected and even owning property would not be easily won. As the Watts riots—which young Walter Mosley witnessed—demonstrated, a similar, disheartening feeling of disappointment was shared by an entire community.

By 1972, Mosley was ready to leave Los Angeles. He told Tom Auer of the *Bloomsbury Review*, "I love L.A., but it was dissatisfying, because you need to have a car, and there's no life on the streets . . . I don't know *where* it is, but it's not on the streets. So I kept looking for different kinds of life." Mosley graduated from a Vermont college, traveled through Europe, and lived in Boston and New York. He also met Joy Kellman, a dancer and choreographer. Although, as the story goes, Kellman's white, Jewish parents disapproved of the couple's relationship, they married in 1987 and eventually settled in New York.

During the 1980s, as Mosley worked as a computer programmer and consultant, he read a great deal. The mysteries of Raymond Chandler, Dashiell Hammett, and Ross MacDonald were included among his favorites, and he also read Albert Camus's dark novel, *The Stranger*, and Alice Walker's *The Color Purple*. This last book inspired Mosley to begin a new career.

One day, Mosley sat down and wrote a sentence "about people on a back porch in Louisiana." He told the *New York Times*'s D. J. R. Bruckner, "I don't know where it came from. I liked it. It spoke to me." Mosley continued to write in the little spare time he had. It was not long before his passion for writing led him to quit his computer programming job and write full-time.

Attracted by the presence of the Harlem writers he'd always admired, Mosley began graduate school at the City College of New York. There, he studied under Frederic Tuten, William Matthews, and Edna O'Brien. Mosley submitted his first novel, *Gone Fishin'* (which featured Easy Rawlins), to various agents; it was rejected fifteen times. Finally, in 1989, Mosley presented *Devil in a Blue Dress*, written as a screenplay, to Tuten. As McCullough related, Tuten secretly passed it along to his own agent, Gloria Loomis. Loomis

was so impressed that she immediately acquired Mosley as a client and sold his manuscript to Norton.

The *Devil*'s Success

In *Devil in a Blue Dress*, according to *Library Journal* contributor Rex E. Klett, Mosley presents an "unusually refreshing protagonist." Ezekiel, or "Easy," Rawlins is a World War II veteran who, along with many of his friends, has come from Houston to live and work in Los Angeles. Easy is disturbed by the prejudice he confronts despite his veteran status, and by the fact that life in L.A. is much more difficult than he had been led to

Denzel Washington portrayed Easy Rawlins in the 1995 film adaptation of *Devil in a Blue Dress*.

believe. After he loses his job at a defense plant in 1948, Easy worries that he will not be able to pay the mortgage on his home in Watts.

Then DeWitt Albright, a rich, well-dressed white man, offers Easy one hundred dollars to find a missing white woman, Daphne Monet. Albright knows that Rawlins is not a professional detective, but he understands that Easy knows the black jazz clubs Monet frequents. Despite a few initial problems, Rawlins finds that he has a decided advantage: for a time, no one white or black suspects that he, a black man, would be working as a detective.

Soon enough, however, Easy learns that his new job is dangerous, as he is caught in what Digby Diehl of the *Los Angeles Times Book Review* described as "a complicated series of intrigues involving other rich white men, other women, more money, and a remarkable number of dead bodies." After Easy meets Daphne, he finds himself implicated in a crime, and develops his detective skills further in order to defend himself.

With *Devil in a Blue Dress,* Mosley contributed something to mystery and crime literature that had been missing: an African-American perspective. While the structural constraints and emotional burdens racism places on the black community are apparent in *Devil in a Blue Dress,* the issue of racism is not limited to the black and white color line. The Jewish owners of a liquor store in a black neighborhood remind Easy of his days in the war, when he helped rescue Jews held in a Nazi death camp.

Critics welcomed the settings, characters, and dialogue Mosley convincingly presented in his first novel. Diehl especially appreciated the "social history" Mosley offers readers, and noted that the author "takes us down some mean streets that his spiritual predecessors [mystery writers Dashiell Hammett, Raymond Chandler, and Cain] never could have because they were white." Marilyn Stasio of the *New York Times Book Review* commented on Mosley's narrative style: "Mr. Mosley writes in a talking-blues style that is its own kind of music."

The setting of Mosley's next book, *A Red Death,* is 1953, in the midst of the anti-Communist McCarthy era. Easy is now the owner of two apartment buildings and a house, which he pur-

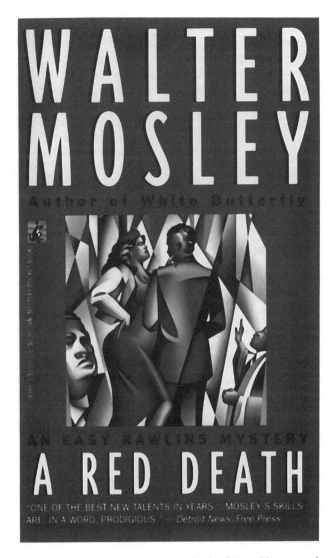

In 1953 Los Angeles, Easy finds himself trapped between a racist IRS agent and an FBI deputy who needs a big favor.

chased with the stolen money he discovered in *Devil in a Blue Dress.* Although Easy has fooled his tenants into thinking he is just the janitor, the Internal Revenue Service finds him and demands to know how he paid for the buildings. The Federal Bureau of Investigation offers him a way out—he must investigate a Jewish union leader suspected of being a communist.

Easy contends with the ethics of completing his assignment for the FBI, but he must also deal with a wrenching personal decision. Easy's murderous friend Mouse is in town looking for his wife, EttaMae, and their son. But EttaMae does not want Mouse to find her, and Easy is desperately in love with EttaMae.

Like *Devil in a Blue Dress, A Red Death* presents a vivid and convincing picture of Watts in the 1950s. As a critic for the *Washington Post Book World* observed, Mosley's "novels evoke in rich and persuasive detail the lives" of Watts' black residents. And in the opinion of a *Publishers Weekly* critic, the story in *A Red Death* is "secondary" to Mosley's "portrait of a time and place."

When Easy Rawlins appears in *White Butterfly,* it is 1956 and he is now a married man with a baby. Easy gets involved in an investigation when the police want to know how a white college student from the University of California at Los Angeles, the daughter of a city official, ended up murdered in Watts. Although Easy is angry that police had failed to investigate the similar deaths of three black women, or "good-time girls," in Watts until the discovery of the murdered white woman, he agrees to work on the case. After sorting through stories from people in clubs and flophouses, Easy finds that the white woman was a stripper—the "White Butterfly."

Another Triumph with *Black Betty*

According to Malcolm Jones, Jr. in *Newsweek, Black Betty* is Mosley's "best book yet." This story is set in 1961, in the era of President John F. Kennedy and Martin Luther King, Jr. Easy Rawlins has a home in West L.A., where he lives with his two adopted children. Recognizing that he can't support his family with the income from his real estate holdings any longer, Easy takes a job searching for a black domestic worker who has mysteriously disappeared.

Easy's need for money is not the only reason for his interest in the case. He remembers Elizabeth Eady, or "Black Betty," as the missing woman was known, from his youth in Houston. She was the woman every man wanted, and the woman who, twenty-five years before, gave Easy a kiss he would never forget. Easy works hard to find Betty despite the prejudice of her employers and the Beverly Hills police.

While he is preoccupied with his search for Elizabeth, Rawlins is engaged in a number of personal dilemmas. Jesus, the fifteen-year-old boy Easy saved from a squalid life and adopted, is a champion long distance runner. But "Juice," as the boy is called, saddens Easy by speaking only to Easy's

other adopted child, a little girl named Feather. At the same time, Rawlins's friend, Mouse, is out of prison and out for revenge, and other friends call upon Easy for help. Rawlins's real estate trouble also worries him. According to Malcolm Jones, Jr. of *Newsweek,* however, the family and friends that threaten to "drag" Easy under also "keep him afloat."

Although *Black Betty* is set in a time of supposed progress for minorities, racism continues to affect Rawlins's life. "It is . . . Easy's somber exhaustion in an era of supposed change that gives this book its special chill," wrote V. R. Peterson in *People Weekly.* As John Rebchook of *Bloomsbury Review* noted, "Mosley reminds us that while life was changing, life went on as before for the too many poor blacks."

Critics applauded Mosley's fourth book. "In a city that's lousy with fictional detectives—almost all white—Easy Rawlins stands out," remarked *Newsweek*'s Malcolm Jones, Jr. Writing in the *New York Times Book Review*, Barry Gifford asserted that Mosley "beats hell out of most of today's contenders for consideration as a top-ranking writer in the mystery division. . . . His words prowl around the page before they pounce, knocking you not so much upside the head as around the body, where you feel them the longest."

Mosley intends to write nine or ten Easy Rawlins books in all, gradually moving Easy from the late 1940s into the 1980s. Mosley told McCullough that he loves "writing about Easy," who is "always changing." He also loves to write about his murderous character, Mouse. Mosley pointed out to Auer that Easy is "the hero of the *book,* but the hero of the world that Easy inhabits is Mouse. He's the guy. He's the man." Fans may look forward to reading upcoming installments in the series, including *The Little Yellow Dog* and *Bad Boy Bobby Brown,* the latter of which is, as McCullough noted, a "homage to Malcolm X."

According to John Rebchook in a *Bloomsbury Review* assessment of *Black Betty,* Mosley "uses Rawlins to say what needs to be said." Yet Mosley is willing to voice his social concerns through other characters as well. *R. L.'s Dream* features a man who is dying of cancer in the 1980s in New York and who recalls playing alongside the great blues musician, Robert Johnson, in the Mississippi black motorist, Rodney King, received "not guilty" verdicts in their first trial and an intense riot ensued on the streets of L.A. Mosley had hoped that the violence demonstrated in the riot could have been avoided. Urban black communities have problems that must be addressed, he asserted, and the rioters sent a loud message only after their other, nonviolent requests had gone unheeded.

Mosley also wrote an editorial for the *Los Angeles Times Book Review* in which he called attention to the subtle racism in mainstream publishing. He asserted that the industry remains predominantly white despite the growing numbers of people of color in the United States. As the chairmen of the Open Book Committee of PEN (an international writers' organization), Mosley continues to challenge mainstream publishers to hire people of color. "Things *can* change and *are* changing," he told Auer. "There are a lot of writers and readers today who come outside of that generally accepted truth about what literature is and what culture is. There are a lot of people like me. So all we have to do is keep talking about it."

Mosley continues to work on his political goals, as he told Auer, "as a writer and through writing." His fans may look for his work in yet another medium—*Devil in a Blue Dress* has been adapted as a motion picture produced by Jonathan Demme, directed by Carl Franklin, and starring award-winning actor Denzel Washington. Mosley is pleased with this development, which will make Easy Rawlins's story accessible to those who haven't had a chance to read his books. "There's a real shortage of male role models in black culture right now," Mosley told McCullough, "and Easy seems to have hit a bit of a nerve in that sense."

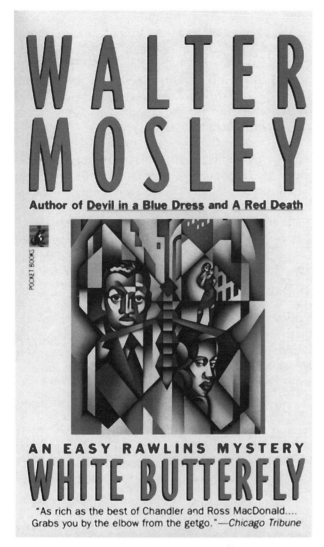

Although he has retired from detective work in favor of being a husband and father, Easy is drawn into the search for a serial killer in this 1992 series entry.

of the 1930s. Mosley told McCullough that he is intrigued with Robert Johnson and his music. "Music is fiction, and fiction is music. This isn't a music novel per se, but there's a rhythm to language and a beat to it."

Fighting Racism on a Variety of Fronts

Mosley does not limit his battle with racism to his novels. Instead, he has taken advantage of the status his works have earned him to speak out about racism lurking in a variety of contexts. Mosley penned an editorial for the *Los Angeles Times* after the four white Los Angeles police officers who were captured on videotape beating a

■ Works Cited

Auer, Tom, "Walter Mosley Meets the Mainstream," *Bloomsbury Review,* November/December, 1994, pp. 3, 10.

Bruckner, D. J. R., interview with Mosley in *New York Times,* September 4, 1990, pp. C1, C16.

Diehl, Digby, "A Stiff Shot of Black and White," *Los Angeles Times Book Review,* July 29, 1990, p. 3.

Gifford, Barry, "L.A. Raw," *New York Times Book Review,* June 5, 1994, p. 13.

Jones, Malcolm, Jr., "Easy Streets," *Newsweek,* July 4, 1994, pp. 66-67.

Klett, Rex E., review of *Devil in a Blue Dress, Library Journal*, June 1, 1990, p. 188.

McCullough, Bob, "Walter Mosley," *Publishers Weekly*, May 23, 1994, pp. 67-68.

Peterson, V. R., review of *Black Betty, People Weekly*, June 20, 1994, p. 31.

Rebchook, John, review of *Black Betty, Bloomsbury Review*, November/December, 1994, p. 3.

Review of *A Red Death, Publishers Weekly*, May 17, 1991, p. 57.

Review of *A Red Death, Washington Post Book World*, September 20, 1992, p. 12.

Stasio, Marilyn, review of *Devil in a Blue Dress, New York Times Book Review*, August 5, 1990, p. 29.

■ For More Information See

PERIODICALS

Booklist, June 15, 1991, p. 1936.

Book World, July 21, 1991, p. 12.

Entertainment Weekly, June 24, 1994, pp. 94-95.

Essence, January, 1991, p. 32.

Kirkus Reviews, January, 1991, p. 766.

Los Angeles Times Book Review, July 12, 1992, p. 2.

New York Times, August 15, 1990; August 7, 1991; August 7, 1992.

Publishers Weekly, May 4, 1992, p. 43.

—Sketch by R. Garcia-Johnson

Gary Paulsen

REVISED ENTRY

■ Personal

Born May 17, 1939, in Minneapolis, MN; son of Oscar and Eunice Paulsen; married third wife, Ruth Ellen Wright (an artist), May 5, 1971; children: James Wright. *Education:* Attended Bemidji College, 1957-58; and University of Colorado, 1976. *Politics:* "As Solzhenitsyn has said, 'If we limit ourselves to political structures we are not artists.'" *Religion:* "I believe in spiritual progress."

■ Addresses

Home—Leonard, MI. *Agent*—Jonathan Lazear, 430 First Ave. N., Suite 516, Minneapolis, MN 55401.

■ Career

Has worked variously as a teacher, electronics field engineer, soldier, actor, director, farmer, rancher, truck driver, trapper, professional archer, migrant farm worker, singer, and sailor; currently a full-time writer. *Military service:* U.S. Army, 1959-62; became sergeant.

■ Awards, Honors

Central Missouri Award for Children's Literature, 1976; New York Public Library's Books for the Teen Age citations, 1980, 1981 and 1982, for *The Green Room*, and 1982, for *Sailing: From Jibs to Jibing*; American Library Association Best Young Adult Books citation, 1983, for *Dancing Carl*, and 1984, for *Tracker*; Society of Midland Authors Award, 1985, for *Tracker*; Child Study Association of America's Children's Books of the Year citation, and Newbery Honor Book, 1986, for *Dogsong*; Newbery Honor Book citations, 1988, for *Hatchet*, and 1990, for *The Winter Room*; Parents' Choice citation (story book), 1991, for *The Boy Who Owned the School: A Comedy of Love*; ALAN award, 1991; Western Writers of America Spur award, 1991, for *Woodsong*.

■ Writings

NOVELS

The Implosion Effect, Major Books, 1976.
The Death Specialists, Major Books, 1976.
The Foxman, Thomas Nelson, 1977.
Winterkill, Thomas Nelson, 1977.
Tiltawhirl John, Thomas Nelson, 1977.
C. B. Jockey, Major Books, 1977.

The Night the White Deer Died, Thomas Nelson, 1978:

Hope and a Hatchet, Thomas Nelson, 1978.

(With Ray Peekner) *The Green Recruit,* Independence Press, 1978.

The Spitball Gang, Elsevier/Nelson, 1980.

The Sweeper, Harlequin, 1981.

Campkill, Pinnacle Books, 1981.

Clutterkill, Harlequin, 1982.

Popcorn Days and Buttermilk Nights, Lodestar Books, 1983.

Dancing Carl, Bradbury, 1983.

Tracker, Bradbury, 1984.

Dogsong, Bradbury, 1985.

Sentries, Bradbury, 1986.

The Crossing, PLB, 1987.

Hatchet, Orchard Books, 1987.

Murphy (western), Walker & Co., 1987.

The Island, Orchard Books, 1988.

Murphy's Gold (western), Walker & Co., 1988.

Murphy's Herd (western), Walker & Co., 1989.

Night Rituals, Donald I. Fine, Inc., 1989.

The Boy Who Owned the School: A Comedy of Love, Orchard, 1990.

Canyons, Delacorte, 1990.

Kill Fee, Donald I. Fine, Inc., 1990.

Woodsong, illustrated by Ruth Wright Paulsen, Bradbury, 1990.

The Cookcamp, Orchard Books, 1991.

Monument, Delacorte, 1991.

The River, Delacorte, 1991.

The Winter Room, Dell, 1991.

A Christmas Sonata, Delacorte, 1992.

Clabbered Dirt, Sweet Grass, paintings by R. Paulsen, Harcourt, 1992.

The Haymeadow, Doubleday, 1992.

Dogteam, Delacorte, 1993.

Eastern Sun, Winter Moon: An Autobiographical Odyssey, Harcourt, 1993.

Murphy's Stand (western), Walker & Co., 1993.

Nightjohn, Delacorte, 1993.

Sisters/Hermanas, Spanish translated by Gloria de Aragón Andújar, Harcourt, 1993.

The Car, Harcourt, 1994.

Legend of Red Horse Cavern, Dell, 1994.

Rodomonte's Revenge, Dell, 1994.

Winterdance: The Fine Madness of Running the Iditarod, Harcourt, 1994.

Call Me Francis Tucket, Delacorte, 1995.

The Tent: A Tale in One Sitting, Harcourt, 1995.

SHORT STORIES

The Madonna Stories, Van Vliet & Co., 1989.

NONFICTION

(With Raymond Friday Locke) *The Special War,* Sirkay, 1966.

Some Birds Don't Fly, Rand McNally, 1969.

The Building a New, Buying an Old, Remodeling a Used, Comprehensive Home and Shelter Book, Prentice-Hall, 1976.

Farm: A History and Celebration of the American Farmer, Prentice-Hall, 1977.

(With John Morris) *Hiking and Backpacking,* illustrated by R. Paulsen, Simon & Schuster, 1978.

Successful Home Repair: When Not to Call the Contractor, Structures, 1978.

(With John Morris) *Canoeing, Kayaking, and Rafting,* illustrated by John Peterson and Jack Storholm, Simon & Schuster, 1979.

Money-Saving Home Repair Guide, Ideals, 1981.

Beat the System: A Survival Guide, Pinnacle Books, 1983.

Father Water, Mother Woods: Essays on Fishing and Hunting in the North Woods, Delacorte, 1994.

JUVENILE

Mr. Tucket, Funk & Wagnall, 1968.

(With Dan Theis) *Martin Luther King: The Man Who Climbed the Mountain,* Raintree, 1976.

The Small Ones, illustrated by K. Goff and with photographs by W. Miller, Raintree, 1976.

The Grass Eaters: Real Animals, illustrated by Goff and with photographs by Miller, Raintree, 1976.

Dribbling, Shooting, and Scoring Sometimes, Raintree, 1976.

Hitting, Pitching, and Running Maybe, Raintree, 1976.

Tackling, Running, and Kicking—Now and Again, Raintree, 1977.

Riding, Roping, and Bulldogging—Almost, Raintree, 1977.

The Golden Stick, Raintree, 1977.

Careers in an Airport, photographs by Roger Nye, Raintree, 1977.

The CB Radio Caper, illustrated by John Asquith, Raintree, 1977.

The Curse of the Cobra, illustrated by Asquith, Raintree, 1977.

Running, Jumping and Throwing—If You Can, photographs by Heinz Kluetmeier, Raintree, 1978.

Forehanding and Backhanding—If You're Lucky, photographs by Kluetmeier, Raintree, 1978.

Downhill, Hotdogging, and Cross-Country—If the Snow Isn't Sticky, photographs by Willis Wood and Kluetmeier, Raintree, 1979.

Facing Off, Checking, and Goaltending—Perhaps, photographs by Melchior DeGiacomo and Kluetmeier, Raintree, 1979.

Going Very Fast in a Circle—If You Don't Run out of Gas, photographs by Kluetmeier and Bob D'Olivo, Raintree, 1979.

Launching, Floating High, and Landing—If Your Pilot Light Doesn't Go Out, photographs by Kluetmeier, Raintree, 1979.

Pummeling, Falling, and Getting Up—Sometimes, photographs by Kluetmeier and Joe DiMaggio, Raintree, 1979.

Track, Enduro, and Motocross—Unless You Fall Over, photographs by Kluetmeier and others, Raintree, 1979.

(With Art Browne, Jr.) *TV and Movie Animals*, Messner, 1980.

Sailing: From Jibs to Jibing, illustrated by R. Paulsen, Messner, 1981.

Voyage of the Frog, Orchard Books, 1989.

Harris and Me: A Summer Remembered, Harcourt, 1993.

"CULPEPPER ADVENTURES" SERIES

The Case of the Dirty Bird, Dell, 1992.
Dunc's Doll, Dell, 1992.
Culpepper's Cannon, Dell, 1992.
Dunc Gets Tweaked, Dell, 1992.
Dunc's Halloween, Dell, 1992.
Dunc Breaks the Record, Dell, 1992.
Dunc and the Flaming Ghost, Dell, 1992.
Amos Gets Famous, Dell, 1993.
Dunc and Amos Hit the Big Top, Dell, 1993.
Dunc's Dump, Dell, 1993.
Amos's Last Stand, Dell, 1993.
The Wild Culpepper Cruise, Dell, 1993.
Dunc's Undercover, Dell, 1993.
Dunc and Amos and the Red Tatoos, Dell, 1993.
Dunc and the Haunted House, Dell, 1993.
Cowpokes and Desperadoes, Dell, 1994.
Prince Amos, Dell, 1994.
Coach Amos, Dell, 1994.
Amos and the Alien, Dell, 1994.
Dunc and Amos Meet the Slasher, Dell, 1994.
Dunc and the Greased Sticks of Doom, Dell, 1994.
Amos's Killer Concert Caper, Dell, 1995.
Amos Gets Married, Dell, 1995.
Amos Goes Bananas, Dell, 1995.
Dunc and Amos Go to the Dogs, Dell, 1995.

"GARY PAULSEN WORLD OF ADVENTURE" SERIES

Escape from Fire Mountain, Dell, 1995.

Rock Jockeys, Dell, 1995.

PLAYS

Communications (one-act play), first produced in New Mexico by a local theater group, 1974.

Together-Apart (one-act play), first produced in Denver, Colo., at Changing Scene Theater, 1976.

OTHER

Author, with Roger Barrett, of *Athletics, Ice Hockey, Motor-Cycling, Motor Racing, Skiing*, and *Tennis*, all 1980. Also writer of *Meteor* and more than two hundred short stories and articles.

■ Adaptations

"Dogsong" (listening cassette: filmstrip with cassette), Random House/Miller-Brody, 1986; *Dancing Carl* was made into a narrative ballet for two dancers with original music by John Collins and choreography by Nancy Keller, and a seven-minute version of it was aired on Minnesota Public Television.

■ Overview

"I was an 'army brat,' and it was a miserable life," Gary Paulsen told Marguerite Feitlowitz in an interview for *Authors and Artists for Young Adults (AAYA)*. "School was a nightmare because I was unbelievably shy, and terrible at sports. I had no friends, and teachers ridiculed me. . . . One day as I was walking past the public library in twenty below temperatures . . . I went in to get warm and to my absolute astonishment the librarian . . . asked me if I wanted a library card. . . . When she handed me the card, she handed me the world." Now a prolific author of coming-of-age stories, Paulsen has also written nonfiction works on such topics as hunting, trapping, farming, animals, medicine, and outdoor life, as well as a collection of stories lauding women for their ability to handle so much responsibility and adversity with equanimity (a book inspired, in part, by the author's aunts and grandmother).

Paulsen trapped and hunted as a youth and ran the Iditarod (a 1200-mile dogsled race that goes from Iditarod, Alaska, to Nome, Alaska) in 1983, and the subjects of most of his books reflect this "outdoors" theme. *Tracker* tells the story of a

This acclaimed 1993 novel focuses on the relationship between two slaves, John and Sarny, and John's secret attempts to teach Sarny to read.

thirteen-year-old boy who must hunt alone for the first time to put meat on the table. Paulsen describes the spiritual relationship that develops between the hunter and his prey and how the deer's acceptance of death helps the boy come to terms with his grandfather's imminent death. *Dogsong* is a story of a boy's coming of age on the northern tundra. Russell, a fourteen-year-old Eskimo, takes a dog team across Alaska and back, encountering and aiding a girl who is suffering from exposure and about to give birth. Eugene J. Linehan in *Best Sellers* praised Paulsen's writing style, noting: "There is poetic majesty in the descriptions without a touch of condescension to the young."

The pilot of a single-engined plane has a heart attack and dies, crashing his plane in the Canadian wilderness in Paulsen's *Hatchet*. Brian Robeson, the sole passenger, must put aside his troubled thoughts about his parents' divorce and try to survive with just the hatchet that his mother had given him as a parting gift. Brian uses his hatchet in numerous ways, such as striking it against rock to make sparks for a fire and to sharpen sticks to use as tools.

Dancing Carl deviates from Paulsen's adventure stories and focuses on interpersonal relationships. When two twelve-year-old boys first meet an enigmatic man in the flight jacket, they think he is an alcoholic and a bum. They quickly learn that Carl is much more than that; he takes over the local skating rink with the power of his presence, and over the course of the winter he becomes the topic of the whole town's conversations. He expresses his emotions with dance-like movements, and the people who watch are made to feel things too, such as repentance for a violent act, happy memories of someone who just died, the pain and terror of Carl's war experiences, and his love for a woman.

Another book that touches on the subject of war and its effect on lives is *Sentries,* a collection of stories about four young people who are given the opportunity to make their lives a success. The stories of a girl who chooses between her Indian heritage and the white world, a migrant worker who commits to working with beet harvesters, a daughter who proves that she is as capable as any son, and a gifted rock musician who creates a new music are juxtaposed with four battle hymns set during such wars as World War II and the Vietnam War. The purpose of these veterans' tales of mental and physical suffering and the threat of nuclear war are to ensure that readers don't take their choices and opportunities for granted and to encourage them to be sentries to protect their rights and freedoms. *The Island* is also more of a reflective than an action-packed novel. Fourteen-year-old Wil Neuton moves with his parents to the north woods in Wisconsin and discovers a floating island that he secretly visits and uses as a place to meditate on the world and his relation to it.

Paulsen, too, has reflected on his life. "It's like things have come full circle," he declared in his *AAYA* interview. "I felt like nothing the first time

In this 1994 adventure, a fourteen-year-old separated from his family's wagon train survives in the wilderness with the help of a one-armed fur trader.

I walked into a library, and now library associations are giving me awards. It means a lot to me."

■ Update

Paulsen's recent novels continue to reflect the author's interest in nature and people who love it. In *The Cookcamp*, a young boy learns some valuable lessons about life and love from his grandmother, who works as a cook for a deep-woods road crew. "This short novel has almost unbelievable poignancy," commented Patty Campbell in the *New York Times Book Review*. Susan M. Harding, writing in *School Library Journal*, concurred by noting that *The Cookcamp* offers a "depth of imagery and emotion" that makes the book "superb for readers just old enough to look back."

In books like *Nightjohn* and *Mr. Tucket*, Paulsen draws on history for literary inspiration. The twelve-year-old heroine of *Nightjohn* is a slave named Sarny who awaits the day when she will be designated a "breeder" by her master. As Sarny tries to deal with this unpleasant eventuality, she surreptitiously takes reading lessons from an older slave named John. John pays a high price for being Sarny's teacher—two of his toes are cut off—but he is eventually able to escape and establish an underground school. In *Mr. Tucket*, fourteen-year-old Francis Tucket has a number of hair-raising adventures when he is captured by a Pawnee tribe after drifting away from his family's Oregon-bound wagon train. After Francis escapes from the tribe, a one-armed fur trader named Jason Grimes undertakes the young teen's frontier education.

The traumas that go hand-in-hand with coming of age are also present in *The Car*, Paulsen's 1994

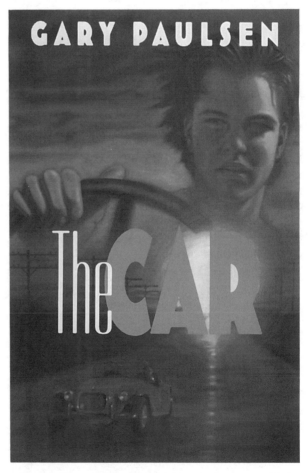

A distraught teenager assembles a kit car and begins a cross-country pilgrimage to find his uncle in this 1994 novel.

novel about a teen who deals with emotional upheaval by working on a car kit. Terry pours the frustration and anger he feels about his parents' separation into long hours with his tools, building the convertible his father never finished. In his review of *The Car* for *School Library Journal*, Tim Rausch called the author's characters "interesting to [young adults] . . . the action is brisk."

Rosa and Traci of *Sisters/Hermanas* have little in common—at least on the surface. Rosa is an illegal immigrant who turns to prostitution in order to survive; Traci is a well-liked junior high schooler whose biggest concerns revolve around cheerleading tryouts and new clothes. Both teens, however, are deeply obsessed with beauty and its impact on their future happiness. The two young women's lives ultimately intersect at a mall, where both girls are forced to face some unpleasant realities. This tale of culture clash and youthful dreams is especially unique in that the entire text appears in both English and Spanish. *Los Angeles Times Book Review* contributor Yvonne Sapia termed the work "brief, ambitious, and told quite poetically."

Paulsen's own colorful life was the basis for the author's 1993 autobiographical book entitled *Eastern Sun, Winter Moon: An Autobiographical Odyssey*. Among the events chronicled are Paulsen's journey by car across the country to meet his long-absent father, his family's unsettling life in the Philippines, and the dissolution of his parents' marriage. While noting that the memoir lacked a certain depth of introspection, Tim Winton of the *Los Angeles Times Book Review* nevertheless found the book to be "no less powerful and dignified for its painful silences."

"I write because it's all I can do," Paulsen once commented. "Every time I've tried to do something else, I cannot." The author continues to write—even though the task is often daunting to him—because he wants his "years on this ball of earth to mean something. Writing furnishes a way for that to happen. . . . It pleases me to write—in a very literal sense of the word."

■ Works Cited

Campbell, Patty, review of *The Cookcamp, New York Times Book Review,* May 5, 1991, pp. 22-23.

Harding, Susan M., review of *The Cookcamp, School Library Journal,* February, 1991, p. 82.

Linehan, Eugene J., review of *Dogsong, Best Sellers,* July, 1985.

Paulsen, Gary, interview with Marguerite Feitlowitz for *Authors and Artists for Young Adults,* Volume 2, Gale, 1989, pp. 165-73.

Rausch, Tim, review of *The Car, School Library Journal,* May, 1994, pp. 131-32.

Sapia, Yvonne, "Sisters in Search of America," *Los Angles Times Book Review,* February 27, 1994, pp. 2, 13.

Winton, Tim, "His Own World War," *Los Angeles Times Book Review,* March 21, 1993, pp. 1, 11.

■ For More Information See

PERIODICALS

Library Journal, February 15, 1993.
Los Angeles Times, December 12, 1987.
New York Times Book Review, May 22, 1988.
Voice of Youth Advocates, June, 1994.
Writer's Digest, January, 1980.*

Gus Van Sant

■ Personal

Born Gus Green Van Sant, Jr., 1952, in Louisville, KY; son of Gus Green (an apparel company executive) and Betty (Seay) Van Sant. *Education:* Rhode Island School of Design, B.F.A., 1975.

■ Addresses

Home—Portland, OR. *Agent*—William Morris Agency, 151 El Camino Drive, Beverly Hills, CA 90212.

■ Career

Screenwriter and director. Director of films, including *The Discipline of D.E.* (short; based on a short story by William S. Burroughs), 1978; *My Friend*, 1983; *My New Friend*, 1985; *Ken Death Gets Out of Jail*, 1987; *Five Ways to Kill Yourself* (short), 1987; *Junior*, 1988; *To Die For*, Columbia, 1995; and *Alice in Hollywood.* Assistant to film director Ken Shapiro, Los Angeles, starting 1975; Cadwell Davis (advertising agency), New York City, commercials producer, 1981-83.

■ Awards, Honors

Los Angeles Film Critics' Award for best independent film, 1987, for *Mala Noche;* Los Angeles Film Critics' Award, New York Film Critics Circle Award, and Independent Spirit Award, all 1989, all for screenplay (with Daniel Yost) *Drugstore Cowboy;* National Society of Film Critics Award for best screenplay, director, and film, 1989, for *Drugstore Cowboy.*

■ Writings

SCREENPLAYS

(And director) *Mala Noche* (adapted from the novella by Walt Curtis), Northern Film Company, 1986.

(With Daniel Yost; and director) *Drugstore Cowboy* (adapted from an unpublished novel by James Fogle), Avenue Pictures, 1989.

(And director) *My Own Private Idaho*, Fine Line Features, 1991.

(And director) *Even Cowgirls Get the Blues* (adapted from the novel by Tom Robbins; includes screenplay for *My Own Private Idaho*), Faber & Faber, 1994.

■ Sidelights

Screenwriter and director Gus Van Sant has a reputation for bringing the seamier side of life to the movie screen. Van Sant's early films are set primarily in the Pacific Northwest and are populated by illegal aliens, drug addicts, petty thieves, and homosexual male prostitutes. When asked about this seeming affection for the fringes of society, the openly gay Van Sant explained to Thomas J. Meyer of the *New York Times Magazine* that his examination of life on the margins was a matter of economics: Van Sant wanted to direct films with a definite aspect of realism, and skid-row Portland, Oregon, was the only place he could afford to shoot. Van Sant's work, however, suggests something deeper. He presents the disenfranchised and downtrodden in unvarnished detail, yet he does so with a sense of humor and compassion that keeps their humanity intact. "Van Sant's films are an antidote to wholesomeness," proclaimed Pauline Kael of the *New Yorker;* "he's made a controlled style out of the random and the careless. He rings totally unexpected bells."

Van Sant's upbringing provides a marked contrast to the subject matter and situations of his films. The filmmaker was born to wealthy parents in Louisville, Kentucky, in 1952. His father was an executive of the McGregor Doniger sportswear company, and his work required frequent relocation. The Van Sant family spent time in Denver and Chicago before settling in Darien, Connecticut, when Van Sant was ten years old. As a child Van Sant showed an early talent for music and the visual arts; he developed an intense interest in painting when he was twelve. "Sometime during adolescence I just buried myself in my work," he told the late actor River Phoenix in *Interview.* "Before then I was pretty much like a normal neighborhood kid." Van Sant also made short animated films with an 8mm movie camera that his parents had given him. "They were more about painting than filmmaking," Van Sant explained to Meyer. As a junior high school student Van Sant saw *Citizen Kane,* a film long considered one of the masterpieces of American cinema, and was impressed by the film's bold imagery and the commanding presence of the young director and leading man Orson Welles.

When Van Sant was a senior in high school his father accepted a job as the president of a company in Oregon. The family lived in an exclusive Portland neighborhood, and Van Sant attended the private Catlin Gabel School. In collaboration with classmate Eric Edwards, Van Sant attempted his first sound film, "The Happy Organ." The twenty-

minute black-and-white film follows a brother and sister on a weekend excursion. When the sister is hit and killed by an automobile, Van Sant's film exhibits the "unsettling sensibility that has persisted in his work," noted Meyer.

Enrolls at Rhode Island School of Design

After graduating from high school Van Sant and high school associate Edwards enrolled at the Rhode Island School of Design. Van Sant initially majored in painting but soon switched to film. Explaining his decision to Phoenix in *Interview,* he confessed that painting, which he had pursued deliberately throughout high school, no longer challenged him. "But filmmaking was a big mystery," Van Sant continued, "and I thought to get anywhere in the business I'd have to work hard and forget about painting for a while. And that's what I choose to do." Van Sant was also influenced in this decision by a viewing of Stanley Kubrick's *A Clockwork Orange* and a subsequent reading of the Kubrick screenplay. The screenplay's unique format opened new frontiers for the aspiring filmmaker.

Van Sant graduated from the Rhode Island School of Design in 1975. He then moved to Los Angeles where he found employment as an assistant to Ken Shapiro, director of the 1974 film *The Groove Tube,* a collection of comic sketches lampooning television. Normally reserved to the point of being laconic, Van Sant had difficulty adjusting to the production of comic scripts. "There were 800 funny things happening a day," he told Meyer, "and I would say one thing." Although his eccentric sense of humor didn't exactly fit Shapiro's style of comedy, Van Sant was shaped by Shapiro's experiences within the movie industry. Following the success of *The Groove Tube,* Shapiro had difficulty getting another project produced; he had a hit with *Modern Problems,* but completed the project cynical about the possibility of retaining control over his films. Convinced that a strong-willed, independent director couldn't realize his vision in studio-controlled Hollywood features, Shapiro told Van Sant to forget about making movies.

Around this time, Van Sant visited Beat generation novelist William S. Burroughs, whom he had located in the New York City phone book. After the meeting Van Sant obtained the rights to pro-

A small group of friends roam the Oregon countryside, robbing pharmacies to feed their drug addictions in *Drugstore Cowboy*, a 1989 film featuring Matt Dillon and Kelly Lynch.

duce one of Burroughs's short stories, "The Discipline of D.E. [Do Easy]." Van Sant shot the black-and-white film in 1977, and it was shown at the New York Film Festival.

Returning to the East Coast, Van Sant worked as a commercials producer for the New York advertising firm Cadwell Davis. In his spare time he wrote screenplays, including *Corporate Vampire* and *Fizzle,* an account of an honor student's collapse. While he was living in New York, a friend sent Van Sant a copy of "Mala Noche," a short story by Portland poet Walt Curtis. Van Sant was captivated by the story, Meyer reported. "But it was the kind of thing that I remember keeping under my bed," Van Sant confessed, "because it was real explicit sexually and it just seemed like a dirty book." Van Sant wrote a screenplay based on the story and returned to Portland in 1983. Working out of a Volkswagon van with a crew of three and a budget of $20,000, Van Sant began filming *Mala Noche,* his first feature-length film.

Directs First Feature

Set in a squalid Portland neighborhood, *Mala Noche* revolves around a homosexual convenience store clerk's attempts to win the affections of Johnny, a young Mexican immigrant. Johnny teases the clerk, Walt, accepting his gifts and favors with no intention of returning Walt's romantic advances. Walt's obsession with Johnny grows deeper as the plot develops. At one point an increasingly frustrated Walt reflects on his unrequited love, remarking, "Johnny will never, never go anywhere with me; I find that sad and absurd." Despite his humiliation, Walt pursues Johnny to the film's tragic conclusion.

Work on *Mala Noche* was completed in 1985, and Van Sant circulated numerous videotape copies of the 16mm black-and-white film, one of which found him an agent. The film was entered in a Los Angeles film festival in 1987; that year it was awarded the Los Angeles Film Critics Award for best independent film. Terrence Rafferty of the *New Yorker* praised the technical proficiency displayed by Van Sant in *Mala Noche,* observing "that what made the picture particularly exciting was that he appeared to be using his skills in an unusually honest, exploratory way." Rafferty proclaimed the film "a stunning debut." "*Mala Noche* has a wonderful fluid, grainy look—expressionist

yet with an improvised feel," Kael similarly stated, concluding: "It has an authentic grungy beauty."

The success of *Mala Noche* brought Van Sant the financial backing of Avenue Pictures, an independent company with a reputation for producing films that fall outside the boundaries of the mainstream. With a budget of five million dollars and a crew of seventy, Van Sant began filming his second feature, *Drugstore Cowboy.* The screenplay was adapted by Van Sant and Daniel Yost from an unpublished novel by convict and drug addict James Fogle, who was sentenced to twenty-two years in a Washington State prison for charges stemming from a series of drug-related crimes. The film follows the exploits of Bob Hughes and his companions as they make their way through the Oregon countryside in 1971, robbing pharmacies and committing petty crimes to feed their drug addiction. Told from Bob's point of view, the film presents the sordid details of the addict's life as facts worthy of consideration and examines addiction without condemning it. Several critics have pointed out that these themes conflicted with anti-drug trends during the socially conservative 1980s.

As the leader of the group, which includes his wife Dianne, his bumbling friend Rick, and Rick's teenage girlfriend Nadine, Bob organizes criminal undertakings with workman-like efficiency. Tense robbery scenes are broken-up by images of Bob's subsequent drug-induced visions, allowing the audience to recognize Bob's descent from the closely ordered world in which he must find drugs to the dreamy world in which he takes them. While this cycle is seemingly endless, Bob must make crucial decisions about the future when the inexperienced Nadine dies of an overdose. With a callousness that belies his paternal nature, Bob buries Nadine's corpse in the woods. After failing to convince Dianne to join him in an attempt to go straight, Bob abandons her and Rick. Shortly after enrolling in an addiction recovery program Bob is shot by a teenage drug pusher. The film closes on Bob's ambulance ride to the hospital, presenting hope for redemption, perhaps, in the mere fact that he is still alive.

With the purchasing power of his first real budget, Van Sant was able to cast Matt Dillon in the role of Bob and Kelly Lynch as Dianne, both of whom won the praise of critics for their performances. William S. Burroughs also appears in the film, as the defrocked, drug-addicted priest who introduces Bob to drugs.

Drugstore Cowboy Earns Awards

Newsweek reviewer David Ansen raised the possibility that *Drugstore Cowboy* "may be the most honest movie about drug addicts ever made." Ansen added that "Van Sant has an unforced lyrical touch and a feel for low life that's free of both condescension and macho romanticizing." While *Rolling Stone* reviewer Peter Travers had reservations about the overall quality of the film, he credited Van Sant with exposing the "very real attraction of drugs." Characterizing the film as "astonishing lyrical and quick-witted," *Film Quarterly* reviewer Steve Vineberg wrote: "What Van Sant looks for in his characters are surprises, the unanticipated twists that people are always capable of . . . Bob's capacity for lonely contemplation, Dianne's blurry vulnerability, Nadine's bravado, Rick's tenderness." In 1989 *Drugstore Cowboy* took the National Society of Film Critics awards for best film, best screenplay, and best director.

Despite the commercial and critical successes of *Drugstore Cowboy* Van Sant encountered difficulty securing financial backing for his third film. Offers to direct a large-budget picture for a major studio arrived steadily, but Van Sant was committed to producing his original screenplay, *My Own Private Idaho,* a contemporary retelling of William Shakespeare's Henry IV plays with the principal roles filled by male prostitutes. Producers hesitated to lend support to the ambitious appropriation of Shakespeare and the potentially controversial subject matter. Finally, Van Sant received a budget of $2.7 million from New Line Cinema to make the picture. He cast Keanu Reeves and River Phoenix as his leads and began filming.

Mike Waters, played by Phoenix, and Scott Favor, played by Reeves, are a pair of Portland street hustlers who share a peculiar friendship. Mike is a child of the streets, long since separated from his mother and family, and a narcoleptic who is prone to falling asleep during moments of duress. Scott, on the other hand, is the son of Portland's wealthy mayor who rebels against his father by slumming as a male prostitute. Obsessed with finding his mother, whom he knows only from a handful of hazy memories and a few worn-out snapshots, Mike begins a search that takes Scott

and him to Idaho and as far afield as Rome. Between clients and excursions there are confrontations with the film's Falstaff, Bob Pigeon, which precipitate Shakespearean soliloquies. As the Henry IV themes of betrayal of friends and loyalty to family develop, it becomes clear that Scott intends to assume his father's legacy and abandon the streets for the security of the world into which he was born. Mike's maturation takes a more dramatic turn as he finds and confronts his mother.

My Own Private Idaho is a complex film, veering widely between fantasy and reality, from the squalor of the streets to garish mansions, and from images of nature to symbols of destruction. In one of the film's more hallucinatory sequences, Mike and Scott are transported to the covers of pornographic magazines, where they carry on a dialogue about the nature of their sexuality. Mike's recurring vision of a house crashing to the ground provides another example of the film's rich visual fabric. Similarly, elements of Shakespearean plotting and acting are thrown together with more naturalistic scenes. It is Van Sant's effort to bring these disparate parts together which distinguishes this film from the sober clarity of his two previous works.

Noting that Van Sant had exceeded the boundaries of conventional filmmaking with *My Own Private Idaho,* David Ansen of *Newsweek* wrote: "Some of the risks he takes are cockeyed magic, and some are so daffy maybe nobody could have pulled them off." Ansen concludes that the film is a "far cry from seamless, but I would gladly trade a dozen well-made studio movies for one of its vital parts." *Maclean's* reviewer Brian D. Johnson found Van Sant's narrative maneuvers more interesting than his subject matter and proclaimed that the "movie is not really about prostitution or homosexuality. It is about the loyalties of family and class, the amnesia of childhood and the outlaw affections of adolescence." In a much less laudatory assessment of the film, a *Time* reviewer characterized Van Sant's plot as a "nonstory" and panned the use of Shakespearean language as a "desperate imposition." Several reviewers reserved similar criticism for the Shakespearean motifs, citing their distracting incongruity with the rest of the film. "But before this trippy, mesmerizing movie swerves out of control, it delivers an exhilarating and challenging ride," wrote Travers in *Rolling Stone.*

Van Sant's fourth film is an adaptation of the Tom Robbins novel, *Even Cowgirls Get the Blues*, which Van Sant described in *Interview* as one of the first novels "tracing the notion of a female hero." The film follows a part-time fashion model as she hitchhikes from coast to coast. Carmella, played by actress Uma Thurman, arrives at an exclusive spa for overweight women just as the cowgirls who staff the resort rebel against their employers. Thurman's character has an affair with a cowgirl played by River Phoenix's sister, Rain. Throughout the film, the pair encounter various representatives of the counterculture of the 1970s. A reviewer for *People* speculated that film was intended to have a dream-like air, "but it's closer to a nap, what with its twinkly feel-goodedness, its karmic, bubbleheaded cuteness."

In 1995, Van Sant directed the black comedy *To Die For*, his first film for a major studio. A satirical look at the media and the national obsession with turning criminals into celebrities, *To Die For*

paired Van Sant with writer Buck Henry, who based his screenplay on the novel by Joyce Maynard. Told in flashback using a psuedo-documentary style, with the actors speaking directly to the camera at times, the film stars Nicole Kidman as Suzanne Stone, a vivacious weatherperson at the local cable station in Little Hope, New Hampshire, who feels trapped in a dead-end marriage to bartender Larry Maretto, played by Matt Dillon. The devilish, ambitious Stone, a careerist who lives by the motto "you aren't anybody in America if you're not on TV," plots to murder her husband and recruits three local teenagers to help. One of the teens, Larry (played by River Phoenix's brother, Joaquin), is seduced by Stone, then shoots and kills Larry while Suzanne, on TV, wishes her husband a happy anniversary.

Boistered by a strong showing at the 1995 Cannes Film Festival, *To Die For* drew rave reviews from critics when released to theaters. In *Rolling Stone*, Peter Travers declared that "Van Sant sets up the

Uma Thurman and Lorraine Bracco starred in Van Sant's 1994 film adaptation of Tom Robbins' novel, *Even Cowgirls Get the Blues*.

media as a poison pinata" and later observed, "although Van Sant makes wicked sport of television, he doesn't underestimate its power to blind us to its faults and bring us to our knees." Todd McCarthy in *Variety* felt that Van Sant's move to a major studio did not dilute the power of his work, stating, "the film fully retains the highly idiosyncratic, charmingly ragged feel of his previous, lower-budget productions."

Van Sant's future projects include a film about the life of pop artist Andy Warhol. Describing the process he goes through in making a film, Van Sant explained in *Interview:* "I see an image that represents the whole film. And so I start to work toward that image, and then I fill it all out, and it becomes very complicated, because you have to have a lot of elements to make the image come to life." Following this method, Van Sant has challenged the movie industry and audiences with his offbeat, visually arresting films. His motion pictures stand as icons of his independent directorial spirit.

■ Works Cited

Ansen, David, "Back in the Low Life Again," *Newsweek*, October 23, 1989, p. 84.

Ansen, David, "Turning Shakespearean Tricks," *Newsweek*, October 7, 1991, p. 66.

Review of *Even Cowgirls Get the Blues*, *People*, May 30, 1994, p. 19.

Johnson, Brian D., "A Hustlers' Odyssey," *Maclean's*, October 28, 1991, p. 101.

Kael, Pauline, "Floating," *New Yorker*, October 30, 1989, pp. 74-78.

McCarthy, Todd, review of *To Die For*, *Variety*, May 29-June 4, 1995, p. 53.

Meyer, Thomas J., *New York Times Magazine*, September 15, 1991, pp. 51, 62, 64.

Review of *My Own Private Idaho*, *Time*, October 28, 1991, p. 101.

Phoenix, River, interview of Gus Van Sant, *Interview*, March, 1991, pp. 126-31, 144.

Rafferty, Terrence, review of *My Own Private Idaho*, *New Yorker*, October 7, 1991, p. 100.

Travers, Peter, review of *Drugstore Cowboy*, *Rolling Stone*, October 19, 1989, p. 29.

Travers, Peter, review of *My Own Private Idaho*, *Rolling Stone*, October 17, 1991, p. 100.

Travers, Peter, review of *To Die For*, *Rolling Stone*, October 19, 1995, pp. 155-6.

Van Sant, Gus, *Mala Noche*, Northern Film Company, 1986.

Vineberg, Steve, review of *Drugstore Cowboy*, *Film Quarterly*, Spring, 1990, pp. 27-30.

■ For More Information See

PERIODICALS

Library Journal, June 1, 1992, p. 201.

Los Angeles Magazine, October, 1991, pp. 206-08.

Newsweek, April 15, 1991, pp. 68-69.

New York, October 9, 1989, pp. 82-83.

New Yorker, May 30, 1994, p. 99.

Rolling Stone, November 11, 1993, pp. 58-61.

—*Sketch by D. P. Johnson*

Acknowledgments

Acknowledgements

Grateful acknowledgement is made to the following publishers, authors, and artists for their kind permission to reproduce copyrighted material.

SANDY ASHER. Cover of *Everything is Not Enough.* By Sandy Asher. Copyright © 1987 by Sandy Asher. Reprinted by permission of Delacorte Press, a division of Bantam Doubleday Dell Publishing Group, Inc./ Jacket from *Things Are Seldom What They Seem.* By Sandy Asher. Copyright © 1983 by Sandy Asher. Jacket illustration copyright © 1983 by Jim Matthewuse. Reprinted by permission of Delacorte Press, a division of Bantam Doubleday Dell Publishing Group, Inc./ Jacket from *A Senior Class Yearbook, Out of Here.* By Sandy Asher. Copyright © 1983 by Sandy Asher. Jacket illustration copyright © 1993 by Lino Saffioti. Reprinted by permission of Lodestar Books, an affiliate of Dutton's Children's Books, a division of Penguin Books USA Inc./ Mayfield, Jim. Photograph of Sandy Asher. Jim Mayfield.

CHARLOTTE and EMILY BRONTË. From the cover of *Jane Eyre.* By Charlotte Brontë. Signet, 1960. Copyright © 1960 by New American Library. Used by permission of Dutton Signet, a Division of Penguin Books USA Inc./ Richmond, G. Portrait of Charlotte Brontë. The Granger Collection, New York. Reproduced by permission./ Top Withens, photograph of. Yorkshire Post Newspapers Ltd. Reproduced by permission./ From the cover of *The Complete Poems.* By Emily Jane Brontë. Penguin, 1992. © The Brontë Society. Reproduced by permission of The Brontë Parsonage Museum./ McGuiness, Bob. From the cover of *Wuthering Heights.* By Emily Brontë. Bantam Books, 1981. Used by permission of Bantam Books, a division of Bantam Doubleday Dell Publishing Group, Inc.

JAMES L. BROOKS. Cast of *Room 222,* photograph of. © 1995 CAPITAL CITIES/ABC, INC. Reproduced by permission./ Cast of *Mary Tyler Moore Show,* photograph of. Reproduced by permission of MTM Entertainment, Ed Asner, Georgia Engel, Gavin Macleod, Mary Tyler Moore, Betty White, and the Estate of Ted Knight./ Hayes, Kerry. From *Broadcast News.* Reproduced by permission of Twentieth Century Fox Film Corporation./ Sennet, Mark. Photograph of James L. Brooks. Reproduced by permission of Onyx Enterprises./ Groening, Matt, from *Greetings from The Simpsons.* © 1990 Matt Groening Productions, Inc. All Rights Reserved. The Simpsons © and ™ Twentieth Century Fox Film Corporation. Reproduced by permission.

JIM CARROLL. Carroll, Jim, portrait of. Reproduced by permission of William Morris Agency, Inc.

ALDEN R. CARTER. Garrick, Jacqueline. From the dust jacket of *Sheila's Dying.* By Alden R. Carter. G.P. Putnam's Sons, 1987. Reproduced by permission of The Putnam Publishing Group./ Thompson, Ellen. From the dust jacket to *Up Country.* By Alden R. Carter. G.P. Putnam's Sons, 1989. Jacket art copyright © 1989 by Ellen Thompson. Reproduced by permission of The Putnam Publishing Group./ From the cover of *Dancing On Dark Water.* By Alden R. Carter. Scholastic, 1990. Illustration copyright © 1992 by Scholastic Inc. All rights reserved. Reprinted by permission of the publisher./ Young, Dan. Photograph of Alden R. Carter. Reproduced by permission.

GARY CREW. Crew, Gary, photograph of. Reproduced by permission of Gary Crew./ From the cover of *Strange Objects.* By Gary Crew. Simon & Schuster, 1990. Jacket illustration copyright © 1993 Kam Mak. All rights reserved. Reprinted with the permission of Simon & Schuster Books for Young Readers.

OSSIE DAVIS. Davis, Ossie, portrait of. Reproduced by permission./ Cooper, Floyd. From the cover of *Just Like Martin.* By Ossie Davis. Simon & Schuster, 1992. Jacket illustration copyright © 1992 by Floyd Cooper. All rights reserved. Reprinted by permission of Floyd Cooper./ Cast of *Purlie Victorious,* photograph of. AP/Wide Word Photos. Reproduced by permission./ Davis, Ossie, Coretta Scott King, Percy Sutton and Ruby Dee, photograph of. AP/Wide Word Photos. Reproduced by permission.

THOMAS M. DISCH. Disch, Thomas M., portrait of. Jerry Bauer. Reproduced by permission./ From the cover of *On the Wings of Song.* By Thomas M. Disch. Carroll & Graf Publishers, Inc., 1979. Copyright © 1979 by Thomas M. Disch. All rights reserved. Reprinted by permission of Thomas M. Disch./ From the cover of *The M.D.: A Horror Story.* By Thomas M. Disch. Berkley, 1992. Cover photograph © 1991 by Geoffrey Spear. Cover construction © 1991 by Archie Ferguson. All rights reserved. Reprinted by permission of The Berkley Publishing Group.

CAROLE NELSON DOUGLAS. Douglas, Carole Nelson. From an illustration in *Rengarth the Lost.* Reproduced by permission of Carole Nelson Douglas./ Sweet, Darrell K. From the cover of *Seed Upon the Wind.* By Carole Nelson Douglas. Tom Doherty Associates, Inc., 1992. Copyright © 1992 by Carole Nelson Douglas. All rights reserved. Reproduced by permission of the publisher./ DeVito, Joe. From the cover of *Catnap.* By Carole Nelson Douglas. Tom Doherty Associates, Inc., 1992. Copyright © 1992 by Carole Nelson Douglas. All rights reserved. Reproduced

FELICE HOLMAN. Cover of *Slake's Limbo.* By Felice Holman. Copyright © 1974 by Felice Holman. Reprinted by permission of Macmillan Books for Young Readers, an imprint of Simon & Schuster Children's Publishing Division./ Cover of *Secret City, U.S.A.* By Felice Holman. Copyright © 1990 by Felice Holman. Reprinted by permission of Macmillan Books for Young Readers, an imprint of Simon & Schuster Children's Publishing Division./ Cover of *The Wild Children.* By Felice Holman. Copyright © Felice Holman, 1983. Reprinted by permission of Charles Scribner's Sons.

GALE ANN HURD. Foreman, Richard. From *The Abyss.* Reproduced by permission of Twentieth Century Fox Film Corporation./ Kirkland, Douglas. Photograph of Gale Ann Hurd's Malibu home. Reproduced by permission of SYGMA Photo News.

BELINDA HURMENCE. Harris, Marty. Photograph of Belinda Hurmence. Reproduced by permission./ Hamilton, Ken. From the jacket of *Dixie in the Big Pasture.* By Belinda Hurmence. Clarion Books, 1994. Jacket illustration copyright © 1994 by Ken Hamilton. All rights reserved. Reproduced by permission of Houghton Mifflin Company./ Assel, Steven. From the jacket of *A Girl Called Boy* by Belinda Hurmence. Clarion Books, 1982. Jacket art © 1982 by Steven Assel. All rights reserved. Reproduced by permission of Houghton Mifflin Company./ From the jacket of *We Lived in a Little Cabin in the Yard.* Edited by Belinda Hurmence. John F. Blair, 1994. Copyright © 1994 by Belinda Hurmence. All rights reserved. From the Penn School Collection. Permission granted by Penn Center, Inc., St. Helena Island, SC.

STEPHEN KING. From the photograph on the cover of *Gerald's Game.* By Stephen King. Signet, 1993. Copyright © Stephen King, 1992. All rights reserved. Reprinted by permission of the author./ From the cover of *Needful Things.* By Stephen King. Signet, 1992. Copyright © 1991 by Stephen King. All rights reserved. Used by permission of Viking Penguin, a division of Penguin Books USA Inc./ From the cover of *Drawing of the Three.* By Stephen King. Signet, 1990. Copyright © 1987 by Stephen King. All rights reserved. Used by permission of Dutton Signet, a division of Penguin Books USA Inc./ From the cover of *Four Past Midnight.* By Stephen King. Signet, 1991. Copyright © 1990 by Stephen King. All rights reserved. Used by permission of Viking Penguin, a division of Penguin Books USA Inc./ The cast of *Delores Claiborne,* photograph of. Castle Rock Entertainment. Reproduced by permission./ Cast of *The Stand,* photograph of. Copyright © 1995 CAPITAL CITIES/ABC, INC. Reproduced by permission.

EARVIN "MAGIC" JOHNSON. Johnson, Magic, photograph with Michael Jordan. Andy Bernstein/NBA Photos. Reproduced by permission./ Johnson, Magic, photograph of he and young boys practicing basketball. Andrew Bernstein/NBA Photos. Reproduced by permission./ Leifer, Neil. Photograph of Magic Johnson, wearing Olympic jacket. Neil Leifer. Reproduced by permission./ Jacket from *My Life.* By Earvin "Magic" Johnson, with William Novak. Copyright © 1992 by June Bug Enterprises. Front jacket photo copyright © 1992 Neil Leifer. Reprinted by permission of Random House, Inc.

JULIAN MAY. Herring, Michael. From the cover of *The Surveillance.* By Julian May. Ballantine Books, 1987. Copyright © 1987 by Julian May. All rights reserved. Reproduced by permission of Ballantine Books, a division of Random House, Inc./ Whelan, Michael. From the cover of *The Golden Torc.* By Julian May. Ballantine Books, 1983. Copyright © 1982 by Julian May. All rights reserved. Reproduced by permission of Ballantine Books, a division of Random House, Inc./ Whelan, Michael. From the cover of *The Adversary.* By Julian May. Ballantine Books, 1985. Copyright © 1984 by Julian May. All rights reserved. Reproduced by permission of Ballantine Books, a division of Random House, Inc./ Whelan, Michael. From the cover of *The Nonborn King.* By Julian May. Ballantine Books, 1984. Copyright © 1983 by Julian May. Reproduced by permission of Ballantine Books, a division of Random House, Inc./ Julian, May. From *The Many-Colored Land.* By Julian May. Ballantine Books, 1983. Copyright © 1981 by Julian May. All rights reserved. Reproduced by permission of Ballantine Books, a division of Random House, Inc./ May, Julian, photograph of, from *Jack the Bodiless.* By Julian May. Alfred A. Knopf, 1991. Copyright © 1991 by Starykon Productions, Inc. All rights reserved. Reproduced by permission of Barbara Dikty.

ROBERT MCCAMMON. From the picture of Robert McCammon in *Boy's Life.* By Robert McCammon. Pocket Books, 1992. Copyright © 1991 by the McCammon Corporation. All rights reserved. Reprinted by permission of Gerber Studio./ From the cover of *Boy's Life.* By Robert McCammon. Pocket Books, 1992. Copyright © 1991 by the McCammon Corporation. All rights reserved. Reprinted by permission of Gerber Studio./ Morrill, Rowena. From the cover of *Swan Song.* By Robert McCammon. Pocket Books, 1987. Cover art copyright © 1987 Rowena Morrill. All rights reserved. Reprinted by permission of Rowena Morrill./ Warren, Jim. From the cover of *Blue World.* By Robert McCammon. Pocket Books, 1990. Cover art copyright © 1990 Jim Warren. All rights reserved. Reprinted by permission of Jim Warren./ Morrill, Rowena. From the cover of *The Wolf's Hour.* By Robert R. McCammon. Pocket Books, 1989. Copyright © 1989 by The McCammon Corporation. All rights reserved. Reprinted by permission of Rowena Morrill.

WALTER MOSLEY. Mosley, Walter, portrait of. Jerry Bauer. Reproduced by permission./ Jinks, John. From the cover of *Devil in a Blue Dress.* By Walter Mosley. Pocket Books, 1991. Copyright © 1990 by Walter Mosley. All rights reserved. Reprinted by permission of John Jinks./ Jinks, John. From the cover of *A Red Death.* By Walter Mosley. Pocket Books, 1992. Copyright © 1991 by Walter Mosley. All rights reserved. Reprinted by permission of John Jinks./ Jinks, John. From the cover of *White Butterfly.* By Walter Mosley. Pocket Books, 1993. Copyright © 1992 by Walter Mosley. All rights reserved. Reprinted by permission of John Jinks./ Washington, Denzel, photograph from *Devil in a Blue Dress.* Courtesy of TriStar Pictures, Inc.

Cumulative Index

Author/Artist Index

The following index gives the number of the volume in which an author/artist's biographical sketch appears.